Rape Crisis Network Ireland (RCNI) is the national representative body for Rape Crisis Centres in Ireland. The RCNI role includes the development and coordination of national projects, supporting Rape Crisis Centres to reach quality assurance standards, using our expertise to influence national policy and social change. The RCNI is a national information and resource centre on all aspects of sexual violence, with a proven capacity in strategic leadership including contributing and advising on the necessary infra-structure for a national response to all aspects of sexual violence.

ABOUT THE AUTHORS

Conor Hanly is a Lecturer in the School of Law, NUI Galway.

Deirdre Healy is IRCHSS Post-Doctoral Fellow, Institute of Criminology, University College Dublin.

Stacey Scriver is a Post-Doctoral Researcher, Women's Studies Centre, School of Political Science and Sociology, NUI Galway.

Rape and Justice in Ireland

Conor Hanly
Deirdre Healy
Stacey Scriver

The Liffey Press

Published by
The Liffey Press
Ashbrook House, 10 Main Street
Raheny, Dublin 5, Ireland
www.theliffeypress.com

© 2009 Rape Crisis Network Ireland

A catalogue record of this book is
available from the British Library.

ISBN 978-1-905785-74-2

All rights reserved. No part of this publication may be reproduced or transmitted in any form or by any means, including photocopying and recording, without written permission of the publisher. Such written permission must also be obtained before any part of this publication is stored in a retrieval system of any nature. Requests for permission should be directed to The Liffey Press, Ashbrook House, 10 Main Street, Raheny, Dublin 5, Ireland.

Printed in the Republic of Ireland by Colour Books.

Contents

List of Tables and Figures xi
Acknowledgements xv
Preface xix
Executive Summary xxiii

Chapter 1: Introduction 1
Defining Rape 1
Overview of the Criminal Process in Ireland 4
Attrition and the Effectiveness of the Criminal Process 7
Rape and the Criminal Process – Attempts at Reform 10
Terminology 12

Chapter 2: The Current State of Knowledge: Rape and Attrition in the Legal System 15
Rape Myths 15
    False Accusations 16
    The 'Real Rape' Stereotype 19
    Rape Supportive Attitudes 29
    Prevalence of Rape Myths 31
Reporting Rape 34
    Theoretical Models of Decision-Making 35
    The Decision to Report 37
    Informal Support Seeking 43
    Contact with Police 43

Prosecuting Rape 47
    Formal Legal Issues – Defining the Act of Rape 49
    The Impact of the Jury on the Prosecutorial Decision 52
    Case Characteristics 54
    Complainant and Defendant Characteristics 63
The Trial Process 70
    Evidentiary Difficulties 70
    Unduly Harsh and Discriminatory Procedural Rules at Trial 72
    Juries 88
    Sentencing 98
    Delay 107

Chapter 3: Methodology 109
Overview of the Research Design 109
Participation in the Study 110
Strand I: Reporting Rape – Methods and Tools 111
    Procedures 111
    Instruments 112
    Limitations 118
Strand II: Prosecuting Rape: Methods and Tools 119
    Questionnaire 119
    Follow Up Questionnaire 119
    Tools of Analysis 120
    Limitations 120
Strand III: The Trial Process – Methods and Tools 121
    Trial Court Records 122
    Trial Court Transcripts 124
    Limitations 125

Chapter 4: Reporting Rape 127
The Sample 127
    Age 127
    Location 128
    Employment Status 129

    Living Arrangements 129
    Case Status 130
Characteristics of Rape 131
    Age at Time of Assault 131
    Location of Assault 132
    Victim-Offender Relationship 133
    Verbal Threat/Use of Force 135
    Victim Resistance 135
    Physical Injury 136
    Alcohol Use 137
Charting the Pathway to Justice 139
    Reasons for Not Reporting 140
    Reasons for Reporting 148
    Delayed Reporting 156
    Victim Withdrawal 157
    Informal Support Networks 162
    Response from Gardaí 163
    Garda Investigation and Follow-up 172
    Summary and Conclusion 181
Follow-up Survey 184
    General Health Questionnaire (GHQ-12) 184
    Post-Traumatic Life Change Questionnaire 185
    Post-traumatic Stress Disorder Symptom Scale-Self Report
       (PSS-SR) 186
    Levenson's Locus of Control Test 187
    Time and Recovery 190
    Discussion 192
The Qualitative Interview 195
    The Initial Decision to Report 196
    The Importance of Privacy 200
    Sensitivity of the Gardaí 201
    The Influence of the Media 202
    The Impact of the Decision to Report 203
    Dealing with the Gardaí 205

Experience with the Legal System 208
The Impact of the Rape 209
Victim Recommendations 213
Conclusion 216

Chapter 5: Prosecuting Rape 219
Describing Rape 220
   Case Characteristics 220
   Complainant/Suspect Relationship 220
   National Distribution of Rape Cases 221
   Other Characteristics 223
   Complainant Characteristics 224
   Suspect Characteristics 226
   Aggravating and Consent Features 228
   Risk Factors 229
   Evidential Factors 231
   Prosecutions for Rape in Ireland 232
Influential Factors in the Decision to Prosecute 233
   Offence Location 233
   Complainant Characteristics 233
   Suspect Characteristics 234
   Intoxication 235
   Aggravating and Consent Features 236
   Risk Factors 239
   Evidentiary Factors 242
   Reason not to Prosecute 243
Withdrawing the Complaint 243
   Who Withdraws? 243
   Reason for Withdrawal 245
   The Effect of a Delay on Withdrawal 248
False Reports 249
Discussion 250
Conclusion and Recommendations 256

Chapter 6: The Trial Process 259
The Trial Court Records 259
- *The Parties* 259
- *The Allegations of Rape* 268
- *The Legal Process* 277

Discussion and Recommendations 317
- *The Parties* 317
- *The Case Characteristics* 318
- *Bail* 321
- *Juries* 325
- *Attrition* 328
- *Sentencing* 329
- *Delay* 334
- *Victims' Rights* 336

The Trial Transcripts 338
- *Order and Nature of the Evidence* 339
- *The Complainant's Evidence* 340
- *The Defendant's Case* 345
- *The Judge's Charge* 347
- *Sentencing Factors* 348

Discussion and Recommendations 353
- *The Nature and Severity of the Complainant's Ordeal* 353
- *Protecting the Complainant* 354

Chapter 7: Conclusion 359
Summary of the Study 359
- *Purpose* 359
- *Profile of Rape in Ireland* 359
- *Operation of the Criminal Justice System* 360
- *Causes of Attrition in Ireland* 362

Dealing with Attrition 365
The Way Forward 368

Appendix 1: Ethical Guidelines.. 373
Appendix 2: Survey Questionnaire... 375
Appendix 3: DPP File Survey... 401
Appendix 4: Withdrawal of Complaint Supplementary
  Questionnaire.. 407
Appendix 5: Rape Trial Records Questionnaire................................... 409
Appendix 6: Trial Transcripts.. 423
Bibliography 431
Index 471

List of Tables and Figures

Tables

2.1 Stranger Rapes 22
2.2 Location of Rape Incidents 22
2.3 Stereotype versus Truth... 28
2.4 Average Sentences in England and Wales.............. 102
2.5 Average Sentences in Victoria 102
2.6 Average Sentences in New Zealand 102
2.7 Sentences for Rape Imposed in Ireland 104
2.8 Ordinary Sentence Characteristics 105
2.9 Severe Sentence Characteristics 106
2.10 Condign Sentence Characteristics 106
2.11 Average Delays, by Jurisdiction 108
3.1 Review of Cases Received by Central Criminal Court........... 124
4.1 Age at Time of Survey 127
4.2 Current County of Residence.................................... 128
4.3 Employment Status 129
4.4 Living Arrangements 130
4.5 Age at Time of Assault.. 132
4.6 Location of Assault.. 133
4.7 Relationship to Offender 134
4.8 Use of Physical Force or Threats 135
4.9 Victim Resistance... 136
4.10 Physical Injuries 137
4.11 Alcohol Use by Victim 137

4.12 Alcohol Use by Offender 138
4.13 Victim's Role in Attrition 140
4.14 Reasons for Not Reporting 140
4.15 Reasons for Reporting 149
4.16 Timing of the Complaint 156
4.17 Reasons for Delay 157
4.18 Reason for Considering Withdrawing a Rape
     Complaint 159
4.19 Source of Pressure to Drop Rape Complaint 161
4.20 Formal and Informal Sources of Support 162
4.21 Where Statement was Made 164
4.22 Gender of Interviewing Officer 165
4.23 Manner of Interviewing Officer 166
4.24 Garda Obligations 173
4.25 Reasons for satisfaction 176
4.26 Reasons for Dissatisfaction 178
4.27 High/Low GHQ Scores and the Stage of Attrition 185
4.28 Furthest Point of Attrition 192

5.1 Nationality of Suspects 226
5.2 Defence Offered by Suspects 228
5.3 Evidence and the Decision to Prosecute 242

6.1 Gender of the Complainants 260
6.2 Complainants' Ages 260
6.3 Age Bands of the Complainants 261
6.4 Complainants' Employment Status 261
6.5 Complainants' Employment, by Industry 262
6.6 Defendants' Ages 264
6.7 Age Bands of Defendants 264
6.8 Defendants' Ages 265
6.9 Age Bands of Defendants 266
6.10 Relationship between Defendants and Complainants 269
6.11 Location of the Rapes 270
6.12 Timing of the Incidents 271
6.13 Complainants' Consumption of Alcohol, in Standard
     Drinks 272

6.14 Defendants' Consumption of Alcohol, in Standard Drinks 273
6.15 Physical Injuries Reported by Complainants 274
6.16 Authorship of Victim Impact Statements.............................. 275
6.17 Issues Mentioned in Victim Impact Statements 276
6.18 Levels of Bail 281
6.19 Levels of Sureties 282
6.20 Dominance of Juries, by Gender... 287
6.21 Frequency of Male/Female Breakdown of Juries 288
6.22 Employment Status of Jurors 288
6.23 Employment of Jurors, by Industry 289
6.24 Employment Status of Jury Foremen.................................... 290
6.25 Employment of Jury Foremen, by Industry........................... 291
6.26 Frequency of Deliberation Times 292
6.27 Results of Jury Deliberations on Rape Charges 294
6.28 Results of Jury Deliberations on Lesser Sexual and Non-Sexual Charges 295
6.29 Results of Jury Deliberations on Charges of Rape under Section 4 296
6.30 Results of Jury Deliberations on Rape Charges, by Gender Dominance 297
6.31 Results of Charges, by Defendant 299
6.32 Attrition, by Defendant... 300
6.33 Attrition, by Charge 302
6.34 Range of Sentences Imposed for Rape.................................. 303
6.35 Range of Sentences by Charge, Trial and Guilty Plea 303
6.36 Frequency of Sentences... 305
6.37 Range of Suspension Periods.. 308
6.38 Frequency of Suspension Periods 308
6.39 Effect of Suspension Periods... 310
6.40 Periods of Post-Release Supervision 311
6.41 Frequency of Supervision Periods 312
6.42 Mention of Defendant or Sentencing in Victim Impact Statements 314
6.43 Median Time Periods, by Stage 317
6.44 Average Sentences for Rape, by Jurisdiction........................ 330

6.45 Delays, by Study 335
6.46 Elements of Transcripts Available 339
6.47 Separate Representation Sought, 2002-2005 341
6.48 Questions on Behaviour.. 344
6.49 The Primary Defence Strategy 346
6.50 Mitigating Factors Highlighted by Defence Counsel 349
6.51 Mitigating Factors Identified by Judiciary 351
6.52 Aggravating Factors Identified by Judiciary 352

Figures

4.1 Life Changes and the Stage of Attrition 186
4.2 Internality and the Stage of Attrition 188
4.3 Powerful Others and the Stage of Attrition 189
4.4 Chance and the Stage of Attrition 190
4.5 PTSD and the Passage of Time 191

5.1 Complainant/Suspect Relationship 221
5.2 Frequency of Rape Offences by County 223
5.3 Outcome of Cases Received by Central Criminal Court,
    2000-2004.. 232
5.4 Comparison of Suspect and Complainant's Levels of
    Intoxication... 235
5.5 Complainant/Suspect Relationship and the Use of
    Physical Force 237
5.6 Complainant/Suspect Relationship and the Use/Threat of
    a Weapon 238
5.7 Complainant/Suspect Relationship in Withdrawn
    Complaints 245
5.8 Primary Stated Reason for Withdrawal of Complaint 246
5.9 Secondary Reason for Withdrawal of Complaint 247

6.1 Defendants' Background Factors 267
6.2 Forensic Tests Conducted in Rape Cases 279
6.3 Bail Conditions.. 283
6.4 Attrition, by Defendant... 301

ACKNOWLEDGEMENTS

This was a hugely complex project that required the breaking of a great deal of new research ground. The Law School at NUI Galway relished the challenge of bringing it to a successful conclusion. Regardless of our best efforts, however, the project would never have been completed had we not received the support, assistance and encouragement of a large number of people. We would like to take this opportunity to publicly acknowledge our debt to all of the following people and organizations for all of their help.

Strand I required the participation of a large number of people who have suffered the indignity of rape. We are indebted to all those who trusted us enough to come forward and complete our questionnaires. We are especially grateful to those people who were willing to relive their experiences by participating in the interview stage of Strand I in addition to completing all the questionnaires. We would also like to acknowledge those members of the various Rape Crisis Centres who assisted in the difficult process of recruiting participants.

Strand II would have been impossible to complete without the support of the Director of Public Prosecutions and his staff. The Director, James Hamilton, and the Deputy Director, Barry Donoghue, were both unstinting in their support from the very beginning of the project and agreed to allow us indirect access to their files. They also agreed to deploy the research resources of their office to assist us. Clara Connolly, Legal Researcher, was of great assistance in developing the questionnaire, and we would acknowledge the researchers in the Office of the DPP who completed the questionnaires: Yvonne Daly, Colin King, Eimear Spain, Mary Rogan, and especially Angela Cleary. Rebecca Coen, Deputy Head of the Prosecution Policy Unit, coordinated the work of these researchers, answered all of our questions and ensured that we fully understood the operation of the Office. We are also grateful to Helena Kiely, Directing Officer, for taking the time to explain the mechanics of the prosecutorial role.

Strand III required the support of the judiciary and the Courts Service. We are grateful to the Honourable Mr. Justice John Murray, Chief Justice of Ireland, and the Honourable Mr. Justice Richard Johnson, President of the High Court, for their gracious permission to access both the trial transcripts and the trial court records, respectively. We would like to acknowledge our particular debt to Nuala McLoughlin, Chief Registrar and Director of Operations for the High and Supreme Courts, for ensuring truly outstanding hospitality in addition to making the practical arrangements for our access to the Four Courts. We are grateful to Frank Lyons for setting us up with an office in the Four Courts complex without which this part of the project would have been impracticable. Liam Convey, Registrar of the Central Criminal Court, and Eamon O'Dwyer were of great assistance in getting us used to the operations of the Central Criminal Court. Geraldine Manners, Registrar of the Court of Criminal Appeal, and Sinead Hogan did all they could to help us locate trial transcripts. We also owe a great deal to Aoife Ní Fhearghaíl of Doyle Court Reporters for arranging access to more trial transcripts.

We would like to acknowledge Molin Ryan, Chief Executive Officer of the Legal Aid Board, for his willingness to answer our questions and supply us with data on applications for separate legal representation. We would also like to acknowledge Professor Ian O'Donnell, Director of the Institute of Criminology at UCD, for his invaluable advice and guidance.

We would like to thank Fiona Neary, Executive Director, and Clíona Saidléar, Policy & Communications Director, at Rape Crisis Network Ireland for their willingness to entrust this project to us and for their support and patience. Particular thanks to Kate Mulkerrins, formerly Legal Coordinator of the RCNI, now Head of the Prosecution Policy Unit at the Office of the DPP, who acted as our contact with the RCNI and the Rape Crisis Centres.

Finally, we would be remiss if we did not acknowledge the immense contribution to this project of all those who acted as research assistants: Nóra Ní Loideain, Senior Research Assistant, Dominic Burke, Michael Coyne, Ingrid Cunningham, Christopher Dwyer, Damien Guihen, Alice Harrison, Tom Hickey, Frances Morrow, Bríd Nic Shuibhne, Ciara Staunton and Aisling Wall.

Conor Hanly
Deirdre Healy
Stacey Scriver

PREFACE

The contradictions between women's reality [of rape] and the legal definitions of that same reality are often so extreme that they effectively bar women from participation in the formal structures of justice. Women learn quickly that rape is a crime in theory only. – J.L. Hermann, *Trauma & Recovery*, 1992.

'No point [reporting the rape]. His word against mine and I had been drinking.' – *Rape and Justice in Ireland*, participant 80.

'So helpful and supportive [Gardaí], brilliant.' – *Rape and Justice in Ireland*, participant 26.

It is relatively recently that Ireland has come to recognise the reality of sexual violence. Largely due to the women's movement, rape crisis centres and victims speaking out, we are beginning to appreciate the scale of crimes of sexual violence in Ireland, within institutions, families and social settings. Many gaps remain in our knowledge, however, especially the extent to which our legal system can deliver justice and restitution.

This unique research is exceptionally wide-ranging, including data from three separate and distinct locations. Strand I researched 100 individual rape victims and their experience of the legal process, Strand II researched 597 files from the office of the DPP and Strand III researched 173 Central Criminal Court cases and 35 transcripts of contested trials. None of these three viewpoints have ever been examined to this degree in Ireland before. This provides us with extensive insight into the reality of rape, the pervasiveness of 'real rape' myths, and the realities of our legal system. Along with insightful findings and a programme of far-reaching recommendations, this research signposts further critical research which must be undertaken. The recommendations concern law reform, policy and protocol development and implementation, allocation of resources and services, awareness raising and education programmes.

Many rape victims in Ireland have a positive experience of our legal system; equally, many do not. Many rape victims consider invoking the legal system, and, on balance decide that it is not worth it. This decision bears no correlation to the seriousness of the crimes perpetrated against them, nor the traumatic impact of those crimes. Thanks to Conor Hanly and his research team Ireland now has solid ground on which to build a programme of legal system reform, combined with targeting the 'real rape' myths and social barriers which prevent access to justice for many rape victims. It is imperative that attention and commitments are given to these recommendations.

In presenting this report for consideration I, on behalf of the RCNI, would like to record our appreciation for the hard work by the lead researcher Conor Hanly and his research team in NUI Galway. The Rape Crisis Network is grateful to The Atlantic Philanthropies for its contribution to this study.

As co-funders, the RCNI recognises and appreciates the contribution of Cosc, the Executive Office of the Department of Justice, Equality and Law Reform with responsibility for the prevention of domestic, sexual and gender-based violence, who generously agreed to provide extra funding in relation to Strand II of the project.

The RCNI wishes to express very special sincere gratitude to the women and men who participated in the research and who shared their experiences of rape and the legal system in Ireland.

From the RCNI perspective, this project has been a team effort, involving expert and valued contributions from all staff, in particular Clíona Saidléar and not least as current Legal Director, Caroline Counihan.

Fiona Neary
Executive Director
Rape Crisis Network Ireland

EXECUTIVE SUMMARY

PURPOSE OF STUDY

There is a dearth of information about the causes of attrition in rape cases in Ireland. It is difficult to develop a coherent response to the problem of rape in society when there is insufficient information to allow for a comprehensive review of existing structures. The primary aim of this study is to fill that lacuna by reviewing materials from different points of the criminal justice system. Secondary aims include the development of a more precise profile of rape in Ireland, and an evaluation of the experiences of those victims who choose to engage with the criminal justice system

METHODOLOGY

The three primary attrition points in the criminal justice system were identified: the decision by victims whether to make a formal report to the Gardaí, the decision by the Director of Public Prosecutions whether to initiate a prosecution, and the trial process. Each of these points was the focus of a specific element, or Strand, of the study and each Strand had its own eligibility criteria. All Strands, however, were confined to acts that fit the legal definition of rape provided by section 2 of the Criminal Law (Rape) Act 1981 and section 4 of the Criminal Law (Rape) (Amendment) Act 1990.

Strand I concerned the decision by victims of rape whether to make a complaint to the Gardaí. Participants were eligible if they were aged at least 18 at the time of the incident, and the incident occurred in Ireland since 2002. One hundred victims of rape participated by completing a questionnaire that contained questions about the incident, their decision whether to report and, if they did make a report, their experiences with the criminal justice system. Participants were also invited to participate in a follow up quantitative study, and fifty people did so. This follow up study employed a series of psychometric devices to assess the impact of the rape and reporting decision on the participants' mental health and attitude. Finally, a small number of participants volunteered for an in-depth qualitative interview designed to elicit narrative accounts about their experiences.

Strand II concerned the decision by the DPP whether or not to initiate a prosecution. A detailed questionnaire was developed which was then completed by researchers in the Office of the DPP in respect of each of 597 files received by the DPP between 2000 and 2004. The purpose of the questionnaire was to elicit information about the complainant, defendant and case characteristics of the cases, and the presence of a series of 'risk factors' – factors identified by the literature as having an effect on the prosecutorial decision. The effect that these characteristics and risk factors had upon the DPP's decision-making was investigated. A further quantitative study exploring the reasons for complaint withdrawal was also conducted.

Finally, Strand III focused on the trial process. Detailed questionnaires were completed in respect of 173 Central Criminal Court cases received by that court between 2000 and 2005. These questionnaires provided an enormous amount of information on how rape is dealt with in the criminal justice system. Additionally, the transcripts of 35 contested trials were analysed to elicit information about the conduct of rape trials in Ireland.

Results

Strand I: Reporting Rape

The Sample

- The participants were all female, half were single and the median age was 27. Nearly 60 per cent were in paid employment

Executive Summary

and there was a fairly even split among those who lived in cities, towns and villages.

The Rape Incidents

- Over two-thirds of the incidents occurred in houses, with the victim's own home being the single most common location.

- One-third of the rapes were committed by strangers, 39 per cent by friends or acquaintances and 18 per cent by current or previous intimate partners. All told, two-thirds of the participants were raped by someone known to them.

- Force was used in over 70 per cent of cases while threats were made in just under one-half of cases. Two-thirds of participants attempted to resist in some way, and nearly the same proportion reported some physical injury. Only 15 per cent reported serious injuries, however, and one-third stated that they did not suffer any physical injury.

- Some 70 per cent of participants had been drinking at the time of the incident; 30 per cent had consumed in excess of six drinks.

Reasons for Not Reporting

- Thirty-four per cent of participants had not made a report to the Gardaí. Concerns about the criminal justice system figured prominently, but the single most commonly stated reason was that the victim did not want others to know what had happened. Four participants claimed to have been drugged and therefore felt that they did not have sufficiently detailed information to make a complaint.

Reasons for Reporting

- Sixty-six per cent of victims had contacted the Gardaí but only 58 per cent made a statement and 9 per cent subsequently withdrew their complaints. The two primary reasons for making a report were that the victim wanted justice (23 per cent) and the influence of family and friends (22 per cent).

- Two-thirds of those who made a report did so within 24 hours of the incident, with half of them making a report within an hour of the incident. The longest delay in making a report was 18 months. By far the most common reason for a delay in making the report was shock.

Withdrawing the Complaint

- Over 40 per cent of those who made a report seriously considered withdrawing their complaint, and the primary reason for this was a poor reaction from the Gardaí.
- Twenty-one participants reported that they had been encouraged to withdraw their statements, with family and friends and Gardaí being almost equally implicated. Nine participants did in fact withdraw their complaints.

Contact with the Gardaí

- Almost two-thirds of the complainants who made a complaint did so in a Garda Station. A female Garda was present in over 85 per cent of interviews, and nearly half of the interviews were conducted solely by a female Garda.
- Most complainants found the interviewing Garda to be warm and sympathetic and most rated the atmosphere during the interview as warm and supportive. Two-thirds of complainants were satisfied or very satisfied with the interviewing officer. Those complainants who had been physically injured and those who had been raped by a stranger tended to give higher satisfaction ratings than those who were not injured or whose attacker was known to them. The prime reason for dissatisfaction with the interviewing Garda was stated to be their unsupportive attitude.

Executive Summary

- The complainants were largely dissatisfied with the Gardaí overall, with poor ongoing contact being the most common reason for this dissatisfaction.

Strand II: Prosecuting Rape

The Sample

- The complainants were overwhelmingly female (96 per cent), Irish (87.2 per cent) and young (77.1 per cent were under the age of 35).

- The defendants were all male and predominantly Irish (76.6 per cent). Nationals from Africa and Eastern Europe were especially over-represented. Two-thirds of defendants were aged under 35.

- There was a high level of alcohol consumption: nearly two-thirds of complainants and 57 per cent of defendants reported being either severely or moderately intoxicated at the time the incident occurred.

The Rape Incidents

- Over two-thirds of incidents occurred in a private setting such as a home or a hotel room.

- Nearly 62 per cent of complainants knew the man accused of raping her/him.

- The incidents were spread over the entire country; counties with easy access to a Sexual Assault Treatment Unit tended to be overrepresented which might indicate that the presence of such a unit improves the rate of reporting.

- The vast majority of cases (95 per cent) involved single perpetrators. While physical force was used in two-thirds of cases and the complainant reported physically resisting in nearly 50 per cent of case, physical injuries were reported by one-quarter of complainants which suggests that the level of force used is usually relatively minor.

- The most common risk factor was the complainant willingly going to the defendant's residence, car or hotel room (24.7 per cent), while another 10.4 per cent had invited the defendant back to her place of residence.

Prosecution Rate

- The DPP prosecuted just under one-third of prosecutable cases (i.e., the total number of cases excluding those cases in which the complainant had withdrawn the complaint).

- Of those cases that went to trial, nearly 60 per cent resulted in a conviction or a guilty plea in respect of at least one charge, sexual or non-sexual.

Impact of Risk Factors

- Regression analysis showed that most risk factors had little impact on the DPP's prosecutorial decision. This finding indicates that the DPP's decisions are being made primarily on evidentiary grounds. A history of alcohol abuse and especially the presence of a mental illness were shown to be related to not prosecuting, however. There were 78 cases involving a complainant with a history of mental illness and only two were prosecuted, the primary explanations being insufficiency of evidence (45 per cent) and it being unsafe to proceed (30.4 per cent).

Complaint Withdrawal

- Over one-quarter of rape complainants withdrew their complaints. One-quarter of these complainants suffered from substance abuse (primarily alcohol). Nearly one-quarter of complainants who withdrew their complaint had a history of mental illness. There was a significant relationship between mental illness and the withdrawal of the complaint on the grounds that the rape did not happen.

- The most common stated reasons for withdrawal concerned the trial and appearance in court.

- Either the Gardaí or the DPP indicated that approximately six per cent of cases might be false. This was most likely in cases in which the complainant made an admission (just under four per cent of complainants, or 13 per cent of those who withdrew their complainants).

Strand III: The Trial Process

The Sample

- Complainants were overwhelmingly female (97.67 per cent), young (median age of 23) and employed in a manual or unskilled job primarily as a shop assistant, waitress or barmaid.

- Defendants were male, slightly older than complainants (median age of 27) and also employed in manual or unskilled jobs especially as construction labourers.

- Probation Reports on 70 convicted defendants indicated a troubled background for most. In particular, three-quarters had a history of alcohol abuse.

The Rape Incidents

- Stranger-rapes made up less than 18 per cent of all cases, with the largest categories of perpetrators being acquaintances (25.82 per cent) and those who had met the complainant within 24 hours of the incident (21.43 per cent).

- Over 60 per cent of rapes occurred in a building, and three-quarters occurred between midnight and six o'clock in the morning.

- There were high levels of alcohol consumption by both complainants and defendants. Looking at those who specified how much they had consumed, nearly two-thirds of complainants and 88 per cent of defendants had been binge-drinking.

- Physical injuries were common, but they were overwhelmingly minor in nature. The primary effect of the rape was psychological, with psychological issues being mentioned in all but two victim impact statements.

The Legal Process

- Three-quarters of defendants were admitted to bail, usually conditionally. Only eight defendants out of the 112 who were admitted to bail absconded, and one of them was subsequently caught and stood trial. Bail is not a significant cause of attrition.

- Juries were numerically dominated by men: nearly 60 per cent of jurors and three-quarters of jury foremen were male. Over 90 per cent of juries contained at least three members of each gender, thereby allowing the minority gender to force a hung jury if they so chose. Jurors were predominantly employed in manual or unskilled positions, with the most common position being a clerical job in the financial services sector. Those who held professional or skilled occupations were disproportionately represented among the jury foremen.

- Juries were reluctant to convict defendants of rape (only 20 out of 84 that were free to do so), and even more so in cases of rape under section 4 (only four out of 29). Eleven juries acquitted the defendants of rape charges but convicted them of lesser sexual or non-sexual offences.

- Female-dominated juries did not convict any defendants of rape charges. Male dominated juries were most likely to convict a defendant of rape.

- Seventy defendants were convicted of rape, a further 29 were convicted of a lesser sexual offence and nine were convicted of a non-sexual offence; excluding the seven defendants for whom the result of their case was unclear, 108 defendants out of 181, or 60 per cent, were convicted of something.

- The median sentence for rape after a trial was 96 months or 102 months after a guilty plea. In cases of rape under section 4, the median sentence after a trial was 84 months and 114 months after a guilty plea. Three-quarters of sentences for rape were for between five and ten years imprisonment.

- Multiple sentences imposed upon the same offender always ran concurrently; in one case, the defendant was sentenced to consecutive terms, but this arrangement was altered by the Court of Criminal Appeal.

- There was no evidence that victims were abusing their right to address the court as to the impact that the rape had upon them. Defendants and punishment were mentioned in 17 and 19 statements, respectively, out of 107 statements.

- The median length of a rape case was 33 months from date of incident to date of final disposition. Cases disposed of by guilty plea typically lasted nine months less than cases that went to trial.

- Sexual history evidence was admitted in 13 cases out of the 35 for which we had transcripts; in 10 cases the prosecution asked the complainant about her sexual history. By contrast, the complainant was questioned about her behaviour in 24 cases, and usually at greater length.

- The primary defence in rape cases was that the complainant consented to sexual intercourse.

- Corroboration warnings appear to be given in a minority of cases only.

MAIN SPECIFIC RECOMMENDATIONS

The Reporting and Investigation Stage

1. The Gardaí must develop protocols to initiate and maintain ongoing contact with rape complainants. This is the primary cause of complainant dissatisfaction with the Gardaí once the initial stages of the investigation are over.

2. The Gardaí should ensure that all rape victims are adequately informed as to all the key developments in the prosecution of their allegations, as required by the Victims' Charter.

3. It is recommended that a greater emphasis be placed on personal sensitivity and compassion towards rape victims during Garda training

4. Serious consideration should be given to specialist training for Gardaí who take statements from those with mental illness, as this group may need to be treated with extra sensitivity in order to discourage withdrawal of genuine complaints.

5. Attempts to dissuade complainants from maintaining their complaints must end. It is not for the Gardaí to make this decision. The Gardaí should explain what is involved in the trial system, but this should be done in as positive a manner as possible.

6. It is recommended that, where possible, victims be allowed time to recuperate before their full statement is taken in order to reduce the impact of shock and post-traumatic stress disorder.

7. Improvements should continue to be made in the provision of support services to complainants from the very beginning of their involvement with the judicial system. Doing so might result in fewer cases being withdrawn. It is therefore recommended that a SATU be established ideally within 80 kilometres of any given location, and that there be a media campaign to educate the public about such supports.

8. It is further recommended that there be a nationally co-ordinated approach to the planning, delivery and ongoing evaluation of support services for victims of sexual violence.

9. It is recommended that the Victims' Charter be amended to include, in addition to the complaints' procedure, an explicit commitment by all criminal justice agencies to take active

measures to ensure that their responsibilities under the Charter will be properly discharged.

10. It is recommended that the Victims' Charter be placed upon a statutory footing

The Prosecuting Stage

11. The DPP should investigate the overrepresentation of non-national defendants to ensure that these prosecutions are being brought for proper reasons.

12. The DPP should develop a protocol for dealing with complainants with a history of mental illness to ensure that complaints by such people are not being dropped simply because they have a mental illness.

The Court Proceedings Stage

13. Bail in rape cases should always be subject to strict conditions which are swiftly and rigorously enforced. At a minimum, defendants should be required to be of good behaviour, to stay away from the complainant unless absolutely necessary and to stay within the jurisdiction of the Irish courts. Bail should not be granted to a defendant who has been convicted of rape.

14. A research project should be commissioned into the jury's deliberative process as soon as possible.

15. Gender quotas should not be imposed on rape juries as there is no evidence that increasing the number of female jurors would have any effect on the conviction rate.

16. There should be a statutory obligation on judges to instruct juries that a conclusion that the complainant acted foolishly does not of itself make her wholly or partially responsible for the rape.

17. The apparent judicial hostility to consecutive sentences needs to be justified or abandoned.

18. The interaction between suspended sentences and post-release supervision orders should be examined.

19. A booklet giving directions on what is inappropriate to mention in a victim impact statement should be produced and distributed, especially to complainants who wish to produce their own statement.

20. A defendant in a rape case should be forbidden by statute to conduct a personal cross-examination of the complainant.

21. The restrictions on the introduction of sexual history evidence should be extended to the prosecution. In the alternative, if the prosecution is to be permitted to continue to introduce such evidence, the complainant must be consulted in advance of any such introduction.

22. With regard to every stage of the process, but particularly once the case is returned for trial, every possible means of reducing delay should be explored, and pursued where appropriate. It is recommended, therefore, that the National Crime Council research recommendations on delay set out in this report are followed, and that there be an implementation strategy by all the relevant agencies in relation to these recommendations.

23. It is recommended that section 6 of the Criminal Justice Act 1993 be amended to clarify and strengthen the victim compensation procedures. Compensation should be considered in every case in which a crime has been shown to have been committed. To ensure that this is done, it is recommended that a statutory obligation to seek compensation on behalf of the complainant be imposed upon the DPP.

24. It is recommended that an expert group be convened to consider the acceptable limits of cross-examination and defence strategy in criminal cases generally, and rape cases in particular. The expert group should consider also whether there is a need to introduce specialist training for lawyers involved in rape cases.

Outside the Criminal Justice Process

25. It is strongly recommended that dealing with Ireland's drinking culture, particularly as it affects the behaviour of potential perpetrators, be seen both as a part of any anti-rape campaign and a prerequisite for the success of any such campaign.

26. It is recommended that there be a media campaign aimed at men, particularly young men, to make them aware that rape is a possible consequence of binge-drinking. They need to be reminded that they are responsible for their own actions, and that voluntary intoxication does not relieve them of that responsibility, morally or legally.

Chapter 1

INTRODUCTION

A comparative European study published in 2003 stated that based on figures provided by the Department of Justice, Equality and Law Reform for three periods between 1977 and 2000, the conviction rate in Ireland had fallen from 9 per cent between 1977-1981 to 1 per cent between 1998-2000 (Regan and Kelly, 2003: 13). This constituted the lowest conviction rate, and therefore the highest attrition rate, from reporting to conviction among all the European countries that provided data (17 countries provided this data). On foot of this finding, the Rape Crisis Network Ireland commissioned the School of Law at the National University of Ireland Galway to investigate the causes of attrition in rape cases in Ireland.

DEFINING RAPE

Rape is a crime in Irish law by virtue of section 48 of the Offences against the Person Act 1861, but this provision does not define the elements of the offence. Irish law is unusual in that there are two parallel definitions of rape. The traditional definition is set out in section 2 of the Criminal Law (Rape) Act 1981:

A man commits rape if:

a) he has unlawful sexual intercourse with a woman who at the time of the intercourse does not consent to it, and

b) at that time he knows that she does not consent to the intercourse or he is reckless as to whether she does or does not consent to it.

This definition is limited in two respects: it is limited by gender in that only a man can commit the offence and only a woman can suffer the offence, and it is limited in that the act punished under this provision is non-consensual penile penetration of the woman's vagina. Section 4 of the Criminal Law (Rape) (Amendment) Act 1990 was enacted to deal with these limitations:

1) In this Act 'rape under section 4' means a sexual assault that includes –

   a) penetration (however slight) of the anus or mouth by the penis, or

   b) penetration (however slight) of the vagina by any object held or manipulated by another person.

2) A person guilty of rape under section 4 shall be liable on conviction on indictment to imprisonment for life.

Officially, rape is rape. Officially, no distinction is made between rapes exhibiting a high level of physical force, the use of weapons and/or multiple assailants and those committed by a single, unarmed individual with no evident physical injury to the complainant. While rape may be rape in the letter of the law, however, studies conducted in other jurisdictions have consistently found that different types of rape are treated differently by prosecutors and juries, and that extra-legal factors influence the outcome. The literature tends to divide rape cases into two categories: simple cases and aggravated cases (e.g., Kalven and Zeisel, 1966; Estrich, 1987; Temkin, 2002). Aggravated cases are those in which various aggravating factors are present:

- It is committed by a stranger;
- It is committed by more than one offender;

- The commission of the rape involved the threat or use of a weapon; or
- The rape results in evident physical injury.

A simple rape, by contrast, is one in which 'a woman is forced to have sex without consent by only one man, whom she knows, who does not beat her or attack her with a gun' (Estrich, 1987: 10). A woman is deemed to have known her attacker if she has had any previous dealings with him. Thus, in a situation in which a woman encounters a man in a pub, converses with him, and then either goes home with him, accepts a lift from him or walks with him to her car, the woman will be deemed to know this man. If the man subsequently rapes the woman, the rape will be classified as 'simple'. There are obvious, evidential reasons why simple rapes are more difficult to prosecute than aggravated rapes. Consent is a thorny issue, and often comes down to a 'he-said/she-said' scenario in simple rapes. If a weapon is produced or a beating is administered there is generally little issue about consent. Forensic evidence may also be easier to attain in aggravated cases.

Complicating matters for both the prosecutor and the jury are the bewildering possibilities of combinations between simple/aggravated, stranger/acquaintance rapes. A woman may be raped by one man she knows and sustain severe injuries; she may be raped by multiple men she knows and sustain severe injuries; she may be raped by one man she does not know and receive no injuries; by multiple men, some she knows and some she does not, and receive injuries or not; she may be raped vaginally, anally or orally, or all three ways, or a combination of ways, by one or more penises, or with an object by one or more people whom she may or may not know, or whom she knows somewhat; and the list goes on. This almost inexhaustible catalogue of possible rape scenarios belies the notion that there is anything that could be considered a 'typical' rape. Yet, despite this reality, both prosecutors and juries have notions of 'real rape' (see e.g., Estrich, 1987; Frohmann, 1991; Kalven and Zeisel, 1966; Dripps, 2008). Juries, it would appear, maintain the mythical notion of the violent stranger rape as the typical rape. Where rapes differ from this norm, as do the majority of rapes, the literature suggests that juries are reluctant to convict, and prosecutors are thus reluctant to prosecute.

OVERVIEW OF THE CRIMINAL PROCESS IN IRELAND

The criminal process in a rape case begins with the complainant making a formal allegation against the defendant. The first possibility of attrition is thus the decision *not* to report the incident to the Gardaí. If an allegation is made shortly after the incident occurred, the complainant will be brought for a medical examination, during which forensic evidence will be collected and sent for analysis. The person against whom the allegation is made will normally be arrested, cautioned and questioned by the Gardaí shortly after the complainant makes a formal complaint. The Gardaí will also visit the scene of the incident and take statements from any witnesses. Once the Gardaí have completed their investigations, a file will be sent to the Solicitor's Division of the Office of the Director of Public Prosecutions (or to a local State Solicitor if outside the capital) who will in turn pass the file on to the Directing Division within the same Office. The Directing Division will determine whether and what charges should be brought against the defendant. In making this decision, the Directing Officers must consider whether there is sufficient evidence to warrant a prosecution and whether the public interest is served by initiating a prosecution (Prosecution of Offences Act, 1974). Assuming these tests are met, the defendant will then be formally charged by the Gardaí, on foot of a Statement of Charges. In some cases, usually where there is some urgency involved, it is possible for the Gardaí to bring initial charges prior to the full file being sent to the Director of Public Prosecutions (DPP), although only after a consultation with a Directing Officer. The charges can be amended later when the full file has been assembled and passed onto the DPP.

Once charges have been brought against the defendant, the trial process begins. The trial process is the procedure by which those charges are formally presented and determined before the judiciary. The process is based either upon a summons for minor offences, or upon an indictment for more serious matters. Rape is one of the most serious offences in Irish law, and can only be prosecuted on indictment (*People (DPP) v. Tiernan*, 1988). The process begins in the District Court, which has three major decisions to make. First, and most important, the District Court returns the defendant for trial in the appropriate court, which in the case of rape is the Central Criminal Court (Criminal Law (Rape) (Amendment) Act 1990, section 10). The District Court formerly made this decision on foot of a preliminary examination (Walsh, 2002: 677), the purpose of which was to determine whether there was sufficient evidence to warrant a trial. The preliminary hearing was abolished by the Criminal Justice Act 1999 with effect from October 2001 (Walsh, 2002: 678). By virtue of section 4A(1) of the Criminal Procedure Act 1967, as amended by the 1999 Act, the District Court must now return the defendant for trial, providing two requirements have been met: the Director of Public Prosecutions consents and the Book of Evidence has been served on the defendant or his solicitor. The Book of Evidence consists of all the evidence on which the prosecution may rely at trial, and will include the Statement of Charges, statements from the complainant and all witnesses, statements from investigating members of the Gardaí, lists of exhibits, medical reports, etc. (Walsh, 2002: 715-6). The evidence contained in the book can be supplemented with further evidence if the prosecution files a Notice of Additional Evidence. Second, the District Court will generally decide whether to admit the defendant to bail pending the full trial of the issues against him. Finally, the District Court may also decide whether the defendant should receive financial assistance in the form of legal aid.

Once the defendant has been returned for trial by the District Court, a date must be fixed for his trial before the Central Criminal Court, and the defendant will usually be arraigned on that date (National Crime Council, 2006: 25). Arraignment is the process by which the indictment is read out to the defendant and he is asked to formally respond to the charges by pleading guilty or not guilty (Walsh, 2002: 777). If the defendant pleads guilty to the charges, there will be no trial and the matter can proceed straight to the sentencing process. If the defendant pleads not guilty to the charges, or to some of them, he must stand trial and all trials in the Central Criminal Court are heard before judge and jury. A jury of twelve citizens will be empanelled and the trial will begin. The case for the prosecution is presented first, invariably in the form of testimony elicited in the form of answers to questions. Each of the prosecution's witnesses are called in turn and examined by counsel for the prosecution, and then cross-examined by counsel for the defence. At the conclusion of the prosecution's case, the defence may seek a direction to acquit. Essentially, the defence will argue that the prosecution's evidence, even when viewed in the most favourable light, is insufficient for a conviction. If the trial judge agrees, he will direct the jury to acquit the defendant and the case will end. If the trial judge disagrees, the defence must present its evidence in the same manner as the prosecution. Once all the evidence has been heard, both prosecution and defence make closing speeches in which they essentially summarise their respective cases. The trial judge then charges the jury by explaining the relevant law and summarizing (and commenting upon) the evidence presented. The jury will then retire to deliberate, following which the jury renders its verdict. If the jury votes to acquit, the case is over and no further action generally can be brought against the defendant in respect of those charges. If the jury fails to reach a verdict, the jury is said to have hung and the prosecution will have the option of initiating the prosecution before a new jury. If the jury votes to convict, the court will usually adjourn proceedings to allow for the production of pre-sentence reports, the most important of which are Probation Reports on the defendant and Victim Impact Statements from or in respect of the complainant. Once these reports have been presented, the trial judge can proceed to impose sentence upon the defendant. The defendant then may seek leave to appeal to the Court of Criminal Appeal, initially from the trial court, or from the Court of Criminal Appeal itself if the trial court refuses the application. The appeal can be against the conviction, the sentence or against both. The Criminal Justice Act 1993 also allows the DPP to appeal against sentences that he feels are unjustifiably low. In both cases, the decision of the Court of Criminal Appeal is usually final, although a further appeal to the Supreme Court is possible if the Court of Criminal Appeal, the Attorney General or the DPP certifies the case as being of exceptional public importance.

ATTRITION AND THE EFFECTIVENESS OF THE CRIMINAL PROCESS

Attrition refers to the process by which cases fall out of the criminal justice system (Gregory and Lees, 1996; Lea et al., 2003). In essence, then, attrition refers to the difference between the number of cases that are brought to the attention of the police and those that result in a conviction. There are a myriad of ways in which this might happen: the victim might not report the incident to the police or she might choose to withdraw her cooperation; the police might be unable to identify or locate the offender; the prosecutorial authorities might decide not to bring a prosecution for a variety of reasons; or, the jury might decide to acquit the person charged. Thus, 'the criminal justice system has been likened to a giant sieve, filtering out cases at every stage of the process' (Bryden and Lengnick, 1997: 1208). This process is a feature of the prosecution of all crimes, but there is evidence that the attrition rate in the prosecution of rape is higher than in the prosecution of other crimes (Roberts, 1996; Phillips and Brown, 1998).

The effectiveness of the criminal justice system in dealing with the problem of rape is typically measured by the conviction rate – the greater the conviction rate (or the lower the attrition rate), the more effective the system is thought to be. This is a problematic method of measuring effectiveness: it suggests that acquittals should be seen invariably as a failure of the system, when acquittals may well be entirely justified. Thus, the acquittal of a person against whom the evidence is too weak to justify a conviction is in truth a success story rather than a failure. Nevertheless, the conviction rate remains the principal means of assessment of the administration of criminal justice. On this form of assessment, the criminal justice system has proven to be a poor response to the problem of rape.

The conviction rate is usually attained in one of two ways. First, from official statistics, the conviction rate can be expressed as the number of convictions in a given year as a percentage of the incidents reported to the police in that year. Thus, using figures from the Home Office, Temkin and Krahe (2008: 20) note that the conviction rate in England and Wales for rape fell from 32 per cent in 1979 to 5.3 per cent in 2004/5. This method of expressing the conviction rate is problematic for two reasons: first, it involves a comparison of convictions with reported incidents even though those convictions almost certainly relate to incidents reported in a previous year because of delays within the criminal justice system. Second, these convictions usually record only the fact of conviction; therefore, the fact that a defendant in a rape case might have been convicted for an offence other than rape would be disguised. The second method of attaining a conviction rate avoids both of these problems: by tracking (either prospectively or historically) a series of cases through the criminal justice system, researchers have been able to determine the precise percentage of cases that result in a conviction for rape. The conviction rate using this methodology is typically higher than that found using the first method. In their joint study of the investigation and prosecution of rape cases in England and Wales, the HMCPSI/HMIC (2002) found a conviction rate of 60.8 per cent of all cases actually prosecuted but only 29.6 per cent of cases that actually went to the jury (i.e., guilty pleas were excluded). These figures were derived from 88 cases that were actually prosecuted as rape; the total sample was 230 cases submitted by the police to the Crown Prosecution Service. The conviction rate (including guilty pleas) from the total sample was some 23 per cent. Kelly et al. (2005: 71) found that of 2, 244 cases in which the result was known, only 322 (14 per cent) were scheduled for trial. Of these, 89 (28 per cent) were determined through guilty plea; convictions for rape were recorded in 66 (20 per cent); convictions for other offences were recorded in 11 (3 per cent); and 104 (32 per cent) resulted in an acquittal. Of the total sample, therefore, the overall conviction rate was 7.4 per cent. Kelly et al. (2005: 28) also summarise in tabular form the results of six earlier studies (four in England and Wales and two in Scotland):

	Chambers & Millar (1983)	Grace et al. (1992)	Lees & Gregory (1993)	Jamieson et al. (1998)	Harris & Grace (1999)	Lea et al. (2003)
Sample (n)	196	464	109	47	483	379
Prosecuted	38 %	33 %	25 %	32 %	20 %	-
Rape Conviction	15 %	19 %	9 %	15 %	6 %	5 %
Other Conviction	10 %	8 %	2 %	4 %	7 %	6 %
Acquittal	9 %	7 %	14 %	4 %	7 %	-

More recently, Feist et al. (2007) found an overall conviction rate of 10.7 per cent out of 676 cases, although this figure dropped to 4.7 per cent if convictions for lesser offences were excluded.

Most British studies, therefore, show a conviction rate of between 10 per cent and 20 per cent, and a large number of other studies from around the common law world show broadly similar results (Russell, 1984: 101; Majority Staff of the U.S. Senate Judiciary Committee, 1993; Frazier et al., 1994; New South Wales Department of Women, 1996; Fitzgerald, 2006; Taylor, 2007). Yet even these low figures are misleading in that they give a conviction rate only out of the cases known to the police. It is well established, however, that the majority of rape cases are not reported to the police (e.g., Myhill and Allen, 2002; Gartner and McMillan, 1995; Tjaden and Thoennes, 2006). When applied to the estimated prevalence of rape in society, the conviction rate drops to dramatically low levels. An American commentator (Feild, 1979) and a

New Zealand commentator (Young, 1983) both estimated that in their respective jurisdictions a rapist had only a four per cent chance of being convicted. The Majority Staff of the U.S. Senate Judiciary Committee (1993) agreed: they estimated that a rape victim had only a two per cent chance of seeing her rapist incarcerated. Accordingly, it is difficult to contest Wright's conclusion (1984: 100) that a rapist who is sent to prison for rape must consider himself very unfortunate.

RAPE AND THE CRIMINAL PROCESS – ATTEMPTS AT REFORM

Rape is not a rare event in our society. Recent studies (Myhill and Allen, 2002; Walby and Allen, 2004) estimate that the total number of women in England and Wales who have suffered rape as adults is around 4 per cent, with 61,000 new victims in 1999 and 47,000 in 2000 (including attempts). Irish figures are not quite so detailed, but the Sexual Abuse and Violence in Ireland study (SAVI) (McGee et al., 2002: 65-6) found that over 6 per cent of women and just under 1 per cent of men had suffered experiences that fit the current legal definitions of rape. These respondents have suffered a violent crime that can cause significant personal injury in addition to the violation of the person inherent in the offence. Additionally, a large number of studies have shown that rape can cause serious psychological effects for the complainant (e.g., Burgess and Holmstrom, 1979; Shapland et al., 1985; Walby and Allen, 2004). Further, Duborg et al. (2005) have shown that rape imposes significant financial costs both to the victim and to society in general. Consequently, there are compelling reasons for society to ensure that the criminal justice system's response to the problem of rape in our society is as effective as possible. The materials cited above show that this has not been the case. Commentators in the 1970s and 1980s pointed out that the law had developed a series of rules related specifically to rape that made successful prosecution more difficult (e.g., Brownmiller, 1976; Estrich, 1987). Further, these rules 'all too often resulted in the victim's being violated a second time – by the criminal justice system' (Estrich, 1987: 42). Three factors combined to bring about reform of the rape laws in common law jurisdictions in the 1980s and 1990s. First, rape victim advocacy groups such as Rape Crisis Centres began to highlight the treatment of victims. Second, the problem of crime control became a dominant theme in the political arena with broad agreement among politicians that the criminal justice system was unduly protective of criminal defendants (Ashworth, 2000; Elias, 2003). Finally, there was increasing recognition among lawyers that victims had in fact been treated poorly by the criminal justice system, a treatment that ultimately could undermine the system itself (e.g., Royal Commission on Criminal Justice, 1993: para. 5.44; Scottish Executive, 2000).

Efforts to reform the rape laws are generally taken to have begun with the formation in 1972 of the Women's Task Force on Rape in Michigan (Temkin, 2002: 150). This Task Force drafted what was then considered an ideal rape statute (March et al., 1982), an effort that was subsequently replicated in other states in the United States, Canada and Australia. Temkin (2002: 151) notes that these reform efforts typically contained five characteristics. First, the traditional single offence of rape was replaced by some form of gradation scheme based on differing levels of offence severity. Second, very often, this gradation scheme dropped the word 'rape' entirely in favour of 'sexual assault', the rationale being that by dropping the word all the historical baggage that went along with that word would also be dropped. Third, attempts were made to alter the manner in which the law treated the issue of consent, such as in Michigan whose model statute dropped all references to consent and focused instead on the circumstances in which the offence occurred (Schulhofer, 1998). Fourth, long-standing common law exemptions from the law of rape for certain categories of males were abolished, principally those concerning husbands and young males under the age of fourteen. Finally, alterations were made to the laws of evidence, especially through the introduction of what became known as Rape Shield Laws. These laws attempted to provide some measure of protection to rape complainants from the kind of intimate questioning that had hitherto characterised a rape trial. There were high expectations that these reforms would revolutionise the trial of rape, leading to much higher rates of reporting, prosecution and conviction (Spohn and Horney, 1996). A series of studies determined, however, that these reforms had achieved little in terms of conviction rates (Department of Justice Canada, 1990; Bachman and Paternoster, 1993-4; March et al., 1982; Schissel, 1996, Horney and Spohn, 1991; Spohn and Horney, 1996), but were nevertheless important in symbolic terms (Berger et al., 1988; Spohn, 1998-9).

TERMINOLOGY

The criminal justice system makes extensive use of labels to denote both the position that individuals hold and the stage within the system that they have reached. Strictly speaking, these labels are just words with formal meanings. Words, however, also carry connotations, and the connotations attached to the terms used to denote those who make allegations of rape have led to a considerable debate on the most appropriate form of reference. The primary choices are 'victims' and 'survivors'. Koss and Harvey (1991: ix) explain the distinction between these terms:

> [The victim] is one who is acted upon and usually adversely affected by a force or agent, one who is subjected to oppression, hardship or who is tricked or duped. It can also denote one who is injured, destroyed or sacrificed. The survivor is the victim who not only has endured, but who has also prevailed and who has rebuilt the meaning shattered by rape.

In other words, referring to those who have been raped as victims denigrates them, whereas referring to them as survivors empowers them. Other commentators disagree, arguing that these distinctions prevent a full understanding of what those who have been raped go through, both at the time of the rape and afterwards in trying to cope with the experience (e.g., Kelly and

Regan, 2001: 47). In other words, anyone who has been raped is both a victim *and* a survivor. This debate, while no doubt important, is not an appropriate subject for this study. Accordingly, the labels used in this study are used in their strict legal sense. Those who allege rape are referred to as victims until they make a complaint, at which point they are referred to as complainants. Those against whom complaints are made are referred to as suspects until charges are laid against them at which point they become defendants. If convicted, defendants become offenders. These terms are used in a strictly neutral sense, and no connotations are intended by their use. Similarly, the chair of a jury is referred to as a foreman as this is the term employed in the controlling legislation; such usage is not intended to suggest that only men can hold this position.

One other issue of nomenclature needs airing. In this study victims of rape are referred to in the feminine gender unless otherwise indicated. This has been done simply for linguistic convenience, and is not meant to deny the existence of male rape, which has been formally recognised by Irish law since 1990. Nor is this practice intended to denigrate the suffering that male victims of rape go through. All the available evidence, however, indicates that men and women do not face an equal threat of sexual violence, and that rape is a crime that is overwhelmingly committed against women. Using the feminine rather than the masculine therefore better reflects the reality of the crime of rape.

Chapter 2

THE CURRENT STATE OF KNOWLEDGE: RAPE AND ATTRITION IN THE LEGAL SYSTEM

There is a dearth of information relating to rape and the legal system in Ireland. Recent studies – Leanne et al.'s (2001) qualitative study, Bacik et al.'s European study (1998) and McGee et al. (2005) – have attempted to address this issue. These studies used in-depth qualitative assessments and quantitative analysis, but such Irish studies remain in very short supply. In order to situate this study within the larger state of knowledge on rape attrition, it is necessary to look at research conducted in other jurisdictions. This chapter assesses the current state of knowledge on reporting rape, prosecuting rape, the trial process and the associated stages of attrition. The starting point, however, is a discussion on the nature and prevalence of so-called 'rape myths', which the literature has shown to be influential at all stages of the criminal process (e.g. Kelly, 2001; Temkin and Krahe, 2008; Myhill and Allen, 2002).

RAPE MYTHS

From the 1970s onwards, sociological researchers began to investigate the impact upon the criminal justice system of widespread cultural misconceptions about rape (Payne et al., 1999: 27). These misconceptions have been labelled 'rape myths' and are defined as 'prejudicial, stereotyped, or false beliefs about rape, rape victims, and rapists' (Burt, 1980: 217). These beliefs depend for their survival 'not on evidence but on constant reiteration' (Kennedy, 1992: 32). Today, virtually all commentators accept that the existence of such rape myths makes convictions in rape cases more difficult to achieve (e.g., Scottish Executive, 2000; Kelly, 2001; Office of Criminal Justice Reform, 2006; Temkin and Krahe, 2008). Rape myth acceptance impacts the criminal justice system in three ways. First, all decision-makers have to base their decisions on their assessment of the information before them, but that assessment takes place within the context of the decision-maker's own value system. Decision-makers who subscribe to rape myths are more likely to view the victim in a negative light (and therefore to decide against her interests) if her actions or behaviour breached the decision-maker's value system (e.g. Acock and Ireland, 1983; Adler, 1985; Muehlenhard, 1988; La Free et al., 1985; Whatley, 2005). Second, decision-makers are called upon to decide whether or not an incident constituted the crime of rape. Because the information before them will rarely be complete, decision-makers may be tempted to depart from the evidence and to fall back upon schematic or stereotypical views of what constitutes rape in order to help them make their decision (Temkin and Krahe, 2008: 42-3). Finally, rape myth acceptance among legislators and judges (at least in common law jurisdictions) can lead to the development of discriminatory legal rules.

Rape myths can be broken into a number of different categories for ease of analysis: a belief in the prevalence of false accusations, a belief in the 'real rape' stereotype, and more general rape-supportive attitudes.

False Accusations

Writing in the eighteenth century, the great English jurist Lord Matthew Hale declared:

> It is true rape is a most detestable crime, and therefore ought severely and impartially to be punished with death; but it must be remembered, that it is an accusation easily to be made and hard to be proved, and harder to be defended by the party accused, tho never so innocent (1736: 635).

Implicit in this statement is an assumption that false allegations of rape are easily made, an assumption that has continuing vitality today. Burt (1980) found that 50 per cent of her respondents endorsed the view that false reports of rape are common, motivated either by revenge or a desire to hide a sexual indiscretion. Hans and Vidmar (2001) cite an opinion poll published in the London *Times* in which one quarter of the 1,056 respondents believed that men were often convicted of rapes that they did not commit. Burton et al. (1998) found that 81 per cent of male respondents and 68 per cent of female respondents agreed that women cry rape the next day because of second thoughts about their earlier sexual activities. In a review of existing studies, Olsen-Fulero and Fulero (1997) found that between 50 per cent and 78 per cent of respondents agreed that most reported cases of rape are false and are promoted by revenge or a desire to disguise 'promiscuous' behaviour.

These attitudes have also been found among police officers, judges and lawyers. Among police officers, researchers in several jurisdictions have found evidence of widespread disbelief of rape complainants. The Law Reform Commissioner of Victoria (1976) noted a study conducted among four Victorian police departments that concluded that 50 per cent of rape reports were considered by police to be unfounded. Similarly, Chambers and Millar (1983) found that Scottish police officers believed false reports to be common, although they noted that few officers were able to provide any actual examples of false reports from their own experiences. Similar police attitudes were reported by Temkin as a result of interviews with officers in London (1999) and Sussex (1997). Out of concern that police officers were 'no-criming'[*] rape reports too easily, the Home Office in Britain introduced Circular 69/1986, which provided that a rape report could be no-crimed only if the complainant retracted the complaint and admitted to falsification (Rumney, 2006: 131). Notwithstanding these instruc-

---

[*] No-criming refers to a process in which police officers formally determine that no crime occurred and that therefore the complainant's allegations should receive no further attention.

tions, Harris and Grace (1999) found evidence of widespread continuing misuse by the police of their no-criming power. As for lawyers and judges, Temkin and Krahe (2008) interviewed 17 judges and seven barristers, all with experience in rape cases. Three judges and one barrister stated their opinion that false reports were a particular problem in rape cases.

Why might a rape complainant make a false report? In most studies, respondents believed that false reports were motivated either by a desire for revenge or to disguise promiscuous behaviour (Burt, 1980; Burton, 1998; Olsen-Fulero and Fulero, 1997). The Law Reform Commission of Victoria (1976) considered this matter in some detail and set out several instances in which they thought a woman might be tempted to make a false complaint:

- If she needs an excuse for coming home late and there is evidence of sexual intercourse;
- If she is found in the act of sexual intercourse and important rights such as custody of children are concerned;
- If she needs to explain a pregnancy or the contraction of a venereal disease;
- If she wants to gain revenge for a husband or boyfriend's infidelity or wants to be rid of a former boyfriend; or
- If she wants to justify an abortion.

Hanly (2001: n. 65) summarises some of the other reasons that have been advanced to explain women's perceived willingness to make a false report: sexual neuroses, sexual fantasies, extortion, attempts to coerce a man to marry her, a desire for notoriety or sympathy, or for no reason at all. It is noteworthy that empirical support for any of these supposed explanations is rarely provided.

Empirical evidence for the prevalence of false reporting in rape cases is inconclusive. Rumney (2006: 136-7) reviews the available empirical evidence on the rate of false reporting, and notes rates running between 1.5 per cent to 90 per cent. Notwithstanding this range, since the late 1970s there has been a broad consensus among scholarly commentators that the rate of false reporting in rape cases is low and is no higher than the rate in other offences (Rumney, 2006: 143). The usual authority for this assertion is Brownmiller (1976: 366), who refers to a review by female police officers of rape complaints made to the New York Police Department that found that two per cent of the complaints were false. The source for this information is stated to be a speech by a New York appellate judge to the New York Bar Association. Regrettably, Brownmiller gave no details as to the methodology employed in this review, and its accuracy has been questioned (Greer, 2000). Part of the difficulty in quantifying the rate of false reporting is definitional (Rumney, 2006) – should one, for example, include as a false report those that are made in good faith (i.e., the complainant was drunk at the time of the incident and honestly thought that something untoward had happened)? A further difficulty lies in identification (Hanly, 2001) – by what criteria is a false report to be identified? Clearly, the mere fact that a prosecution is not brought or, if a prosecution is initiated, is unsuccessful, is not evidence of falsification. Accordingly, an empirical finding must be based on clear and reliable criteria before it can be accepted, a requirement that few empirical studies have met (Rumney, 2006: 139). Thus, the true rate of false reporting in rape cases is unknown, but there is as yet no conclusive evidence that false reports are common.

The 'Real Rape' Stereotype

Perhaps the most pernicious myth surrounding the trial of rape offences concerns the so-called 'real rape' stereotype. As its name suggests, this is a stereotypical view of the characteristics of a typical rape attack that decision-makers expect to see in a rape allegation. In describing her own rape experience, Estrich (1987: 47) commented that the 'most important thing is that [the rapist] was a stranger; that he approached me not only armed but uninvited; that he was after my money and car, which I surely don't give away lightly, as well as my body'. In other words, if those characteristics are present in a given incident, the decision-maker is much more likely to label the incident as rape (Kalven and

Zeisel, 1966: 249-254; Burt and Albin, 1981; Kerstetter, 1990; Lees and Gregory, 1993; Frazier and Haney, 1996; Du Mont et al., 2003). This has been confirmed through interviews with criminal justice professionals, most of whom claim not to subscribe to the stereotype themselves but who nevertheless accept its power especially over jurors and act accordingly[*] (Brown et al., 2007). Thus, the real rape stereotype is not only descriptive but is prescriptive as well at least in its effect (Temkin and Krahe, 2008: 32). Interestingly, the power of the real rape stereotype not only affects the decision-maker; it may also affect the complainant's view of the incident. A number of researchers have found significant proportions of their respondents experiencing incidents that met their legal definition of rape who did not themselves view those experiences as rape (Koss and Oros, 1982; Scronce and Corcoran, 1995; Myhill and Allen, 2002: 53-7; Du Mont et al., 2003; Walby and Allen, 2004:51-2). Peterson and Muehlenhard (2004) note that there might be a number of reasons for this, but argue that even victims will have been exposed to rape myths and must have been influenced by them. Consequently, victims are more likely to report a rape to the police if the incident fits the stereotype. As a result of this and the issue of downstreaming, stereotypical rapes are more likely to be prosecuted which in turn 'shape[s] the social perception of what genuine rape cases are like' (Temkin and Krahe, 2008: 40). Thus the stereotype becomes self-perpetuating.

There are several characteristics traditionally associated with the real rape stereotype:

1. The rapist is a stranger to the victim;

2. The rape will occur outdoors, usually at night;

3. The rape will be perpetrated by force, usually with a weapon;

4. The victim will resist physically and will suffer physical injuries as a result; and

---

[*] This is a process known as downstreaming – i.e., decisions are made at early stages of the criminal process in anticipation of decisions that are perceived to be likely further downstream in the system.

5. The victim will be highly emotional after the rape.

To this list, a further, more modern characteristic should be added due to its prominence:

6. Drugs such as Rohypnol and GHB are the date rape drugs of choice.

Each of these characteristics will be considered in turn.

Stranger Rape

This is perhaps the strongest element of the real rape stereotype: prosecutors are more likely to initiate proceedings, and proceedings are more likely to be successful, in stranger attacks than in attacks in which the victim has a prior relationship with the attacker (Kalven and Zesiel, 1966: 252-4; Adler, 1987: 47; Estrich, 1987: 47; U.S. Senate Majority Staff, 1993: 21, 32-3 (citing Vera Institute of Justice, 1981); Leviore, 2004; Temkin and Krahe, 2008: 91). Yet, virtually every study confirms that the overwhelming majority of rapes are committed by assailants who are known to the victim (Adler 1987: 46-7 (citing Sanders, 1980: 61; Wright, 1980: 124); Harris and Grace, 1999; Kelly, 2001: 8 (citing National Victim Center, 1992; Tjaden and Thoennes, 1998); Myhill and Allen, 2002: 30; Walby and Allen, 2004: 59-60; Kelly et al., 2005: 20; Feist et al, 2007: 12). Table 2.1 sets out the percentage of stranger rapes as found in several of the most recent studies.

Further, some studies have found a very high incidence of rape by intimates: Harris and Grace (1999), for example, found that intimates made up 43 per cent of assailants; Myhill and Allen (2002) found that current and former partners accounted for 56 per cent of all alleged rapists. Additionally, Walby and Allen (2004: 59) found that the more serious the assault the more likely it was that the assailant was well known to the victim.

Table 2.1: Stranger Rapes

Studies	% of Rapes by Strangers
Harris and Grace (1999)	12
Myhill and Allen (2002)	8
Ruparel (2004)	36
Kelly et al. (2005)	28
Feist et al. (2007)	14

Location and Time of the Rape

The real rape stereotype assumes that rapes take place outdoors and at night. This assumption is correct as far as timing is concerned. Amir (1971: 84) found that almost half of all rapes occurred between the hours of 8.00 pm and 2.00 am. Ruparel (2004: 3) found that the majority of rapes occurred between 9.00 pm and 4.00 am. Feist et al. (2007: 16) found that 30 per cent of rapes occurred between midnight and 1.00 am.

The stereotype is utterly incorrect, however, as far as location is concerned. The majority of rapes are committed indoors, as Table 2.2 shows.

Table 2.2: Location of Rape Incidents

Studies	% of Rapes Indoors	% of Rapes Outdoors	% of Rapes in Vehicles
Amir (1971)	67	18	15
Adler (1987)	72	37	N/A
Harris and Grace (1999)	73	18	8
Myhill and Allen (2002)	75	13	N/A
Ruparel (2004)	32*	14	15
Feist et al. (2007)	70	14	5**

* Figure refers to victim's home only
**Figure refers to defendant's car only

The overwhelming majority of rapes are committed in private locations, usually either the victim's home, the defendant's home or a home shared by both parties. Research in Ireland agrees. McGee et al. found that adult female sexual abuse was most likely to occur in private locations, with only 24.2 per cent of incidents occurring in a public place, outdoors or in a garden (2002: 101). For male victims, the corresponding figure was 24.1 per cent. Just over 34 per cent of female sexual abuse victims reported that their experiences occurred in their own or the offender's home; the corresponding figure for male victims was 21.2 per cent (ibid.).

There is an obvious link between the location of the rape and the relationship between the parties. Out of simple opportunism, a stranger rape is more likely to occur in outdoor locations, and this was confirmed by Feist et al. (2007: 9) who found that 75 per cent of stranger rapes occurred outdoors, over half of which occurred in a public area. Opportunism also explains why the majority of rapes occur indoors: as most rapes are committed by someone known to the victim, the perpetrator will likely have more opportunities to take advantage of a private setting for the rape.

Force and Use of Weapons

Jurors appear to attach a great deal of importance to evidence that the defendant used physical force in order to have sex with the complainant (Reskin and Visher, 1986). This is not surprising; the use of force is generally incompatible with a suggestion that the intercourse was consensual, and the more force that was used the greater the likelihood of securing a conviction (Adler, 1987: 116). There is some truth to this aspect of the stereotype in so far as some degree of physical force beyond that required to commit the rape is not unusual. In an early study by Amir (1971: 154), force was used in 550 out of the 646 cases in the sample under examination (or 85 per cent). More recent studies tend to confirm this finding: Myhill and Allen (2002: 32, 34) found that force was used in 74 per cent of cases with violent threats being used in 75 per cent of cases; Walby and Allen (2004: 36) found that force was used in

71 per cent of cases and threats were used in 29 per cent of cases; and, Feist et al. (2007) found that some level of force was used in 68 per cent of cases.

Nevertheless, the levels of force used are usually quite low. While Feist et al. (2007) found that force was used in 68 per cent of cases, only 9 per cent of victims were actually beaten by their attacker. Similarly, Ruparel (2004) found that three-quarters of cases involved little extra violence beyond what was needed to accomplish the rape. Thus, while rape is an inherently violent crime, the use of severe extraneous violence is comparatively rare. Similarly, the use or display of weapons is also quite rare. Walby and Allen (2004: 36) found that a weapon was displayed or used in only 10 per cent of cases, while Feist et al. (2007: 20) found that a weapon was produced in only 4 per cent of cases. Nevertheless, if evidence of the use of a weapon is produced at trial, the chance of securing a conviction is doubled (Kelly et al., 2005: 72).

Resistance and Injury

Allied to the assumption that a genuine rape will be accompanied by violence and/or the use of a weapon is the assumption that the victim will physically resist and will be injured as a result. The assumption that rape victims will physically resist is one of the most durable rape myths (Ellison and Munro, 2009: 371-2). Yet studies show that most victims do not fight back. Amir (1971) found that the principal strategy employed by victims was submission, with only 18 per cent actually attempting to fight off their attacker. Over thirty years later, Feist et al. (2007: 21) came to a similar conclusion. Out of a total of 676 cases, they were able to extract information on the victim's response in 440 cases. The victim attempted to fight back in only 12 per cent of cases; by contrast, the victim employed verbal dissuasion in 63 per cent of cases and attempted to get away in 47 per cent of cases. Physical resistance was found to be most likely in the case of a rape committed by a partner or an ex-partner.

Physical injuries are not uncommon, and this is not surprising given that some degree of physical force is used in the majority of rape cases (see above). In some cases, the injuries are severe: Amir (1971: 176) found that nine victims were in hospital at the time of his study while one had died, all as a result of injuries sustained in the attack. A significant proportion of victims can become pregnant (Adler, 1987: 12 (citing a report from the London Rape Crisis Centre in which it was stated that 13 per cent of their clients who had contacted them over a two-year period had become pregnant as a result of their experiences)). Physical effects of such severity tend to be relatively rare: the most common physical injury suffered by victims consists of bruising (Holmstrom and Burgess, 1978). The primary form of injury suffered by rape victims tends to be psychological, which can be very severe (Holmstrom and Burgess, 1978; Shapland et al., 1985; Resick, 1987). In the 1970s, this psychological injury was termed Rape Trauma Syndrome (RTS), a label coined by Burgess and Holmstrom (1979). They postulated that RTS had two phases: the acute phase, dominated by the victim's fear for her personal safety, and the reorganisation phase, in which the victim's lifestyle underwent changes due to anxiety, depression, insomnia, phobias and interpersonal difficulties. More recent studies have confirmed that rape victims do indeed typically make long-term changes to their lifestyles. Myhill and Allen (2002: 43) found that two-thirds of victims reported avoiding certain people or places as a result of the rape, 45 per cent went out less then before the rape and over half were taking extra security precautions. Today, RTS is treated as one form of Post-Traumatic Stress Disorder (Shapland and Hall, 2007).

Evidence of resistance to the attack and injuries arising therefrom is powerful proof of non-consent, thereby making conviction more likely (Adler, 1987: 116). This is a perfectly proper use of evidence. The difficulty, however, is that jurors tend to view negatively complainants who do not appear to have resisted or suffered injury (Krulewitz and Payne, 1978; Krulewitz and Nash, 1979). As a result, juries are reluctant to convict in the absence of such evidence (Brereton, 1993). This is problematic given that most physical injuries are relatively minor and will heal relatively quickly; as a result, there is likely to be little evidence of physical injury in cases that are not reported very quickly. Further, psychological injury, which can be severe and long-lasting, cannot be seen by jurors.

Victim's Evidence

That rape victims will suffer serious and ongoing psychological effects has been well-demonstrated (see above). There are common assumptions as to how these effects will manifest themselves, especially when the victim gives her evidence. Jurors tend to assume that a genuine rape victim will be highly emotional in court, and accordingly will be less likely to believe a complainant who gives her evidence in a calm or unemotional manner (Winkel and Koppelaar, 1991).

Drug Assisted Rape

A modern addition to the real rape stereotype concerns the phenomenon of drug-assisted rape. The common belief is that a rapist will surreptitiously insert exotic chemical substances such as GHB or Rohypnol into an unsuspecting person's drink in order to knock that person out so that the rapist can then engage in sexual intercourse with her (Finch and Munro, 2005). It would seem that this belief is so strong that the presence of GHB or Rohypnol in a scenario is sufficient for mock jurors to automatically label the incident as rape (Finch and Munro, 2005). This view of drug-assisted rape has also achieved official sanction: the Sexual Offences Index compiled by the Metropolitan Police in London, for example, classifies an incident as drug-assisted if the complainant was administered a drug or noxious substance with the intent of impairing his or her ability to consent to a sexual act (Ruparel, 2004: 4). On this basis, Ruparel (2004: 4) reported that drug-assisted rapes made up six per cent of all rapes recorded on the Sexual Offences Index between 2001 and 2003.

This view of drug-assisted rape is both incorrect and unduly narrow. It is incorrect as to the effect that Rohypnol and GHB have on the victim. They do not in fact cause unconsciousness in the victim; rather, they have an amnesiac effect that the victim's brain interprets as unconsciousness. To the outside observer, however, the victim simply appears to be drunk (Finch and Munro, 2005: 27, citing Slaughter, 2000). The stereotypical view of drug-assisted rape is also unduly narrow in that it excludes what several studies have shown to be the drug of overwhelming choice in rape cases: alcohol (El Sohly and Salamone, 1999; Sturman, 2000; Slaughter, 2000; Bellis et al., 2008). Thus, Ruparel (2004) found that drug-assisted rape, as defined for the purposes of the Metropolitan Police's Sexual Offences Index, accounted for 6 per cent of cases, but 27 per cent of victims reported that they had been drinking at the time of the incident. El Sohly and Salamone (1999) examined 1,179 specimens from rape cases and found GHB in 4 per cent and Rohypnol in 8 per cent; alcohol, by contrast, was found in nearly 41 per cent. Similarly, Slaughter (2000) examined 2,003 specimens and found GHB present in 5.4 per cent and Rohypnol in 0.5 per cent; alcohol was found in 63 per cent. Yet the stereotypical (and official) view of drug-assisted rape excludes cases in which the complainant was intoxicated from alcohol, despite alcohol having almost identical effects upon the complainant's ability to form consent as GHB and Rohypnol (Slaughter, 2000). This distinction between alcohol and other chemical substances reflects the level of acceptance that alcohol has achieved in western societies as a social lubricant. Mock jurors have been shown to try to distinguish between alcohol-fuelled sex and alcohol-fuelled rape: Finch and Munro (2005) found that mock jurors were willing to accept the surreptitious use of alcohol by a man to 'loosen up' a woman, and if sexual intercourse resulted, it would likely be deemed legitimate unless the man intended to take advantage of her. Interestingly, the mock jurors paid little attention to the effect that the alcohol had upon the complainant, focusing instead upon the defendant's intention. Thus, alcohol has been deemed to be a legitimate tool in a man's sexual armoury and may be used to lower another person's inhibitions. Not surprisingly then, Masher and Anderson (1986) reported that 75 per cent of their respondents admitted using alcohol in their attempts to persuade a woman to have sex with them. Similarly, an Australian paper has suggested that the use of alcohol as a spiking agent is not viewed as spiking in the conventional sense (Neame, 2003).

Summary: 'Real Rape' v. Real Rape

Empirical studies show that the 'real rape' stereotype is almost entirely misleading; Table 2.3 contrasts the stereotype with the findings from these studies:

Table 2.3: Stereotype versus Truth

	Real Rape Stereotype	**Truth**
Stranger Rape	Rapes usually committed by strangers	Majority of rapes committed by someone known to victim
Location of Rape	Outdoors	Indoors
Use of Force	High levels of force required	Usually low levels of force used
Use/Display of Weapons	Frequent	Rare
Resistance	Typical	Infrequent
Serious Injury	Usual	Comparatively rare; usually low level injuries such as bruising
Victim's Reaction	Highly emotional	No typical reaction
Use of Drugs	GHB or Rohypnol	Alcohol

Empirical studies also show that the victims of rape are usually quite young (Amir, 1971; Harris and Grace, 1999; Myhill and Allen, 2002; Walby and Allen, 2004; Feist et al., 2007). Harris and Grace (1999: 7) reported that of the 446 victims in their study whose age was known, over one-third were aged between 16 and 25. A further 21.3 per cent were aged between 26 and 35. Feist et al. (2007: 8) found that 60 per cent of the victims in their study were aged between 16 and 35. Myhill and Allen (2002: 21) calculated that people in the 16-19 age bracket were four times more likely to be raped than any other age group. Given these results, it is scarcely surprising that most victims of rape are also single; Harris and Grace (1999: 6), for example, found that two-thirds were single. Similarly, Myhill and Allen (2002: 23) found that women who were married or in a long-term relationship were the least likely to be victimized. Also not surprising is the finding by several studies that the majority of rape victims are from the lower socio-economic bracket (e.g., Myhill and Allen, 2002; Walby and Allen, 2004; Kelly et al., 2005; Feist et al., 2007). The majority of victims are young and single and are therefore not likely to have accumulated any great degree of wealth.

Rape Supportive Attitudes

Rape supportive attitudes are more general social and cultural perceptions and beliefs that are supportive of rape in that they make dealing with rape, rape victims and those accused of rape more difficult. Researchers have found that those who hold such attitudes are more likely to exonerate the defendant and blame the victim (e.g., Wenger and Bornstein, 2006; Temkin and Krahe, 2008: 81). Experimental researchers have also found a correlation between rape supportive attitudes and traditional attitudes towards sex roles (Acock and Ireland, 1983; La Free et al., 1985; Muehlenhard, 1988; Whately, 2005). One of the major rape supportive attitudes arises in cases in which the victim has a prior relationship with the defendant. Experimental studies have shown that when subjects learned of a prior relationship, they were less likely to believe that the incident constituted a rape (Klemmack and Klemmack, 1976; La Free et al., 1985; Johnson, 1994; Willis and Wrightsman, 1995; Yescavage, 1999; Krahe et al., 2008). Further, evidence of a prior relationship tends to reduce the seriousness with which the incident is viewed by participants in such studies. L'Armand and Pepitone (1982) reported that their subjects viewed the rape as less serious and less damaging if the victim had a prior sexual relationship with the defendant. Similarly, Johnson (1994) reported that subjects assessed the victim's probability of enjoyment as higher in a case of acquaintance rape than in a case of stranger rape.

Many rape supportive attitudes concern what is known as victim-precipitation. Amir (1971: 259) defined victim-precipitation as a situation in which 'the victim is the one who is acting out, initiating the interaction between her and the offender, and by her behaviour she generates the potentiality for the criminal behaviour of the offender or triggers this potentiality, if it existed before in him'. In other words, by her behaviour or appearance, the victim brings about the rape and therefore must bear at least partial responsibility for it. Temkin and Krahe (2008: 81) summarise some of the more common victim-precipitation beliefs:

Rape is caused by:

- Women who tease men;
- Women who allow men to touch them intimately;
- Women who allow the situation to get out of control;
- Women who use alcohol or drugs;
- Women who dress in a sexy way; and
- Women who engage in unsafe conduct.

The first three of these beliefs arise in situations in which the victim can be said to have engaged in flirtatious or sexual behaviour with the defendant prior to the rape. In common parlance, the victim is said to have led the defendant on. Yescavage (1999) conducted a study among 46 male undergraduate students who were presented with a series of vignettes involving sexual intercourse in which several factors were varied, including the timing of a refusal to have sexual intercourse (i.e., after light petting only or after heavy petting). The subjects were required to indicate their perceptions of each party in each vignette. Yescavage found that women who engaged in sexual behaviour and then later refused to engage in sexual intercourse faced a drastic increase in perceptions of their accountability for what followed, with a corresponding decrease in perceptions of the defendant's accountability. Yescavage speculated that in certain situations, a woman's refusal was deemed to be unacceptable; that she is 'judged to have relinquished her right to refuse if she allows sexual activity to continue past a certain point' (1999: 807).

The fourth belief concerns the accountability of a victim using alcohol or drugs. A series of experimental studies show that participants in these studies judged such victims quite harshly, with higher levels of accountability being applied to them than to women who had not been drinking (La Free et al., 1985; George et al., 1988; Wild et al., 1998; Wenger and Bornstein, 2006). The most recent of these studies (Wenger and Bornstein, 2006) presented to 152 students a series of vignettes in which substance use by the victim was varied. The researchers reported that the sober victim was perceived by the participants as being more credible than a victim intoxicated through the use of alcohol or LSD.

The fifth belief concerns the victim's appearance, both physical and dress. Deitz et al. (1984) reported that their subjects were less positive towards an unattractive victim than towards an attractive one, both of whom resisted the attack. The authors speculated that the subjects had difficulty in believing that an assailant would persist in his attempts to have intercourse with an unattractive woman who resisted his advances. As for the woman's dress, Whately (2005) found that subjects attributed greater responsibility for a rape to suggestively dressed woman than to a woman who was more sombrely dressed.

The last belief concerns victims whose actions placed them in danger. Muehlenhard (1988) found that subjects were harsher to a woman who had visited the defendant's apartment. Other kinds of dangerous activity might include hitch-hiking and walking home alone at night (Temkin and Krahe, 2008).

Prevalence of Rape Myths
The first attempt to measure the prevalence of rape myths was made by Burt who developed the Rape Myth Acceptance Scale

(1980). Essentially, this scale allows researchers to measure the level of acceptance among subjects of a series of popular misconceptions about rape. Since then, other researchers have developed a plethora of other measuring instruments – Payne et al. (1999) counted at least 24 such instruments before developing yet another one – but Burt's scale remains the most popular (Payne et al., 1999: 28). Using instruments of this nature, researchers have found widespread acceptance of rape myths in adult populations in different jurisdictions (e.g., Burt, 1980; Giacopassi and Dull, 1986; Ward, 1995; Taylor and Mouzos, 2006). A telephone survey among one thousand adults in the United Kingdom conducted by Amnesty International in 2005 demonstrated the continuing vitality of victim-precipitation myths in that jurisdiction (cited in Amnesty International UK, 2008). Thirty per cent of respondents agreed that a victim was partially or totally responsible for a rape if she was drunk at the time. Two-thirds felt that the victim was at least partially to blame for being raped if she had not clearly stated her non-consent, while almost the same proportion placed some blame upon the victim if she had behaved in a flirtatious manner. Wearing revealing clothing was sufficient for over one-quarter to attribute some blame to the victim, while having many sexual partners or walking alone at night allowed over one-fifth of respondents to attribute some blame to her. More recently, Temkin and Krahe (2008) conducted a survey among 2,176 adults resident in England (one-fifth of respondents were not British) to test the prevalence of victim-precipitation beliefs and general rape myths. Using a 7-point Likert scale,* they found that one-quarter of respondents scored above the mid-point on the scale for victim-precipitation beliefs, thereby indicating a fairly high level of acceptance. Nearly one-half of respondents scored similarly with respect to rape myths. While accepting that the participants overall tended to disagree with both sets of myths, the authors con-

---

* A Likert scale is a widely used scale in which respondents indicate their level of agreement with a stated proposition. Typically, respondents will be asked if they strongly agree, agree, neither agree nor disagree, disagree or strongly disagree with the proposition.

cluded that a 'substantial minority of participants showed support for female precipitation beliefs and modern rape myths' (2008: 108). In Ireland, an opinion poll commissioned by the *Irish Examiner* found very high rates of rape myth acceptance (Ryan, 2008). One-third of respondents felt that a woman is at least partly to blame if she had been flirting with the defendant prior to the rape, while one in ten respondents ascribed total responsibility to the complainant if she had had multiple sexual partners. One-third of respondents ascribed partial responsibility to the complainant if she wore revealing clothing or was raped while walking in a deserted area. One in twelve respondents blamed the woman entirely if she was drunk or had consumed illegal drugs, while over half of male respondents under the age of 25 felt that she bore some responsibility for the rape in these circumstances.

Some feminist authors argue that the prevalence of rape-myth acceptance is due to the inherently patriarchal nature of modern society in which men actively attempt to subordinate women. Representative of this view is Susan Brownmiller (1976). She argues that '[rape] is nothing more or less than a conscious process of intimidation by which *all men* keep *all women* in a state of fear' (1976: 15 – italics in the original). As most decision-makers within society in general, and within the criminal justice system in particular, are male, it is not surprising that the dominant view of rape is one that is male-supportive. To change this situation, it is essential to increase the number of women in positions of authority, especially in law enforcement, because '[w]omen believe the word of other women. Men do not' (1976: 387).

There may, however, be a more innocent explanation for the continued vitality of rape myths at least as far as the real rape stereotype is concerned. Most people probably derive their view of rape from media reports and representations. As reports that correspond to the real rape stereotype are more likely to be prosecuted, such incidents are also more likely to be reported in the media, thereby creating a self-perpetuating process (Temkin and Krahe, 2008: 40). Further, the real rape stereotype is also quite dramatic and lends itself to media reporting. Soothill et al. (1990)

examined the reporting of rape in six British newspapers at five points between 1950 and 1985 (five newspapers were examined across all five points; one newspaper was added for the last three points). They found that by the 1980's, there were fewer cases being reported than in the earlier decades but those that were reported tended to be more sensational. They concluded that the dominant image of rape presented in the newspapers, especially in the tabloids, was of rapes committed by strangers who terrified and humiliated women. As far as media representations of rape are concerned, Bufkin and Eschholz (2000) examined the portrayal of rape scenes in the top 50 grossing films of 1996. They found five rape scenes, all violent and three resulting in severe injuries. All but one of the victims was portrayed as being entirely innocent, and four of the five rapists were strangers (the fifth was a grocery man vaguely acquainted with the victim). The authors concluded that while representations of rape in films are relatively rare, those that are shown depict the 'stranger-danger' scenario that lies at the heart of the real rape stereotype. Given such reports and representations, it is scarcely surprising that large proportions of the population continue to harbour misconceptions of rape.

REPORTING RAPE

The first potential stage of attrition occurs with the victim's decision to report to the police. There is substantial evidence to indicate that the majority of rapes do not come to the attention of the criminal justice system. The British Crime Survey (Myhill and Allen, 2002), for example, found that only around one-fifth of sexual assaults are reported. Australian research suggests that around a third of sexual assault victims report (Australian Bureau of Statistics, 1999). In the US and Canada, it is estimated that around 15 per cent of rape victims contact the police (Tjaden and Thoennes, 2006; Gartner and MacMillan, 1995).

Irish research also reveals low rates of disclosure. Highlighting the silence that surrounds sexual violence, McGee et al.'s (2002) survey of 3,000 Irish men and women found that almost half of the respondents who experienced sexual victimisation never spoke to anyone about the assault. Even fewer had utilised formal sources of support. For example, less than 10 per cent reported to the Gardaí and only 12 per cent disclosed to mental health professionals. Reporting rates are low even among people who have disclosed their abuse to support agencies. Statistics published by the Rape Crisis Network Ireland (RCNI, 2005) show that approximately a quarter of their clients who had experienced adult sexual abuse notified the Gardaí.

These findings reveal that non-reporting by victims constitutes a significant source of attrition. Non-disclosure of rape entails several consequences for the victim and society. When a rape is not reported, the victim may not have access to support services; the offender will not be apprehended, punished or treated; and knowledge about the characteristics and impact of sexual violence will remain incomplete (Feldman-Summers and Norris, 1984). It is important then to understand why so few people report rape to the police. This section reviews existing literature on victim decision-making, including theoretical perspectives and empirical research investigating the factors associated with reporting rape. It concludes by examining alternative help-seeking strategies utilised by victims.

Theoretical Models of Decision-Making

To date, little theoretical or empirical work has examined decision-making among victims of crime. Much of the theoretical work in victimology to date has focused on identifying the causes and precipitators of victimisation, although some have begun to investigate the processes involved in deciding to contact police.

Theories of victim decision-making are predicated on an essentially rational choice framework (e.g., Gottfredson and Gottfredson, 1988). According to this perspective, victims carefully consider the range of available options and choose the one that will best achieve their goals when deciding whether to report. The decision to report is determined by the seriousness of the crime and the amount of financial, psychological or physical harm suffered as a result. These rational theories have been disputed, however, by models of human decision-making that show that people rarely make rational decisions derived from well-formulated cost-benefit calculations. Research shows that decision-making is vulnerable to error, bias and cognitive shortcuts (Kahneman, Slovic and Tversky, 1982). Among crime victims, rationality may be compromised further by the emotional distress associated with criminal victimisation.

Greenberg and Ruback (1992: 195) conceptualised victim decision-making as 'semi-reasoned action'. Drawing on their extensive empirical research, they proposed a three-stage model of victim decision-making. First, victims establish whether their experience is 'criminal' by comparing the incident against their personal definitions of what constitutes a crime. Second, victims decide whether the incident is serious enough to report. This decision depends on the extent to which they feel they have been wronged (expressed as a sense of injustice or anger) and the extent to which they view themselves as vulnerable to repeat victimisation (expressed as fear and uncertainty about the future). Finally, they decide whether to report the crime, deal with matter themselves, or do nothing. Social influence plays a role at each stage: others can influence the victim in labelling the incident as a crime and by exerting pressure to report.

Greenberg and Beach (2004) studied decision-making among a sample of 422 property crime victims. They found evidence that three independent processes – cognitive, affective and social – were involved. Victims were more likely to report crimes with greater financial costs when they experienced emotional arousal (especially fear) after discovering the crime and when they were advised by others to make a report. Social influence was particularly important, as victims who were advised to call the police were almost 12 times more likely to report than victims who were advised against it or received no advice at all. Goudriaan et al. (2004) criticised the neglect of social and contextual factors in existing theories of victim decision-making. They argued that the situational characteristics (such as victim-offender relationship, losses experienced) are important but a comprehensive theoretical account must also consider the role of contextual factors (such as the level of social disorganisation in the neighbourhood, confidence in the police) and the influence of social norms (for example, beliefs about the appropriateness of calling the police) on the reporting decision.

It is now generally accepted that human behaviour emerges from a complex interaction between individual factors and the social world (see Henriques et al., 1984). These ideas have influenced recent thinking about decision-making among victims of sexual violence. Lievore (2005: 10) observed that the decision to report a sexual offence to the police is 'the outcome of an active process that takes into account a range of complex social and personal contingencies.' In other words, decisions are facilitated or constrained by the social context in which they are made.

Adopting a social ecology perspective, Menard (2005) argued that it was important to take account of social and structural factors in any model of victim decision-making. She surveyed over 600 clients attending rape crisis centres in Pennsylvania and found that both individual and contextual factors played a role in the decision to contact the police. Women were more likely to report when the offence was severe or the assailant was a stranger. However, social factors (such as poverty and availability of victim services) also influenced decision-making.

The Decision to Report

Crime surveys show wide variations in reporting rates for various crimes, and rape and sexual assault are among the least likely crimes to be reported (see van Kesteren, Mayhew and Nieuwbeerta, 2000). Lizotte (1985) compared rape reporting to the reporting of ordinary assaults. In his study, the decision to report a rape was more likely to be influenced by the severity of the incident and factors that make a strong case for the prosecution (for example, rapes by offenders known to the victim were less likely to be reported). A number of studies have attempted to identify which, if any, variables might predict a victim's decision to make a report to the police. Some surveys ask victims directly why they did not report and these provide further insight into victims' motivations for disclosure or non-disclosure. In her literature review, Lievore (2003) categorised disincentives to reporting into two groups, personal and criminal justice factors. Personal obstacles included feeling the offence was too trivial to report, not regarding it as a 'real' crime, considering it a private matter, wanting to deal with it themselves, self-blame, shame, and not wanting others to know. Criminal justice factors included fear of the legal system, fear of not being believed, of hostile treatment, lack of evidence. Felson et al. (2002) found that victims' motives for reporting incidents of violence varied according to the gender of the victim and the victim-offender relationship.

Socio-Demographic Factors

Research on the impact of socio-demographic variables has returned mixed results. Gartner and MacMillan (1995) found that age was significant with older women being more likely to report. Comparisons of reporting rates for male and female victims have shown that women are more likely than men to contact the police (see Pino and Meier, 1999). These authors also suggested that there are gender differences in reasons for non-disclosure. Male victims did not report unless seriously injured in order to protect their masculine identity, while women's decisions were influenced by whether their assault fit the 'real rape' stereotype. There is some evidence that victims of lower socio-economic status are more likely to report (for example, Bachman, 1993). Other studies have found that ethnic minorities are more likely to make a complaint to the police (Ullman and Filipas, 2001). Finally, Lizotte (1985) found that married women were more likely to contact the police while highly educated women were less likely to report. On the other hand, Golding et al. (1989) found that, while gender was significant, age, ethnicity, and education were not. Similarly, Feldmann-Summers and Norris (1984) found no support for the influence of socio-demographic variables on the decision to report. In their review, Greenberg and

Ruback (1992) concluded that socio-demographic variables are not strong predictors of reporting.

Psychological Factors

A number of studies have focused on the impact of psychological factors on disclosure. The psychological consequences of sexual violence are widely documented in the literature. For example, Lees' (1996) interviews with women who had experienced sexual violence vividly depicted the emotional aftermath of rape, which included severe depression, suicide attempts, and relationship difficulties. In fact, acute Post-traumatic Stress Disorder (PTSD) is considered a normal response to interpersonal violence (Foa and Riggs, 1995). Studies reveal that several psychological variables are associated with a reduced likelihood of reporting. These include: self-blame (Ruch et al., 2000), shame (Easteal, 1994), denial and personal disorder (Peretti and Cozzens, 1983), feelings of guilt (Wiehe and Richards, 1995) and emotional upset (Golding et al., 1989). Ruch et al. (2000) studied the decision to report sexual assault among 741 women who were contacted through a sexual assault treatment centre in Hawaii. Victims were more likely to report in cases involving threats of harm or where they had employed particular resistance strategies (i.e. screaming for help, trying to escape). Factors that decreased reporting were self-blame, ethnicity, and physical injury. Ruch et al. concluded that the most important variables related to the victim rather than the assault.

Perceptions of the Criminal Justice System

Other studies have found that perceptions of the criminal justice system are strong determinants of disclosure. Feldman-Summers and Norris (1984) found that decision-making was not influenced by socio-demographic factors or attitudes and beliefs about self, others or rape. Although incident characteristics (such as injury, victim-offender relationship) and social pressure to report were significant, the strongest predictors concerned the perceived benefits of reporting. These were psychological rather than tangible and included the belief that the victims would receive positive treatment from police and that reporting would help them to feel safe.

Severity of the Rape

One of the strongest predictors of reporting crime to the police is the severity of the incident (see Greenberg and Ruback, 1992). Research confirms that incident severity is associated with reporting among victims of sexual violence. In a randomised survey involving 447 sexual assault victims, Golding et al. (1989) tested the impact of a range of victim and incident characteristics on the decision to report to police. Women, victims of stranger assaults, victims of completed rapes and those who experienced more severe emotional upset were more likely to report. Similarly, Ullman and Filipas (2001) found that women who were injured during an assault or attacked by strangers were more likely to call the police. Using data collected for the 1992 National Crime and Victimisation Survey, Bachman (1998) found that injured victims were more likely to report even when other variables were controlled. Clay-Warner and Harbin-Burt (2005) found that victims of aggravated assaults were seven times more likely than victims of simple assaults to report.

Victim–Offender Relationship

The impact of victim-offender relationships on the decision to report has received extensive attention in the literature. In the British Crime Survey (Myhill and Allen, 2002), 36 per cent of stranger rapes were reported to the police, compared to 15 per cent of partner rapes and 8 per cent of date rapes. Rapes by offenders known to the victim were also less likely to be disclosed to anyone. Stranger rapes were twice as likely to be disclosed as assaults by partners or ex-partners. Similar findings have been reported in Australia ((Mouzos and Makkai, 2004) and the United States (Mahoney, 1999). Evidence relating to the impact of victim-offender relationship on reporting is mixed. Some researchers have found that women raped by men they knew were equally likely to report as those raped by non-intimates (Tjaden and Thoennes, 2006).

Rapes within intimate relationships are generally treated separately in the literature. Non-consensual intercourse between a husband and his wife has only recently been recognised by the law as rape in many jurisdictions.* There are unique characteristics of rapes within marriage compared to other types of rape. In particular, the rape often forms part of an ongoing pattern of physical, emotional and sexual abuse rather than a single event. Most women involved in abusive relationships are ambivalent about ending it and often move in and out of the relationship before ending it completely (Campell et al., 1998; Watson and Parsons, 2005). Reporting sexual violence is complicated by additional issues, such as concerns about the impact of disclosure on children, or the victim's financial dependency on the perpetrator (Shoham, 2000). In a landmark study, Russell (1990) found that less than 10 per cent of victims of marital rape reported to the police. Although many do not report to police, victims of domestic abuse are not passive and often deploy alternative coping strategies to deal with the violence (such as seeking advice or fighting back) rather than ending the relationship (Campbell et al., 1998).

Gartner and MacMillan (1995) suggested a number of explanations for the inconsistent findings regarding the impact of victim-offender relationship on reporting. They highlighted methodological issues with victimisation survey design, such as the tendency to conflate victim-offender relationships into broad categories (e.g. stranger/ non-stranger), which may obscure nuances and subtle variations in relationships. In their study, using data collected for the Canadian Violence Against Women Survey, Gartner and MacMillan found that violence by offenders known to the victim was significantly less likely to be reported even when victim characteristics (e.g. age), incident characteristics (e.g. physical or sexual violence) and seriousness (physical or psychological harm, weapon use) were controlled.

---

* In Ireland, this recognition came with the Criminal Law (Rape) (Amendment) Act 1990.

Impact of Rape Myths

Williams (1984: 460) hypothesised that assaults corresponding to the 'classic' or 'real' rape template were more likely to be reported to the police. In a study involving 246 female rape victims, she found that the police were more likely to be notified about incidents that were perpetrated by a stranger or acquaintance, involved injury, threat or force, or where the offender broke into the victims' home or car. Tomlinson (1999: 86) concluded that non-reporting emerges 'directly from rape myths that are deeply embedded in our general culture'. In her study, victims were less willing to report sexual assaults involving known assailants (particularly those involving previous sexual relations), assaults that did not involve threats, force or injury, and cases where victims had engaged in risky behaviours (e.g. substance use) beforehand. Similarly, Du Mont et al. (2003) found, in a study of 186 sexual assault victims presenting to a sexual assault treatment centre, that the presence of 'real rape' factors increased the likelihood that a victim would report. Interestingly, however, women who did not conform to the perfect victim stereotype (for example, because they were members of minority groups, had experienced mental health difficulties, had a history of victimisation, were unemployed, or had consumed alcohol at the time of the assault) were equally likely to report.

Irish Studies

A number of Irish studies have explored reasons for disclosing sexual violence. In *The SAVI Report*, the most common reasons given by respondents for non-disclosure were that the offence was not serious enough to report or that the Gardaí could not do anything about it (McGee et al., 2002: 131). In Watson and Parsons' (2005) study, victims of domestic violence who did not report believed the offence was not serious enough or cited embarrassment. In Leane et al.'s (2001) study, two of the interviewees had never reported to the Gardaí. They did not report because of their close relationship to the perpetrator. A more general Irish crime survey (Central Statistics Office, 2004) found that only 51 per cent of assaults were reported compared to 90 per cent of motor vehicle thefts. Reporting rates varied according to the perceived seriousness of the offence and the victims' perceptions of whether the Gardaí could do anything about it.

Informal Support Seeking

Kaukinen (2002) observed that the emphasis placed on the decision to report crime to the police potentially characterises non-reporters as 'passive and helpless'. In reality, she argued, victims actively seek help following victimisation with informal social networks (particularly family and friends) often being at the forefront of help-seeking. It is important to take these alternative strategies into account, particularly since social influence plays such an important role in victim decision-making.

Research shows that most rape victims tell family and friends and rely on their social networks (and to some extent, counsellors and medical professionals) to help them deal with the incident. Tjaden and Thoennes (2006) found that 59 per cent spoke to friends about the assault (15 per cent reported to police). Golding et al. (1989) found that almost half of victims told friends or relatives compared to 10 per cent reporting to police. In Ireland, around half of those who did disclose sexual violence did so to family or friends (McGee et al., 2002). Similarly, Watson and Parsons found that victims of domestic violence were more likely to tell a friend (49 per cent) or family member (43 per cent) than the Gardaí (22 per cent).

Contact with Police

During the 1970s and 1980s, the interrogation techniques used by police when questioning rape victims came under harsh scrutiny (see Lees, 1996). In a Scottish study, for example, over half of the participants expressed critical views about the police (Chambers and Millar, 1983). Many experienced a lack of sympathy from the interviewing officer, perceived a sense of disbelief, felt they were being blamed for the assault and believed the information provided about their cases was insufficient. The experience of going to court can be even more distressing. Research suggests that attitudes and beliefs about police may influence decisions to report (e.g. Hattem, 2000).

Contact with the Police in the United Kingdom

Temkin (1997) evaluated the police response to rape complainants in the UK. She interviewed 23 women who reported rape to Sussex police between 1991 and 1993. Although over half said that they found the experience of giving a statement highly distressing, almost all were positive about the officer who took their statement: victims appreciated being able to give their account in a supportive environment. They were less satisfied with the investigation process, although positive ratings remained high. The main reasons for dissatisfaction were lack of follow-up contact, support or information. Victims whose cases fit the 'real rape' template were more likely to express positive views about the police. Other UK studies also show that victims have positive experiences of police particularly in the early stages of an investigation (for example, Lees and Gregory, 1993; Adler, 1991) although there is evidence of a decline in satisfaction over time (see Shapland et al., 1985).

Contact with the Police in the United States

In the US, Frazier and Haney (1996) surveyed 90 victims who were sexually assaulted between 1990 and 1994. Most had positive attitudes towards the police. They described officers as being concerned and believing, and they felt the officers explained things clearly and took the complaint seriously. With regards to their experience of the legal system overall, victims felt they did not have enough control over how cases were handled or did not receive enough information about their cases.

Contact with the Police in Australia and New Zealand

A number of Australian studies have investigated sexual assault victims' satisfaction with the police. Edwards (1996) surveyed 43 victims of sexual assault whose cases had reached completion. Overall, the majority felt that the police were sympathetic. In Lievore's (2005) study, around half of the women who reported their assault expressed positive views about the police response. Specifically, they cited supportive attitudes and behaviours, believing attitude, and the provision of information. Negative features included disbelief, blame, insensitivity and lack of action. Around half said they were not sure if they would report a similar offence in the future. In New Zealand, Jordan (2001) conducted a survey of 48 women who had lodged a complaint with the police between 1990 and 1994 in order to examine the experience of reporting rape in New Zealand. In a situation that she characterised as a 'rape lottery' (ibid: 700), she found that half were satisfied with their treatment by the police and half dissatisfied. Factors that increased satisfaction included being treated with sympathy and understanding, feeling believed, receiving support and achieving a successful outcome. Victims were dissatisfied when officers showed them a lack of empathy or belief or treated their complaint as unimportant.

Contact with the Police in Ireland

O'Keefe (2003) researched Garda decision-making in rape investigations in Ireland. In a survey of over 300 Gardaí, she discovered that the course of investigations was influenced by investigators' beliefs and attitudes about rape and their perceptions of the appropriate victim response to such an attack. Many believed false allegations were common and perceived their role as deciding the veracity of an allegation rather than looking for proof. The final deliberative stage of investigation was characterised by assumptive based reasoning (if the story fits their assumptions) and predictive forecasting about likely outcomes.

Nevertheless, other studies indicate that the Irish public have a positive perception of the Gardaí. Findings from the Garda survey have been fairly consistent since 2001, revealing that over three-quarters of respondents were satisfied with Garda performance. However, satisfaction ratings were lower among those who had contact with the Gardaí. Of those who reported a crime, less than half were satisfied with the provision of information about their case. In spite of this, around three-quarters described the Gardaí who dealt with their complaint as helpful, competent, sensitive, polite and interested. In the Central Statistics Office survey, while over half of the respondents rated the Gardaí's work as 'good' or 'very good', actual victims were less likely to have positive perceptions of the Gardaí (one in four rated their work as 'poor' or 'very poor') (Central Statistics Office, 2004).

Other studies have examined satisfaction among sexual assault victims. In the SAVI survey, almost half expressed positive views about the service they received. They felt the Gardaí treated their case seriously and did not blame them for the assault (McGee et al., 2002: 132). Nevertheless, a significant minority were dissatisfied with the sensitivity of the Gardaí and the level of information they received about procedures and auxiliary support services (ibid.). The women interviewed by Leane et al. (2001) concurred with these findings. Overall, their perceptions of the Gardaí were positive. Despite finding the process of making a statement difficult, three commented on the caring, sympathetic approach taken by the Gardaí. At a later stage, three were dissatisfied with the level of information received about the progress of their cases.

Bacik et al. (1998) undertook a survey of 20 adult women who had experienced sexual violence and consequently participated in the legal process. They were drawn from five EU countries: Ireland (6), France (5), Belgium (4), Germany (4) and Denmark (1). The experience of Irish women was compared to that of the five other member states. While Irish participants were more likely to have a positive experience during initial contact with the police, their experience of court was significantly more negative than in any other countries. Specifically, they felt less confident and articulate when testifying, were more dissatisfied with the legal system, and felt it was unfair. Overall, Irish participants were more negative about their involvement in the criminal justice system.

Overall, international and Irish research shows that satisfaction with the police response has increased yet reporting rates remain low and attrition rates high. Studies show that even among victims who do report, many remain ambivalent about pursuing their complaint (Chambers and Millar, 1983; Lievore, 2005). Given that people are often unsure about pursuing a case, it is vital that they have a positive experience with the criminal justice system and receive ongoing support to encourage them to remain engaged in the legal process.

Prosecuting Rape

In Ireland the decision to report a rape is only the first step within the legal system, and one of the only steps the complainant takes herself. Once the rape has been reported to Gardaí, and barring a subsequent decision to withdraw the complaint, the complainant's role is reduced to that of a witness, and it is the Directing Officers within the Office of the DPP that take responsibility for the progression of the case within the justice system. In the simplest terms, it is the responsibility of the Directing Officers to decide, first, whether the case is prosecutable and second, whether it is worth prosecuting. In satisfying the first condition the Directing Officer will decide whether there is a *prima facie* case, that is that the body of evidence is such that a 'jury, properly instructed on the law, could conclude beyond a reasonable doubt that the accused person is guilty of the offence charged' (Director of Public Prosecutions, 1999: 14). While some prosecutorial authorities require that a case have at least a 51 per cent chance of resulting in a conviction before it can be prosecuted, Ireland has no such formal regulations (ibid.: 15). The second consideration requires the Directing Officer to decide whether the evidence is credible and reliable. As detailed in the 1999 Annual Report of the DPP, '[s]tatements made cannot simply be accepted and acted upon at their face value without considering whether or not they are truthful and reliable' (ibid. p. 15). This, however, requires that a judgment is made 'on matters of fact without having had the benefit of seeing the evidence tested in the manner in which it would be tested in a trial' (Walsh, 2002: 611). Very often the Officer's decision will rely on subjective criteria, especially the Officer's perception of how the evidence will be received by judge and/or jury.

Because the DPP represents the State, rather than the victim of a crime, the decision to prosecute a case must reflect the public interest. Certainly it is only in the public interest to prosecute credible and reliable *prima facie* cases, but considerable further discretion is used in deciding which cases will go to trial. Generally speaking, it is not in the public interest to prosecute cases with little or no chance of resulting in a conviction (Director of Public Prosecutions, 2001: 10), regardless of whether the DPP believes an offence has been committed. Thus a primary consideration for prosecutors is whether there is a 'reasonable prospect of securing a conviction before a reasonable jury or a judge in cases heard without a jury' (ibid.). There is no precise or defined method for the DPP to make such an assessment, although the 2001 *Statement of General Guidelines for Prosecutors*, sets out some indicative factors including:

- The reliability and consistency of the complainant;

- The existence of independent evidence; and

- The potential defences open to the accused including any motivation on the part of the complainant to lie (ibid.: 13-15).

In some situations a case may arise that is considered so outrageous and abhorrent that it is in the public interest to prosecute the case even when there is a low probability of securing a conviction (ibid.: 11).

In the UK and US, police have a 'gatekeeper' role. Police can 'no-crime' or 'unfound' a rape complaint and thus limit which complaints are passed on to prosecutors. In Ireland, Gardaí have no formal 'gatekeeping' function in that the DPP has directed that all allegations of sexual crimes be referred to his office for a decision on prosecution. The existing international literature is complex and often contradictory, but certain patterns do emerge that provide some sense of the structure that informs prosecutors' decision to prosecute rape cases. Prosecutors are interested in pursuing cases that are likely to result in convictions and will thus consider juries' potential reactions to legal issues, and case and character evidence. Beyond the basic formal legal criteria, including the identification of the defendant and the fact of rape, certain case and character issues are influential. Complainant cooperation is perhaps the single most important factor in deciding to pursue a rape case, but the presence of injury and any other corroborating evidence, such as an independent witness or forensic evidence, are also influential. Where the complainant has been drinking or using drugs, there is a negative impact on the decision to prosecute, reflecting both evidentiary and character issues.

The literature suggests that prosecutors appear to create a picture of the complainant based on extra-legal considerations such as age, class, risk-taking behaviour, and general believability, and compare this to the picture that they know from experience the jury is likely to hold of a genuine rape victim. If a complainant falls short of this expectation, the literature suggests that prosecutors are less willing to bring the case to trial. Finally, defendant characteristics appear to play a minor role in the decision to prosecute, with past criminal convictions now being the most significant factor. This review of the literature on prosecutorial decision-making in rape cases concurs with Spohn et al.'s view that

> prosecutors consider, not only the legally relevant indicators of case seriousness and offender culpability, but also the background, character, and behaviour of the victim, the relationship between the suspect and the victim, and the willingness of the victim to co-operate as the case moves forward (2001: 208).

Whether the DPP conforms to this representation of decision-making in rape trials will form the basis of the fifth chapter of this study.

Formal Legal Issues – Defining the Act of Rape

The first consideration for prosecutors in deciding whether to prosecute a rape complaint is whether the act of which the individual complains meets the legal definition of rape set out in section 2 of the Criminal Law (Rape) Act 1981 or section 4 of the Criminal Law (Rape) (Amendment) Act 1990.* Therefore, the prosecutor must be reasonably certain that one of the forms of penetration set out in the legislation occurred, that the offender has been properly identified, that the penetration occurred without the complainant's consent, and that the offender acted either intentionally or recklessly.

Identity of the Offender

Identity is rarely going to be an issue in cases in which the suspect is known to the complainant. Identity is most problematic in cases of stranger rape. Identifying the suspect may rely on victim identification, forensic identification or an independent witness. Spohn and Holleran found that the presence of physical evidence connecting the defendant to the crime had a strong and significant effect on charging decisions, particularly in stranger cases (2004: III-5-6). Studies of prosecution rates in rape cases that include all stranger cases, such as cases where the identity of the assailant is unknown, consistently note that stranger cases are less likely to go to trial (see, e.g., Spohn et al., 2001: 226; Frazier and Haney, 1996: 617). Once the identity of the defendant is established, however, a stranger case is more likely to be prosecuted and to result in a conviction (Frazier and Haney, 1996: 617; Beichner and Spohn, 2005: 484; Lievore, 2005: 4). Gregory and Lees found that of the 27 rape cases that resulted in a conviction in their 1994 study based in the UK, only five were acquaintance cases (1996: 90). Considering that only 88 of the 301 reported cases made it through police screening to the Crown Prosecution Service (CPS), and the CPS took no further action in 17 more cases (ibid.), there is a strong suggestion that acquaintance cases are weeded out along the legal pathway, and that stranger cases are perceived as stronger cases by police and prosecutors. Once identity is established in a stranger rape case the literature demonstrates that stranger rapes are more likely to go to trial.

---

* These definitions are set out in Chapter 1.

Consent

The law in most common law jurisdictions does not require formal proof of resistance, but the presence of injury and defensive wounds does help to establish the absence of consent. Hence, 'the victim's claim that she did not consent to sex is corroborated by injury, use of force, the severity of the assault and the availability of additional evidence linking the defendant to the assault' (Lievore, 2005: 4). Genital injury can be strong evidence of forceful penetration, but such evidence occurs in a minority of cases (McGregor et al., 2002). In a study at a hospital-based Sexual Assault Service, forensic evidence from over 350 individuals who alleged vaginal, anal or object rape showed that even with a colposcopy genital injury was found in just over 40 per cent of individuals and just over one-third (38.2 per cent) tested positive for sperm-semen. In the majority of cases, therefore, there was no evidence of the presence of semen or genital injury. This can present the prosecutor with difficulty – in such cases, the court may be 'left with the false impression that negative results negate the possibility that a sexual assault occurred' (ibid.: 645). Accordingly, the study found 'significant positive associations of documented injury with charge filing' (ibid.). This association was not limited to genital injury, however. Further, it was found that over one-third (35.9 per cent) of participants in the above study suffered either no injuries of any kind (12.1 per cent) or only mild injuries (23.8 per cent) (such as redness or tenderness), which could legitimately occur during consensual sex. Therefore, relying upon physical evidence of non-consent could have a detrimental affect on the rate of attrition at the prosecutorial stage. Without physical evidence, prosecutors may look to witnesses, although independent witnesses are exceedingly rare in rape cases. More likely, the prosecutor will have to rely upon the complainant's testimony. In so doing, the prosecution moves away from strictly objective legal criteria and into the more subjective area of extra-legal victim and case characteristics which will be considered in more detail shortly.

Mens Rea

The law effectively decriminalises the act of rape if the defendant committed that act without the required state of mind. Irish law requires proof of a subjective state of mind: the defendant must have known that the complainant was not consenting or was reckless as to whether or not she consented. Thus, the prosecution must find a way to show the jury what was going on in the defendant's mind at the time of the rape. Even on the best of evidence, this is going to be difficult. Further, if the defendant genuinely believed that the complainant had been consenting, the defendant must be acquitted, even if that belief was entirely unreasonable on any objective grounds (*DPP v. Morgan*, 1976). As Tur (1996) points out, the effect of this is that an entirely narcissistic defendant who cannot conceive of any woman refusing to have sexual intercourse with him cannot be convicted regardless of the circumstances in which the rape occurred. Thus, the law formally permits a defendant to shelter behind the most objectionable of rape myths providing his belief in those myths is genuine.

Formal-legal factors are necessarily significant in the decision to prosecute a rape case. It is undoubtedly true that 'statutory elements of a crime are the primary determinates of official decision-making in processing sexual assault complaints' (Kerstetter, 1990: 269). It is questionable, however, whether the statutory elements are the *sole* primary determinate. Certainly, without complying with the basic formal legal criteria of rape, a case cannot result in a conviction and a prosecution would be a waste of the State's resources. The literature suggests, however, that the formal legal requirements set only the minimum threshold that must be met; other non-legal factors such as particular case characteristics, jury expectations and predicted jury bias mediate these formal legal requirements in the decision of whether or not to prosecute.

The Impact of the Jury on the Prosecutorial Decision

The DPP is under a statutory duty to consider the public interest when deciding whether or not to prosecute a case, and the public interest is unlikely to be served by bringing a case that has no prospect of a conviction. In Ireland, as in all common law jurisdictions, the ultimate decision on the defendant's guilt lies with the jury. In order to fulfil his public interest obligation, therefore, the DPP must consider not only the legally relevant issues, but also any extra-legal considerations that may influence a jury's decision. Spohn et al. note that 'in deciding whether to go forward with a case ... prosecutors attempt to predict how the background, behaviour, and motivation of the suspect and victim will be interpreted and evaluated by other decision makers, and *especially by jurors*' (2001: 207 – emphasis added). Lisa Frohmann concurs and argues that prosecutors adopt a 'downstream orientation' in which they are 'actively looking for "holes" or problems that will make the victim's version of "what happened" unbelievable or not convincing beyond a reasonable doubt, hence unconvictable' (1991: 214).

In Kalven and Zeisel's landmark study of the American jury, the authors conclude that the rate of disagreement between judges and juries as to verdict is five times greater in non-aggravated cases than in aggravated cases (1966: 252-253). They suggest that juries are liberated from the formal rule of the law where objective evidence is weak, thereby allowing the jury to fall back on bias and social convention in coming to their verdict. They argue that:

> The law recognizes only one issue in rape cases other than the fact of intercourse: whether there was consent at the moment of intercourse. The jury, as we come to see it, does not limit itself to this one issue; it goes on to weigh the woman's conduct in the prior history of the affair. It closely, and often harshly, scrutinizes the female complainant and is moved to be lenient with the defendant whenever there are suggestions of contributory behaviour on her part (ibid.: 249).

A succession of commentators has concurred in this position (see, e.g., Weninger, 1978; Albonetti, 1987; Frohmann, 1991, 1997; Spohn et al., 2001; Beichner and Spohn, 2002). There is also some support for it in Ireland; the principal judge of the Central Criminal Court, Carney J., has stated that, '[i]n these situations [acquaintance rapes], the most horrific sexual attacks have been described in evidence but there has been a hostile reaction to the prosecutrix from the jury' (quoted in Leanne et al., 2001: 29).

Bryden and Lengnick suggest that when evidence is not conclusive, jurors will 'try to take account of the potential impact of an erroneous verdict. That is, they will seek to minimize their expected regret from having reached an erroneous decision' (1997: 1376). In other words, it follows from the usual absence of independent evidence in rape cases that juries usually will be conservative in assigning guilt. Dripps argues, however, that juries represent 'popular opinion, rather than elite opinion, and popular opinion in rape cases can be decidedly pro-defence' (2008: 971). He argues that popular opinion is primarily influenced by 'sexual mores and gender roles' rather than evidential considerations (ibid.). This view is supported by a great deal of experimental research, which will be considered in more detail later. The Office of the DPP has indicated that a case should not be prosecuted unless there is a reasonable prospect of securing a conviction (Director of Public Prosecutions, 2001: 10), thereby effectively requiring his Directing Officers to consider the jury's likely reaction to the evidence. This, in turn, requires the Directing Officers to consider the factors that are likely to sway the jury, including extra-legal factors.

Case Characteristics

There are many particular case characteristics involved in the decision to prosecute a rape and these characteristics often reflect the blend of evidential requirements, legal-formal issues and perceived jury bias as are evident in the literature considered above.

Complainant Non-Cooperation

Of the variables listed above, studies have consistently noted that the single most significant factor in the attrition of reported rape cases is the victim's decision not to pursue the case (see, for instance, Bryden and Lengnick, 1997: 1377; Brown et al., 2007: 357; Temkin, 2002: 21; Lievore, 2005: 4). Although prosecutors have the formal power to pursue cases in the public interest without the victim's consent, in practice it is virtually impossible to do so. Prosecutors in both Ireland and in England and Wales have formally accepted that the victim's interests are a proper issue for consideration in making the decision to prosecute. The DPP thus argues that in deciding whether the public interest requires a prosecution, 'the likely effect on the victim or the family of the victim of a decision to prosecute, or not prosecute' must be assessed (Director of Public Prosecutions, 2001: 11). Similarly, the Crown Prosecution Service in England and Wales details that a prosecution is less likely where it 'is likely to have a bad effect on a victim's physical or mental health' (Crown Prosecution Service, 2005: 8). This suggests that proceeding without the complainant's cooperation, and even forcing the complainant's attendance through a witness summons, is a possibility. In practice, however, such a possibility is likely to occur only very rarely: the scarcity of independent evidence largely precludes the possibility of taking a case to trial without the victim's support. Indeed, 'to ignore victims' wishes as an important piece of data in deciding whether to prosecute invites a caseload of unwinnable cases, disgruntled victims, and (in extreme cases) prosecution of innocent defendants' (Davis et al., 1997: 107).

Victims retract complaints and refuse to cooperate with prosecutors for a number of reasons. Lea et al. (2003: 593) found that victims who were previously intimate with their attacker were more likely to retract their complaint (see also Lievore, 2005). One Crown Prosecutor asserted that victim retraction was most common in cases of marital rape, and that the rate of retraction in these cases 'is about as likely as it is in any domestic violence situation' (in Brown et al., 2007: 365). Yet, it is not only complainants in acquaintance rape cases who retract their complaints or refuse to cooperate; victims of both stranger and acquaintance rapes are likely to withdraw their support from a rape prosecution (Spohn et al., 2001: 230). Prosecutors have suggested that this is due to a reluctance to go through the invasive process of a court trial and disillusionment with the legal system itself. Spohn et al.

record prosecutor opinions that 'once [the victim] knows what it is going to mean to proceed with the case through the criminal justice system, she may decide it's not worth it' and that 'quite a number of people are petrified about having to describe the gory details of the violation to strangers'(ibid.). Even with stranger rape cases, victims may feel that their behaviour on the night in question, or other extra-legal factors, may be used to discredit them and complainants may wish to avoid the prolonged and distressing process of a trial. Holmstrom and Burgess found that only 41 per cent of rape complainants in their landmark study 'clearly and unequivocally wished to press charges' (Holmstrom and Burgess, 1978: 56) and recorded a list of reasons that complainants gave for refusing to proceed, including (in order of commonality):

- The desire to avoid the ordeal of court;
- A fear of the assailant taking revenge;
- They felt sorry for the defendant; and
- They just wanted 'to forget the whole thing' (ibid. 58).

These are not unreasonable considerations, and prosecutors who attempt to compel the complainant's involvement thus run the risk of causing substantial harm to the complainant's interests.

Victim Injury and the Use of Weapons

Where a victim decides to make a complaint of rape, the prosecutor must consider the effectiveness of the evidence and the likelihood of a conviction. Evidence of victim injury rates highly among factors that positively influence the decision to prosecute. The HMCPSI study, for example, found that medical evidence of injury was relevant in 58 out of 75 cases in their sample, thereby underlining the importance of such evidence (HMCPSI, 2006: 89). Evidence of injury allows prosecutors to prove force (and thus, potentially, absence of consent) and penetration (Bryden and Lengnick, 1997: 1247), and evidence of violence is strongly related to the successful outcome of a rape case (Brown et al., 2007: 367).

Injury tends to indicate resistance, and even though resistance is no longer required to constitute a rape in most common law countries, it is nevertheless influential in achieving a conviction (Horney and Spohn, 1991: 151). In fact, it has been found that there is a positive association between the degree of injury sustained and the likelihood of charges being filed and a conviction being secured (McGregor et al., 2002: 645). It is also interesting to note, however, that victims appear to recognise the association between weapons and injuries and prosecution/conviction: Kerstetter found that the use of a weapon was associated with victim willingness to prosecute (1990: 308). Temkin similarly asserts that where violence was not used or threatened the victim was 'most likely to withdraw her complaint' (2002: 21). Perhaps, like prosecutors, complainants are also looking for greater odds of conviction than acquittal before they are prepared to proceed down the arduous path of a trial. Alternatively, victims may feel compelled to pursue more aggravated cases to prevent the brutalization, and possible death, of other women.

Multiple Assailants

In detailing the rape of a nurse by three doctors with whom the nurse was acquainted, Estrich argues that in her opinion and that of the defence attorneys, 'the numbers were critical to the result' (1987: 99). This case characteristic involves issues of both credibility and case seriousness. Convention would hold that a woman is unlikely to consent to sexual intercourse with a group of men. The jury is thus more likely to perceive the encounter as non-consensual. Further, the fact that multiple men participated in the rape is seen as a greater violation to the victim, and that where more than one man raped the victim, the victim is deemed to have suffered multiple, repeated rape. Thus 'gang rapes' are perceived as more serious and may therefore be more likely to be prosecuted, although the literature is not clear on this point.

Repeated Rape

A rape is repeated where a single act occurs more than once or where multiple forms of rape occur, such as the penetration of the mouth *and* vagina by a penis. There is anecdotal evidence in the literature that suggests that prosecutors *expect* a rape to be repeated, at least in some circumstances. As DDA Tracy Timmerton stated in Frohmann's study, 'my experience has been that when a rapist has a victim cornered for a long period of time, they engage in multiple acts and different types of sexual acts and very rarely do just intercourse' (Frohmann, 1991: 217). Using prosecutorial accounts such as this, Frohmann argues that where rape cases diverge from the expected pattern (i.e., where only one count of vaginal rape occurs), prosecutors may discredit the claim and be disinclined to prosecute (ibid.). This argument is not backed, however, by any empirical studies and Spohn et al.'s study found that out of 58 cases that were rejected by prosecutors, only four were rejected for being atypical scenarios (2001: 214). The fact of a repeated rape, whether by one assailant or multiple assailants, may however interact with the perceived seriousness of the crime, the impact on the victim, and the presence of injury. Therefore, while studies do not conclusively indicate whether repeated rape *directly* influences prosecutor's decision to prosecute, there may be indirect or associated connections. This is likely to be also true of the infliction of other sexual indignities on the victim.

Relationship between Complainant and Defendant

As discussed earlier, the relationship between the complainant and the defendant has been shown in the majority of studies to have a significant impact on the prosecutorial decision. In most of these studies, stranger rapes are more likely to be prosecuted once the identity of the defendant has been established (see, e.g., Harris and Grace, 1999; Kingsnorth et al., 1999; Tellis and Spohn, 2008; Frazier and Haney, 1996; but see Spohn et al., 2001, in which the opposite effect was found). Albonetti found that cases involving strangers had an 84 per cent chance of being prosecuted and puts this down to the perception among prosecutors that acquaintance rapes involve greater uncertainty (1987: 309). Adler argues that prosecutors are also more likely to doubt the victims of acquaintance rape cases (1987: 30) and Weninger similarly notes that the probability of prosecution was highest in cases of strangers (1978: 389). A previous relationship between victim and accused has been shown also to have a significant impact on whether the victim will withdraw her complaint. Lievore's Australian study found that the majority of the cases in which the complainant withdrew her cooperation involved current partners, former partners and other known defendants (2005: 4).

Location of Initial Contact and Rape

The location of the rape, as well as the location of the initial contact between the complainant and the defendant, has been shown to influence the decision to prosecute. Lea et al. found that in cases that were given no further action by the CPS, the initial contact between the complainant and the defendant was most likely to have occurred in a private space (2003: 595). Similar results were found by Brown et al. (2007, 359) and Spohn et al. (2001: 226): cases are more likely to be prosecuted if they occurred in a public place. The influence of location is likely linked to the issue of relationship. In most cases, rapes that occur in the complainant's home will likely follow an invitation to enter given by the complainant to the defendant, and such an invitation is most likely to occur in the context of some kind of prior relationship. As already noted, most studies show that acquaintance cases are less likely to be prosecuted or to result in a conviction.

Time-Lapse between Rape and Report

A number of studies have shown that the greater the lapse of time between the incident and the report to the police, the less likely a prosecution becomes (Kingsnorth et al., 1999: 287; Brown et al., 2007: 361; Lievore, 2005: 41) although results have been mixed (see, e.g., Spohn et al.: 226; Frazier and Haney, 1996: 624). Such a lapse raises both evidential and credibility issues. If there is a delay in making the report, there is likely to be a significant impact on the evidence available to the prosecution. Documenting any injuries, recording the presence of semen, and conducting other forensic tests are time-limited processes; thus, the greater the time-lapse the less physical evidence will be available to successfully prosecute the case. Not surprisingly, the presence of physical evidence has been shown conclusively to increase the likelihood of prosecution in rape cases (e.g., Horney and Spohn, 1996: 145; McGregor et al., 2002: 640; Brown et al., 2007: 363; Spohn et al., 2001: 207).

A complainant's credibility may be questioned where she delayed in reporting the rape. Temkin quotes Boyce's judgment that 'the failure to complain at the first reasonable opportunity is a circumstance which tells against the truthfulness of the complainant's evidence' (2002: 90). Evidence of recent complaint is permitted in court to provide credibility for a complainant's story (ibid.: 188), but in doing so the inverse is also implied – that late complaints reflect poorly on credibility (Adler, 1987: 118-119; Brown et al., 2007: 365). Prosecutors must take into account the possible defences that will be mounted by the accused, and the impact of a late complaint is thus likely to influence their decision about whether or not to prosecute. Adler's study concluded that those who delayed reporting their rape for between one day and three months, had a case conviction rate of 38 per cent, compared to 73 per cent for those who reported immediately (1987: 119). Similarly, Brown et al.'s more recent study suggests that prosecutors still associate immediate reporting with credibility (2007: 365). The *degree* to which a delay in reporting a rape is influential in terms of evidence or of credibility remains uncertain, but the fact that a delay *is* influential is significantly represented in the literature.

Other Case Characteristics

There are a number of other case characteristics that appear in the literature as being influential in the decision to prosecute. These include the rare cases in which an independent witness is able to provide corroboration for the complainant's account; the existence of such a witness has a positive association with the decision to prosecute (Kingsnorth et al., 1998: 366). The complainant's ability to accurately recall events and important details, her consistency in relating the event, and her attempts to escape are also positively related to prosecution (HMCPSI/HMIC, 2002: 54), while reconciliation between complainant and defendant has a negative impact (Lievore, 2004: 41).

Alcohol and Drug-Use

Research has proven that the use of alcohol in rape contexts is very high (see, for instance, Cowan, 2008; Klippenstine et al., 2007; HMCPSI and HMIC, 2007). Studies record the use of alcohol by the complainant in rape cases at between 38 per cent of rape complainants aged sixteen or older in the United Kingdom (Finney, 2004: 2) and 81 per cent among American student complainants. Other American studies indicate that rape defendants used alcohol in between 57 and 61 per cent of cases (ibid.). British studies record a similar rate of drinking by convicted rapists (ibid.). In Ireland, McGee et al. noted that alcohol was involved in 45.3 per cent of cases of unwanted sexual experiences by adult women in Ireland; cases in which both parties were drinking accounted for 26 per cent of cases (2002: 101). The correlation between alcohol use and the incidence of rape has thus been demonstrated beyond doubt.

Alcohol consumption is an especially important prosecutorial consideration with respect to the issue of consent and the perception of the complainant by the jury. As regards consent, the use of alcohol by the complainant may result in her being unable to recall whether or not she gave consent (Hingson et al., 2005, cited in Howard et al., 2007; see also Spohn et al., 2005). The defendant might also use the complainant's drinking to argue the issue of consent. He might also attempt to use his own intoxication as the basis of a defence. Intoxication is not a defence to rape charges in most common law jurisdictions (Temkin, 2002: 130), but the defendant could argue that their own intoxication contributed to their genuine belief that the complainant consented to intercourse.

Further, some experimental studies have shown that mock jurors found the complainant less credible if she was sober when raped by an intoxicated defendant (Klippenstine et al., 2007: 2636). Other studies have concluded that individuals generally found intoxicated defendants less blameworthy than sober ones, while intoxicated complainants were judged more harshly (see Cameron and Stritzke, 2003; Schuller and Stewart, 2000). A recent study that tested the affect of rape myths on undergraduate law students and post-graduate trainee lawyers in Germany found that except in cases where a former partner raped his intoxicated ex-partner, both groups of students associated decreased liability with an intoxicated defendant, and increased responsibility with an intoxicated complainant (Krahé et al., 2008: 469, 475). Further, a poll conducted by Amnesty International among adults in England and Wales found that some 30 per cent believed that a woman who had been drinking was in some way to blame for her sexual assault (2008).

The literature indicates a correlation between the consumption of alcohol by complainants and the decision not to prosecute (Tellis and Spohn, 2008: 260). In strict legal terms, having sexual intercourse with a partner who is insensible through intoxication constitutes rape (Temkin, 2002: 90). Nevertheless, there is a wide range of levels of intoxication, between freely giving consent (while intoxicated) and being incapable of giving consent (due to intoxication). It is popularly accepted that alcohol breaks down inhibitions, and that both men and women engage in activities (including sexual activities) while intoxicated that they would be unlikely to do while sober. Any law that purports to respect autonomy must protect 'the autonomy of drunken women to choose to have sex' (per Sir Igoe Judge, in Cowan, 2008: 909). That alcohol acts as a disinhibitor, however, has led to the perception that women who engage in such acts may later regret them and thus falsely claim to have been raped. Thus, the complainant's drinking may impact some assumptions that prosecutors and jurors might otherwise make: that a woman is unlikely to have consented to sex with a stranger, with multiple men, to very rough sex, to certain sexual acts, and so forth.

Complainant and Defendant Characteristics

Evidence of physical injury has been shown to exercise considerable influence on prosecutors' decisions, mostly because this evidence tends to support the complainant's allegation that she did not consent to intercourse. When there is no such objective evidence, the prosecutor's decision is made more difficult. Since Kalven and Zeisel's landmark study (1966), a significant number of studies have echoed their conclusion that when objective evidence is lacking, the jury will rely on their perception of the complainant and the defendant in coming to a verdict (see, e.g., Beichner and Spohn, 2005: 489, Tellis and Spohn, 2008: 258). As the prosecutor's perception of the jury's likely reaction to the evidence is a factor in his decision, the prosecutor must also consider the characteristics of the complainant and the defendant. Studies do differ, however, on exactly which characteristics are influential. Some of the complainant characteristics considered include sexual history, risky behaviour, status, race, and 'believability' involving factors such as mental health, age, intelligence, appearance and even the complainants' reaction to the rape; and defendant characteristics including past criminal activity, status, and race.

Sexual History

The use of sexual history in rape trials is a highly charged subject. Bryden and Lengnick note that 'abundant anecdotal evidence suggests that American juries, like their English counterparts, are powerfully influenced by the complainant's sexual habits, and that, despite rape shield laws, defence counsel often manage to get such evidence before the jury' (1997: 1355). Prosecutors must consider this fact when deciding whether to prosecute a rape case, and it would not be particularly surprising to find that prosecutors were reluctant to proceed in cases where the complainant had been involved in numerous previous sexual relationships, had a history of involvement in prostitution, been involved in sex work or had been behaving 'lasciviously' on the occasion of the rape. Further, attrition at this stage may also occur when the complainant withdraws the complaint out of fear of the trial and cross-examination (Temkin, 2002: 197). Indeed, Holmstrom and Burgess listed fear of trial as the second most common reason for victim non-cooperation (1978: 58).

The literature indicates that prosecutors are strongly influenced by the complainant's sexual history, although this is largely anecdotal (Frohmann, 1991; Adler, 1987; Estrich, 1987); there is surprisingly little statistical evidence to support this claim (Kingsnorth et al., 1999: 290; Beichner and Spohn, 2005: 486-7, found some correlation between case rejection and the complainant's moral character but only in cases that were evidentially weak anyway). Frohmann (1998) asserts that prosecutors actively discourage complainants with a questionable sexual history from pursuing their complaint. She maintains that various devices are mobilised, including the presentation of negative 'downstream' consequences of pursuing the case, to encourage the withdrawal of complaints that are considered unwinnable (1998: 399). In this way the prosecutor can avoid formally rejecting the case, making it appear instead that the prosecutor is merely acceding to and reinforcing the complainant's own decision. There are also suggestions in the literature that sexual history evidence might be hidden as the official reason for rejecting a case. Spohn et al. (2001) note a case that was officially rejected due to the complainant's inability (due to self-induced intoxication) to recall whether or not she consented; however, the prosecutor also noted that the complainant was taking medication for AIDS (a formally irrelevant fact). Spohn et al. interpret this comment as revealing the prosecutor's perception 'that the victim is sexually promiscuous' (2001: 217), and suggest that this extra-legal factor influenced the decision not to prosecute.

Evidence that the complainant had a pre-existing sexual relationship with the defendant may form the basis of the defence strategy (e.g., consent, honest belief or ulterior motive), and the prosecution might decide to pre-empt that defence by rejecting the case. Spohn et al. cite two instances where the prosecution rejected cases due to the presence of consensual sexual acts between the complainant and the defendant immediately prior to the rape. In the first case the complainant allowed the defendant to kiss her, lie on top of her, and remove her underwear with 'a little struggle' (2001: 216). In the second case the complainant allowed the defendant to perform oral sex on her (ibid.). Both cases were dropped by prosecutors on the basis of the prior sexual relationship; the prosecutor apparently believed that the relationship would form the basis of a successful consent defence. The decision to drop a case in these circumstances is problematic in that it requires the prosecutor to accurately anticipate the jury's likely view of societal sexual norms. Naturally, prosecutors are expected to draw upon their experience, but there is a danger that in their prosecutorial decisions the prosecutor might simply reinforce outdated social beliefs about sex and consent. Further, as Bryden and Lengnick have noted, sexual history evidence is ambiprobative (1997: 1356).[*] If a woman has had 'twenty instances of prior sexual conduct with rock stars ... without claiming rape, in the absence of other evidence of motivation the most reasonable inference is that she claimed rape this time because she was raped' (Bryden and Lengnick 1997: 1356, citing Wright and Graham, 1980: 594). Qualitative studies show, however, that prosecutors are slow to test this view (see, for instance, Frohmann, 1991; 1998; 1999).

Risky Behaviour

There are a number of actions that a complainant might take that the literature suggests are regarded as involving a high degree of risk by prosecutors and jurors, and may influence a prosecutor's decision to prosecute. These actions include hitchhiking, attending parties or bars alone, being out alone after dark, accepting lifts in a stranger's car, and inviting the defendant to her home or accompanying him to his home (e.g., Kalven and Zeisel, 1966; Ker-

---

[*] Ambiprobative evidence is evidence that potentially supports the competing claims of the prosecution and the defence. Bryden and Lengnick suggest that as ambiprobative evidence supports both sides, in fact it offers support to neither side (2002: 1356).

stetter, 1990; La Free 1981; Spohn et al., 2001). Spohn et al. found that prosecutors were more likely to reject cases if the complainant willingly accompanied the defendant to her home or his home, or where drugs and/or alcohol were involved (2001: 227-228; see also Spohn and Holleran, 2004 and Spohn and Tellis, 2008). This is especially pronounced in cases that are already quite weak either because of its characteristics (Spohn and Holleran, 2004: III-5-6) or because of the absence of corroborative evidence (Brown et al., 2007: 367). The influence of evidence of the complainant's risky behaviour may be ameliorated, however, by evidence of aggravating factors such as injury or the use of weapons

Race and Status

The influence of race upon prosecutors' decisions in rape cases is a contentious issue. Some analysts maintain that race has a significant and ongoing influence in these decisions (e.g., Irving, 2008), while others have no found no such effects (e.g., Horney and Spohn, 1996). According to the US Department of Justice's statistics, between 1996 and 2005 black women were raped somewhat more frequently than white women; further, the vast majority of rapes were intra-racial in nature (US Department of Justice, 2005: Table 42). According to the conviction statistics, black men are also somewhat more likely to commit a rape (or perhaps are just more likely to be convicted) than white men (ibid.: Table 40). However, these statistics represent convictions, and cannot thus explain prosecutorial decisions. S'Alessio and Stolzenberg studied rapes perpetrated by single individuals in 17 states, and found that black defendants accused of rape were proportionally no more likely to be arrested for forcible rape than white defendants accused of rape (2003: 1391), but black men were proportionally more likely to be *accused* of rape (ibid.: 1388). In the United Kingdom a similar result was found, with Afro-Caribbean men being marginally over-represented among rape offenders (Muir and MacLeod, 2003: 349; also see Smith, 1989; Wright, 1980). Sentencing statistics in the United States support the notion of a racial hierarchy, with white offenders who rape white women receiving longer sentences than black offenders who rape black victims (Maxwell et al., 2003, cited in Irving, 2008: 111-12). A comparison between statistics would suggest that prosecutors are not unduly influenced by the race of the defendant or the complainant in deciding whether to prosecute a rape case, but that race is an issue in the reporting of rape. It is worth noting that the majority of studies that have examined the influence of race in rape cases have been conducted in North America, where racial issues have long been recognised within the legal system and society generally, and have focused on the black/white dichotomy. Ireland represents a very different situation, where multiculturalism is in its first generation. Thus, the influence of race may be very differently represented in this jurisdiction.

Toni Irving asserts that black women and girls are more likely to have complaints dismissed or re-coded as lesser, often non-sexual, offences (2008: 103) but 'not all black women are de facto ignored' (ibid.: 116): marriage, class and status convey upon some women greater protection by the law (ibid.: 116-117). Thus, status appears to be a relevant factor, and this relevance arises in two respects. First, a number of studies have suggested that those from a higher socioeconomic background are less likely to suffer rape (e.g., Bailey, 1999; Martin et al., 2006). Indeed, Bailey calculated that 'each $1,000 increment in women's average income in 1990 is associated with an average decline of 9.53 rapes per 100 000 women', and suggested that women from a higher economic status may be able to 'purchase' safe and secure living situations (1999: 54).

Second, the literature suggests that prosecutors prefer to prosecute cases in which a woman of high socio-economic standing is raped by a man of low socio-economic standing, possibly reflecting a perception that juries are less likely to believe that consent occurred between members of these different social groups. Brown et al found that rape cases in which the defendant was unemployed were more likely to progress through the criminal justice system successfully (2007: 361). Cases in which the victim was unemployed and non-Caucasian, by contrast, were more likely to receive a decision of 'no further action' (ibid.: 362). In a

British qualitative study, Temkin (2000) noted the comments of two barristers who expressed the view that socio-economic status is relevant to the jury's reception of the case. The first stated: 'if a woman looks like a scrubber she's going to get less sympathy from a jury than someone who looks respectable' (2000: 225), while the second claimed that '[i]f you live in a squat or are a single mother it does impact on juries. I think that they think you are more likely to have got what you deserved' (ibid.). These comments suggest that prosecutors do consider socio-economic factors, at least those that affect the complainant, in making their decision. Further, Brown et al. found that where the defendant was employed, the CPS was more likely to drop the case (2007: 362). These findings are significant as they suggest that certain groups, particularly poor women and non-Caucasian women, are marginalised by the criminal justice system while those groups of women who receive greater legal protection are less likely to need it.

Credibility

There are a number of elusive factors that might affect a prosecutor's perception of the complainant's credibility. Prosecutors are much more likely to prosecute cases in which the complainant has no prior convictions (Brown et al, 2007: 361). In cases in which the complainant has a past history of mental health problems or mental infirmity, the complaint is less likely to proceed to prosecution (Howard League, 1985: 71; Lievore, 2004: 41). Holmstrom and Burgess (1978: 144) found that the most common credibility factor cited by prosecutors concerned the complainant's intelligence. Other factors include the victim's appearance and age, with younger victims more likely to have their cases prosecuted (Tellis and Spohn, 2008: 258). Frohmann's earlier study also highlighted the use of complainants' physical characteristics as factors contributing to the west coast American prosecutors' decision not to prosecute, including the use of such charged terms as 'street-worn' and 'cluckhead' (1991: 218). Some anecdotal evidence suggests that juries are more receptive to attractive, well presented complainants: barristers in Temkin's qualitative study (2000) decried complainants who dressed inappropriately in court, saying that 'it would be useful if they could sit down without showing their knickers' (2000: 225). It is important to note, however, that prosecutors often rely on second-hand descriptions of the complainant recorded on police files in assessing the complainant's credibility (Kelly, 2001: 27).

Police and medical records often contain information about the complainant's emotional state during reporting and medical examination. This information may then be used by the defence to discredit the victim, and can thus pre-emptively influence the prosecutor's decision. Frohmann identified in her study that prosecutors expect certain behaviours and emotions from rape victims, including anger and crying (1991: 220). If these reactions are not present, prosecutors may use the discrepancy between expected and actual behaviour to reject cases (ibid.: 220). Brown et al. record a Crown prosecutor's opinion that 'I have a lot of trouble believing that the victim is a genuine victim of rape ... [if] she appears to be emotionless and acts as if nothing happened to her' (2007: 365). This approach is problematic as studies indicate that almost half of all rape victims are 'non-emotive' (McGregor et al., 2002: 644-45), and is reflective of an element of the real rape syndrome discussed earlier.

'Bad Character' Evidence

Prosecutors are more likely to prosecute cases in which the defendant has previous convictions (Holmstromm and Burgess, 1978: 43). The joint thematic report by the Inspectorates of Crown Prosecution Service and the Constabulary in Britain recommended that prosecutors not only look for previous convictions but also look more generally at 'bad character' evidence (HMCPSI/HMIC, 2002). The 2007 review states that of the relevant 37 charged files considered, prosecutors appropriately considered 'bad character evidence in 21 cases' (2007: 116), indicating that in Britain such evidence does now inform the decision to prosecute.

THE TRIAL PROCESS

In Chapter One, the conviction rate in rape cases was discussed in some detail, and it was noted that the conviction rate in contested rape cases is very low. The literature suggests five primary explanations for this low success rate:

- Evidentiary difficulties inherent in the prosecution of rape cases;

- The development by the law of unduly harsh and discriminatory procedures in rape trials;

- Juries are male-dominated and their members are swayed by rape myths;

- The imposition of unduly lenient and inconsistent sentences, leading to a belief that the crime of rape is not taken seriously; and

- Undue delays in the trial process.

Each of these explanations is considered in turn now.

Evidentiary Difficulties

There are unique evidentiary problems in rape cases (Hanley, 2006). The Advisory Group on the Law of Rape (better known as the Heilbron Committee after Mrs. Justice Heilbron who chaired the Group) noted that an allegation of rape involves an act of sexual intercourse 'which is not in itself either criminal or unlawful, and can, indeed, be both desirable and pleasurable' (1975: para.9). What distinguishes rape from sexual intercourse is the absence of the complainant's consent to the act, and to register a conviction against the defendant the jury must be convinced – beyond a reasonable doubt – that the act was not consensual. To support its allegation that the intercourse was non-consensual, the prosecution must rely upon the testimony of witnesses, especially the complainant, and forensic and medical evidence. In most cases, however, the sexual act will occur in private thereby precluding any direct eye-witness testimony other than that of the complainant (Scottish Executive, 2000: para. 87; Office for Criminal Justice Reform, 2006: 9). As a result, the prosecution case very often stands or falls according to the performance of the complainant in the stand (Temkin, 2000: 224). This performance can be marred, however, by two prominent factors: first, many people feel a natural embarrassment when dealing with matters of an intimate and sexual nature in a public forum (Scottish Executive, 2000: para. 87). Second, and more significantly, it is well documented that a large proportion of rape victims were intoxicated at the time of the sexual act (e.g., Roizen, 1997; Testa and Parks, 1996; Ruparel, 2004; Mohler-Kuo et al., 2004; Feist et al., 2007). Intoxication affects a person's ability to recall exactly what happened, which is, of course, precisely the ability most needed by the complainant when giving evidence in court.

Given the absence of eye-witnesses, corroboration for the prosecution's allegation that the sexual act was non-consensual usually comes in the form of forensic or medical evidence, much of it collected from the complainant's body. Brown et al. (2007: 368) note rather bluntly (but correctly) that in a rape case, the complainant's body is effectively a crime scene and needs to be treated as such. Medical evidence is particularly time-sensitive – bruises on the complainant's body, for example, provide dramatic evidence that the sexual act was non-consensual but bruises heal and disappear within a few days. Forensic evidence, in the form of hair samples, semen samples, etc. can offer positive proof that the defendant had intercourse with the complainant. This kind of evidence is also time-sensitive in that it can be lost easily through degradation or contamination. Making a report to the police so that such evidence can be collected is essential, but it is not unusual for complainants to delay making a report to the police. Further, it is not uncommon for victims of rape to attempt to wash away what has happened by bathing immediately (Law Reform Commission of Victoria, 1988: para. 99; Estrich, 1987: 21). While understandable, these actions can result in the loss of a great deal of corroborating evidence, and the absence of corroboration is identified by many commentators as the single most important evidentiary reason for the low conviction rate in rape cases (e.g., Temkin, 2000: 224; Scottish Executive, 2000: para. 87; Office of Criminal Justice Reform, 2006: 9; Brown et al., 2007: 368).

But even where a complaint is made promptly and all the forensic evidence has been collected, the totality of the prosecution's evidence is often ambiguous (Scottish Executive, 2000: para.87). This evidence may well establish that the defendant had sexual intercourse with the complainant, but this is not sufficient for a rape conviction. Where such ambiguity exists, jurors are more likely to rely on interpretations that fit their own value system (Reed, 1965; Gobert, 1997) or their own knowledge of what constitutes a real rape (Temkin and Krahe, 2008: 42-3), as discussed previously.

Unduly Harsh and Discriminatory Procedural Rules at Trial

Legal redress for a rape is ultimately the province of a court, and to achieve that redress the complainant must overcome a significant number of barriers. The totality of the prosecution's evidence must convince the jury beyond a reasonable doubt of the defendant's guilt (*Woolmington v. DPP*, 1935). It is not uncommon for complainants to feel that they were the ones that were on trial (Bohmer et al., 1975; Advisory Group on the Law of Rape, 1975: para. 12; Estrich, 1987; Lees, 1993; Kelly, 2001: 31) or that the experience of giving evidence was as upsetting as the original rape (Holmstrom and Burgess, 1978). To be sure, complaints about their treatment in court are not limited to rape complainants: Rock (1993: 70), for example, found strikingly similar complaints from prosecution witnesses in non-sexual cases. Nevertheless, the rape complainant is said to be in a particularly invidious position with many victims being surprised at the ferocity of the cross-examination they faced (HMCPSI/HMIC, 2002: 74). In an oft-cited article, Lees (1993) described the court process in a rape trial as amounting to a 'judicial rape' in which 'the woman's account is often discounted or disbelieved, her credibility and reputation undermined' (1993: 11). Four primary reasons have been advanced to account for this phenomenon:

1. The range of defences available to the defendant has become so narrow that he typically has no choice but to attack and undermine the complainant's credibility;

2. As a result, the complainant is at the heart of the prosecution's case;

3. To undermine the complainant, defence counsel is happy to play to prejudices held by the court and especially by the jury; and

4. The influence of rape myths on the law has been so strong as to require the development of special legal rules that apply only to rape cases especially concerning the complainant's prior sexual history and corroboration.

The position of the jury is considered separately below; for now, each of these four reasons will be considered in turn.

The Defences Available to the Defendant

Vasschs (1994) suggests that a person accused of rape has three basic lines of defence: a denial of involvement, a denial that sexual intercourse occurred or an assertion that the intercourse was consensual. A variation on this last possibility is the controversial claim that the defendant honestly believed that the intercourse was consensual (*DPP v. Morgan*, 1976). Koski (2002) points out, however, that the advent of DNA testing has reduced the defendant's options in most cases to an assertion of consent. This has been borne out by empirical studies of the defences used in rape trials in England and Wales (Harris and Grace, 1999: 20; Feist et al., 2007: 44[*]), Scotland (Brown et al., 1993), Australia (Brereton, 1993; Tasmanian Task Force on Sexual Assault, 1998) and New Zealand (Young, 1983: 73).

---

[*] Alone among all of these studies, Feist et al. found that a blanket denial of all charges was the main defence offered in 46 per cent of cases, with consent being the main defence in 44 per cent of cases.

The Position of the Complainant in a Rape Trial

The legal definition of rape requires proof that the complainant did not consent to sexual intercourse, and it is well-established that most contested cases revolve around consent (see above). Accordingly, 'the state of mind of the complainant, her demeanour, words and actions before, during and after rape are of central importance to the criminal justice system' (Rumney, 2001: 898, citing Hall, 1988: 74; see also La Free, 1989; HMCPSI/HMIC, 2002: 74). The complainant is usually the first witness called and can spend anything up to a few days in the stand, although Adler found that the average was between three and four hours (1987: 50). Further, in most criminal trials, the prosecution will have a range of witnesses and professional experts to call upon to prove its case. Rape cases, however, present special difficulties for the prosecution, as already outlined. The effect of these difficulties is to place the complainant at the heart of the prosecution case. A poor evidential performance from the investigating police officer or medical expert, while damaging, will not necessarily be fatal to the prosecution's case; a poor evidential performance from the complainant will almost certainly result in the defendant's acquittal.

Defence Tactics

Given that rape myth acceptance has been shown to be prevalent in modern western societies, it is almost certain that at least some rape myths are accepted by lawyers and judges. It is not necessary, however, for a lawyer to subscribe to these myths to make use of them as a trial strategy. In her study of rape trials, Adler (1987: 53) reported that defence counsel would routinely engage in continual questioning of the complainant to establish consent or that the complainant had not behaved entirely properly. In a series of interviews with judges and barristers, Temkin and Krahe (2008: 134) reported that the barristers in particular had noted that a standard defence strategy in rape cases was to focus on the complainant's behaviour, thereby playing to the possibility that at least some members of the jury would subscribe to rape myths.

Nevertheless, there is evidence that defence barristers today are more subtle in their approach to cross-examination than Adler described in 1987. Temkin (2000) explored the defence strategies more fully in a series of interviews with leading barristers. All denied personally engaging in overt bullying of the complainant, seeing it as counter-productive. This accords with Kelly et al.'s finding that out of 23 observed trials, only three involved lengthy and humiliating questioning of the complainant, and all three of those cases ended in the defendant's conviction (2006: 47).

From her interviews, Temkin (2000: 230-6) was able to identify several distinct strategies employed by defence counsel in rape cases:

- The defence is frequently led by a female barrister;

- Assessing the complainant – the barristers try to adapt their approach to the kind of person he or she is;

- Trapping the complainant – counsel would frequently try to establish some kind of rapport or common ground with the complainant, especially to keep her calm. Some of the interviewees specifically expressed the view that if the complainant gave her evidence calmly the jury would be less inclined to believe her (2000: 231);

- Exploiting inconsistencies – counsel would routinely compare what the complainant said in her statement to the police with what she told other people and with what she had said in evidence. The smallest inconsistencies were then exploited to try to undermine the complainant's credibility;

- Using the medical evidence – medical reports frequently contain a great deal of background information that can be pursued and exploited; and

- Discrediting the complainant – this was the central strategy employed by the barristers; indeed, one female barrister specifically stated that discrediting the complainant was more important than establishing facts (2000: 231). Barristers would try to discredit complainants by focusing on their behaviour, their clothing and their appearance. The purpose of these lines of questioning is to suggest to the jury either that the complainant consented to the intercourse or that she had acted so foolishly that she was to blame for what had happened. The barristers also accepted that they routinely apply to the trial judge for permission to cross-examine the complainant about her prior sexual history, specifically to paint the complainant as a slut. None of the barristers interviewed could recall any real difficulties in getting such questions admitted despite formal restrictions being imposed by legislation (2000: 234-5).

Special Legal Rules in Rape Cases

The common law developed a number of special evidential practices that only applied in sexual cases. Of these, by far the most problematic were the rules that permitted the introduction of prior sexual history evidence and those concerning corroboration. A more rare issue is the power of the defendant to conduct a personal cross-examination of the complainant. Since the 1970s, legislative changes have been made to improve the complainant's position at trial.

Prior Sexual History Evidence. Prior to the 1970s, evidence that the complainant had engaged in sexual relations prior to the alleged rape, especially with the defendant, was routinely introduced during rape trials. This practice was derived from the view that immoral women are likely to be also untruthful women (Law Reform Commission of Victoria, 1988: para. 124). In practice, this view meant that the defence had a 'virtually unconstrained licence to sling sexual mud' (Adler, 1982: 666). The introduction of evidence of the complainant's prior sexual history was said to be the single most important basis for discriminatory effects in a rape trial (Feild, 1979). Demonstrating the complainant's lack of chastity would lead a jury to one of three conclusions: that the complainant likely consented, that she got what she deserved, or that she was not a credible witness (Feild, 1979: 264). Any one of these conclusions would almost guarantee the defendant's acquittal.

Many law reform bodies at least partially defended the introduction of this evidence. Thus, the Heilbron Committee (1975: para. 134) asserted that evidence as to the complainant's relationship with the defendant would always be relevant. Similarly, the Law Reform Commission of Victoria (1988: para.136) argued that juries might find it difficult to assess evidence of consent without knowing the relationship context. Nevertheless, from the 1970s onwards a series of legislative restrictions on the introduction of sexual history evidence – known as 'rape shield laws' – were introduced throughout the common law world. Most of these measures required the permission of the trial judge before introducing this kind of evidence, especially evidence of the complainant's general sexual history. In one of the first empirical studies of the introduction of prior sexual history under a shield regime, Adler (1987: 73) found that formal applications were made in 18 of the 45 cases (40 per cent) in her review that went to trial. The percentage rose to 60 per cent in cases in which consent was the primary defence offered. Three-quarters of these applications were successful. But prior sexual history evidence was also introduced in other ways, including by the prosecution. In total, Adler found that evidence as to at least some aspect of their prior sexual histories was introduced against 96 per cent of the complainants in her study. Studies conducted since then have found similar results in different jurisdictions in the common law world (Brown et al., 1993; New South Wales Department of Women, 1996; Lees, 1996; Henning, 1996; Department of Justice of Victoria, 1997). Interviews with judges and barristers confirmed that many legal professionals continue to hold the view that this evidence is generally relevant (Harris and Grace, 1999: 40; Temkin, 2000).

As a result of these findings, the Home Office in England concluded that the existing shield laws had failed in their primary objective and tougher restrictions were enacted in section 41 of the Youth Justice and Criminal Evidence Act 1999. This provision prohibits the defendant from introducing evidence or asking any questions relating to the complainant's sexual behaviour, subject to four specific exceptions. These exceptions are as follows:

1. The evidence relates to a relevant issue in the case that is not an issue of consent, which is defined to exclude the defendant's belief in consent;

2. The evidence relates to a relevant issue in the case which is an issue of consent and the complainant's sexual behaviour is alleged to have occurred at or about the time of the incident in question. 'At or about', in this context, means within 24 hours (Kelly et al., 2006: 16);

3. The evidence relates to a relevant issue in the case which is an issue of consent and the complainant's sexual behaviour was so similar to any sexual behaviour by the complainant which the defence evidence shows either was a part of the incident in question or occurred at or about the same time, such that the similarity cannot be explained as coincidence; or

4. The defence wishes to rebut any evidence of the complainant's sexual behaviour introduced by the prosecution and goes no further than required to accomplish this rebuttal.

Further, any evidence or questions admitted under these exceptions must relate to specific instances of behaviour, and permission must be denied if the court believes it reasonable to assume that the primary purpose of the evidence or questions is to impugn the complainant's credibility. The defence must make a written request, setting out exactly the evidence they wish to introduce or the questions they wish to ask and the reasons for making the application.

On the face of it, these restrictions appear to remove a great deal of judicial discretion. The House of Lords, however, expanded the third exception (the similarity exception) in *R v. A* (2001) by permitting the introduction by the defence of evidence of a prior relationship that the defendant claimed to have had with the complainant. The defence claimed that this evidence had a bearing on the issue of consent. Exercising its interpretive power under the Human Rights Act 1998, the House of Lords decided that this evidence should be admitted where it was 'so relevant to the issue of consent that to exclude it would endanger the fairness of the trial under Article 6' (2001: para. 46). Kelly et al. (2006: 18) suggest that this ruling is potentially broad enough to allow the admission of any sexual history evidence on the grounds that a fair trial so requires it. In their study of 160 cases for which full data was available, Kelly et al. (2006: 28) found that applications under section 41 were made in one-quarter of cases, and were successful in about two-thirds of those cases. Further, they observed 23 trials and noted section 41 applications being made in nearly a third of them. However, sexual history was raised in three-quarters of the observed trials, which indicates that trial judges are permitting such evidence despite section 41. Temkin and Krahe (2008: 148) found that six of the seventeen judges interviewed actively circumvented the prohibition in section 41 if they thought such evidence was necessary for a fair trial. In effect, they interpreted the decision in *A* to give them the very discretion that Parliament had attempted by section 41 to restrict.

The available research suggests, therefore, that legislative attempts to restrict the introduction of sexual history evidence have not been successful. The literature indicates that two primary attrition effects flow from this failure. First, the possibility that such evidence might be introduced has a dissuasive effect on victims contemplating making a report (Kelly et al., 2005: 76; Kelly et al., 2006: 62). Kelly et al. (2006: 62) interviewed nineteen victims and found that two chose not to report and five others thought seriously about not reporting largely because of the possibility of this evidence being introduced. Consequently, the introduction of prior sexual history evidence was a major issue for over one-third of the victims they interviewed. Second, experimental studies (e.g., Johnson et al. 1995; Schuller and Hastings, 2002) have found that the introduction of this kind of evidence has a negative impact upon mock jurors. This is despite modern sexual mores being such that virtually all adults will have a sexual history of some kind (Kelly et al., 2006: 3). In Ireland, for example, the Crisis Pregnancy Agency found that over 80 per cent of Irish women aged between 18 and 24 had engaged in vaginal sexual intercourse; for women aged between 30 and 34, the applicable figure was almost 98 per cent (2006: 144). Further, Schuller and Hastings (2002) found that subjects used sexual history evidence to evaluate the complainant's credibility and the likelihood of consent even when specifically instructed not to do so. Thus, judicial instructions designed to limit the use of this evidence had no impact of the subjects' decision-making process. Therefore, given the frequency with which such evidence is raised in rape trials and the effect that it has upon juries, Feild's claim (1979), made 30 years ago, that sexual history evidence is the single most important attritional factor in rape cases appears to have continuing vitality.

Corroboration. Rape victims have traditionally been treated by the law with 'unequalled suspicion' (Adler, 1987: 15). Nowhere is this more apparent than in the corroboration rule that developed in sexual cases. Corroboration has been defined as

> [I]ndependent testimony which affects the accused by connecting or tending to connect him with the crime. In other words it must be evidence which implicates him, that is, which confirms in some material particular not only the evidence that the crime has been committed, but also that the prisoner committed it (*R v. Baskerville*, 1916: 667).

With few exceptions, corroborative evidence is not required in a criminal trial but its presence increases the security of a conviction. In sexual cases, the common law developed a rule whereby the jury had to be warned specifically of the dangers of convicting the defendant on the uncorroborated testimony of the complainant (*R v. Graham*, 1910; Hanly, 2001). This rule traces its origins to Hale's well-known comment that rape complaints are easily made but hard to defend and the assumption that women (who make up the overwhelming majority of rape complainants) routinely make false allegations of rape (discussed earlier). Other commentators have defended the rule on the basis of 'no harm, no foul'. The Mitchell Committee in South Australia (1976: 45-6), for example, argued that as a jury is likely to seek corroborative evidence anyway, the corroboration rule merely alerted them to dangers of which they were already aware anyway. An American commentator (Anon., 1970: 460) argued that in many cases, the jury will be forced to choose between two competing versions of events. In these circumstances, the natural sympathy felt for victims of violent crime would lead to the presumption of innocence being overridden, which in turn would force the defendant to disprove the allegation.

Since the 1980s, however, most commentators have consistently argued for the abolition of the corroboration rule, on two principal grounds. First, all the evidence shows that rape victims, rather than making easy allegations, tend to find making a complaint of rape extraordinarily difficult. Second, commentators have taken issue with the 'folkloric assumption' that women are as deceitful as the policy underlying the rule assumes (Temkin, 1982: 417). As noted earlier, there is no conclusive empirical evidence that complainants in rape cases are more likely to lie than complainants in other kinds of cases. Accordingly, there is no justification for the law to single out rape complainants by means of a special warning. A third line of attack held that the corroboration rule was overly complex and did not even accomplish its stated function of protecting men from false complaints (LSE Jury Project, 1973; Hans and Brooks, 1977).

Legislators and commentators alike have generally accepted these arguments, to the extent that it is now difficult to find a modern defence of the old corroboration rule. Throughout most of the common law world, legislative intervention has resulted either in the abolition of the rule or at least in its being watered down. In the United Kingdom, for example, the corroboration rule was abolished by section 32 of the Criminal Justice and Public Order Act 1994. In *R v. Makanjuola; R v. Easton* (1995), the Court of Appeal confirmed that a corroboration warning should be given only where there is an evidential reason for believing that a particular complainant might be untrustworthy. Temkin suggests that with this decision, the law regarding corroboration in rape cases in England is now 'perfectly satisfactory' (2000b: 191). Evidence from other jurisdictions, however, gives ground for pause. In New South Wales, for example, section 405C of the Crimes (Sexual Assault) (Amendment) Act 1981 abolished the corroboration rule in that jurisdiction. This provision was interpreted by the courts as meaning that a corroboration warning should not be given unless the trial judge thought it justified and that if a warning was given, it should not impugn the trustworthiness of sexual complainants as a class (NSW Department for Women, 1996: 186-7). Nevertheless, in its own study of 92 cases in which the judge gave a summing-up to the jury, the NSW Department of Women (1996: 188-9) found that a corroboration warning was given in 80 per cent of cases. Further, an old-style warning was given in just over 40 per cent of cases. In only 14 cases was no corroboration warning of any kind given at any stage in the trial. It is worthy of note that the cases studied were heard between 1994 and 1995 – thirteen or fourteen years after the abolition of the corroboration rule. Thus, it is facile to assume that legislative abolition and recognition by the superior courts of that abolition will necessarily translate into changes in trial practice.

Self-representation by the Defendant. In most common law jurisdictions, those accused of criminal offences are entitled to receive professional legal assistance, at State expense if necessary. On occasion, however, defendants charged with rape have preferred to dispense with the services of professional lawyers and to represent themselves. In 1996, Ralston Edwards was tried for raping Julia Mason. He fired his lawyers and conducted his own cross-examination of the victim, which continued over six days. Mason suggested later that through his questioning, Edwards was 'reliving the rape moment by moment', a suggestion leant some support by the fact that Edwards deliberately wore the same clothes at trial as he had worn at the time of the incident. Edwards was eventually convicted and sentenced to two terms of life imprisonment, but his personal cross-examination of the victim caused a media scandal throughout England (Rock, 2004: 346-52). This case was a particularly egregious example of what is often claimed as the 'right' of the defendant to represent himself at trial, and by extension, to personally conduct the cross-examination of the complainant. Those who make this claim can offer some powerful support: Article 6(3)(c) of the European Convention on Human Rights specifically recognizes the right of criminal defendants to 'defend himself in person or through legal assistance of his own choosing'. Similarly, the United States Supreme Court has recognized the right to self-represent as one of the rights protected by the Sixth Amendment (*Faretta v. United States*, 1975).

Describing the power of a defendant to represent himself as a legal *right* seems a little odd historically. For centuries, trials were conducted without lawyers; the defendant – and the prosecutor – had no legal representation (Langbein, 1985). This practice was defended on the basis that the interposition of lawyers between the parties and the court would obstruct the court's attempts to get to the truth. It was only in 1695 that defendants being prosecuted for treason were given a right to be legally represented at trial (Treason Act 1695), a right that was subsequently extended to all felony defendants in 1836 (6 and 7 Will.IV, c.114). The default position of the common law, therefore, was self-representation – not as a right but as a necessity. The defendant's *right* is to legal representation, not to self-represent. To be sure, the defendant has the power to waive this right either by dismissing his lawyers or by not seeking representation in the first place. If the defendant does waive his right to be represented, his position simply reverts to the default common law position.

Nevertheless, there is little reason for victim-advocates to complain about the defendant's decision to self-represent, whether it be a right or merely a power, except when the defendant proposes to conduct a personal cross-examination of the complainant. It is possible to permit the defendant to represent himself if he so chooses but to require him to conduct a cross-examination of the complainant and other vulnerable witnesses through a professional lawyer. This is the approach adopted or recommended in a growing number of common law jurisdictions – England and Wales (Home Office, 1998: paras. 9.28-9.55; section 34 of the Youth Justice and

Criminal Evidence Act 1999), Scotland (Scottish Executive, 2000: paras. 23-31), New Zealand (New Zealand Law Commission, 1999) and the Commonwealth (Commonwealth Secretariat, 2001: Section IV). The European Court of Human Rights has also recognized that there may be occasions when a defendant might be required to accept a lawyer against his will without any breach of Article 6(3)(c) (*Croissant v. Germany*, 1993). Even the US Supreme Court appears to be having second thoughts, having ruled recently that the right to self-represent applies only to trials and not to appeals (*Martinez v. United States*, 2000).

Protecting the Victim at Trial

The standing of the complainant in a common law criminal trial is that of the 'triggerer-off' (Christie, 1977: 3) of the process and subsequently the principal witness for the prosecution. She has no control over the investigation of the crime committed against her, the prosecution of the defendant or the choice of punishment to be inflicted upon him in the event of a conviction (see generally Walsh, 2002). By the 1970s, the position of the victim at trial was increasingly the source of public anxiety and academic scrutiny, becoming today one of the dominant discourses in criminal justice circles (O'Malley, 2006: 226). Of particular concern was the alienation reported by victims who sought redress through the criminal justice system, especially victims of rape (see Ellison, 2002). To some extent, this was a necessary by-product of the objective adversarial process that had evolved since the eighteenth century. Under this process, a crime is considered to be an assault upon the State, and on that basis, it is the State that prosecutes the offender. This is perhaps the most difficult part of the process for a victim to understand. As a Canadian commentator put it, '[t]ry convincing crime victims that the crime was against the state, not against them.... Victims are the ones whose blood has been shed, whose property has been taken, or whose dignity has been left in tatters, and the Queen [i.e., the State] is unlikely even to know about it' (Paciocco, 1999: 355). Victims also had specific complaints about aspects of the criminal process. As late as the 1980s, for example, it was not uncommon to find police officers referring to their interview of the rape victim as an interrogation (Temkin, 2002: 4, citing Firth, 1975; Chambers and Millar, 1983: 78-85). Victims whose cases went to trial were particularly distressed by their cross-examination by defence counsel (Adler, 1987; Lees, 1996), and incensed by the lack of information on the progress of their case through the system (Law Reform Commission, 1987; Bacik et al, 1998; Leane et al., 2001; McGee et al., 2002). Victims felt aggrieved that the prosecuting lawyer did not act on their behalf. Three factors combined to press for improvements in the lot of victims. Victims themselves began to organize advocacy groups that articulated their concerns more forcefully. Second, the problem of crime control became a dominant theme in the political arena with broad agreement among politicians that the criminal justice system was unduly protective of criminal defendants. Defending victims' rights became one vehicle through which crime control advocates could justify an erosion of due process values (O'Malley, 1993: 43-4; Ashworth, 2000; Elias, 2003). Finally, there was a recognition among lawyers that victims had in fact been treated poorly by the criminal justice system, a treatment that could ultimately undermine the system itself (e.g., Royal Commission on Criminal Justice, 1993: para. 5.44).

Considerable international efforts have been made since the 1980s to improve the lot of victims of crime (United Nations, 1985; European Council, 2001; Commonwealth Secretariat, 2002). These international efforts have been matched by considerable legislative activity on the home front as well; the following list shows some of the measures taken in Ireland to improve the position of complainants in rape trials:

- Guaranteed anonymity of the complainant before, during and after the trial (section 8 of the Criminal Law (Rape) Act 1981 as amended by section 14 of the Criminal Law (Rape) (Amendment) Act 1990);

- Restrictions on the introduction of prior sexual history evidence (section 3 of the 1981 Act as amended by section 13 of the 1990 Act);

- Introduction of limited separate representation for victims when an application has been made to introduce evidence of the complainant's prior sexual history (section 34 of the Sex Offenders Act 2001);

- Exclusion of the public (section 6 of the 1981 Act as inserted by section 11 of the 1990 Act);

- Provision for legal aid for a complainant in a sexual case to seek legal advice (section 26(3) of the Civil Legal Aid Act 1995);

- Corroboration warning made discretionary rather than mandatory (section 7 of the 1990 Act);

- Entitlement to have a friend, relative or parent in court during the proceedings (section 6 of the 1981 Act as amended by section 11 of the 1990 Act);

- Provision for compensation to be payable to the victim (section 6 of the Criminal Justice Act 1993);

- Provision for state appeals against unduly lenient sentences (section 2 of the 1993 Act); and

- Entitlement to address the court prior to sentencing and an obligation on the court to take account of the impact of the crime upon the complainant (section 5 of the 1993 Act).

Additionally, the Department of Justice, Equality and Law Reform published a non-statutory Victim's Charter in 1999 setting out the standards that criminal agencies are expected to achieve when dealing with victims. The fact that the Charter does not purport to create legal rights, however, has attracted a great deal of criticism (e.g., Rape Crisis Network Ireland, 2005; European Commission, 2004). The Irish government also established a Commission for the Support of Victims of Crime in 2005 to establish a framework for the development of victims' services and to support the work of voluntary bodies that supply the bulk of services to victims (Amnesty International, 2004: 7). Further, the Irish government has established a specialist unit within the Department of Justice, Equality and Law Reform called Cosc to co-ordinate research into sexual and gender crime. The Garda Síochána has also established a specialist investigative unit – the National Domestic Violence and Sexual Assault Investigations Unit – based at Garda Headquarters in Harcourt Street, Dublin.

Some of these measures, especially those concerned with victim advocacy during the sentencing process, have been controversial. Complainants have a statutory right to address the court as to the impact of the rape and the court is under a statutory obligation to take that impact into account. Critics have suggested that this might result in sentences being based upon unusual consequences that the defendant could not have foreseen, which they suggest would be unfair (Ashworth, 1993: 506; Guiry 2006: 3; O'Malley, 2006: 162-4; Morgan and Saunders: 21). Ashworth argues that such consequences should be built into the general levels of sentences instead. O'Malley points out that in a sentencing system that is built on the principle of just deserts (as exists in Ireland), it follows that offenders should receive the punishment that they deserve and 'deservedness is determined by the actual culpability of the offender' (O'Malley, 2006: 163). Critics have also suggested that victims might take the opportunity afforded to them by victim impact statement schemes to exercise some degree of vengeance, and that this will make the criminal justice system increasingly punitive (Coffey, 2006: 16; Coen, 2006; O'Malley, 2006: 228). Interestingly, few of these critics have cited compelling empirical evidence to support their claims of victim vengeance. It is true that some studies have found that a minority of victim impact statements do go beyond the permitted boundaries and make references to the defendant (Chalmers et al, 2007: 373). While not spelled out in the studies, it is safe to assume that these references generally were not terribly complimentary. Nevertheless, Hoyle et al. (1998: 28) found in their study of actual victim impact statements that victims tended to understate the severity of the impact of the crime. Perhaps for that reason several empirical studies in other jurisdictions have found that victim impact statements have had no appreciable effect on sentencing patterns (Erez et al., 1997; Muir, 1990; Davis and Smith, 1994; for an overview of this research, see Roberts, 2003: 381-3). It may be that judges have accepted victim impact statements at a rhetorical level but not at the level of action (Morgan and Sanders: 23). Alternatively, Erez and Rogers argue that judges expect certain reactions from certain crimes, and that as most victim impact statements tend to confirm these expectations, the statements lose 'their aura of seriousness' (1999). There is little evidence of vindictiveness on the part of victims, and even if some victims do indulge their desire for revenge, the suggestion that victim impact statements will make the system more punitive is flatly contradicted by empirical evidence. As Rock observes, the 'victim-vigilante has always been more of a demon that haunted the legal imagination than an empirically well-grounded figure' (2004: 181).

Juries

In the common law system, decisions on innocence or guilt are in the hands of a jury – a group of untrained lay people usually chosen at random from among the general populace. The placing of this responsibility into the hands of the jury has traditionally been seen as one of the principal legal mechanisms to ensure fairness and civil liberties (e.g., Blackstone, 1765: 379; Devlin, 1956: 164). Prior to the nineteenth century, it was unusual for a case not to be decided by a jury; since the nineteenth century, ever greater proportions of cases have been dealt with by summary courts and by guilty pleas (Jackson, 1937). Today, only a small fraction of criminal prosecutions actually go before a jury. Nevertheless, as has been shown earlier, the jury casts a longer shadow over the entire process than the actual number of jury trials would suggest. In particular, all sides in a criminal prosecution must assess what a jury might do given the evidence, and that assessment will influence every decision made in the criminal process. How juries arrive at their decisions, and the factors that influence those decisions, are therefore matters of great importance. Attempts to understand these matters, however, are hampered by the fact that all jury deliberations are conducted in secret in order to encourage full and frank discussions (*R v. Connor; R v. Mirza*, 2004; McHugh, 1988). As a result, researchers have had to employ other strategies to determine what goes on in the jury room, usually archival studies or experimental studies (MacCoun, 1989).* Archival studies involve an examination of court records to determine what juries have done. This methodology is useful for discerning verdict patterns, but it throws little light on the factors that lead the juries to those decisions.

Experimental studies with mock juries allow researchers to manipulate certain variables to determine their effect and to control external variables in a way that would be impossible in a real trial (Devine et al., 2001: 626). Nevertheless, these studies have found little favour with the courts, especially when they derive from methods that are neither very realistic nor representative of actual legal processes (Bornstein, 1999: 88). Three primary deficiencies are said to arise from these studies. First, all participants know that the experiment is not real and that there are no consequences to their decisions (Auld, 2001: 166; Koski, 2002). Second, these studies typically involve a group of university students being presented with a vignette and being asked to decide innocence or guilt. Whether real-world conclusions can be drawn from studies using such unrepresentative groups is unclear, although Bornstein (1999) conducted a review of 44 experimental studies over a 20 year period and found no evidence that studies using students subjects differed greatly in their results from studies using more representative groups. Third, while some researchers

---

* A third strategy, peculiar to the United States, is to conduct post-verdict interviews among jurors. This strategy is illegal in England and Wales by virtue of section 8 of the Contempt of Court Act 1981, and in several other common law jurisdictions as well. The law in other common law jurisdictions, such as Ireland and New Zealand, while not expressly prohibiting post-verdict contact with jurors, tends to frown upon attempts to make such contact.

have gone to enormous lengths to replicate realistic conditions – Hastie and his colleagues (1983), for example, used subjects who had been summoned for jury service, conducted the study in real courtrooms and jury rooms, and used a video-taped trial drawn from the transcript of a real trial and performed by a real judge and real lawyers – most are nowhere near as complex or realistic. In particular, few include the deliberative process, preferring instead to allow the subjects to render verdict individually. Kalven and Zeisel (1966: 488) suggested that deliberations play little role as the pre-deliberation majority, as shown by the initial vote, usually prevails in the verdict. More recent studies have shown, however, that deliberations do have an impact (e.g., Diamond, 1997) and most jury scholars tend to place the deliberative process at the heart of the jury's function (e.g., Abramson, 2001).

The limitations of these methodologies need to be borne in mind, but given the absence (and possible illegality) of research into real deliberations, these studies are the only source of information about how juries go about their duties. The primary duties of the jury are to listen to the evidence presented in court, to deliberate upon that evidence and to render a verdict based upon that evidence as instructed by the trial judge. Most importantly, jurors are expected to put aside any personal prejudices and to decide the matter before them impartially. There is research to show that the evidence in a case is of primary importance to the jury in its deliberations (Hastie et al., 1983; Reskin and Visher, 1986; Visher, 1987). Judges have also expressed confidence that they can properly direct juries regarding their duties and that juries will follow those directions (Kibble, 2004). Several experimental studies have shown, however, that jurors are willing to depart from judicial instructions on the definition of the offence, and will administer what they see as the spirit of the law (Feild, 1979; Wissler and Saks, 1985; Horowitz, 1988; Wiener et al., 1991; Schafer and Kerwin, 1992; Steblay et al., 2006). Other studies argue that jurors will fall back on their own knowledge and beliefs and other non-legal factors in coming to a verdict, especially if the evidence presented is weak or leaves apparent gaps (see Temkin and Krahe, 2008: 65-8, for a review). In the context of rape cases, Kalven and Zeisel (1966: 253-4) speculated that jurors in rape cases effectively redefine the offence of rape according to their own notions of fairness and assumption of risk. A complainant who, in the view of a jury, had precipitated the rape would thus be judged very harshly indeed. Brownmiller (1976: 373) agreed, writing that:

> [J]uries are allies of male defendants and enemies of female complainants for reasons that run deeper than their poor grasp of the law or their predominantly male composition. They are composed of citizens who believe the many myths about rape, and they judge the female according to these cherished myths.

This view is shared by many prosecutors and judges who have expressed the view to researchers that the jury is a barrier to conviction in rape cases (Brownmiller, 1976: 373; US Senate Majority Staff, 1993: 34; Temkin and Krahe, 2008: 132).

Juror Attitudes to Rape

Brownmiller's comment suggests that rape myth acceptance is the principal reason for biased decision-making by juries. As noted earlier, studies have shown high levels of rape myth acceptance in society generally. Given that juries are selected randomly from among the general populace it is inconceivable that these attitudes do not find their way on to the juries in rape cases, at least occasionally. But the issue is more complex than that in that levels of rape myth acceptance have been shown to vary according to gender. Studies have consistently shown higher levels of rape myth acceptance and victim-precipitation beliefs among men than among women (e.g., Calhoun et al., 1976; Anderson et al., 1997; Temkin and Krahe, 2008). Anderson et al.'s study is especially worthy of note as it is a meta-analysis of twenty-seven other studies on gender and rape myth acceptance. Not surprisingly, therefore, experimental studies have also shown that male mock jurors attribute higher levels of responsibility to the complainant than do their female counterparts (Feild, 1978; Dietz et al., 1984; Johnson et al., 1995; Gerber et al., 2004; Temkin and Krahe, 2008). By contrast, female mock jurors are more likely than male subjects to empathise with the rape complainant and to find her a credible witness (Schult and Schneider, 1991; Brems and Wagner, 1994; McLendon et al., 1994; Wenger and Bornstein, 2006). Consequently, female mock jurors are more likely than male subjects to vote to convict the defendant (Jacobson, 1981; Schutte and Hosch, 1997). Schutte and Hosch conducted a meta-analysis of thirty-six experimental studies concerning gender and verdict in simulated rape and sexual assault cases. They concluded that the probability of a female mock juror voting to convict was 58.5 per cent as against 41.5 per cent for male mock jurors. These studies appear to confirm Brownmiller's assertion cited earlier that '[w]omen believe the word of other women. Men do not' (1976: 387).

Male Dominance of Juries

For most of its existence, the institution of the jury was exclusively the province of men.* It was not until the twentieth century that women were permitted to serve as jurors, and only comparatively recently that jury composition began to achieve any semblance of gender equality. As late as the 1970s, the Heilbron Committee intimated that male dominance of juries in England was still the norm and that female potential jurors were more likely than male potential jurors to seek excusals. The Committee speculated that this was so due to the desire of married women to care for their young children (Heilbron Committee, 1975: para. 180; see also Sealy and Cornish, 1973). In Ireland, the Law Reform Commission found that 30 per cent of jurors between 1979 and 1986 were female (Law Reform Commission, 1987: Appendix). In almost 90 per cent of rape cases (78 out of 88), there was at least one female juror on the jury. Men were in the majority in 77 per cent of juries (68 out of 88), while women were in the majority in only 16 per

---

* The only time that women could serve on a criminal jury prior to the twentieth century was as part of a jury of matrons empanelled to determine as a matter of fact whether a woman was pregnant.

cent of the juries (14 out of 88). In approximately one third of cases (35 per cent), there were at least four jurors of either gender, but in only seven per cent were the genders equally represented (ibid.). More recently, successive studies in Britain have shown that the gender gap on juries has been closing (Zander and Henderson, 1993; Thomas, 2007). Thomas reported that male and female representation was almost identical (51 per cent women and 49 per cent men), and that 80 per cent of juries had a fairly even split: 6–6, 7–5 or 8–4. She concluded that 'the under-representation of women among serving jurors is another myth of jury service' (2007: 144).

It might be argued that despite the appearance of compositional equality, male jurors still dominate the actual proceedings of the juries. This might occur through the selection of a foreman or by dominating the deliberations. All juries must select one of their number to act as foreman. By tradition, the foreman chairs the jury's deliberations and acts as a conduit between the jury and the judge. Research into jury foremen is limited and much of it is out of date, but those studies that do exist suggest that men are much more likely to be selected than women (Strodtbeck et al., 1957; Mills, 1969; Beckham and Aronson, 1978; Baldwin and McConville, 1980; Deosaran, 1984; Marder, 1987; Diamond and Casper, 1992). Some old research suggests a correlation between the choice of foreman and seating arrangements: those sitting at the head of the table were more likely to be chosen as foreman, and men were more likely to sit at the head of the table (Strodtbeck and Hook, 1961; see also Nemeth et al., 1976, who also found a greater tendency among male subjects than female subjects to take the head seat). Formally the foreman has no greater power than any other juror, but they tend to speak more often than other jurors (Hastie et al., 1983; Marder, 1987) and are perceived by other jurors as being influential (York and Cromwell, 2006). Male jurors generally have also been found to speak more often: Hastie et al. (1983) found that male jurors initiated 40 per cent more comments than did their female counterparts. Nevertheless, in a recent study by York and Cromwell (2006), the researchers could find no evidence that members of historically, culturally or socially dominant groups were still dominating jury deliberations. They speculated that much of the apparent vocal dominance of male jurors found in earlier studies can be attributed to sustained bouts of disagreement with each other.

Increasing the Female Presence

Systemically, there is evidence that male dominance of juries is waning, but this does not mean that a jury in a particular case could not be dominated by men who hold views hostile to the complainant. This is especially true in a jurisdiction in which the power of peremptory challenge exists.* Accordingly, many law reform bodies have suggested that in rape cases, the principle of random selection should be amended to ensure a minimum number of female jurors. The Heilbron Committee (1975: para. 188), for example, recommended that steps be taken to ensure that both sexes would have at least 4 members on any rape jury. Law reformers in Tasmania (Law Reform Commission of Tasmania, 1976: para.13) and Australia (Royal Commission on Human Relationships, 1977: para. 64) took a similar view. In Ireland, the Joint Oireachtas Committee on Women's Rights took a more extreme view, and recommended that rape juries be composed of equal numbers of men and women (1987: para. 8). These proposals all have at their heart the same assumptions: that women are under-represented on juries and that attitudes prejudicial to rape complainants held by male jurors go unchecked as a result of this under-representation, to the detriment of the complainant. Indeed, the Heilbron Committee encapsulated this view by arguing that 'a proper balance of the views of both sexes is of importance, indeed

---

* The power of peremptory challenge allows lawyers to remove potential jurors without providing any justification for doing so. This power, which has existed for centuries, remains in use throughout the common law world, but was abolished in England and Wales by section 118 of the Criminal Justice Act 1988. In the United States, peremptory challenges cannot be used against particular groupings (*Batson v. Kentucky*, 1986).

we feel of paramount importance, in reaching a proper view about the attitude of the man and of the woman' (1985: para. 187).

Each of the assumptions underpinning these proposals are open to challenge. We have seen already that the gender gap on juries is closing, and there is no empirical evidence that female jurors, as a class, are any more sympathetic to rape complainants than male jurors. Indeed, anecdotal evidence from judges and barristers suggests that in their experience female jurors tend to judge the rape complainant more harshly than male jurors (Harris and Grace, 1999: 37; Temkin and Krahe, 2008: 136-7). Further, if female jurors are more sympathetic to the complainant, then one would expect that female dominated juries would have a higher conviction than male dominated juries but empirical studies have found no evidence of this. The Mitchell Committee in South Australia (1976), for example, correlated the gender composition of juries with their verdicts in all rape cases heard in South Australia between 1965 and 1975. They found no statistically significant difference in the conviction rate between female dominated juries and male dominated juries, and concluded that 'women are at least no more likely to convict of the offence of rape than are men' (1976: 54). Similarly, Nelligan (1988) studied 86 rape trials in Hawaii and found no greater propensity to convict among female dominated juries than among male dominated juries. Further, some experimental studies also cast doubt upon the assumption that female jurors are more likely to convict in rape cases (Fischer, 1997; Benlevy, 2000; Koski, 2002; Batchelder et al., 2004). Rumsey and Rumsey (1977) and Fischer (1997) both found that guilty verdicts in a simulated rape trial did not increase by adding more women to the jury until the jury was virtually entirely female. Benlevy (2000) found that male subjects were more sympathetic to the complainant than female subjects, while Batchelder et al. (2004) found that female mock jurors were more likely to disbelieve the complainant in a consent based rape case. Interestingly, Batchelder et al. also found that the female jurors tended to dominate the deliberations and that the male jurors tended to be swayed by them. Koski (2002) also found that in seven out of nine deliberations highly vocal and persuasive females lead the juries to an acquittal.

Thus, there is no evidence that individuals will conform to the general attitudes of the group to which he or she belongs (Abramson, 2000: 145; see also Sealy and Cornish, 1973). As Simon explained:

> It is extremely difficult to predict the response or behavior of a given individual to a concrete situation on the basis of such gross characteristics as occupation, education, sex or age. In any situation what a person thinks or does is a function of who he is, the exigencies of the situation, how strongly he feels about the problem, and a host of other factors (1968: 118).

Temkin and Krahe (2008: 122) agree that a conclusion that female jurors are more likely to convict than male jurors is too crude. Other studies have shown that a variety of factors can affect how a person deliberates and the results of that deliberation – age (Mills and Bohannon, 1980-1; Feild and Bienen, 1980; Higgins et al., 2007), socio-economic background (Adler, 1973; Hastie et al., 1983; Reed and Reed, 1997), levels of educational attainment (James, 1959; Mills and Bohannon, 1980-1; Hastie et al., 1983) and political outlook (Howard and Redfering, 1983; Anderson et al., 1997). Most importantly, a person's attitudes to, and experiences of, rape will affect how they deliberate and vote in a rape case (Feild, 1978; Wiener et al., 1989; Weir and Wrightsman, 1990; Anderson et al., 1997; Temkin and Krahe, 2008). Thus, a woman with traditional attitudes as to sex roles is likely to be more hostile to a rape complainant than a man with more egalitarian values. Accordingly, there is little evidence that simply increasing the number of women on rape juries would improve the conviction rate in rape cases.

Other Measures

Other possible mechanisms to reduce the impact that rape myth acceptance has on jury verdicts have been canvassed in the literature. Temkin and Krahe (2008: 177-80) consider possibly the most extreme solution – abolition of juries in rape cases. They point to Kalven and Zeisel's (1966) finding that judges were seven times more likely to convict in cases of simple rape than were juries. Removing juries would pre-empt counsel's attempts to play to juror prejudices and would obviate the need to educate jurors. They conclude, however, that this is not a realistic option due to a lack of empirical data and the fierce opposition that any such move would undoubtedly face.

Temkin and Krahe (2008; 180-1) also canvass the possibility of introducing some form of pre-selection screening to help in the removal of potentially biased jurors (i.e., those that have high levels of rape myth acceptance or those who have personal experience of rape). This kind of screening, by means of a pre-selection questionnaire, is common in the United States where it is known as *voir dire*. La Free et al. (1985: 402) suggest that a side-effect of this process is to educate jurors about their responsibilities and to encourage them to suppress their personal feelings. There is an absence of research to prove such beneficial effects, and in any case, it is not permitted in England and Wales and many other common law jurisdictions. Indeed, in Ireland, a Divisional High Court specifically rejected a trial judge's use of a pre-trial questionnaire to assist in the identification and removal of biased jurors (*DPP v. Haugh*, 2000).

One other possibility is also canvassed in the literature that has the benefit of working within existing jury trial structures: assisting the jury through expert evidence on reactions to rape. Such evidence is already quite common in the United States (Garrison, 2000; Vidmar and Hans, 2007: 201). In England, the Office for Criminal Justice Reform (2006) has proposed amending the law in that jurisdiction to allow for the introduction of general expert evidence to help provide a proper context in which the jury can evaluate the complainant's behaviour. The proposal differs from the position in the United States; there, it is not uncommon for both sides to introduce expert diagnostic evidence – in other words, experts are presented who then given an expert opinion on whether or not the complainant was suffering from Rape Trauma

Syndrome or Post-Traumatic Stress Disorder. The proposal in England is to permit the introduction of expert evidence of a general nature only – in other words, the evidence will not be related specifically to the complainant in any specific case. This proposal has proven to be controversial (Office of Criminal Justice Reform, 2007). The major argument in principle against allowing such evidence is that it is unnecessary – jurors should be allowed to exercise their common sense in evaluating the complainant's evidence and even if some form of direction is necessary, it would be safer if that direction came either from the prosecuting counsel or the judge. As to the first point, studies have shown that potential jurors are not, in fact, aware of the facts about rape (Frazier and Borgida, 1988; Ellison and Munro, 2009b) and there is accordingly a need to educate them (Feild, 1979). Where this is done, there is evidence that such efforts are successful (Gabora et al., 1993; Nietzel et al., 1999; Ellison and Munro, 2009a).

As to the second point, Lees (1997) found that prosecuting counsel were not especially good at countering rape myths. Ellison and Munro (2009a) found that directions from either an expert or the trial judge helped jurors in overcoming rape myths. Thus, permitting the trial judge to give directions concerning rape myths might be a good alternative to expert testimony, but it would necessarily alter and expand the role of the trial judge.

Sentencing

Traditionally, the common law in Ireland has invested a great deal of sentencing discretion in judges; the legislature typically sets the maximum sentence available for a particular crime and the trial judge is then free to set the sentence imposed on an individual offender anywhere up to that maximum (O'Malley, 2006: 53). The use of that discretion in rape has been the subject of much criticism since the early 1970s (Lloyd and Walmsley, 1989: 25). Criticisms have tended to be directed both at the mode of punishment chosen as well as to the length of sentences imposed. As a result, there have been consistent calls for the introduction of measures to curb the apparent disparity in sentencing practice

(O'Malley, 2006: Ch. 3). In particular, the use of sentencing guidelines has been recommended, and many jurisdictions have introduced some form of guideline regime. At one end of the guideline spectrum is the Federal Sentencing Guidelines prepared by the United States Sentencing Commission under authority granted by the Sentencing Reform Act 1984. The Commission created a grid based on both crime-seriousness and offender-characteristics, from which the trial judge would arrive at an appropriate predetermined sentence. With only a limited power to depart from this sentence, these guidelines were 'probably as close to mandatory guidelines as one can get' (O'Malley, 2006: 54. Following the decision of the United States Supreme Court in *United States v. Booker* (2005), the mandatory nature of the Guidelines has been diluted considerably).

Most common law jurisdictions rely on guidelines developed by the appellate courts. In England, the Court of Appeal set out sentencing guidelines for a number of offences, including rape. In *R v. Billam* (1986), the Court decided that the starting-point for a contested rape case should be five years imprisonment, rising to eight years if there were specified aggravating factors present or fifteen years for a campaign of rape. The process by which the Court of Appeal introduced new guidelines was altered by the Crime and Disorder Act 1998 which established the Sentencing Advisory Panel. This Panel, composed of judges, academics and other experts appointed by the Lord Chancellor, was created to advise the Court of Appeal on existing guidelines and the formation of new ones. The Panel was instrumental in the development of revised guidelines for rape adopted by the Court of Appeal in *R v. Millberry* (2003). These revised guidelines essentially updated those set out in *Billam* but the basic starting points remained the same. In 2000, the Home Office commissioned a review of the sentencing regime in England and Wales, known as the Halliday Report (Home Office, 2001). This Report recommended the creation of a new tier in the sentencing machinery, a recommendation implemented with the creation of the Sentencing Guidelines Council under the Criminal Justice Act 2003. This body, chaired by the

Lord Chief Justice, comprises eight judicial members and four non-judicial members. The Council has effectively superseded the Court of Appeal in its guidelines function, and the Sentencing Advisory Panel now makes recommendations and gives advice to the Council, which in turn formulates guidelines. The Council has already published definitive sentencing guidelines in relation to rape; in effect, the pre-existing guidelines set out by the Court of Appeal in *Millberry* have been extended to all non-consensual penetrative acts that constitute the offence of rape as defined in the Sexual Offences Act 2003 (Sentencing Guidelines Council, 2007). Section 172 of the Criminal Justice Act 2003 obliges all sentencing courts in England and Wales to have regard to these guidelines but the guidelines are not binding.

Disposition

In England and Wales, it is unusual for a convicted rapist to avoid a custodial sentence: Lloyd and Walmsley (1989: 26) found that the percentage of convicted rapists sentenced to imprisonment increased from 92 per cent in 1973 to 96 per cent in 1985. Harris and Grace found that all persons convicted of rape in their study were imprisoned; of 36 who were convicted of offences other than rape, 29 were also imprisoned (1999: 33). They also cite national figures that suggest that anyone convicted of rape will be imprisoned. In 2000, a study by the Sentencing Advisory Panel reported that the imprisonment rate for those convicted of rape was 98 per cent (Sentencing Advisory Panel, 2002: 13). Similarly, Morrison et al. (2008: 74) report that 98 per cent of persons convicted of rape in New Zealand in 2006 were sentenced to imprisonment. In New South Wales, the Department of Women (1996) found that between May 1994 and April 1995, 81 per cent of those convicted of rape were imprisoned and a further 13 per cent were subject to periodic detention (i.e., they were incarcerated only over weekend periods for up to three years). In Victoria, in the five years between 2003 and 2008, 226 people were sentenced for rape and 92 per cent received a custodial sentence. The range for custodial sentences ran from 89 per cent in 2007-08 to 98 per cent in 2006-07

(Sentencing Advisory Council, 2009). Only in the United States is there evidence of large-scale avoidance of imprisonment. Greenfeld (1997: 14) reported that in 1992 only 66 per cent of convicted rapists were imprisoned, 19 per cent were sent to local jails and 13 per cent received probation. Similarly, the United States Senate Majority Staff (1993: 54) reported, on foot of information from 18 States, that one-fifth of rapists received probation. These figures are now well out of date and the current position in the United States might well be different.

Length of Sentences

Just as modes of punishment have become more harsh, so too have average sentences for rape. Lloyd and Walmsley (1989) found that sentences increased in severity between 1973 and 1985. For example, they found that the percentage of rapists sentenced to less than three years imprisonment fell from 55 per cent to 36 per cent, those sentenced to between three years and five years increased from 30 per cent to 39 per cent, and those sentenced to more than five years rose from 15 per cent to 25 per cent (1989: 28). By 1996, however, Harris and Grace reported that half of those convicted of rape were sentenced to at least six years imprisonment or 72 months (1999: 34). In 2000, the average length of determinate sentences (i.e., excluding indeterminate life sentences) imposed on adult rapists was seven years and four months (88 months)* (Sentencing Advisory Panel, 2002: 13). The same study showed that pleading guilty resulted in an average reduction in sentence of some 11 per cent, from 88 months to 79 months. In 2006, the Parliamentary Under-Secretary for the Home Office, Vernon Coaker, MP, gave the House of Commons the average sentences for adult rape, excluding indeterminate life sentences, as shown in Table 2.4.

These sentences are more severe than sentences imposed in Australia and less severe than those imposed in New Zealand.

---

* For offenders under the age of 18, the average sentence was three years and nine months, or 45 months (Sentencing Advisory Panel, 2002: 13).

The Sentencing Advisory Panel in Victoria found that between 2003-04 and 2007-08 the average sentences imposed were as shown in Table 2.5.

Table 2.4: Average Sentences in England and Wales

Year	Average Sentences in Months
2000	85.4
2001	84.6
2002	87.7
2003	90.5
2004	87.9

Table 2.5: Average Sentences in Victoria

Year	Average Sentences in Months
2003-04	66
2004-05	69
2005-06	61
2006-07	62
2007-08	61

By contrast, Morrison et al. (2008) found that average sentences imposed for rape in New Zealand were considerably more severe than those imposed in either England and Wales and Victoria.

Table 2.6: Average Sentences in New Zealand

Year	Average Sentences in Months
2000	95.9
2001	92.7
2002	99.9
2003	106.9
2004	99.0
2005	98.8
2006	104.9

In the United States, Greenfeld reported that in 1992, the average prison sentence imposed for rape was 164 months, or just under 14 years, while the average jail term was eight months and the average probation period was just under six months (1997: 14). Greenfeld also noted a huge disparity in sentences depending upon the defendant's plea: the average prison term imposed after a jury conviction of rape was 'nearly 13 years longer than the average sentence received by those pleading guilty to rape' (1997: 15). Thus, while the percentage of rapists in the United States receiving a prison sentence appears to be considerably lower than in the rest of the common law world, when such a sentence is imposed, it is likely to be substantially more severe than anywhere else, especially if the defendant contested the charges.

Sentencing in Ireland

Ireland has a relatively unstructured system of sentencing (O'Malley, 2006: 53). As long as the sentencing judges do not exceed the maximum sentence set by legislation, they are generally free to impose whatever sentence appears to them to be appropriate. Unlike in England, there are no judicially-created sentencing guidelines in this jurisdiction, and there have been calls for the introduction of such guidelines either generally (Law Reform Commission, 1996) or specifically in the context of rape (e.g., Joint Oireachtas Committee, 1987: para. 10.1, Rape Crisis Network Ireland, 2005). To date, the judiciary has resisted such calls, on the basis of both the absence of empirical research on sentencing patterns in Ireland and the constitutionally protected independence of the judicial function (see *People (DPP) v. Tiernan*, 1988).

The only data that exist in Ireland on sentencing in rape cases comes from the Annual Reports of the Courts Service as shown in Table 2.7.

These figures are deficient in at least two respects. First, they provide only sentencing bands, which makes the calculation of average and median sentences impossible. Second, two of the bands themselves were altered: from 2000 to 2002, the number of sentences for between two and five years' imprisonment was given; from 2003, that band changed to include all sentences under five years' imprisonment. Similarly, from 2000 to 2004, the number of sentences imposed for between five and ten years and more than ten years were given; in 2005, these bands were changed to between five and 12 years and more than 12 years, respectively. These alterations, on top of the wide sentencing bands used, make tracking sentencing patterns very difficult.

Table 2.7: Sentences for Rape Imposed in Ireland

Year	Life	<10 Years	5-10 Years	2-5 Years	>2 Years	Other
2000	0	6	17	36	5	23
2001	0	6	31	27	9	25
2002	1	5	24	22	5	20
2003	2	7	28	16*	N/A	8
2004	2	8	14	7*	N/A	7
2005	0	3**	20***	13*	N/A	7
2006	1	3**	20***	9*	N/A	4
2007	2	2**	34***	7*	N/A	3

*Figures are for a new category of Up to 5 Years
**Figures are for a new category of <12 Years
***Figures are for a new category of 5-15 Years

The Courts Service's figures indicate a general trend of increasing severity. In 2000, the majority of sentences imposed by the Central Criminal Court in rape cases were for periods of less than five years. By 2007, the majority of such sentences were for periods in excess of five years. In an opinion poll published by the *Irish Examiner* in 2008, 13 per cent of respondents felt that rape should attract a minimum sentence of between three and six years' imprisonment, 38 per cent felt between six and ten years' imprisonment was more appropriate, and 39 per cent demanded life imprisonment (Ryan, 2008: 10-11).

A further analysis of sentencing decisions in Irish rape cases was provided by Charleton J. in *People (DPP) v. Drought* (2007). The judge considered a large number of cases in three categories: those that attracted ordinary punishments, those that attracted severe punishments and those that attracted condign punishments.

Ordinary Punishments (Three to Eight Years' Imprisonment). Fully suspended sentences for rape were rare – in 2006, only four such sentences were found, and they were imposed almost certainly for sexual assault rather than rape. Out of 42 sentencing decisions that had resulted in sentences for rape of between three and eight years' imprisonment, Charleton J. noted the following characteristics as shown in Table 2.8 (the tables below were derived from the judge's discussion):

Table 2.8: Ordinary Sentence Characteristics

Sentences Imposed	Characteristics
8 Years	Unusual degree of violence; or particularly unfortunate effect on victim; or conviction on a number of different counts; or incidents occurring over several years to young victims.*
7 Years	Serious cases reduced to seven years due to mitigation such as: early guilty plea, defendant's age, health and lack of prior convictions, or the incident occurred long ago. Cases aggravated by effect on victim or level of violence.
6 Years	Aggravated by threats/violence, even with a guilty plea.
5 Years	Cases mitigated by defendant's age and circumstances.
4.5, 4 or 3 Years	All have strong mitigating factors. All but one involved guilty pleas.

*Regarded as lenient sentences that in other cases have attracted more severe sentences.

Severe Punishments (9 to 14 Years Imprisonment). Charleton J. then considered 22 cases in which sentences of between 9 and 14 years imprisonment were imposed. Five cases concerned single counts of rape, nine involved a single incident that resulted in several counts and the remainder involved multiple counts, usually perpetrated over many years.

Table 2.9: Severe Sentence Characteristics

Sentences Imposed	Characteristics
9-12 Years	Serious ordinary cases contested by defendant; or multiple counts with young victims, usually old cases and defendant pleads guilty.
10-12 Years	Multiple counts and defendant has prior convictions for violent offences. Unusual for single count of rape unless especially violent or degrading.
12-14 Years	Exceptionally violent violation; or exceptional humiliation or degradation.

Condign Punishments (15 Years to Life). In this category, Charleton J. examined 22 cases. Nine cases concerned a single incident that usually lasted for several hours, two involved a gang rape and the remainder involved multiple incidents or multiple victims or both.

Table 2.10: Condign Sentence Characteristics

Sentences Imposed	Characteristics (several of the following)
15- 20 Years	Gang rape; prior convictions for violent offences; incidents lasting for several hours; constant threats of death; multiple counts; victim very young or very old; excessive violence. Guilty plea may mitigate slightly.

Life Imprisonment	Need to protect the community, shown by: Very serious, vicious and degrading sex crimes over a period of years; or serious breach of trust; or pre-meditation; or systematic campaign.
	Usually many prior convictions and long periods in prison for violent offences.

Delay

A series of studies have shown that delays in the processing of criminal trials are a source of concern to complainants (e.g., Adler, 1987: 50; Temkin, 2000: 222; Kelly et al., 2005: 73). Prosecuting barristers interviewed by Temkin noted how traumatic it can be for a complainant who has tried to get on with her life but then has to relive the experience at trial after a long delay (2000: 222). Temkin goes on to note that in Victoria, Australia there is a statutory obligation to bring the defendant to trial within six months of the date on which he was charged, and recommends that consideration be given to the enactment of similar legislation in England and Wales (2000: 239).

In Ireland, the Annual Reports published by the Courts Service show a continuing reduction in delays in cases coming to trial in the Central Criminal Court.* In 2002, the time from the return for trial until the start of the first hearing was 18 months; by 2007, this delay was reported to have fallen to eight months (Courts Service, 2003 and 2008). These figures, of course, only show part of the story with delays; they give no indication of how long the investigative period was. The National Crime Council recently completed an in-depth study of delays in cases coming before the Central Criminal Court (National Crime Council, 2006). They examined all cases disposed of between 1 January 2002 and 31 March 2004, a total of 332 cases (10 of which were excluded due to insufficient data). Of these cases, 198 were rape cases and of these, only 88 went to trial. The Council discovered that the median rape case was disposed of just over 28 months after the defendant's

---

* These figures include both rape and homicide cases.

initial arrest and 20 months after his charge (National Crime Council, 2006: 9). Typically, the period from arrest to return for trial would last for 11 or 12 months (National Crime Council, 2006: 12), while the time from return for trial to final disposal would typically take over 16 months (National Crime Council, 2006: 22). These delays were substantially longer than those recorded by the Crown Courts or the Central Criminal Court in England, as shown in Table 2.11.

Table 2.11: Average Delays, by Jurisdiction

Court and Country	Average Delay, from Return for Trial until Final Disposal (weeks)
Central Criminal Court, Ireland	81
Crown Courts, England and Wales	27
Central Criminal Court, London	32

The authors note that there is unlikely to be any great substantive difference in the applicable laws, so the difference in delay must be accounted for in the different procedural rules and practices (National Crime Council, 2006: 41). The Rape Crisis Network Ireland has voiced the opinion that delays of this nature in the criminal justice system add to the attrition rate, harm the viability of the prosecution and further traumatize victims (RCNI, 2007: 9).

Chapter 3

METHODOLOGY

OVERVIEW OF THE RESEARCH DESIGN

To date, Irish studies of sexual victimisation have employed either large-scale quantitative designs (McGee et al., 2002) or small-scale qualitative approaches (e.g., Leane et al., 2001) to measure rape prevalence and attrition. This study combines the best of both approaches by adopting a mixed-methods design. The first element of the research design, presented in Chapter 4, consists of three sub-components. The first part of the investigation involved a quantitative survey of rape victims. This was supplemented with in-depth interviews with a sub-sample of participants. Third, participants were surveyed, and psychometric tests were administered, on a subsequent occasion with a view to documenting their experiences with the criminal justice system. The second element of the research design, presented in Chapter 5, involves a large-scale quantitative examination of, and regression analysis on, material provided by the Office of the DPP. The purpose of these analyses was to ascertain which factors influenced the prosecutorial decisions of the Directing Officers. An analysis of withdrawn complaints was also conducted. Finally, the third element of the study, presented in Chapter 6, is a quantitative analysis of the judicial and trial process for rape complaints based upon 173 rape trial court records and 35 trial transcripts.

Quantitative research uses structured designs to collect objective and reliable information from a large number of people. Its findings can be replicated and may be representative of the population as a whole. Qualitative data, however, can provide rich insights into respondents' understandings of their social worlds. Some researchers have argued that, while national surveys provide invaluable information on the prevalence of sexual assault, smaller targeted surveys are more appropriate for studying the experiences of victims (e.g., Gardner, 1990). In addition, in-depth interviews with rape victims are largely absent from the literature. This qualitative component has the potential to provide a valuable addition to knowledge in Ireland and further afield.

PARTICIPATION IN THE STUDY

Specific criteria were put in place for participation in this study. These were:

1. **Offence:** The definition of rape used in this study followed the legal definition as defined under the Criminal Law (Rape) Act 1981 and the Criminal Law (Rape) (Amendment) Act 1990. Only individuals who experienced one or more of the following were eligible to participate:

   a) penetration of the vagina by penis without consent, or

   b) penetration (however slight) of the anus or mouth by the penis without consent, or

   c) penetration (however slight) of the vagina by any object held or manipulated by another person without consent.

2. **Age:** Participants must have been 18 or over at the time of the assault to participate. Rapes committed against children, while prosecuted under the same legislation, raise a different set of strategic, legal and ethical issues.

3. **Time limit:** The first phase of the study focused on rapes that occurred since 2002. It was important to start at 2002 because new legislation was enacted in 2001 which might have had the effect of altering the experiences of victims. The second phase of the study, examining the prosecutorial decision, included rapes reported to Gardaí between 1 January 2000 and 31 De-

cember 2004. Finally, the third aspect of the study, the trial process, utilised trial court records from the Central Criminal Court Register recorded between 2000 and 2005 and court transcripts from rape cases that were prosecuted between 2002 and 2005.

4. **Jurisdiction:** All rapes must have occurred in Ireland.

STRAND I: REPORTING RAPE – METHODS AND TOOLS

The study involved a national survey of 100 women who experienced rape in Ireland since 2002. The survey had three primary aims: (a) to profile the characteristics of rape in Ireland, (b) to identify the factors that influenced the reporting or non-reporting of rape to the Gardaí and (c) for those who reported, to document their experiences as their cases progressed through the criminal justice system. This chapter outlines the methods, design and procedures used in this aspect of the study. It also describes the instruments and questionnaires used to obtain information. Finally, it concludes with a socio-demographic profile of respondents.

Procedures

Data collection took place between August 2005 and October 2006. Three main strategies for recruitment were used. First, participants were contacted through Rape Crisis Centres, all of whom agreed to assist the research including the centres not affiliated with the Rape Crisis Network Ireland. This produced the largest response (n = 85). Second, posters and leaflets were designed and distributed to agencies that had contact with potential rape victims, such as doctors' surgeries, hospitals, universities, other educational institutes, and women's refuges. These materials contained information about the participation criteria, assurances about the confidentiality of the survey and details about how to participate. This proved a largely unsuccessful strategy, resulting in only three responses. Finally, a media campaign involving both national and local media was undertaken. This consisted of interviews with the researchers, letters to editors, and articles describing the research and requesting participation. This strategy generated eleven eligible responses. One respondent did not explain how she heard about the survey.

Within the RCCs, counsellors made the initial contact with eligible clients using a prepared script, which set out the purpose of the study, what participation involved and the ethical guidelines.[1] If the client agreed to participate, their name and contact details were forwarded to the researcher who then contacted them directly. Three methods of participation were offered to participants: post, telephone or on-line. A research helpline and website were set up for the study. A covering letter that reiterated information about the research was enclosed with the survey pack (and read to telephone interviewees). Respondents who wished to remain anonymous were given the option of having the survey posted to them care of their local Rape Crisis Centre. Respondent located through other means contacted the researcher directly by phoning the research helpline. No payment was offered for participation in the survey. Participants in the face-to-face interviews were paid €50 to cover expenses. In total, 71 respondents said they were willing to be contacted for the follow up survey, resulting in 50 participants. The follow-up questionnaire was sent to participants on two occasions, facilitating a prospective study of contact with the criminal justice system and the impact of rape. Finally, a sub-group of participants was asked to participate in face-to-face interviews, producing twelve interview scripts.

Instruments

Three questionnaires were designed for the study: the initial survey, the follow-up survey and the qualitative interview schedule. In designing the questionnaire, existing guidelines for conducting research on sexual violence were consulted. Early drafts of the questionnaires were reviewed externally and modified on the basis of advice received. The pilot studies offered further opportuni-

---

[1] See Appendix 1 for description of the ethical guidelines used in the research.

Follow-up Survey

Of the original sample of 100 respondents, 50 completed a follow-up questionnaire designed to assess the impact that the rape and their experiences within the justice system had on their mental health and attitude. In particular, it was intended to examine the relationship between the stage of attrition and mental health and recovery. The questionnaire involved four psychometric tests aimed at understanding incidences of possible psychological dysfunction, the impact the incident had on the individuals' 'outlook' on life, their perception of the 'locus of control' or the extent to which the individual feels they have control over the outcomes of their life, and indications of Post-Traumatic Stress Disorder (PTSD) among rape survivors.

General Health Questionnaire (GHQ-12). People who have experienced sexual violence are also likely to suffer significant psychological and physical consequences, as is widely documented in the literature (see Foa and Riggs, 1995). The General Health Questionnaire was designed to detect psychiatric disorders within respondent populations in community settings and non-psychiatric clinical settings (Goldberg, 1978: 1). The questionnaire used in this study is the GHQ-12. The GHQ-12 is the shortest version of the General Health Questionnaire available and has been identified as a good measure of psychological wellbeing (Goldberg and Williams, 2004). This is a twelve question self-reported survey that asks respondents to give a score of 1 to 4, (1 = 'not at all', 2 = 'no more than usual', 3 = 'rather more than usual' and 4 = 'much more than usual') to questions designed to assess variations from the normal state of mind of the respondent over the past weeks. The questionnaire therefore focuses on 'breaks in normal function, rather than upon lifelong traits' (ibid.: 5). The GHQ-12 may be assessed in two ways:

- According to the GHQ scale in which scores of 0 are given to the answers 'not at all' and 'no more than usual', and a score of 1 is given to 'rather more than usual' and 'much more than usual'; or

- According to a Likert scale which produces results ranging from 1-4, with one representing 'not at all' and four representing 'much more than usual'.

The first score can be used to identify a split in the sample (i.e., whether individuals who made a report to the Gardaí are more likely to have indications of poor mental health than those who did not make such a report), while the Likert scale is useful for establishing a gradation in poor mental health indicators among those who did and those who did not report their rape.

Post-Traumatic Life Change Questionnaire. There is growing awareness that positive changes can occur after a negative life event (Tedeschi, Park and Calhoun, 1998). Research suggests that the perception of a positive effect may be linked to better mental and physical health among victims of sexual violence (Frazier et al., 2001; Connor et al., 2003). Frazier et al.'s (2001) post-traumatic life change questionnaire was used to examine the positive and negative changes that occurred in survivors' lives as a result of the rape. Although there are other validated instruments that measure post-traumatic growth, this scale was chosen because it incorporates both positive and negative changes and because it has previously been used with sexual assault victims. The self-administered questionnaire consists of 17 items that measure life changes on several dimensions:

- Changes in self (e.g. sense of self worth, faith in own judgement);

- Relationships (e.g. with family and friends);

- Life philosophy (e.g. sense of purpose in life, spiritual well-being);

- Empathy (e.g. concern for others in similar situations); and
- Beliefs about the world (e.g. belief in the goodness of people, about the safety of the world).

The 17 items were rated on a five-point scale with '1' representing 'much worse' and '5' representing 'much better'. Scores were tallied on a Likert scale, with higher scores indicating positive life changes and lower scores indicating negative life changes.

Post-Traumatic Stress Disorder Symptom Scale – Self Report (PSS-SR). The PSS-SR was developed to measure the presence and severity of Post-Traumatic Stress Disorder. It is a self-report questionnaire consisting of 17 items, which correspond to the DSM-III-R diagnostic criteria for Post-Traumatic Stress Disorder (PTSD). The PSS-SR is used to measure the frequency of symptoms associated with Post-Traumatic Stress Disorder using a four-point Likert scale (0 = 'Not at all' to 3 = 'five or more times per week/very much/almost always') (Foa et al., 1993). Foa et al. (1993) found this scale to be both a reliable and valid measure of PTSD. The scale was chosen over other measures of post-traumatic stress disorder for a number of reasons. First, it has been validated with female rape victims. Second, whereas most PTSD scales consist of professionally administered interviews, the PSS-SR has been validated as a self-report instrument. Finally, it takes account of the revised DSM-III diagnostic criteria.

Symptoms are organised into three categories: re-experiencing the event or intrusion (e.g. nightmares, flashbacks), avoidance-numbing (e.g. avoiding trauma reminders, detachment from others), and increased arousal/hyperarousal (e.g. hyper-vigilance). Those respondents who record a '1' or higher on at least one intrusion, three avoidance/numbing, and two hyperarousal items, were determined to have a probable diagnosis of PTSD (Foa et al., 1993).

Locus of Control Test. Locus of control is 'a generalised expectancy pertaining to the connection between personal characteristics and/or actions and experienced outcomes' (Lefcourt, 1991: 414). Individuals with an internal locus of control believe that their actions directly affect events, while people with an external locus of control believe that their destinies are controlled by luck or the influence of powerful others. In the literature, belief about self-efficacy has been identified as an important factor in recovery from traumatic episodes (see Benight and Bandura, 2004). In order to establish whether the stage of attrition was affected by the respondent's perception of her ability to control a situation, Levenson's Locus of Control test was used (Levenson, 1981). This test assesses beliefs about the operation of control and is measured on three scales: Internality (I scale), Powerful Others (P scale) and Chance (C scale). The I scale measures the extent that individuals feel they have control over their own lives and is related to an internal locus of control, while the P scale measures the belief that powerful others have control in their lives. The C scale measures the extent to which individuals feel that fate or chance controls what happens to them (Levenson, 1981: 17). The P and C scales are thus related to an external locus of control. A Likert scale ranging from 1 (strongly disagree) to 6 (strongly agree) recorded the respondents' answers to questions. Each scale produces results that range from 8–48, with a score of 24 indicating no real feeling either way. It is empirically possible for an individual to score high or low scores on all three scales as they are unrelated to one another, although this is uncommon (ibid.: 18).

Statistical Tools for the Analysis of Psychometric Tests. Due to the small sample size, the variety of statistical tests and their degree of accuracy were impaired. ANOVA tests required a sample size of 76 to achieve a power of 0.80. Our sample was too small for this test. The sample size was marginally large enough, however, to qualify for Chi Square tests for independence, with a power of 0.80, indicating a 20 per cent probability of a type II error. Type II errors, also called false negatives, occur when the null hypothesis is not rejected despite being false. In lay terms this means that statistical tests may indicate that there is no statistical significance to a relationship, when, in fact, there is. Although a power of 0.80 is lower than desired, it is conventionally held among social researchers to be acceptable (Cohen, 1988). Independent samples *t*-tests allowed for the smallest sample size, but were also run at a power of 0.80. Again, this means that there is a 20 per cent probability of not identifying significant results, suggesting that this analysis may provide an incomplete picture of the relationship between attrition and recovery from rape.

Qualitative Interview Schedule

The primary aim of the qualitative interview was to elicit in-depth narrative accounts of the decision to report rape to the Gardaí. The interview also offered an opportunity to study the process of recovery, including the impact of rape, respondents' coping strategies and their use of support services. Elements of the Life Story Interview (McAdams, 1995) were incorporated into the design. This questionnaire is designed to uncover participants' personal stories, motivations, goals and sense of self. The interview covered four main areas:

- Section I: The decision to report (e.g. reasons for reporting/not reporting);
- Section II: Impact of the rape (e.g. changes experienced, impact on relationships. employment);
- Section III: Recovery process (e.g. key events, positive and negative influences on recovery); and
- Section IV: Coping strategies (e.g. internal resources, role of social supports).

The analysis of the interviews aimed to identify themes relevant to those who reported their rape, those who did not, and themes common to both groups. Furthermore, it attempted to understand the context in which the decision to report was made and the long-term impact that such a decision had on the victim. Although parts of the interview were structured, priority was given to allowing the interviewee to describe their experiences in their own words and time, and thus to allow as much relevant information as possible to be shared.

In order to examine, in depth, the factors involved in making the decision of whether or not to report a rape, discourse analysis was used to analyse the interviews. Discourse analysis 'concentrates on the analysis of knowledge formations, which organize institutional practices and societal reality on a large scale'; thus, 'interview data are analyzed on the macrosociological level, as social texts' (Talja, 1999: 460). In this way, the interview analysis attempted to reveal underlying social conditions that may influence a rape victim's decision to report.

Because of the large amounts of data produced through qualitative interviews, the sample size was necessarily small. Care was taken, however, to ensure that victims of different ages, socioeconomic backgrounds and experiences were included. Consequently, the sample for the interviews does adequately represent the variation in victims present in the larger data samples used for the initial survey. Further, as individual interviews varied greatly in length and participants were allowed to stop the interview whenever they felt necessary, not all of the interviews were completed to the same extent. Thus, victim recommendations, the final part of the interview, were not supplied by all those interviewed. Despite this, the interviews did provide a wide-ranging and spontaneous source of data that has the potential to provide texture and context to the quantitative data and, in some cases, has produced results that explain and/or challenge the results of the quantitative studies.

Limitations

This study had a number of shortcomings. The first related to the sample size (n = 100). Small numbers make it hard to detect statistical differences unless they are very large. Second, the sample is not representative of all rape victims. Existing statistics show that most rape victims do not report (McGee et al., 2002; RCNI, 2004).

The number of non-reporters in the current sample (n = 34) is low, suggesting that this group may be under-represented. Also, although efforts were made to recruit men, only three were located. Nevertheless, despite its limitations, this sample is one of the largest obtained for an Irish study of this kind and offers valuable insight into the experience of rape in Ireland and victim decision-making. It is also a national study and so can provide insight into rural and urban experiences.

STRAND II: PROSECUTING RAPE – METHODOLOGY AND TOOLS

Questionnaire

For this section of the study, a quantitative analysis was performed on materials received from the Office of the DPP on 597 reported rapes received by the DPP from the beginning of 2000 to the end of 2004. Questionnaires were completed by researchers in the Office of the DPP, with questions relating to basic factual information including relevant dates, classification of offences, the DPP's final decision and the outcome of the case. A copy of the questionnaire is appended in Appendix 3. In total, 623 questionnaires were returned by the DPP, which resulted in a total of 597 usable case files. Nine case files were excluded as they were not rape cases and eighteen files were found to be duplicates. The data was recorded by reference to victims, resulting in two cases being aggregated into one as they both referred to the rape of one woman by two men. Two further files (each representing the rapes of two women on a single occasion by one man) were recorded to represent the complainants and were thus documented as four files. Of the 597 usable case files, one further file was excluded from the regression analysis as the decision to prosecute was still pending.

Follow-up Questionnaire

A second questionnaire was prepared in respect of the complainant's decision to withdraw, a copy of which is shown in Appendix 4. A total of 161 questionnaires were returned. Along with factual information, the DPP's researchers provided the answers as recorded by Gardaí relating to false reporting and complainant vulnerability, such as poverty, homelessness, substance abuse or dependency, the complainant's relationship with the accused, prostitution and mental illness, and the complainant's stated reason for withdrawal. Additional information from the Garda files was also included where relevant.

Tools of Analysis

Data from the original and follow-up questionnaires were entered into the Statistical Package for the Social Sciences (SPSS) program, version 15.0. This program was then used to assess potential relationships and significant associations between various case, complainant, and suspect factors recorded on the questionnaires. Further, relationships and associations between these factors and the ultimate decision on prosecution were also assessed. Descriptive statistics were also generated which could then be compared to population demographics for the state of Ireland.

The 2002 Census was used to compare population demographics with the population of suspects and complainants in this study. The 2002 Census was chosen over the 2006 Census as the earlier Census was a better comparative match to the date range of 2000-2004 for the complaints used in the analysis. If different groups and regions were proportionally represented then the percentages from this study and the population demographics from the Census should be roughly equal. Where this was not true, certain groups and/or regions of the country can be seen to be over or under represented.

Limitations

Researchers were not permitted to access the DPP's files directly, and instead had to rely on the DPP's own research staff to complete the surveys in respect of the files. This restriction created some difficulties, especially in respect of the consistent interpretation of the questions asked. Further, the initial intention was to examine a small sample of questionnaires as a pilot study and to then examine and re-work the questionnaire as necessary, before submitting the questionnaire to the entire sample. However, time constraints negated this possibility. In consequence, some questions that could have been included in the questionnaire were absent. However, the questionnaire did address the vast majority of concerns noted in the literature regarding prosecutorial decision-making, and the large sample size allowed for a good variation of statistical tests with a high power, indicating a very low probability of attaining false results.

STRAND III: THE TRIAL PROCESS – METHODOLOGY AND TOOLS

The third and final section of the study, presented in Chapter 6, concerns rape attrition occurring during the trial processes. To properly investigate this form of attrition, it was necessary to gain access to court records. An immediate decision was made between retrospective and prospective methodologies. A retrospective methodology focuses on cases that have been completed, and the investigation would therefore require access to official records. A prospective methodology focuses on cases still making their way through the judicial system, and would require ongoing contact with the courts and court personnel. The literature contains numerous examples of both strategies being employed, and they both have their advantages. It was decided that a retrospective methodology would better suit the needs of this analysis, for a variety of methodological and logistical reasons:

- In order to investigate attrition, it was necessary that the cases in the sample be completed to allow for identification of the attrition point, and a retrospective study of completed cases would give the best overview of the entire criminal justice system;

- A retrospective study would minimize the level of disruption caused to the operations of the Courts Service and the courts themselves;

- The Annual Reports of the Courts Service indicate that there are comparatively few rape cases being heard by the courts – an average of 35 per year between 2000 and 2005 (Courts Service, 2000-2005). Many of these would deal with child rape and therefore would not fit the study's eligibility criteria. Accordingly, a methodology that relied upon direct observation would not return a sufficient number of cases for analysis within an acceptable time-frame; and,

- Rape trials are no longer heard only in Dublin; rather they can be heard in cities and larger towns around the country, making their observation by researchers more difficult in logistical terms.

A discussion with the Courts Service indicated that their records fall into two categories:

- Trial Court Records, which typically contain all the formal paperwork concerning cases such as the Book of Evidence, the Order Sending the Defendant forward for Trial, bail documents, the jury's verdict, the Certificate of Conviction and sentencing documents such as Victim Impact Reports, Probation Reports and details of the sentence itself

- Trial Transcripts, which would include a verbatim record of the evidence presented at trial, and possibly counsel's closing arguments, the judge's charge to the jury.

Both categories of documents were of interest to this analysis.

Trial Court Records

The Chief Justice and the Courts Service granted the research team unrestricted access to the trial court records held by the Central Criminal Court, subject to a Confidentiality Agreement under which it was agreed not to identify any individual case and to allow the Courts Service to verify, in advance of publication, that this requirement had been adhered to. The Courts Service also provided a small office in the Four Courts complex in which to conduct the examination of the files.

The analysis began with the Register of the Central Criminal Court, a very large book in which is recorded (by hand) all cases referred to the Central Criminal Court for trial. The Register contains basic information on each case, such as the case number, the defendant's name, the principal charges involved, the county in which the case occurred, whether or not bail was granted and the name of the defendant's solicitor. From the Register a list of all cases in which sexual charges were noted were extracted according to the year in which the case was referred to the Central Criminal Court. Interestingly, we discovered that while most cases were assigned numbers according to the year of referral, this was not always the case. Thus, some cases were received in one year but were assigned a number from the preceding year or from the following year. There were also several instances of cases being consolidated into other cases, sometimes in different years.

In total, the Central Criminal Court received 661 cases between 2000 and 2005, of which 432 had at least some sexual element and were included on our list. The initial list was not confined to those cases listed in the Register as being rape cases; rather, note was taken of all sexual cases so as to include any cases that involved allegations of rape but which were not prosecuted or listed as such. Each of these cases was sought from the Central Office archive and reviewed to determine whether or not they met the eligibility criteria:

a) The victim was aged at least 18 at the time of the incident. The age of the defendant was irrelevant;

b) The gender of the victim was irrelevant;

c) The case involved at least an allegation of non-consensual penetration that would meet the legal definition of rape as contained in either section 2 of the Criminal Law (Rape) Act 1981 or section 4 of the Criminal Law (Rape) (Amendment) Act 1990; and

d) The incident occurred in Ireland.

The majority of sexual cases involved allegations of sexual offences against children, but some others involved allegations of sexual offences against adults that did not legally amount to rape. Both categories of case were excluded. A number of cases involving multiple allegations of sexual abuse and rape that began when the victim was a child but continued after he or she reached majority were encountered. These cases were included initially but ultimately were excluded as they were in reality cases of child abuse and were of a materially different nature to those cases that were the focus of this study. The end result of this review is shown in Table 3.1.

Table 3.1: Review of Cases Received by the Central Criminal Court

No. of Cases Received by CCC	661
No. of Cases with a Sexual Element	432
No. of Cases Located	416
No. of Cases Excluded	243
Total No. of Cases Included	173

Each of these 173 cases was then reviewed in detail and a questionnaire, set out in Appendix 5, was completed in respect of each case. Each questionnaire was then double-checked, with a random sample being checked in detail to ensure accuracy. The resulting data were then inputted into a specially designed database, and the inputting was double-checked to ensure accuracy. The data were then analysed.

Trial Transcripts

The Chief Justice granted the research team permission to access trial transcripts, subject to the same Confidentiality Agreement as with the Trial Court Records. From the Registrar of the Central Criminal Court a list of all rape cases that went to trial between 2002 and 2005 were obtained. We did not go back to 2000 as we were informed that transcription protocols changed that year to include closing arguments. The Trial Court Record for each of the cases on the list was then checked to ensure that it fell within the eligibility criteria; those that involved allegations against child victims and allegations of offences that did not meet the legal definition of rape were excluded. Cases that went to retrial were counted as separate cases. In total, 75 cases that went to trial between 2002 and 2005 that fell within our eligibility criteria were identified. The Courts Service was approached for copies of the transcripts in each of these cases but we were informed firstly that the stenographers in court do not work for the Courts Service but for commercial firms of Court Reporters, and that formal transcripts are only prepared in respect of cases that are appealed to the Court of Criminal Appeal. The Registrar of the Court of Criminal Appeal supplied all of the transcripts of the cases that had been appealed – thirteen in all. We then sought, and received, permission from the Chief Justice to approach the Court Reporters to produce transcripts especially for the study. They agreed to do so and supplied all of the outstanding transcripts on the list that they were able to locate, and in as complete a condition as possible. A brief questionnaire was then completed in respect of each transcript, a copy of which is presented in Appendix 6. The resulting data were then analysed.

Limitations

Regrettably, a large number of transcripts were incomplete, but virtually all had a complete transcript of both the complainant's evidence and the defendant's evidence. Only a minority contained counsel's closing speeches and the judge's charge to the jury. Even fewer contained the judge's comments at sentencing. This limited the quantity and in some cases the quality of the information that could be gleaned from the transcripts.

Chapter 4

REPORTING RAPE

THE SAMPLE

The survey data was collected from a sample of 100 adult rape victims, who had experienced rape in Ireland since 2002. This section describes the key socio-demographic characteristics of the respondents. Although the sample was not designed to be representative of the population as a whole, the sample will be compared to the Irish population (CSO, 2002) and the SAVI sample, where appropriate.

Age

The majority of participants were relatively young. Around 30 per cent were under 22 years and a further 20 per cent were aged 23 to 27 years. Nevertheless, there was a wide variation in ages. The youngest participants were 18 years old at the time of the survey, while the oldest was 62 years.

Table 4.1: Age at Time of Survey

	Age in Years
Minimum	18
Maximum	62
Median	27
Mode	22
Mean	30.3
Standard Deviation	10.8

Location

Participants were also asked to classify their current area of residence as either rural, town or city. Numbers were fairly evenly divided between the three, although slightly more lived in cities (39 per cent) than villages (29 per cent) or towns (32 per cent). The Census figures for 2002 (CSO, 2002) showed that 40 per cent of the population lived in rural areas and 60 per cent in urban areas (including large towns). In SAVI, around half lived in rural areas. A lower number of respondents in the current sample than in the general population were living in rural areas.

Respondents were also asked in which county they were currently residing (see Table 4.1). Eighteen of the 26 counties were represented in this survey. However, the majority came from Kerry (12 per cent), Limerick (12 per cent), Dublin (11 per cent) and Galway (11 per cent). In the 'other' category, two gave current addresses outside Ireland. Seven per cent did not answer this question.

Table 4.2: Current County of Residence

	%
Cork	6
Donegal	6
Dublin	11
Galway	11
Kerry	12
Limerick	12
Mayo	6
Waterford	6
Other	23
Not given	7

Respondents were also asked about their nationality. The vast majority (89 per cent) were Irish. A further five per cent were born in the UK. The remainder were born in other European countries (two per cent) and outside Europe (three per cent). One respondent did not provide this information. These proportions are similar to census figures.

Employment Status

Table 4.3 shows the employment status of the respondents. The unemployment rate was 19 per cent (women who were on disability allowances were also classed as unemployed). Census figures for 2002 show that 3.8 per cent of Irish women were unemployed and a further 4 per cent were on disability. The percentage unemployed in this sample is therefore greater than in the general population.

Table 4.3: Employment Status

	%
Paid Employment	59
Student	14
Homemaker	8
Unemployed	19

Census figures (2002) show that higher proportions of the current sample (59 per cent) were in full employment compared to the Irish population as a whole (43.3 per cent). Similar rates described themselves as students (14 per cent compared to 11 per cent in the total population), while fewer were homemakers (8 per cent compared to 27 per cent in general population). In McGee et al. (2002), 7 per cent were students, 48 per cent were in paid employment and less than one per cent worked in the home.

Living Arrangements

The living arrangements of the respondents are shown in Table 4.4. Just over half (51 per cent) described themselves as single.

Seventeen per cent were either married (4 per cent) or living with a partner (13 per cent). A fifth were living with their parents. Finally, nine per cent were separated or divorced and two were widowed. One person did not answer this question.

Table 4.4: Living Arrangements

	%
Single	51
Married/Cohabiting	17
Living with Parents	21
Other	11

Census figures (CSO, 2002) show that 42 per cent of the population was single and 47 per cent were married. Percentages of single women in the present study were higher (51 per cent) and married much lower (four per cent). The breakdown was very different from the SAVI sample, where 19 per cent of female respondents were single and 69 per cent were classified as married/co-habiting/divorced or separated (McGee et al., 2002).

Case Status

Respondents were asked about the status of their case at the time of the interview. Around two-thirds of the sample (n = 66) reported the rape to the Gardaí and a third (34 per cent) did not. Among those who reported, eight women did not make a statement. Of the remainder who made a statement (n = 58), the offender had been charged in nine cases and cases had been dropped in 30 cases. Fourteen files were with the DPP at the time of the interview and were awaiting a final decision. The remaining four participants did not know the status of their cases. Among the nine cases in which the offender had been charged, trials had been completed in four cases.

CHARACTERISTICS OF RAPE

This section gives an account of the experience of rape, as described by the survey respondents. It provides details about the victim, the offender, the nature of the assault and the context in which it occurred. This information is important for two reasons. First, few Irish studies to date have explored the experience of rape. Second, existing evidence suggests that the type of assault often impacts on victims' decisions to report and criminal justice agents' decisions to pursue a case (see Estrich, 1987). It is therefore important to account for these factors in a study of victim decision-making. Findings are compared, where appropriate, with patterns found in Irish (e.g. McGee et al, 2002; RCNI, 2004) and international (e.g. Myhill and Allen, 2002; Tjaden and Thoenes, 1998) studies.

Age at Time of Assault

Table 4.5 shows the age of respondents at the time of the assault.[*] The range of ages at the time of the rape was broad, with ages ranging between 18 and 62 years (respondents had to be over 18 to participate). The results indicate that the majority were relatively young at the time of the assault, with over a third (38 per cent) aged 22 or under. Nevertheless, a significant minority (10 per cent) were aged 48 or over. Overall, the average age at which the assault occurred was 28.9 (SD = 10.7). The median age was 26 years and the mode was 19 years.

The age profile of respondents is comparable to that reported in other studies. Age has been identified as an important risk factor for sexual violence, with women in their late teens and early twenties most vulnerable to rape and sexual assault (Myhill and Allen, 2002; Mouzos and Makkai, 2004; Tjaden and Thoennes, 1998). Similar patterns have been found in Ireland. For example, the majority of clients treated for sexual assaults at the Rotunda

---

[*] Two women reported experiencing rape over a period of several years so were excluded from the age analysis. Both reported that the abuse occurred during their twenties and thirties.

Sexual Assault Treatment Unit in 2003 were aged 16 to 29 (Rotunda, 2003).

Table 4.5: Age at Time of Assault

	Age
Minimum	18
Maximum	62
Median	26
Mode	19
Mean	28.9
Standard Deviation	10.7

Location of Assault

Respondents were asked where the rape had occurred. (Four people mentioned more than one location so the total exceeds 100.) As can be seen in Table 4.6, the majority of rapes occurred indoors. Around a third (n = 32) of reported assaults occurred in the victim's home. Other common locations were homes belonging to the offender (n = 24), non-relatives (n = 13) and relatives (n = 4). A significant minority reported that they had been raped outdoors, either in a public area (n = 9) or on the street (n = 12).

This confirms patterns found in Ireland and other jurisdictions, which show that women are most likely to be raped in their own homes (see for example, Myhill and Allen, 2002; McGee et al, 2002). In Ireland, McGee et al. (2002) found that female victims of adult sexual violence were most likely to have been assaulted in their own home (20 per cent), outdoors (24 per cent) or in the offender's home (14 per cent).

Table 4.6: Location of Assault

	Number
In Your Own Home	32
At the Offender's Home	24
On the Street	12
Friend's or Other Non-relative's House	13
In a Park/Other Open Public Space	9
B&B/Hostel/Hotel	5
Relative's House	4
At Work	1
At School/University	1
In a Pub/Nightclub	1
Other	4

Victim-Offender Relationship

Almost all of the incidents involved just one offender. Eight respondents reported incidents involving more than one offender and two did not answer this question.

Looking at the victim's relationship to the offender, the results show that the majority of women were raped by someone they knew. The largest categories involved friends (14 per cent) and acquaintances (25 per cent). Only a minority of respondents were raped within intimate relationships. Five per cent of rapes were perpetrated by spouses or partners, and three per cent by boyfriends. Around one in ten involved former relationships. Ex-boyfriends perpetrated seven per cent of rapes and ex-spouses and partners perpetrated three per cent. Just over a third (n = 34) involved assaults by strangers.

Table 4.7: Relationship to Offender

	%
Stranger	34
Acquaintance	25
Friend	14
Ex-boyfriend	7
Spouse/Partner	5
Workmate/Colleague	3
Date	3
Boyfriend	3
Ex-spouse/ex-partner	3
Family member	2
No response	1
Total	100

The rate of stranger rapes found in this sample is higher than has been reported in victimisation surveys. In Britain, for example, stranger rapes accounted for only eight per cent of all rapes (Myhill and Allen, 2002). Slightly higher rates of stranger rapes have been found elsewhere, although they are generally still quite low. Seventeen per cent of rapes and assaults are perpetrated by strangers in Australia (Australian Bureau of Statistics, 1999), 23 per cent in Canada (Johnson and Sacco, 1996) and 14 per cent in the USA (Tjaden and Thoennes, 1998).

The Rape Crisis Network Ireland national statistics indicate that only 6.8 per cent of their clients were assaulted by strangers while the majority were assaulted by friends, acquaintances or partners (2007). This suggests that victims of intimate partner violence are under-represented in this study. Nevertheless, one of the largest category of unwanted sexual experiences documented in the SAVI report concerned assaults by strangers (21 per cent of incidents) (McGee et al., 2002). It is not clear whether these differences reflect actual patterns of sexual violence or differential disclosure to researchers and support services. There is some evidence to suggest that victims of non-stranger rape are less likely to label their experiences as rape and do not always disclose such incidents to researchers (see Gartner and MacMillan, 1995).

Verbal Threat/Use of Force

A significant number of the rapes reported in this survey involved force or threat of force beyond that required to commit the rape. Just under half, or 47 per cent, of respondents stated that they were verbally threatened or intimidated by the offender at the time of the incident.

Table 4.8: Use of Force or Threats

	Physical Force (%)	Threat (%)
Yes	71	47
No	24	48
Missing	5	5

A significant proportion (71 per cent) also reported that the offender used physical force against them. Some respondents (14 per cent) said that the offender used a weapon in the attack. The most common was a knife or other stabbing implement (reported by eight women). These results reflect the findings of victimisation surveys, which show that the majority of rapes are accompanied by physical force and threats (e.g. Myhill and Allen, 2002).

Victim Resistance

Respondents were asked whether they had attempted to resist the attack, either physically (by force or trying to escape), verbally (by screaming or persuading the attacker) or by other means. The majority (66 per cent) reported offering some form of resistance. Among those who did not resist, three explained that they had been unable to do anything because they were unconscious, drugged or tied up at the time of the assault. Three others froze or felt they could do nothing. It is important to note that resistance can result in additional physical injury; as one respondent explained, 'I told him to fuck off, he got very violent so I went quiet'. It is also important to note that, although almost two-thirds of respondents attempted to resist their attackers using physical and verbal means, these strategies did not prevent the rape.

Table 4.9: Victim Resistance

Resistance	%
Yes	66
No	33
Don't know/unsure	2

In general, studies show that people are more certain that a rape has occurred when the victim engages in obvious physical resistance (Krulewitz and Nash, 1979). Further, victims who do not resist rape are less likely to label their experience as rape (Peterson and Muehlenhard, 2004). Under Irish law, however, failure to resist does not, of itself, indicate consent and the same is true in most of the common law world.

Physical Injury

Respondents were asked whether they had been physically injured as a result of the assault. Around a third (37 per cent) reported that they suffered no physical injury during the assault. This means that a little less than two-thirds suffered some physical injuries. Rates of physical injury in this sample were higher than have been reported in national surveys, in which around a third of victims report injuries (e.g. Myhill and Allen, 2002; Tjaden and Thoennes, 1998).

Respondents' injuries were classified as either minor (e.g. bruises, cuts, scratches) or severe (e.g. knocked unconscious, broken bones, internal injuries). In most cases, the physical injury was relatively minor (44 per cent suffered injuries such as cuts and bruises), while 15 per cent reported experiencing more severe injuries. Respondents who reported any physical injury, minor or severe, were asked whether they had required medical care or hospitalisation. In total, 24 respondents (a quarter of the sample) received medical treatment for their injuries and five of these reported that their injuries were severe enough to require hospitalisation. Although the physical injuries documented here are significant, it does not account for the significant emotional, psychological and social trauma of rape that is frequently recounted by victims (see Lees, 1996).

Table 4.10: Physical Injuries

Severity of Injury	%
None	37
Minor (e.g. bruises, cuts, scratches)	44
Severe (e.g. knocked unconscious, broken bones, internal injuries)	15
Other	3
Missing	1

Alcohol Use

Respondents were asked whether they or the offender had been drinking at the time of the incident and the results indicate that alcohol use was common. In half of the cases, the respondent reported that both she and the offender had been drinking. Levels of alcohol use were also examined and these will be explored next.

Table 4.11: Alcohol Use by Victim

	%
None	30
Two Drinks or Less	16
Three to Five Drinks	25
Six Drinks or More	29

Over two-thirds (70 per cent) of women reported that they had been drinking. In order to provide a more detailed picture of alcohol use, respondents were asked how much alcohol they had consumed. The breakdown shows that 16 per cent had imbibed two drinks or less, 25 per cent had consumed three to five drinks, and 29 per cent six or more. The majority had therefore consumed three drinks or more at the time of the assault.

These findings are in line with patterns found in other Irish studies. The Dublin Sexual Assault Treatment Unit records that 58 per cent of clients seen in 2003 had consumed more than four units of alcohol (Rotunda, 2003). Other Irish estimates suggest that alcohol is involved in around half of all cases of adult sexual violence (McGee et al., 2002).

Respondents were also asked whether the offender had been drinking. Over a quarter did not know. Of the remainder, respondents stated that the offender had not been drinking in 16.7 per cent of cases. Over half of the cases (58 per cent) therefore involved some degree of alcohol use by the offender. Details about the offenders' level of intoxication were also probed. Respondents said that the offender had been drinking a little in 10 per cent of cases, and had consumed a moderate amount in 24 per cent of cases. The respondent said the offender had been drinking a lot at the time of the assault in 24 per cent of incidents.

Table 4.12: Alcohol Use by Offender

	%
None	16
A Little	10
Moderate	24
A Lot	24
Unknown	26

CHARTING THE PATHWAY TO JUSTICE

One of the primary aims of this survey was to shed light on the factors that influence victims' decisions to report rape to the Gardaí. It is widely accepted that reporting rates for rape and sexual assault are extremely low. In Ireland, for example, *The SAVI Report* estimated that only around one in ten rapes are reported to the Gardaí (McGee et al., 2002). Non-reporting therefore constitutes the largest source of attrition in cases of rape, yet the processes and factors involved are poorly understood.

This section examines the victim's role in attrition, using the information provided by survey respondents about the factors they considered when making their decision. First, the explanations given by the 100 survey respondents for their decisions to report or not to report are examined. Among victims who make a report, a significant number later withdraw their complaint (Kerstetter, 1990), and the next section examines the reasons given by victims in this sample for withdrawing their complaint. Finally, existing research indicates that, for many victims of rape and sexual assault, the main source of assistance comes, not from official agencies but from informal social networks (e.g. Greenberg and Rubrack, 1992; Kaukinen, 2002). The final section therefore focuses on the alternative sources of help utilised by the respondents.

Before addressing the reasons for reporting, non-reporting and case withdrawal, the victim's role in attrition is described. Table 4.13 shows the victim's role in attrition, expressed as a percentage. As can be seen, around a third did not report; a further eight per cent reported but did not make a statement, and nine per cent made a statement but later withdrew their complaint. Around half (n = 49) pursued their complaint.

Table 4.13: Victim's Role in Attrition

Status	%
Did Not Report	34
Reported, No Statement	8
Made Statement, Withdrew	9
Case Pursued	49
Total	100

Reasons for Not Reporting

Thirty-four respondents stated that they had not informed the Gardaí about the rape. They were asked to give reasons for their answer. This question was open-ended to allow respondents to express the full range of factors that influenced their decisions. Many gave more than one reason, giving a total of 60 responses.

Their reasons can be summarised under five broad headings: (a) psychological factors (b) social considerations (c) criminal justice factors (d) incident characteristics, and (e) other reasons. In most cases, more than one factor was involved and it is likely that multiple factors are considered by victims in making their decisions. This section will explore these factors in detail.

Table 4.14: Reasons for Not Reporting

Reason	Number
Criminal Justice (N = 18)	
No Evidence	8
Fear of Legal Process	5
Lack of Faith in Justice System	5
Social (N = 12)	
Didn't Want Others to Know	8
Fear of Disbelief	3
Got Negative Response	1

Incident Characteristics (N = 15)	
Alcohol/Drug Use by Victim	6
Drug-Assisted Rape	4
Victim–Offender Relationship	5
Psychological Factors (N = 12)	
Embarrassment/Shock/Fear	10
Blamed Self	2
Other (N = 3)	
Fear of Perpetrator	3

Criminal Justice Factors

Concerns about the legal system are regularly cited by victims as reasons for non-disclosure to police (see Kelly et al., 2005; Lievore, 2003). Victims variously cite fear that they will not be believed (Lees, 1997), the belief that the police cannot help (Van Kesteren, Mayhew and Nieuwbeerta, 2000) or perceive the incident as a private matter (Mouzos and Makkai, 2004). In total, 18 women in this study cited factors relating to the criminal justice system as reasons for non-reporting. Several specific aspects were mentioned: concerns about lack of evidence, fear of the legal process and lack of faith in the justice system.

No Evidence. Eight women stated that they did not report because they felt there was not enough physical evidence that the crime had occurred. In three cases, this was because the women did not report straight away. By the time they considered reporting, they felt it was too late as the physical evidence of the crime was gone. In one case, the respondent's drink was spiked on a night out and by the time she realised what had happened the evidence was gone. The remaining two respondents, both in their twenties, described how the shock and trauma they experienced immediately after the rape meant they initially tried to deal with it themselves by suppressing or minimising what had happened. The following respondent, raped by a stranger, wrote:

> *Didn't report because at the time of the incident I was in shock. I tried to put it down to just a bad experience and thought it wasn't as bad as it seemed. Blamed myself for putting myself in the situation with the guy. Also didn't think anyone would believe me. And after a day or two had passed, all physical evidence was gone. All that was left were fading bruises (107).*

Others were aware that determinations in rape cases centre on one person's word against another. In Irish law, the onus of proof is on the prosecution. Two had had prior sexual contact with the offender and feared the Gardaí would not believe that they had not consented on this occasion. Two others had been drinking at the time of the assault and their answers suggested a fear that this would impact on their credibility. The following quote from a 26-year-old woman, raped in her own home by a friend, illustrates this:

> *I was drunk and a little unsure as to what exactly had happened. A friend came into my bedroom while I was sleeping after having been drinking. I spoke to other friends about it the following day and confronted the guy a couple of days later. I didn't expect any joy from talking to the Gardaí as I knew it would be his word against mine (32).*

Fear of Legal Process. Five women were concerned about certain aspects of the legal process. Many were concerned about the impact the process would have on themselves, their family and their friends. Research suggests that fear of 'secondary victimisation' by the criminal justice system may not be unfounded (e.g., Campbell et al., 2001).

> *I felt it would make things worse because I thought it would prolong the way I was feeling. Because I was drugged and didn't remember a lot and didn't know who did this to me (60).*

One woman was misinformed about the nature of the Garda interview and this discouraged her from reporting. She had been drugged and raped by a stranger in her home and explained her fears:

> *I was afraid of the impact it would have on those close to me and me as a victim. I heard that the Gardaí make you sit in a room with the offender and make your statement. I couldn't do that (81).*

Lack of Faith in Justice System. Feldmann-Summers and Ashworth (1984) argued that people are less likely to report a crime if they believe it will not result in a positive outcome. In this study, five respondents had little faith that the criminal justice system could help them. Two believed that offenders would not be punished. Both were concerned about the traumatic nature of the court process. They felt it would not be worth enduring as the process was unlikely to result in justice for them. As one respondent, a 21-year-old woman who was raped by a stranger at a party, put it:

> *I didn't think there was any point, they would have gotten off without being convicted and I would have had to go through the whole thing again over and over, describing every time what happened to me. I wanted to forget about it as soon as it happened (114).*

The remaining two did not believe that the Gardaí could do anything. The following extract, from a 19-year-old, who was drugged and raped by a stranger, wrote:

> *I was at a festival. There were no cameras. My drink was spiked. Trying to find him would be like trying to find a needle in a haystack (99).*

There is some evidence to suggest that contact with the criminal justice system can be damaging to victims. In some cases, it can intensify existing psychological distress (see Campbell et al., 2001). Many victims also rate their experience at court negatively

(Holmstrom and Burgess, 1978). Further, few who report rape achieve a conviction (see Regan and Kelly, 2003) suggesting that this group's lack of faith may be justified.

Social Factors

Did Not Want Others to Know. Four respondents mentioned the impact disclosure would have on their family and friends as a reason for not reporting. In two cases, respondents felt that the criminal justice process would be distressing for them to endure. Another woman who was assaulted by a work colleague was concerned that members of her family might retaliate against the offender and be arrested themselves:

> *[I was] protecting myself and my family – if I said anything they would have got upset, might have talked to offender and ended up in jail (39).*

Where the offender is part of the victim's inner circle, the effects of reporting on family and friends becomes more germane. The following example illustrates how a personal relationship with the offender can impact on disclosure. The woman was raped by an ex-boyfriend with whom she had a child. She explained:

> *We have a son so I didn't want to cause problems that would affect his relationship with his father or for me, problems with friends/relatives not believing me (98).*

Others were concerned about the wider consequences of reporting. They did not want people in their areas to know what had happened to them. They felt that the benefits of reporting would not outweigh the costs of people finding out. This may be a particular concern for people living in small or close-knit communities. This is illustrated by the quote below from a 21-year-old student raped at a house party:

> *[It] happened in local area. I didn't want anyone to know what happened (83).*

Fear of Disbelief. To some extent, this category overlaps with fear of disbelief by Gardaí but is given as a separate category because it related to a more general fear of disbelief. Two of the respondents in this category were raped by someone they knew. The following explanation was provided by a woman who was raped by a friend in her own home.

> *I did not report the rape because I was too ashamed at what happened to me at my age. I didn't think anyone would believe me and I did not want my children to find out what had happened to me (89).*

Negative Response. Greenberg and Ruback (1992) stressed the significance of social influence in decisions to report crime. They argued that negative responses from trusted others can impede disclosure. In this study, two respondents stated that a negative response was the reason for non-disclosure. In one case, a 19-year-old woman who was raped by an acquaintance did not receive support when she told her friends what happened. In another case, the respondent felt ignored by the Gardaí, thereby illustrating Jordan's observation that initial contact with the police is important in encouraging victims to come forward (2001). In her answer, this woman explained how she was treated and the impact it had on her.

> *When I finally decided to report this crime, I went to the local Garda Station and stood at the window inside, completely ignored by male and female guards for 20 [minutes]. In the end, I was so distraught I left. It astounded me that I was left there though at least five guards saw me as they walked past drinking coffee (95).*

Incident Characteristics

Research suggests that the nature of the rape itself impacts on the decision to report. Studies have found that rapes conforming to the 'real rape' template are more likely to be reported. In other words, rapes by strangers, where the victim has been injured or where the offender used force beyond that required to commit the rape, threats or a weapon are more likely to be reported (see Williams, 1984; Tomlinson, 1999; DuMont et al., 2003). Thirteen women explained that features of the assault influenced their decision to not report. The features they identified were their own alcohol or drug use, the fact that they were drugged during the assault and their relationship to the offender.

Alcohol/Drug Use. Studies have shown that alcohol use decreases the likelihood of reporting (Clay-Warner and Harbin-Burt, 2005), and increases the likelihood of blame being attributed to the victim (e.g., Scronce and Corcoran, 1995). Six respondents referred to their own alcohol or drug use in their explanations for non-reporting. Generally, the respondents felt that their alcohol or drug use might be judged negatively by the Gardaí and would impact on whether they would be believed. Five of these had consumed six drinks or more. There concerns are illustrated by the following comments:

> *I was drunk that time when it happened and wasn't sure how they [Gardaí] would respond (64).*

> *No point. His word against mine and I had been drinking (80).*

In another case, the victim was unsure about the details of the rape due to alcohol consumption. Finally, one respondent who had been raped by a stranger blamed herself for the assault. She had voluntarily taken recreational drugs earlier that evening. She explained:

> *I felt the incident was my fault. That I had intentionally gone out that night to take ecstasy though later on I was given drugs that I took but did not know what I was taking. So I felt I could not do anything, like I had let the situation happen (97).*

Drug-assisted Rape. The phenomenon of drug-facilitated sexual assaults has recently begun to gain attention in the media. Date-rape drugs can impair memory and decision-making ability and reduce victims' ability to recognise a dangerous situation or resist attack (Negrusz et al., 2005). Four women stated that they had been drugged. All stated that they had been raped by strangers. One had no recollection of the attack and only discovered that she had been raped after a positive pregnancy test. Three cited difficulties recalling details of the attack as reasons for not reporting. One respondent explained how such attacks impact on the decision making process:

> *Because not much happens thereafter if you've been spiked. You slowly remember what has happened. By the time it all comes together, it's too late (29).*

> *Because I was drugged and didn't remember a lot and didn't know who did this to me (60).*

Victim/Offender Relationship. Research suggests that rapes involving offenders that are known to the victim are less likely to be reported, although there has been a rise in reporting rates for non-stranger rapes in Britain (Harris and Grace, 1999). A prior relationship also brings with it additional considerations, such as breach of trust and the impact of disclosure on family and friends. In this survey, four respondents cited their relationship with the offender as a factor in their decision not to report. Their relationship to the offender took a variety of levels of intimacy. In three cases, the women had prior consensual sexual contact with the offender and were concerned that this would cast doubt on the veracity of their complaint. In one case, the offender was an ex-partner.

> *We had continued a sexual relationship for a couple of years after the relationship. I felt that because people would view our relationship as being on a strictly sexual basis then the Gardaí wouldn't believe that I hadn't consented or that it wasn't me leading him on.*

Three had met the offender socially or on a date. As one explained:

> *I felt very ashamed as I was drinking and left the disco with him (65).*

A final respondent, a woman in her mid-twenties had been raped by a friend, and the emotional impact made her unable to report:

> *A friend of mine inflicted this on me, so a mixture of shock, unacceptance of what occurred, etc. would be my reason (102).*

Psychological Factors

Twelve respondents mentioned psychological factors as reasons for not reporting. They explained how they felt embarrassed, ashamed or shocked about the assault. These feelings left them unable to confront or deal with what had happened to them. Such emotions are common responses to sexual violence (see Easteal, 1994). One respondent, who was raped at a party, explained why she did not report and this is illustrative of these issues:

> *I wanted to forget about it as soon as it happened. I'm also so ashamed of what they did to me; they made me feel like a piece of dirt. In a way, reporting it would seem like admitting they had got the better of me (114).*

Reasons for Reporting

Two thirds (n = 66) of respondents reported the rape to the Gardaí. Of these, 48 women reported the offence themselves, someone else made the disclosure in 17 cases and one respondent could not remember who had contacted the Gardaí. They were asked to explain why they had decided to report. Again, the question was open-ended and many gave more than one reason. Seven women did not provide any reasons.

The reasons given are presented in Table 4.15, and have been categorised under four main headings: (a) wanting justice (b) social influence (c) security concerns and (d) other reasons. This section provides an in-depth account of these reasons.

Table 4.15: Reasons for Reporting

Reason	Number
Wanted Justice (N = 23)	
Righting a Wrong	12
Seeing Justice Done	8
Serious Crime	3
Social Influence (N = 22)	
Make Report	14
Offer Advice/Persuasion	6
Help Label Experience as Rape	2
Security (N = 15)	
Fear/Self-protection	9
Protection of Others	6
Miscellaneous (N = 15)	
Incident Characteristics	5
Psychological Distress	4
Faith in Criminal Justice System	4
Other (N = 2)	

Wanted Justice

Existing studies suggest that victims are more concerned with getting public validation for the crime and the harm it caused than engaging in retribution (Lewis Herman, 2005). In total, 23 respondents cited a desire for justice as their reason for reporting. There were several themes expressed within this category: belief that what had happened was a wrong that needed righting, needing to see justice done and a recognition that a serious crime had been committed.

To Right a Wrong. Victims are more likely to report if they believe they have been wronged (see Greenberg and Ruback, 1992). Twelve respondents expressed a desire to obtain justice for what had happened to them. Responses in this category were generally expressed using phrases like 'it shouldn't have happened to me' or 'it was an offence towards me'. The following respondent was raped by a stranger. She told her partner immediately and they reported the offence to the Gardaí together. She explained her reason simply:

> *Because I wanted justice for what was done to me (106).*

Others expressed a strong belief that what had happened was 'wrong.' The following respondent, raped by an ex-boyfriend, illustrated this.

> *Because I was violated. This man was wrong, what he did was wrong. I said no but he didn't listen. Nobody has the right to take what isn't theirs (17).*

Seeing Justice Done. In Hattem's study (2000), victims made a report in order to punish the offender. They were aware that what had happened was wrong, considered it an offence and felt the offender should not get away with it. Similar sentiments were expressed in this study. Eight respondents expressed a desire that the offender should not get away with what he had done:

> *At the time I thought it was the right thing to do. No one should get away with such a thing and I wanted something done about it (15).*

> *Wasn't going to but friend saw me upset and told guards. When I thought about it, it was the right thing to do. He shouldn't be getting away with it (87).*

Within this category, three respondents expressed a wish that the offender be punished for what he had done. One woman described how she felt lucky to escape with only minor injuries after being raped by a stranger. She reported immediately.

[I] wanted to report straight away. I was lucky to be alive. Wanted to stop him doing it to someone else. Wanted him punished (26).

Serious Crime. The literature shows that crimes that are perceived as serious are more likely to be reported (Greenberg and Ruback, 1992). The answers given by respondents in this category suggested that they expected a positive outcome from reporting – for example, getting justice or having the offender punished. The following response was given by a woman who was raped outside her own home:

Serious crime – the only thing to do. Never crossed my mind not to. Believed the law would give me the answers I need at the time (4).

Social Influence

Social influence was the second most important reason given for making a report. Other people played several roles: some provided concrete help by making the report when the victim was too distressed, some offered advice and confirmed that the incident was a crime. Feldmann Summers and Norris (1984) found that victims who reported had experienced more social pressure to report from family and friends.

Make Report. The most frequently mentioned role of other people was to make the report to the police. Chambers and Millar (1983) found that the majority of victims talked to someone else before deciding to report (mostly friends and relatives), and that many of these people made the decision to report. In this study, 14 respondents explained that the decision to report was made by others. In two cases, the decision to report was made by a nurse and a friend. In three other cases, the victims were found by a passerby who alerted the Gardaí. The following explanation was provided by a woman who was drugged and raped by acquaintances.

> *I was found by a cab driver in a very distressed state, partially dressed and brought by the cab driver to the police station (20).*

Respondents explained how the initial impact of the rape left them in distress or shock. Some respondents felt too upset or distressed to make the report themselves and another person stepped in to help. Others said they didn't have time to think about reporting. This woman was raped by a stranger in her own home; her comments highlight the chaos and upheaval that often accompany such attacks:

> *It was reported straight away. He broke into my house in the middle of the night. My boyfriend was there. It was hectic. I didn't make a conscious decision to report. It just happened (48).*

In other cases, the experience of disclosure was less positive. Three respondents felt pressured into reporting by the person to whom they initially disclosed the incident. The following respondent, a 22-year-old who was raped by a stranger, told her mother who then called the police. As a result of this, the respondent initially did not reveal the full details of her attack to the Gardaí:

> *I didn't want to. Rang my mother and she told the guards. I would have preferred if they weren't involved. The guards made me feel worse. Were abrupt. I was upset. Didn't want to talk to two men. I didn't tell them about the rape - the full story. I knew they weren't going to get him anyway. I was too upset so I told them I was attacked (50).*

Persuasion. Six respondents indicated that they were advised or persuaded to make a report by others. In the following example, the victim first disclosed the assault to a friend who persuaded her to report. She explained that she was in shock, was trying to deal with it by herself and initially was unsure whether to report:

> *I wasn't sure what to do at first, but when I told my friend about it she was very angry and upset. She said that the possibility of him doing it again if he thought he got away with it was very*

> *high and so I did it for this reason. In this I mean doing it to other women (93).*

Below, the respondent described how she blamed herself for the assault. She had been knocked unconscious during the assault and did not remember all the details. When she confided in a friend and her doctor, both confirmed that reporting was an appropriate response. She stressed the importance of having someone confirm that what had happened was a crime. She explained:

> *At first I went home and slept. Next morning I woke up and thought it was my fault for going out on my own. But couldn't remember anything but knew it had happened. I called on my best friend and sat through the whole thing word for word and she told me to go to the doctors and he made same sense as my friend did. Decided to report the incident (112).*

Defining Experience as Rape. Lievore (2003) explains that, in order to report, a victim must first recognise herself as a victim and also believe that others will view her in that way. Research suggests that a significant number of rape victims do not classify their experiences as rape (see, e.g., Myhill and Allen, 2002). Immediately after a rape, victims are in shock and are not always certain that what happened to them was rape or even a crime. Other people can act as an external gauge and help the victim to label her experience appropriately. The following respondent, who was 18 at the time of the assault, did not report immediately because she was in shock. After speaking to her family, she confirmed for herself that what had happened to her was wrong:

> *I knew I had to, still raw at the time. My sister influenced me to report. I knew it was wrong, didn't really know what happened. My brothers said it was rape (18).*

Security

Fifteen respondents expressed the desire to protect either themselves or others from future attacks by the offender. There is evidence to suggest that victims of sexual violence are at risk of future violence. Research has shown that women who have experienced previous incidents of sexual abuse have a higher risk of being re-victimised as adults (Coid et al., 2001). Walby and Allen (2004) found that half of reported incidents of sexual violence by husbands or partners were repeat victimisations. In this study, nine respondents expressed concerns about their safety. In three cases, the respondent stated that they feared retaliation from the offender. All knew their attacker and two had already experienced harassment or threats. The following explanation was given by a 22-year-old who was raped by an ex-boyfriend and suffered severe physical injury as a result of the attack.

> *I wasn't living my life – not going to college. Under constant threat and harassment from offender. I couldn't live with what he'd done. What he did was wrong. He tried to do it again a second time, just walked into my house (16).*

Four cases involved offenders with whom the victims were involved in a relationship. The first concerned a one-off incident with a boyfriend. In the remaining three cases, the respondents stated that the most recent incident was part of a pattern of ongoing abuse. The following respondent explained how her husband had begun to abuse her daughter and this gave her the incentive she needed to make a complaint:

> *Because my husband had raped me as a form of control – submission and it worked and he thought he had me ground down so he started on our daughter. Couldn't cope with so I went to the Gardaí, social services, my doctor and left the family home (84).*

In the final two cases, the respondents reported a more general sense of fear. Rape often engenders a new sense of vulnerability in victims (see Greenberg and Ruback, 1992).

Six women were concerned about protecting others from future attacks by the offender. Although reconviction rates among sex offenders is low, Falshaw et al. (2003) found a higher rate of re-offending (around 20 per cent) when re-offending measures included reconvictions for sexual offences, undetected sexual offending and other offence-related behaviour. This suggests the respondents' concerns may be justified. Two respondents in this study stated that they wanted the offender brought to justice to prevent further offending. In a third case, the respondent agreed to report after her friend pointed out that the offender might re-offend. Two women were violently assaulted and feared for their lives. They went to the Gardaí in order to protect others from undergoing such brutal attacks. The following explanation is illustrative of this attitude:

> *I was in shock when I reported. How premeditated and heinous it was. He was a professional and predatory rapist. I wanted to stop him from doing it to anyone else (45).*

Miscellaneous

Other explanations for reporting included incident characteristics, psychological factors and faith in the legal system. Four respondents mentioned factors concerning the assault as reasons for reporting. All four cases involved significant levels of violence and this prompted their reports. The presence of additional violence appeared to heighten the sense of injustice, the desire to protect others from such serious attacks and helped the respondents to realise that something serious had happened. This respondent, who was raped by her partner, described her injuries, which required medical care:

> *Because as well as being raped, he broke my arm in two places, fractured my jaw and tooth, also ribs. Want him jailed (111).*

As for psychological distress, respondents explained that they could not live with what the offender had done and went to the Gardaí to alleviate some of the distress. This comment, from a 19-year-old assaulted by a friend, highlights the distress and fear experienced in the aftermath of sexual violence.

I felt frightened and didn't know what else to do (76).

Finally, others felt that the criminal justice system would provide support, security and answers. This comment illustrates the fear felt by victims of rape and the need they feel to have the Gardaí do something about it.

I would be afraid to go outside if I didn't. I was hoping the guards would do something about it (41).

Delayed Reporting

This section describes the timing of the report to the police and outlines the reasons respondents gave for not reporting straightaway. Table 4.16 shows that the majority of individuals that did report contacted the police within 24 hours. Twenty-two (33.3 per cent) reported the offence within one hour, while a further 22 notified the Gardaí within 24 hours of the assault occurring. Eighteen per cent (n = 12) waited a month or more before reporting. The longest delay was 18 months after the assault. One respondent did not provide this information.

Table: 4.16: Timing of the Complaint

	Number
Within One Hour	22
Within 24 Hours	22
Within One Week	9
Within One Month	6
Within One Year	5
Over a Year	1

Respondents who did not report immediately were asked to give reasons for the delay. In total, 36 women answered this question. Multiple responses were allowed and are listed below in Table 4.17. The most common reasons related to the psychological trauma of rape. Many (n = 17) were in shock or felt numb following the assault. Others (n = 7) tried to cope with what had happened privately before deciding to go to the Gardaí. Social factors were also important. Nine women said they were unsure whether or not to report until someone else suggested it, and eight were concerned about how others would respond to disclosure. Five were concerned about the Garda response.

Table 4.17: Reasons for Delay

	Numbers
In Shock/Numb	17
Unsure Whether to Report Until Someone Else Suggested It	9
Scared about Other People's Reactions	8
Thought I Could Handle It Myself	7
Scared of Garda Response	5
Scared of Offender	5
Unconscious/No Memory	5
Was Not Sure If It Was a Crime at First	4
Other	3

Victim Withdrawal

Studies have shown that victims' unwillingness to proceed with a complaint is a major factor in attrition (e.g., Kerstetter, 1990; Harris and Grace, 1999). Studies exploring the nature of the victim's decision to make a complaint indicate that fear of the legal process is a common reason for subsequent non-cooperation (Holmstrom and Burgess, 1978; Kelly et al., 2005). Others suggest that victims might be influenced by the behaviour of police and prosecutors (Frohmann, 1991; Chambers and Millar, 1983) or concerns about the nature and quality of the evidence supporting their complaint (Kerstetter and van Winkle, 1990). This survey aimed to examine the factors that influenced victims' decisions to withdraw their complaint. They were divided into two groups: those who made an initial report but did not make a statement; and those who made a statement but later withdrew their complaint.

Reported but No Statement

Eight respondents made an initial report to the Gardaí but did not make a statement. The main reasons given for withdrawing at this stage concerned the Garda response to their report. Respondents described how the Gardaí had emphasised the negative aspects of pursuing a case and explained that this deterred them from proceeding. In Kelly et al.'s study (2005), victims who withdrew at this stage also cited unsupportive behaviour by police as a major factor in dropping their complaint. While officers might feel they are simply preparing the victim for what is to come, it may actually put them off pursuing a case (see Harris and Grace, 1999).

The primary disincentives raised by Gardaí included people finding out about the assault and potential delays in the case coming to trial. In one case, for example, the respondent, who was 23 years old at the time of the rape, wrote:

> *Gardaí did say they would organise for me to make a statement but also explained everyone in the town would then eventually hear about it (88).*

Others were unsure about whether their cases could stand up in court. This 31-year-old described her concerns about the quality of the evidence in her case:

> *I had no evidence. I washed myself and my clothes immediately. My recollections of event were vague as I was given date rape drug. He is a top professional with many connections, prone to violence towards men. I was frightened he would find me and hurt me (28).*

The final respondent was too afraid to make a formal statement about the rape, which was perpetrated by an ex-partner and formed part of a pattern of abuse spanning almost a decade. The offender was willing to plead guilty to charges of physical violence if she dropped the rape case and she agreed to this:

Statement made of history of physical abuse but afraid to make it on sexual abuse/rape (44).

Withdrawal of Statement

Research has shown that many victims have second thoughts about pursuing a complaint. Doubts relate to confidentiality, fear of reprisals and reaction from police (Chambers and Millar, 1983). Others have cited concerns about credibility and the quality of evidence supporting their case (Lievore, 2005). This section will examine the decision to withdraw the complaint among the current sample. Respondents were asked whether:

- They had seriously considered withdrawing their complaint, and if so why;
- They had been encouraged to withdraw their complaint, and if so by whom;
- They had withdrawn their complaint.

Twenty-eight women stated that they had seriously considered withdrawing their complaint at some point. This means that of all the women who reported (n = 66), 42 per cent later thought about withdrawing.

Table 4.18 Reason for Considering Withdrawing a Rape Complaint

Reason	Number
Poor Treatment by Gardaí	11
Personal Safety	7
Fear of Court	4
Trauma of Rape	3
Case Factors	3
Other	5

Poor Treatment by Gardaí. The criminal justice system featured strongly in victims' concerns. It is of note that the most common reason given by victims for considered withdrawal was poor treatment by Gardaí (n = 11). Respondents complained that the Gardaí were not doing enough to progress their case, that it was for them difficult to obtain information and that they had to initiate most of the contact themselves. Satisfaction with Garda response will be examined in more detail shortly, but in the meantime, some examples of the difficulties experienced by those who considered withdrawing are discussed here. One respondent, who had suffered a violent assault that resulted in severe injury, withdrew her complaint:

> *Because I found the Gardaí/detective who took charge of the investigation to be very evasive and I was the person who had to keep phoning to check had they found the person. No victim liaison officer assigned to me (70).*

Others felt that the Gardaí had treated them with disbelief. A young student, assaulted by a stranger, described how the Gardaí had responded to her report.

> *I was made to feel ashamed and dirty. Tarnished with the 'she was drinking' label. I was made to feel that it was just 'sex.' It was a devastating blow (61).*

Others found it difficult to deal with the intense nature of the investigation and explained that they felt 'pressured' by the Gardaí. Despite finding the process difficult, this 18-year-old who was assaulted by her boyfriend, was determined to pursue her case. She explained that she found that:

> *the line up experience [was difficult] – but couldn't back out (9).*

Personal Safety. Lea (2003) found that intimidation by the perpetrator was implicated in almost half of cases in which the victim withdrew her allegation. In this study, seven respondents were concerned for their personal safety and feared that the offender would come after them again. Worryingly, some cited intimidation by the perpetrator or his family and friends as their reason for withdrawing. In the first case, the woman was assaulted in her own home by an acquaintance and suffered severe physical injuries as a result. The second woman was raped by a man she had met in nightclub.

> *My family was threatened by the offender and his family. I was very afraid of these people (101).*

> *I just wanted to forget the incident and when they found out who did it they let him go until the DPP gave their result and I was afraid he would come after me again (59).*

Three respondents cited the psychological distress they experienced as reasons for considering withdrawal, describing how the process was becoming too much for them. Three women mentioned case factors. In one case, the respondent had been drinking, and two felt there was not enough evidence to proceed. Finally, four mentioned fear of the court process as a reason. The following response was provided by a young woman who was raped by a stranger.

> *... because I was sick at the thought of going to court and being cross-examined. Offender is the one who's accused – it's unfair to victims (45).*

Twenty-one respondents, or almost one-third of all who had made a report, stated that they had been encouraged to withdraw. Table 4.19 shows who exerted this pressure on them.

Table 4.19: Source of Pressure to Drop Rape Complaint

	Number
Family/Friends	12
Gardaí	10
Suspect/Associates	5

The impact of social influence on the decision to report has been discussed earlier. These findings show that such pressure can also be exerted in the opposite direction. Most pressure was exerted by the family or friends of the victim (n = 12). Again, it is worth noting that the Gardaí were the second most common source of pressure. Interestingly, none of the cases in which the victim felt the Gardaí had encouraged withdrawal involved serious physical injury and four involved intimate relationships. In other words, Garda pressure to withdraw the complaint occurred primarily in cases that did not meet the real rape model. Ultimately, nine respondents withdrew their complaint, and it is worth noting that seven of them had made the report to the Gardaí themselves. Of the other two, one had been pressured by her parents into making the report and had never been committed to the case.

Informal Support Networks

A failure to report to the police does not necessarily indicate passive acceptance by the victim of what was done to her. Studies show that the majority of sexual assault victims disclose their experience to friends or family (e.g., Burgess and Holmstrom, 1978).

Table 4.20: Formal and Informal Sources of Support

	Number	Rating
Friend	50	4.3
Family	20	4.6
Support Agency/Refuge	11	4.7
Boyfriend/Partner	8	4.6
Gardaí	7	3.8
Medical	2	3.5
Other	2	4.0

All respondents in this study had told someone about what had happened and they were asked to identify the first person they told. Their responses reveal that they relied mostly on informal sources of support drawn from their social networks. The most common sources of support were friends, who were the first ones told in half of all cases (n = 50), followed by family members, who were the first ones told in 20 per cent of cases. Support agencies or refuges figured prominently (n = 11), although it is possible that this reflects the fact that the sample in this study was recruited primarily through support agencies. Most studies show that victims under-utilise the services of Rape Crisis Centres (see Campbell et al., 2001; McGee et al., 2002). The Gardaí were the first told in around seven per cent of cases.

Respondents were also asked to rate the level of support received from the person to whom they first disclosed the assault on a scale of 1 to 5. Overall, the majority of people disclosed to were supportive. As can be seen from Table 4.20, support agencies received the highest rating. Gardaí and medical professionals received the lowest ratings. This is consistent with finding reported in other studies (e.g., Campbell et al., 2001).

Response from the Gardaí

During the 1970s and 1980s, there was a growing awareness that many women who reported rape to the police experienced poor and hostile treatment (see Temkin, 2002; Lees, 1996). This led to changes in legislation, police practices and victim services in many countries. Several surveys have evaluated the police response to rape victims since these reforms. Key studies have been conducted in the United Kingdom (see, for example, Chambers and Millar, 1983; Adler, 1991; Lees and Gregory, 1993; Temkin, 1997, 2002), New Zealand (Jordan, 2001), Canada (Hattem, 2000) and Australia (Edwards, 1996). These studies have revealed some improvements in police practice, and there is some evidence that these reforms have improved reporting rates (Bachman, 1993). Irish studies show moderate levels of satisfaction with police among crime victims in general (CSO, 2004) and sexual assault victims in particular (e.g. McGee et al., 2002).

This section describes the experiences of Irish women who reported rape to the Gardaí. As explained in the last chapter, 66 respondents reported the incident to the Gardaí. Eight did not make a statement. This chapter deals only with women who made a statement (n = 58). It begins by examining the process of making a statement. This is followed by an examination of respondents' satisfaction with their treatment. By identifying both good practices and shortcomings, this analysis can help practitioners improve their responses to rape victims.

Making the Statement

After making an initial report of rape, the victim is required to make a formal statement. This is one of the earliest points of contact a victim has with the criminal justice system. The victim's experience at this stage is vital for building trust and motivation to pursue a complaint. Respondents were asked where they had made their statement and Table 4.21 sets out their responses. Almost two-thirds made their statement in a Garda Station. The second most common location was the respondent's home.

Table 4.21: Where Statement Was Made

	Number	**%**
Garda Station	38	65.5
Own Home	12	20.7
Hospital	3	5.2
Other	4	6.9
Missing	1	1.7
Total	58	100

Table 4.22 describes the gender of the interviewing officer. In almost all cases (86.2 per cent) a female Garda was present. Half of all interviews (48.3 per cent) were conducted by a female Garda only and a further 37.9 per cent were conducted by both male and female Gardaí. Only seven respondents stated that they had been interviewed by a male Garda only.

Table 4.22: Gender of Interviewing Officer

	Number	%
Female Only	28	48.3
Male Only	7	12.1
Both	22	37.9
Missing	1	1.7
Total	58	100

Most studies conclude that the gender of the interviewing officer does not impact on satisfaction ratings and that attitude is more important than gender (e.g. Bacik et al., 1998; Temkin, 1997). In this study, 77.8 per cent of women interviewed by a female Garda only and 71 per cent of those interviewed by both a male and female officer stated that they were satisfied or very satisfied with the Garda. Only 42 per cent of those interviewed by a male officer only stated that they were satisfied or very satisfied. This suggests that victims may be less satisfied when interviewed by a male Garda.

Manner of Interviewing Officer

Respondents were asked to rate the attitude and manner of their interviewing officers on three 5-point scales:

- Hostility Scale (where 1 = hostile and 5 = warm);
- Sympathy scale (where 1 = unsympathetic and 5 = sympathetic); and
- Atmosphere scale (where 1 = cold/clinical and 5 = warm/supportive).

Table 4.23 shows the average responses on each of these scales.

Table 4.23: Manner of the Interviewing Officer

	Hostility	**Sympathy**	**Atmosphere**
Mean Result	3.89	3.81	3.36
Standard Dev.	1.14	1.21	1.30

Overall, ratings show that the respondents perceived the Gardaí to be both warm and sympathetic in their approach to taking the statement, although a minority disagreed. The majority (62.1 per cent) rated the interviewing Garda as warm or very warm and only 12.1 per cent gave a rating of hostile or very hostile. The average rating on the Hostility scale was 3.89 (SD = 1.14). Similar positive ratings were given on the Sympathy scale. Again, the results show that victims found the Garda to be sympathetic (m = 3.81, SD = 1.21). In total, most (63.8 per cent) rated the Garda as sympathetic or very sympathetic and 13.8 per cent rated as unsympathetic. Respondents were also asked to rate the atmosphere during the interview on a scale of one to five (1 = cold/clinical and 5 = warm/ supportive). Again, average ratings were quite good (m = 3.36, SD = 1.30). Around half (48.3 per cent) felt that the atmosphere was warm and supportive.

Satisfaction with the Interviewing Officer

Respondents were asked to rate their satisfaction with the Garda who took their statement on a scale of one to five (where 1 = very dissatisfied and 5 = very satisfied). The average satisfaction rating was 3.89 (SD = 1.3), which suggests a good level of satisfaction with the initial Garda response. Looking at satisfaction ratings in more detail, over two-thirds (67.2 per cent) were satisfied or very satisfied with the Garda who took their statement. Nevertheless, a significant minority (13.8 per cent) were dissatisfied or very dissatisfied with the Garda who took their statement.

It has been suggested that the police respond differently to victims of 'classic' rapes (see e.g., Estrich, 1987; Temkin, 1997). If this is the case, then respondents who knew their offender, who were not injured and who had consumed alcohol should be less satisfied with the Garda response. These factors were examined in relation to satisfaction ratings.

Respondents who were injured at the time of the assault (M = 4.14, SD = 1.27) tended to give higher satisfaction ratings to the Garda who took their statement than respondents who were not injured (M = 3.44, SD = 1.20). These differences approached significance (t = 1.93, p = .06). Looked at in relation to requirement of medical care (a measure of severity), respondents who required medical care (M = 4.47, SD = .87) were significantly more likely than respondents who did not require medical care (M = 3.63, SD = 1.34) to give satisfactory ratings to the interviewing Garda (t = 2.76, p = .008). This analysis shows that victims who suffered obvious physical injury were more satisfied with the initial Garda response to their report.

Victims of stranger attacks gave higher satisfaction ratings (M = 4.30, SD = 1.13) than victims of offenders known to the victim (M = 3.65, SD = 1.32) and again these differences approached significance (t = 1.85, p = .07). Victims were slightly but not significantly more likely to be satisfied with the Garda response when the offender was a stranger. There were no differences (t = .232, ns) in satisfaction ratings between victims who were drinking (M = 3.92, SD = 1.34) and those who were not (M = 3.83, SD = 1.15). In other words, victims who had been drinking were as satisfied with the Garda response as those who had not consumed alcohol.

Reasons for Satisfaction

Surveys show that victims are satisfied with their treatment if they feel that they were believed, treated with respect and were allowed to retain some control over proceedings (Jordan, 2001). Respondents were asked to provide reasons for their satisfaction ratings. Three main themes emerged from this analysis: the characteristics of the interviewing Garda, the manner in which the interview was conducted and the provision of additional support.

Characteristics of the Interviewing Garda. Making a statement is a difficult, distressing and lengthy process (Temkin, 1997; Chambers and Millar, 1983), so the Garda attitude is very important. A number of positive adjectives were ascribed to the interviewing Garda: sympathetic, supportive, caring, helpful and genuinely concerned for the victim's welfare. The respondents valued an officer who was on their side and believed them. The following quotes illustrate the ideal approach. The first respondent reported straight away and was interviewed in her home by a female Garda. She described it in positive terms:

> *I was interviewed by female Garda which made the atmosphere for me comfortable to talk to her. She was very nice and sympathetic, told me to relax and take my time to tell my story and for her to tell me that she 'believed me, I was telling the truth (106).*

In this case, an 18-year-old woman who reported immediately found the interviewing officer warm and sympathetic.

> *She [i.e., the Garda] was helpful, she wasn't pushing me. Offered me glass of water. She was nice (69).*

The women interviewed by Leane et al. (2001) concurred with these findings. Overall, their perceptions of the Gardaí were positive. Despite finding the process of making a statement difficult, three commented on the caring, sympathetic approach taken by the Garda.

Interview Techniques. Respondents also cited certain interview techniques as positive features. They appreciated it when the interviewing Garda did not pressure them, let them tell their story in their own time, stopped for breaks and explained procedures. This is important as telling their story can have therapeutic value for victims (McAdams, 1993). In the following example, the respondent had not wanted to contact the Gardaí but her mother did anyway. The Respondent was interviewed by a male officer, who she described as warm and caring. Despite her initial reluctance to report, she did not withdraw her complaint.

> *Rang to see how I was the next day. Acted like they cared. Kept me updated about progress but I didn't want to talk (50).*

In some cases, however, a positive experience could not overcome victim's reluctance to pursue a complaint. The following response was provided by a woman who reported immediately, recognising that what had happened was a serious offence. Despite her positive experience with the interviewing officer, she later withdrew her complaint because she was concerned about people finding out what had happened to her

> *She [i.e., the Garda] understood how I was feeling and told me I could take as long as I needed and free to stop whenever I wanted (57).*

Extra Support. Several respondents appreciated being offered additional practical support by the Gardaí. One respondent was grateful when the Garda rang to check on her welfare after she had made her statement. Two other respondents were accompanied by the Gardaí to the medical examination. In one case, the Garda had given up holiday time to attend. The following respondent delayed reporting her rape despite experiencing serious injury. Again, she had a positive experience and found extra help in ending harassment by the offender to be very useful.

> *Didn't judge me, concerned about my welfare, made it easy to go to college. Gave support on constant basis, explained system very well. They talked to offender and his friends about harassment and it stopped (16).*

Reasons for Dissatisfaction

Respondents who were dissatisfied with the interviewing officer also gave reasons for their answers. Four did not answer this question. Two main themes emerged from their responses: unsupportive attitudes and administrative factors.

Manner and Attitude. In Chambers and Millar's survey (1983), a quarter of respondents cited the manner of the police as a key source of dissatisfaction. They felt that the police responded to their complaint with a lack of consideration, tended to blame the victims for the assault and did not believe them. In this study, twelve respondents referred to the manner and approach of the Garda as reasons for dissatisfaction. They described the Gardaí as lacking in sympathy, were clinical in their approach and were disbelieving. This 18-year-old respondent described her experience of making her statement. This was done in a Garda Station and a female officer took the statement. The respondent reported straight away and described the experience as follows:

> *Lack of sympathy, no warmth, asked loads of questions, treated me like I was lying (18).*

The next respondent was a young woman who was raped while on a date. She reported immediately and was interviewed by a female Garda at the Garda Station. She described the interviewing officer as hostile and unsympathetic, and the atmosphere during the interview as cold and clinical. She stated:

> *I felt she [bean Garda] was very unprofessional. Had no compassion or sympathy (75).*

Others felt that the interviewing Garda did not believe them and engaged in blame. This respondent, who had been assaulted by a man she had met that evening, described the impact of such attitudes. She explained that she considered withdrawing her statement as a result. Her case was later dropped when the suspect was not identified.

> *I was made to feel it wasn't a serious sexual assault. I was phoned a few days later. Garda stated, 'you were seen on CCTV footage*

> *kissing this man'. I was devastated. A kiss did not encourage a sexual assault (61).*

The second comment is from a respondent who had been attacked by a stranger on the street. She delayed reporting for several weeks, partly because of fear of how the Gardaí would respond. From her statement, it appears her fears were justified.

> *I felt she [i.e., the interviewing Garda] thought I was wasting her time and that she didn't believe it was actually a rape because of the fact I was so out of it, I don't remember much. I only reported it in case there were similar cases that it might help (110).*

Some felt that the Gardaí were encouraging them to drop their complaint. One respondent, who did not report until a week after the assault because she tried to deal with it herself, was discouraged from pursuing her case by the male and female Gardaí who interviewed her. Her case was later dropped due to lack of evidence.

> *I didn't feel by the end of the interview that I had done the right thing as they were not seeming to be very positive that I had come to them after a week had gone by (109).*

Administrative Matters. Eleven were dissatisfied with administrative aspects of the interview. They mentioned factors such as the length of time it took to make a statement, the unsuitability of the environment and the gender of the interviewing officer. The following two comments illustrate the difficulties complainants experienced when making a statement. The first respondent, who was attacked by a stranger in her home, reported within 24 hours. She found the female Garda unsympathetic and hostile in her approach.

> *Garda took my statement. It took two hours to get through it. There was no sympathy. They were doing a job that's all (30).*

The second respondent reported her rape by an ex-boyfriend immediately. While she described the female Garda who interviewed her as sympathetic, she found the length of time it took to make the statement difficult.

> *I did not expect to sit in a Garda Station from 8.10 a.m. the morning I was raped until 12.15 in the afternoon. Still in the same clothes. I felt dirty, could not shower (94).*

Two respondents questioned the suitability of the Garda Station as a location for the interview. The following extract illustrates one of the problems:

> *Male detective told me and my daughter to take a seat as they had important work to do, then female Garda interviewed us in the front hall where anyone could listen (5).*

Three mentioned being interviewed by a male Garda as a cause of dissatisfaction. The Victims' Charter specifies that people who report rape will be given the option of being interviewed by a female Garda. In practice, this was sometimes problematic. One respondent felt embarrassed about having a male Garda present when giving personal details. A second explained how the female Garda had to be brought in from another station. This 21-year old respondent, who had specifically requested a female Garda, felt her views were disregarded.

> *I wanted to speak only to a female guard but it was as if it was slightly inconvenient. I gave my statement with the female guard but with a male guard coming in and out as he pleased. Afterwards a male guard from another branch came in and went through the whole statement again. Was annoyed at this as it seemed that it was routine to ask if I wanted a female guard and yet go ahead and have men walking in and having more input than the female guard in the end (93).*

Garda Investigation and Follow-up

Respondents were asked about the investigation of their complaint. The majority (81 per cent) said that the Gardaí had investigated their complaint (e.g. taken witness statements, visited crime scene). In almost two-thirds of cases (63.8 per cent), a suspect was later taken in for questioning. Over three-quarter of respondents (77.5 per cent) underwent a forensic medical examination. The majority of these (n = 28) had their examination conducted in a specialist rape trauma unit. Of the remainder, ten had examinations done in a hospital accident and emergency department, six were conducted in a General Practitioner's surgery and one was conducted in a private hospital. Medical examinations were not performed in cases that were reported too long after the assault (n = 6) or where the victim was unwilling to be examined (n =2).

In the Victims' Charter (Department of Justice, Equality and Law Reform, 1999), the Gardaí make a number of commitments to victims of crime:

- When possible, provide a doctor and Garda of the same gender for victims of sexual offences;

- Offer information about support services and assign a Garda Liaison Officer to assist victims;

- Explain the investigation process to victims and ensure that they are kept informed of any developments in the investigation; and

- Supply information about court procedures and outcomes, such as details about the court hearing, the likelihood of being called as a witness and the trial outcome.

Table 4.24: Garda Obligations

Commitment	Yes (%)	No (%)
Option of a Female Garda	63	37
Information about Support Services	58	42
Explain Investigation	64	36
Explain Proceedings	56	44

Table 4.24 shows the extent to which the Gardaí met their obligations under the Charter. These figures suggest that the Gardaí are

fulfilling their commitments for a majority of victims. Nevertheless, a significant minority – almost 40 per cent – report being treated in a manner contrary to the Charter.

In the Charter, the Gardaí also commit to keeping the victim informed of the progress of their cases. In this survey, respondents were asked how difficult they found it to obtain information. Again, they rated it on a five-point scale (1 = easy to obtain and 5 = difficult to obtain). Almost forty per cent (37.9 per cent) stated that they found it difficult or very difficult to obtain information about the progress of their cases from the investigating Garda. The average rating was 3.27 (SD = 1.52) suggesting moderate levels of difficulty overall (an in-depth analysis of difficulties experienced follows).

Overall Satisfaction

Respondents were asked to rate their overall satisfaction with the investigation of their cases by the Gardaí. The results show that respondents were largely dissatisfied with their treatment. The average rating was 2.77 (SD = 1.5). Two out of five respondents who gave a rating (41.4 per cent) described themselves as dissatisfied or very dissatisfied with the investigation. This result contrasts sharply with the largely positive ratings given to the Gardaí in respect of the first stage in the process, the taking of the initial statement. The difference between satisfaction levels at both points is statistically significant (t = 6.54, p <.001).

As noted earlier, it has been argued that police are more likely to believe and follow up a report that fits the 'classic' rape template (e.g., Grace et al., 1992; Harris and Grace, 1999). Victims' satisfaction ratings were compared with several features of the real rape scenario, namely physical injury, victim-offender relationship and victim alcohol use.

There were no differences (t = .81, ns) between respondents who experienced physical injury (M = 2.88, SD = 1.6) and victims who did not (M = 2.53, SD = 1.26). With regards to requiring medical care, respondents who did require it (M= 3.25, SD = 1.7) were not significantly more likely to give positive ratings (t = 1.54, ns) than respondents who did not (M = 2.57, SD = 1.39). Victim-offender relationship was also examined. Victims of stranger attacks gave higher ratings (M = 3.32, SD = 1.50) than victims of non-stranger attacks (M = 2.52, SD = 1.44). This difference approached significance (t = 1.91, p = .06). Finally, the differences between women who had used alcohol (M = 2.89, SD = 1.5) and women who had not (M = 2.50, SD = 1.5) were not significant (t = .87, ns)

These results suggest that women whose cases conform to the 'real rape' stereotype are slightly, but not significantly, more likely to be satisfied with how the Gardaí handled their case. This suggests that the Gardaí do not treat complainants differently.

The relationship between overall satisfaction and various aspects of the initial Garda interview was investigated. Several significant correlations were found. Overall satisfaction was correlated with ratings of warmth (r = .351, p = .01), sympathy (r = .32, p = .02), atmosphere (r = .410, p = .002) and satisfaction with the interviewing officer (r = .383, p = .005). These results indicate that there was a significant relationship between overall satisfaction, the manner and attitude of the interviewing Garda and the context of the interview.

The links between features of the follow-up and overall satisfaction were also investigated. Respondents were significantly more satisfied with the overall investigation if the Gardaí had provided them with information about support services (t= 3.73, p < .001) and investigation procedures (t = 2.45, p = .018). There were no differences in relation to the provision of information about going to court (t = .883, ns). Overall satisfaction was strongly linked to perceptions of difficulty in obtaining information about the progress of their cases (r = .445, p = .005). In other words, the more difficulty respondents experienced obtaining information about the progress of their cases and procedural matters, the less satisfied they were with the investigation.

In sum, women who did not conform to the 'real rape' stereotype (i.e. stranger rape, injury, no alcohol use) were slightly less satisfied with the Garda response. Respondents were more satisfied with the conduct of the investigation when the interviewing

Garda was warm, sympathetic and supportive. Further, satisfaction was higher when the Gardaí provided information about support services, explained the procedures involved in an investigation and kept them updated with the progress of their cases. There were no differences in satisfaction ratings in relation to whether an investigation had been undertaken, whether anyone was questioned or as regards the provision of information regarding court procedures.

Reasons for Satisfaction with Garda Investigation

Respondents were also asked to give reasons for their satisfaction or dissatisfaction. Only 16 mentioned only positive aspects compared to 31 who cited only negative aspects (a further eleven either gave no response or gave responses that could not be classified). Many gave more than one reason, so the number of responses will not add up to 58.

Table 4.25: Reasons for Satisfaction

	Number
Access to Information	7
Administrative	6
Attitude	5

Access to Information. Victims value being kept informed of the progress of their cases (Temkin, 1997; Jordan, 2001). Irish surveys have also shown that dissatisfaction occurs when information about cases is not provided (Leane et al., 2001). Similarly, in this study, respondents appreciated it when the Gardaí kept in touch and provided information about any developments in the case.

One respondent, for example, explained why she was satisfied with the follow-up contact by the Gardaí. She had been informed about support services, investigative procedures and had no difficulty obtaining information about the progress of her case. In particular, she valued the contact with the investigating Garda.

> *They explained everything and if I ever needed to talk to anyone I only had to pick up the phone. They also called to see how I was doing (8).*

A second respondent, who was 21 years old at the time of the assault, was also satisfied with the investigation. Her assailant was questioned and later charged (although the offence was downgraded to sexual assault despite fitting the legal definition of rape). Again, she valued being kept informed.

> *They have been helpful and inform me of anything significant that they can tell me (93).*

Administrative. Respondents were satisfied when they believed that their case had been thoroughly investigated and when they felt the Gardaí were doing all they could to identify and to catch the offender. The following explanation was provided by a respondent who was assaulted by a friend and suffered severe injuries as a result:

> *Alleged perpetrator questioned and detained, witness statements taken (3).*

In a second case, the respondent was raped by a stranger who had yet to be identified. She reported having no difficulty obtaining information about her case and felt that the Gardaí were doing all they could to catch the offender:

> *Any time a non-national is brought in the Garda investigating my case goes to check out their profile as they have a picture from CCTV (103).*

Attitude. All respondents in this category commented on how supportive their investigating Garda was. The following explanation was given by a woman whose file was with the Director of Public Prosecutions at the time of the interview. She described how the Gardaí had treated her during the investigation.

So helpful and supportive, brilliant (26).

In conclusion, respondents valued having access to information about their cases and ongoing support from the investigating Garda. They appreciated knowing that their cases were being investigated thoroughly and receiving a supportive response.

Reasons for Dissatisfaction with Garda Investigation

Table 4.27 sets out the reasons expressed by respondents for their dissatisfaction with the Garda investigation. Four major themes emerged: lack of information or access to the investigating Garda, criticisms of the investigation process itself, the attitude of the investigating Garda and delays in bringing case to a conclusion.

Table 4.26: Reasons for Dissatisfaction

	Number
Lack of Information/Contact	17
Investigation	9
Unsympathetic Attitudes	8
Delay	7

Lack of Information or Contact. The literature suggests that one of the key sources of dissatisfaction with police follow-up is the lack of information given about the case (Adler, 1991; Lees and Gregory, 1993) or procedures and auxiliary support services (McGee et al., 2002). The most common theme emerging from respondents' reasons for dissatisfaction was lack of information or follow up contact from the investigating officer. Several respondents reported actively seeking contact with the investigating Garda, either by making phone calls or visiting the station. One respondent, a 21-year-old assaulted by a stranger, made a statement after an A&E nurse notified the Gardaí:

> *Never followed up complaint. Anytime I contacted Garda in charge of case she was never there to take calls. She phoned a friend of mine and that was it (61).*

A second respondent found the initial Garda response very supportive but was less satisfied with how they followed up her complaint. She stated that she found it very difficult to obtain information about the progress of her case.

> *Am sick of having to hound Garda only to be told will be in at X hours and on phoning again and not in (111).*

In some cases, a follow-up interview was requested in order to finalise aspects of the statement but this did not happen in some cases. The following comment was provided by a respondent who was raped by an ex-partner. She found it difficult to get any information about her case and described herself as 'in the dark'. She explained further:

> *The bean Garda that took my statement was supposed to return to my home to adjust my statement. Two items were to be amended. Have not seen her since. She never phoned me back to let me know about the case. She said she would (94).*

In some cases, the respondent was upset when the offender was told the outcome of the case first. In the following case, the offender was a stranger but knew the respondent's friends:

> *When accused was granted bail they failed to let me know when they promised me I would be the first to know. I was told by the accused's friends who taunted me and verbally abused me in my home town. Very frightening (13).*

Investigation. Nine respondents were concerned about the quality of the investigation. One felt that Gardaí should have done DNA tests but failed to do so. Another respondent stated that essential witnesses were not interviewed, while three others were concerned at the delays in beginning the investigation (e.g., collecting evidence or interviewing suspect). The following example concerns a respondent who had a positive experience at the initial stage. She was concerned about the Gardaí's failure to collect evidence.

> *Guards waited till next day to cordon off area. Didn't seem interested in collecting evidence – neighbours found my clothes (12).*

Another woman's experience highlighted the anxiety that can occur when people feel that investigations are not thorough. Her case was later dropped by the DPP due to insufficient evidence:

> *As it was one person's word against another it was very relevant that certain people be interviewed as it was premeditated and so he had told people he was going to and often told them he had, yet those people were not interviewed (109).*

Two respondents felt that there were too many Gardaí involved in their cases. One respondent, aged 24, described herself as very dissatisfied with the officer who took her statement because the officer appeared to know little about the case.

Unsympathetic Attitudes. Some felt that the Gardaí were not sympathetic or supportive enough at the follow-up stage. They believed that their complaints were not being taken seriously or that the Gardaí were not interested in those complaints. The following comments highlight the emotional impact on victims when they feel their cases are neglected:

> *More should be done. I was forgotten about. They don't see this as a crime. Not helping people who need help (50).*

> *If I don't keep phoning about my case it appears as if it is gathering dust in the police station. I really feel the Gardaí are not interested (70).*

Delays. Several respondents complained about the length of time it took to deal with their complaints; some had been waiting for over a year and still had heard nothing. The effect of the delay was aggravated by a lack of ongoing contact. One respondent explained:

> *Have heard nothing about the case for a year. Was asked to sign a release form to send clothes to Dublin. This is the last I heard. Any info I've got is from phoning them myself. I feel my case isn't important to them (48).*

Summary and Conclusion

This chapter has revealed that the majority of victims were young. Most were raped by people they knew and many of the attacks occurred in the victims' homes. Alcohol use by both the victim and the offender was a common feature. Research suggests that rapes with these characteristics are less likely to be reported. Nevertheless, one of the strongest predictors of rape reporting is the severity of the incident (defined as use of a weapon, physical injury, force or threat of force). The sample from this study revealed that around half of the rapes involved verbal threats, 70 per cent involved physical violence by the offender and around two-thirds of victims suffered physical injury as a result of the attack.

The incident profile suggests that many of the rapes conformed to some elements of the real rape stereotype since they involved violence, physical injury and resistance. On the other hand, most involved offenders known to the victim, alcohol use and domestic situations. Any of these factors can increase or decrease a victim's willingness to report. The sample was too small, however, to establish clearly whether particular factors were associated with reporting.

Respondents' explanations provided valuable information about the various incentives and deterrents to reporting rape. Among non-reporters, the most significant concerns were fear of the criminal justice system, concerns about the nature of the assault and anxiety about the social implications of disclosure. The primary influences on the decision to report were a desire for justice, social influence to report and protection for self and others.

The decision-making process described by the respondents to this survey corresponds well with Greenberg and Ruback's (1992) model of victim decision-making. These authors theorised that the first step in reporting a crime to the police requires that the victim label the incident as a crime. Next, they must deem it of sufficient seriousness to warrant reporting to the police. Thirdly, they make a decision about what to do. As in their model, social influence permeated each stage of the decision-making process among Irish victims. Friends and family helped victims to define their experiences as rape, then provided support and advice and practical assistance with making the report.

The results suggest that the decision to report is not a single event but is ongoing throughout the case. There are multiple decision points and victims re-assess their choices constantly throughout the criminal justice process. This is shown by the number of reporting respondents who considered withdrawing their complaints. Negative experiences with the criminal justice system might well lead to victims deciding to withdraw their complaints.

The results reveal that concerns about the criminal justice system played an important role at each stage of attrition. Negative perceptions of the criminal justice system, particularly fear of the process and lack of faith in its ability to provide justice, feature strongly in the explanations given by victims who do not report. The most common reason given by respondents who reported but did not make a statement was the perception that they could not deal with the difficult demands of pursuing a case. Finally, women who withdrew their complaint after making a statement cited poor treatment by the Gardaí and fear of the legal process.

In the Victims' Charter (Department of Justice, Equality and Law Reform, 1999), the Gardaí make the following commitment:

> The Gardaí are very conscious of your special place in the criminal justice system and would like to establish a supportive relationship with you. Special regard for your real concerns and needs is a high priority and you will be treated with empathy, courtesy and respect (Department of Justice, 1999: 6).

Satisfaction with the Garda response was investigated at two stages: (a) the initial statement, and (b) follow-up contact. Overall, the majority of victims were satisfied with the initial stage. They valued an approach that was sympathetic and supportive. They were more satisfied when Gardaí used interview techniques that did not involve pressure, allowed them to take breaks, and provided clear explanations of procedures and practical support. Dissatisfaction occurred when interviewing Gardaí were perceived as unsympathetic or disbelieving. The location of the interview, the length of time it took to make a statement and being interviewed by a male Garda all contributed to reduced levels of satisfaction. The quantitative analysis showed some evidence that satisfaction was higher for victims of 'real rape.'

At a later stage, victims' satisfaction with the Gardaí dropped significantly. Positive aspects at this stage included being kept informed about case, belief that their case had been thoroughly investigated and being dealt with by supportive officers. Negative experiences included lack of information, poor investigation, unsupportive attitudes and delays in cases reaching a conclusion. Statistical analysis showed some impact of real rape characteristics on satisfaction ratings.

Shapland et al. (1985) concluded that there were two distinct stages for victims in their interaction with police and that reasons for satisfaction were different at each stage. At the initial report phase, satisfaction is influenced by the level of concern shown by police. Later in the investigation, victims are more concerned about provision of information. The experiences reported by respondents in this study correspond with this analysis.

Overall, respondents' experiences with the Gardaí were akin to a 'rape lottery' (Jordan, 2001: 68). Jordan's study (2001) highlighted the disparity between the needs of victims and the administrative and bureaucratic concerns of the investigating team and concluded that this can lead to dissatisfaction among victims.

> At the very time that a raped woman is seeking to be believed and validated, the police will be intent on obtaining

proof and verification that she is telling the truth (Jordan, 2001: 701).

Jordan argued that this situation is not inevitable and may be minimised if proper training procedures are put in place for police. Victims' recommendations for improving police response to reports of sexual violence include: offering support at every stage of the legal process, including counselling and legal services, and; providing sensitivity training to agents of the criminal justice system (e.g. Edwards, 1996; Hattem, 2000).

THE FOLLOW-UP SURVEY

Of the original sample of 100 respondents, 50 individuals completed a follow-up questionnaire designed to assess the impact that the rape and their experiences within the justice system had on their mental health and attitude. The follow-up survey consisted of a survey pack containing four validated psychometric instruments: the GHQ-12 (General Health Questionnaire), the Post-Traumatic Life Changes Questionnaire, Levenson's Locus of Control Test and the Post-Traumatic Stress Disorder Symptom Scale-Self Report (PSS-SR). In particular, it was intended to examine the relationship between the stage of attrition and mental health and recovery. Few of the tests conducted produced results with statistical significance. This result must be interpreted with some caution, as the small sample size may obscure actually existing relationships. Further, it should be borne in mind that, as the respondents could not be assessed before the experience of the rape, it is impossible to determine with certainty whether, for example, the perception of the locus of control was influenced by the rape and subsequent involvement in the justice system, or if the perceived locus of control influences the extent of involvement in the justice system.

General Health Questionnaire (GHQ-12)

A Chi Square test was run to establish whether the stage of attrition affected the respondent's GHQ score. A low score (0-3) on the GHQ test would indicate few or no indicators of psychological dysfunction, while a high score (4+) would indicate some or many indicators of psychological dysfunction. The results are set out in Table 4.27.

The test result was near to significant at the 0.05 level (χ^2=9.046, df 4, sig. 0.06, V= 0.439).

Table 4.27: High/Low GHQ Scores and the Stage of Attrition

	Low GHQ (none or few indicators of psychological dysfunction)	High GHQ (some or many indicators of psychological dysfunction)
Did Not Report	1	12
Reported (no statement)	2	2
Made a Statement	5	11
DPP Decision: Do Not Prosecute	0	8
Went to Trial	0	6
Withdrew Complaint	2	2

Post-Traumatic Life Change Questionnaire

Frazier et al.'s (2001) post-traumatic life change questionnaire was used to examine the positive and negative changes that occurred in victims' lives as a result of the rape. No statistically significant association was found between the stage of attrition and either positive or negative life changes (χ^2=2.310, df 4, sig. 0.679). Although not significant, when the sample was divided into those who experienced more positive life changes (score = > 51) and those that experienced more negative life changes (score = < 51), it was found that there was an ascending number of individuals that reported more positive changes in life than negative ones, as they moved through the legal system. Thus, while only 35.7 per cent of those that did not report their rape indicated more positive life changes, 66.7 per cent of rape complainants whose case went to trial reported more positive changes than negative changes.

When the total score for life changes was analyzed, the variable for life changes still indicated independence from the stage of attrition ($t(46)=1.478$, $p> 0.05$). It was again found that those who did not report the rape to the Gardaí had the lowest score on the life changes test, indicating a negative influence on their lives (M=47, SD=10.95); however, those whose cases were reported but not prosecuted had the highest score on the test (M= 53, SD=15.88). This result suggests that a decision to prosecute is generally related to positive changes, the strongest positive changes are related to having a reported case not prosecuted. The most likely explanation for this apparent discrepancy is the difficulty and fear that typically surrounds the trial experience.

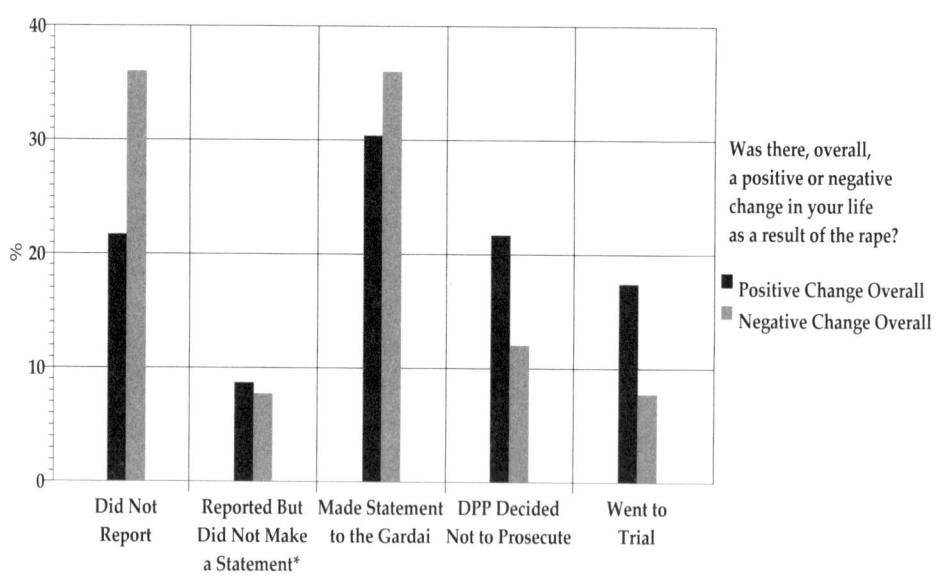

Figure 4.1: Life Changes and the Stage of Attrition

Where in the legal system is the case now?

* This category was excluded from subsequent analyses due to low frequency.

Post-Traumatic Stress Disorder Symptom Scale-Self Report (PSS-SR)

The PSS-SR is a 17-item test designed to measure the frequency of symptoms associated with Post-Traumatic Stress Disorder (PTSD) using a four-point Likert scale (Foa et al., 1993). Those respondents who record a '1' or higher on at least one intrusion, three avoidance/numbing, and two hyperarousal items were determined to have a probable diagnosis of PTSD (Foa et al., 1993).

The Chi Square test was used to determine if there was a significant association between the stage of attrition and the positive presence of PTSD. No significant associations were found between the stage of attrition and the presence of Post-Traumatic Stress Disorder as measured on the PSS-SR test (χ^2=1.176, df 4, sig.0.882). Whether a rape victim reports the incident to Gardaí, or whether a reported case is prosecuted, there is no significant association with PTSD. Although PTSD is very common amongst all victims of rape, there are some minor differences noted between the different stages of attrition. As displayed on the chart below, those who did not report their rape to Gardaí have the highest incidence of PTSD (93.3 per cent), while those who reported the incident but did not make a statement have the lowest incidence of PTSD (75 per cent); the other groups variously fall into the range between 83.3 per cent (went to trial) and 88.9 per cent (DPP decision not to prosecute).

When a total score was obtained by adding answers to the questions on the PSS-SR questionnaire, this score was tested against the binary variables: did you report (yes/no), was the case prosecuted (yes/no), and did you withdraw your complaint (yes/no). None of these relationships expressed a statistically significant variance in their mean results.

Levenson's Locus of Control Test

In order to establish whether the stage of attrition was affected by the respondent's perception of her ability to control a situation, Levenson's Locus of Control test was used (Levenson, 1981). This test assesses beliefs about the operation of control and is measured on three scales: Internality (I scale), Powerful Others (P scale) and Chance (C scale).

The Internality scale was tested against the decision to report. It was found that reporting a rape was statistically independent from the score for the I scale on the Locus of Control test ($t(47)$= -0.016, p> 0.05). The mean result for those who had reported (M 31.54, SD6.07) and that for those who had not reported (M 31.57, SD 5.06) were virtually identical. When the relationship between internality and the DPP's decision to prosecute was examined it was found that, on average, those whose cases were dropped scored slightly higher (M 32.09, SD 5.72) than those whose cases were prosecuted (M 30.50, SD 2.50), although this result was not statistically significant ($t(38)$= - 0.663, p>0.05). When comparing internality scores between those who withdrew their complaint and those who did not withdraw, it was found that the I scale scores were very similar (a mean of 31 as opposed to a mean of 31.6, respectively). Statistical significance was not indicated by the t-test ($t(47)$=-0.198, p> 0.05).

Figure 4.2: Internality and the Stage of Attrition

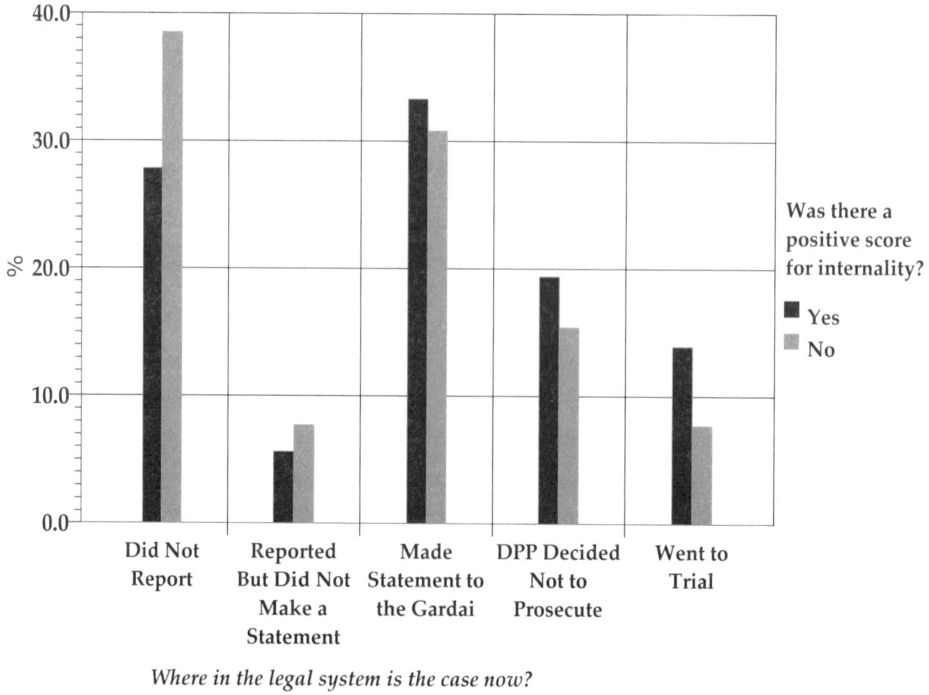

Where in the legal system is the case now?

On the P scale, the difference between those who reported to the Gardaí and those who did not was minute (M 24.4, SD 9.51 as opposed to 24.57, SD8.11) and not statistically significant ($t(47)$= -0.059, p> 0.05). Similarly, the results for the relationship between the DPP's decision to prosecute and the P scale were also insignificant ($t(38)$= -0.111, p>0.05). The relationship between withdrawal, however, and the score on the P scale came close to statistical significance ($t(47)$=1.718, sig. 0.092). On average, those who withdrew their complaint had a much higher score on the P scale (M 31.75, SD 9.53) than did those who did not withdraw (M 23.80, SD8.82).

Figure 4.3: Powerful Others and the Stage of Attrition

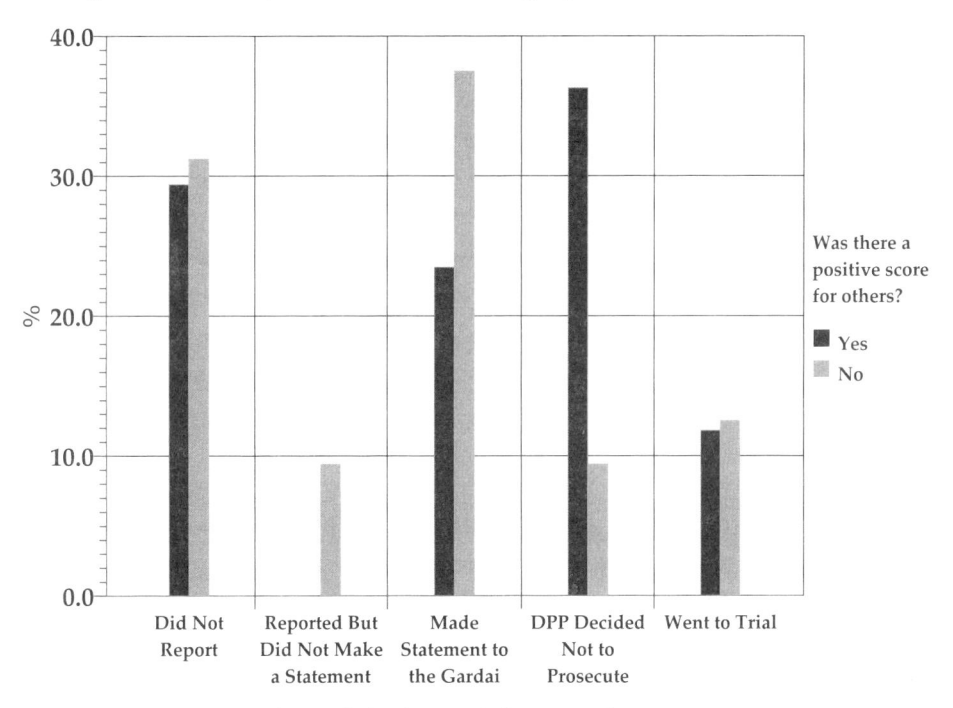

Finally, no significant associations were found on the C scale between the decision to report and the perception of chance as the locus of control ($t(47)$= 0.063, p>0.05); nor was there any significant association between the DPP's decision to prosecute and the score on the C scale ($t(38)$= 0.390, p>o.o5). A significant result was found for the relationship between the score on the C scale and the decision to withdraw the complaint ($t(47)$=2.020, p<0.05).

Those who did withdraw scored considerably higher on the C scale (M 35.00, SD 8.79) than did those who did not withdraw their complaint (M 27.80, SD 6.68). Similar results on the P and C scales are unsurprising as they both relate to an external locus of power. Other studies have also found a correlation between responses on the P and C scales (Levenson, 1981, p. 23).

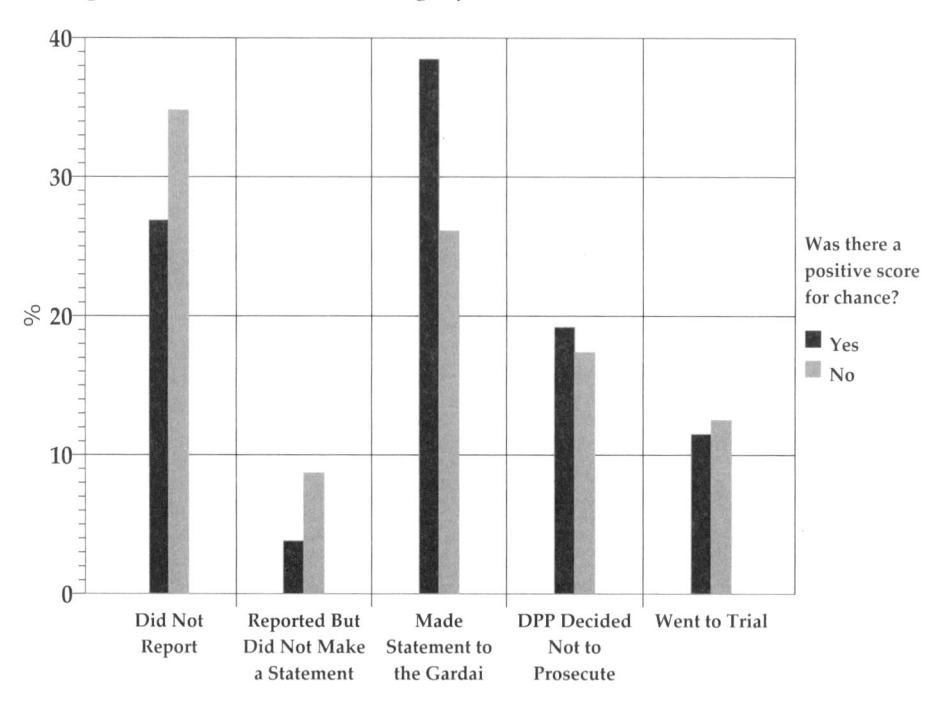

Figure 4.4: Chance and the Stage of Attrition

[Bar chart showing percentages by stage of attrition (Did Not Report, Reported But Did Not Make a Statement, Made Statement to the Gardai, DPP Decided Not to Prosecute, Went to Trial) with two bars each for "Was there a positive score for chance?" Yes/No.]

Where in the legal system is the case now?

Time and Recovery

Recovery from an ordeal such as rape is usually measured in years. Significant correlations were found between the passage of time and the number of symptoms of PTSD present at the time of the survey ($r = -0.323$, $n = 46$, sig. 0.029). The longer the time span since the rape the fewer PTSD symptoms were present, a result also found by McGee et al. in their examination of PTSD and sexual abuse in Ireland (2002: 113). There was also a very notable improvement in PTSD symptoms between the third and fourth year after the rape.

Significant relationships were also found between the total score on the Internality Scale and the total score for PTSD (r = -0.365, n = 48, sig. 0.011), and between the Powerful Others Scale and the PTSD score (r =0.304, n = 48, sig.0.035). However, while an internal locus of control is associated with the presence of fewer and milder PTSD symptoms, where Powerful Others are perceived as the locus of control, PTSD symptoms are more prevalent.

Figure 4.5: PTSD and the Passage of Time

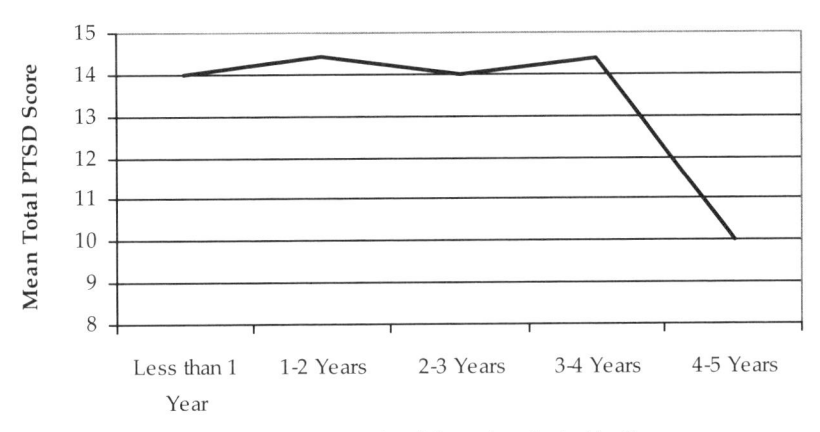

How many years has it been since the incident?

When the sample was divided into those with a positive score for internality (score > 24), and those with a negative score for internality (score < 24), it was found that those with a positive score were more likely to report the rape, more likely to make a statement and more likely to see their case proceed to trial, than those with a negative score.

The trial outcome had no significant effect on the locus of control, the Life Changes test, the GHQ score or indications of PTSD.

Table 4.28: Furthest Point of Attrition

	Positive Score for Internality (%)	**Negative Score for Internality (%)**
Did Not Report	27.8	38.5
Made a Report (did not make statement)	5.6	7.7
Made a Report and Gave a Statement	33.3	30.8
DPP Decided Not to Prosecute	19.4	15.4
Went to Trial	13.9	7.7

Discussion

There is little evidence to suggest that involvement in the legal system or the stage of attrition has any direct influence on the time-frame for the recovery of rape. This result is contrary to the findings of Peretti and Cozzens (1983) who found that women who did not report rape were more likely to experience negative physical, psychological and social symptoms that those who did report. There is some indication in the analysis that suggests that the further the case progresses the more likely the individual will be to suffer from psychiatric disturbances, although this was not found to be statistically significant. The small sample size may be to blame. Those who were the least likely to suffer from psychiatric disorders according to the GHQ test were those who reported their rape but were absolved from further participation in the legal process, either because they did not make a statement or because they withdrew. It is possible that reporting to the Gardaí helps to mitigate mental health problems, while the arduous experience of being involved in the legal system has a negative impact on mental health.

The Life Changes Questionnaire, however, reports a different reaction. More positive life changes were noted as the complainants moved through the justice system. Perhaps the experience of working through this issue encouraged the complainant to take control of other aspects of their life. It is also possible that those whose cases proceeded furthest in the justice system were those who were the most likely to gain possible support resources in terms of family and friends. As with the GHQ-12 test, however, the respondents with the *highest overall* score on the life changes test were those whose cases were dropped by the DPP. This may suggest that while making a report is positively associated with mental health and recovery, the trial experience may delay or negatively impact the life and mental health of rape victims.

Post-Traumatic Stress Disorder was very common amongst all rape survivors: 87.8 per cent of all questionnaire respondents qualified for a diagnosis of PTSD. This condition does not appear to be strongly affected by the decision to report or the point at which the case is determined, although there is some suggestion that those who did not report are somewhat more likely to suffer from PTSD than those who did report. Time did affect the strength of PTSD, however, as recorded on an accumulative Likert scale, with a notable drop in symptoms and severity after the fourth year. Further, those with an internal locus of control were likely to suffer fewer PTSD symptoms and were least likely to qualify for a PTSD diagnosis. Benight and Bandura (2004) similarly found that a belief in self-efficacy was importantly associated with recovery from traumatic events.

There were no statistically significant relationships between the locus of control and the stage of attrition, apart from the decision to withdraw. It was found that a high score on the Chance scale was significantly associated with the decision to withdraw. A high score on the Chance scale was also significantly associated with a high score on the Powerful Others scale, which was in turn significantly associated with a low score on the Life Changes test. Furthermore, a high score on the Powerful Others scale was significantly associated with a high score for PTSD. It is, therefore, possible that the relationship between Chance and Powerful Others and the decision to withdraw is affected by the poor mental health associated with both external loci of control scales. It is also possible that those who have a strong belief in chance or fate may feel that the perpetrator will get what he deserves in the end, regardless of the legal system – a view expressed by one victim during the qualitative interview who did not make a statement to Gardaí.

Prolonged exposure to the legal process may have a detrimental effect on the complainant's mental health. Although falling short of statistical significance, there was some indication that those who made a report but did not see their case proceed to trial were more likely to report positive life changes, to have a lower incidence of PTSD symptoms and to demonstrate an internal locus of control. Respondents in this category would have had the opportunity to avail of services such as the Sexual Assault Treatment Units; they would therefore gain the support, medical attention and validation required for physical and psychological recovery without going through the often harrowing experience of a trial. These factors suggest that changes in the legal system to provide support for rape complainants as their complaint is processed may help the complainant deal with the psychological demands of the legal process and simultaneously assist in their recovery. It is difficult to determine, however, whether it is the complainant's experience with the legal system that affects her mental health and sense of control, or whether it is her sense of control that affects her mental health and experience with the legal system. It is likely that the greater part of a rape victim's recovery relies primarily on social supports and their own coping skills and mechanisms. While the legal system may be able to improve some aspects of its service, particularly in terms of delays, communication and support structures for complainant, it is unlikely that these changes will have a significant impact on the victim's recovery process. Increasing the complainant's sense of control, however, may induce a greater perception of internality in terms of the locus of control, and thereby possibly assist in a more positive recovery process.

THE QUALITATIVE INTERVIEWS

Follow-up interviews were conducted in 2006 with 12 women who were raped between November 2002 and August 2005. Eight women had officially reported their rape to the Gardaí, while four had not reported. Only one of the reports had proceeded to prosecution resulting in a guilty verdict for sexual assault. Of the other reported offences, one case was discontinued due to the defendant's suicide and another was directed 'do not prosecute' by the DPP. The other five cases were still awaiting a decision by the DPP. The women ranged in age from 18 to 55 at the time of the rape. Six of the women who took part in the interview were raped by people they knew, while one woman had been raped by a man she had met that night. One woman reported being raped by her partner, while another was raped by her ex-boyfriend. The majority of the interviewees (five) were employed in clerical work, while two others were students, one a homemaker, one a teacher and three were unemployed with no indication of their previous employment. All but two women reported the use of physical force beyond that required to commit the rape being used against them, with two women sustaining severe injuries. Five of the interviewees had consumed three to five drinks on the occasion of the rape, while two more had consumed six or more drinks. On average, the women who did not make a report had a higher level of alcohol consumption than those who did make a report. Two women offered no resistance to their attacker; one claimed to have been drugged, while the other admitted being too intoxicated to resist. Weapons were present on two occasions – one was a car-jacking and rape, and the other was a false imprisonment and rape.

Although the sample size was small, the qualitative interviews demonstrate similar variations in the suspect, complainant, and case characteristics as were evident in the larger survey and follow-up survey questionnaires. The interviews thus have the potential to provide context and texture to the information gathered through the quantitative processes.

The Initial Decision to Report

The interviewer asked the twelve women involved in the interviews to discuss their reasons for reporting, or not reporting, the rape. This open-ended question inspired narrative accounts of the immediate aftermath of the rape that are enlightening. The interviewer then produced a card that had a number of potential reasons for reporting (because it was a crime, to protect others, to protect myself, to attain justice, etc.), or not reporting (wanted to deal with it myself, blamed myself, didn't want to hurt others, too embarrassed, did not want to involve Gardaí). When the card was produced the interviewees tended to agree with a number of the statements, but there was a notable discord between the reasons given in response to the open-ended question and those selected from the card. The most popular options on the card were those that concerned justice, self-protection, protection of the family and shame. Of the explanations given to the open-ended questions, it is significant that seven were influenced by others or had the situation taken out of their hands completely. In the immediate aftermath of the rape, six of these women describe themselves as being in various stages of shock and disorientation. The following comments are illustrative:

It was my husband who found me ... I was in shock and I was ... having tremors, shakes and I was disoriented and I didn't know where I was ... I remember him shouting to get the phone (4).

The night it happened um ... I suppose I was really ... in a comatose state and my husband took me home and put me to bed and didn't want to ... I suppose alarm me or upset me so he waited until the next morning um ... to talk to me and we made the decision pretty much together to report it (3).

It was just out of shock, the house was broken into, I was raped and ... we woke up and the guy ran out of the house um ... it was just pure out of shock you know? (48).

> *The first thing was, 'no way. Absolutely not'. But I suppose one of my friends was there at the time and she kind of persuaded me – herself and another girl that I actually don't know ... she made me alright call the guards in the end (30).*
>
> *I rang the Samaritans and I spoke to a lady on the Samaritans who told me straightaway to report this and I didn't hesitate in reporting it (1).*

All six of these women reported the rape within 24 hours. These forthright explanations of the context in which the rape was reported suggest that reporting an incident of rape may have less to do with altruistic, justice-seeking or self-preservation motives than with circumstance and the immediate advice of family members, friends and counsellors.

Only one other interviewee who did report the rape appears to have made the decision to report the rape without outside influence. This woman reported being raped by her partner who had long been physically abusive. The decision to report appears to have grown out of a realisation that the defendant had gone too far; reporting the rape to the Gardaí was the first part of a strategy to end the abuse and the relationship.

The four women who did not make a report were alone in the immediate aftermath of the rape. These women were mostly victims of date rape and expressed uncertainty about their own perception of the incident as a rape and concern about how others would perceive it.

> *But even at that stage, I still didn't believe it myself, d'you know? Because it all goes back to how I met him and the circumstances leading up to it... I mean if you were to ask anybody, it would be like 'well, she was with him' ... I believed the Gardaí would do nothing because of the situation I had put myself in (107).*
>
> *I suppose my main factor was in the end, you see in the end I actually consented... I couldn't imagine actually physically having to be forced so I suppose telling him it was okay was making it*

easy on myself... and that's what blocked me for a long time (107).

I didn't want to report it because I didn't... you know. I was so sort of distressed and I didn't want to tell anybody about it. And I didn't want to talk about it and I didn't really know, I hadn't really gathered my thoughts as to what had actually happened for a couple of days because I was thinking about it and thought that couldn't have happened. You know, I must have slept with him or whatever (14).

The respondents who did not report did not tell anyone about what happened to them until days, weeks or even months later.

I went to my doctors for an examination and I think before that, I was just in complete shock and I was just 'no' ... and I just ... I hadn't cried about it. I hadn't coped with it. I hadn't even owned up to it ... I think it was about a week later (88).

The interviews suggest that receiving validation about the rape and support from someone in the immediate aftermath of the incident has a profound effect on the decision to report. Considering the state of shock that most of the rape victims report being in after the incident, it is not surprising that the initial reaction would be to retreat from the trauma of the incident – to go into a state of denial or avoidance, common characteristics of Post-Traumatic Stress Disorder (Survive.Org, 1998). In cases in which the rape did not fit the 'real' rape stereotype, the victim may need extra reassurance that the incident was indeed rape and an objective ear to help her make sense of the event and assuage any sense of self-blame. This finding is consistent with Williams (1984) and Tomlinson (1999), among others, who assert that women whose rape does not fit the classic rape scenario are less likely to report their rape. The presence and influence of another to confirm the status of the incident, and to help direct the victim towards making a report, may act to counteract any desire to retreat.

Three of the four interviewees who did not report still had some contact with the Gardaí. In one instance, a friend of the victim made an unofficial report to a Garda with whom she was acquainted. This Garda encouraged the victim to make a complaint but the victim declined (107). Another victim went to the Gardaí a year after the incident with the intention of making a report. She was motivated by ongoing harassment from the suspect and wanted help from the Gardaí. She described the Garda to whom she spoke as 'attentive' and 'sympathetic', but also 'realistic'. The Garda pointed out that there was no evidence and that 'everyone' would find out. These comments 'just made [her] kind of back out a bit' and she did not make a statement (88). The third victim also went to the Gardaí one week after the incident but declined to make a statement when she was informed that the suspect would be interviewed. The suspect was a former boyfriend, had a criminal history and was violent, and the victim was afraid of retaliation. She also was not impressed with the attitude of the Gardaí and felt that she would receive no protection from them (28).

Frohmann has argued that prosecutors in the US use strategies to manage the reactions of victims of sexual assaults through displays of concern, specifying downstream possibilities and shifting paradigms (1998: 393). There is evidence in these comments of similar strategies being employed by members of the Gardaí. Interviewee 28, for example, was discouraged from making a complaint by an apparent lack of concern from the interviewing Garda. Had reassurance and protection been offered, it is possible that she would have followed through with her original intention and given a statement. Interviewee 88 was discouraged from making a statement when the Gardaí explained to her that she lacked evidence and that her privacy would be compromised. Indeed, the Garda's comments, no doubt offered in good faith, fit exactly the downstreaming strategy identified by Frohmann. Thus, although the Gardaí have no legal capacity to no-crime or unfound a rape complaint, they may have an immediate affect on the complainants decision to make a statement and possibly to pursue the case.

The Importance of Privacy

The issue of privacy was raised, without prompting by the interviewer by all but one interviewee. Concerns about family, friends and others in the community knowing about the rape featured prominently among interviewees who had reported and even more so among those who had not. A simple desire to preserve one's privacy and avoid gossip was significant to a number of the interviewees (3, 39, 88, 107). Many, however, wanted to maintain privacy in order to protect their loved ones. One interviewee, whose mother went through a similar experience, was particularly concerned for her grandparents' wellbeing; she stated that 'it would hurt them because they know what happened to my mum' (88). Another explained that she could not talk to those to whom she was closest as 'it would have broken their heart' (14). Interviewees also expressed concern that members of their family might attempt retaliation against the suspect if they became aware of what had happened. One interviewee pointed out that she wanted her brothers 'to protect me in one instance but I'm trying to protect them as well' (107). Despite the desire to maintain privacy, many interviewees reported feelings of isolation due to not telling their families. One stated that 'I feel that they don't know me anymore, because they don't know this' (107).

Although the interviewees who did make a report also expressed reservations about the loss of privacy regarding the incident, they had mixed reactions to the resulting attention. One had details of her rape, together with judgmental comments about her behaviour including the comment that 'she deserved it', posted to a Bebo page. This major breach of privacy contributed to a major psychological breakdown and incidents of self-harm (50). Another victim discontinued contact with her sister due to lack of support and claimed that her friends were either 'overbearing' or did not care (1). Others had a positive experience, receiving validation and support from family, partners and friends. Some made new friends or had existing friendships strengthened when news of the rape emerged, and people shared their own experiences. Still others experienced a mixture of good and bad reactions. These experiences reinforce the need for those in whom rape victims confide to react in a positive manner. The very act of disclosure can be a major part of a victim's recovery and should be encouraged. Denial, non-disclosure of the event to family and friends, distraction and social withdrawal have been shown to increase the risk of Post-Traumatic Stress Disorder (Ullman et al., 2007: 33). The reverse is also true, however: negative social reactions, such as disbelief, stigmatization and disempowerment are associated with an increased risk of self-blame and PTSD (ibid.: 29).

Four interviewees were involved in radio or television interviews or had their stories published in newspapers with their consent in order to draw attention to their cases when they felt that the legal system had failed them. One interviewee used the media in an attempt to redress an imbalance of power between the suspect and herself. The suspect was described as a well-known, connected businessman, and the interviewee stated that she went public and waived anonymity because 'there was no way I was going to be insignificant when it came to this... I wanted my story told' (39). The other victims similarly wanted a chance to express themselves (4; 3; 1). One stated that she 'wanted to publicise [the rape] because I was so angry and I was so ... hell bent on getting the perpetrator to justice' (4). The strategy backfired somewhat, however, especially when the court case fell through as 'it became a burden that [people] knew because you never got away from it.... People's attitude changed towards me' (ibid.).

Sensitivity of the Gardaí

Some interviewees found members of the Gardaí to be crude and insensitive. A middle-aged rape victim was offended by the specificity of the language the Gardaí used in questioning her, such as asking about the nature and extent of penetration. She explains:

> *The female guard, I found her to be quite rough. I thought she wanted to be too manly doing that kind of thing. Then when it*

came to the fella, he was more gentle but at the same time he still used the same words (39).

Another young victim was horrified to be questioned in front of her entire family about intimate details of the rape by the first Garda who arrived on the scene. She described the Garda as 'rude' (50). A number of the interviewees spoke of the difficulty they had in describing the details of the rape to the Gardaí due to embarrassment. Interviewee 50, for example, noted that she was interviewed by two male Gardaí who were only a few years older than her. Their obvious discomfort at hearing the details of the rape magnified her own discomfort in providing those details. Indeed, she was never able to make a full statement of the incident due to her sense of awkwardness. Another victim similarly related her embarrassment at describing the intimate details of the rape. She also mentioned her surprise at how 'normal' the entire incident seemed to the guards (30).

Other interviewees described the lack of privacy associated with the interview at the Garda Station. One interviewee, who was brought to the Garda Station still wearing the dirty, torn clothes she had on when she was raped, was walked passed a large number of other Gardaí. She was 'embarrassed that they were looking at me deep down' (4). Another victim felt degraded by the experience of handing over the 'knickers' she was wearing at the time of the assault to the guards in the hospital (1).

The Influence of the Media

Literature on the influence of the media in rape cases is often quite negative. In 1982 the London Rape Crisis Centre in London reported that 'we have found that violence against women is frequently glorified by the media whilst the real suffering of women is dismissed or ignored' (Adler, 1987: 63). More recently the media has been accused of selling a distorted account of rape in society by focusing on false allegations, attacks by foreigners and attacks on young girls (Shields, 2008; see also Morway, 2006). However, the media has also been used by Rape Crisis Centres to launch campaigns and to raise awareness. The SAVI study in Ireland found that 76 per cent of participants 'felt that the media coverage of sexual abuse and violence was either somewhat or very beneficial' (McGee et al., 2002: 160).

Perceptions of the media among interviewees were mixed. Of the four interviewees who did not make a report, two had a positive impression of the media and two had a negative view of the influence of the media. Of the eight interviewees who did make a report, three took a positive view of the media, four had a negative view and one was uncertain about the influence of the media. Thus, there is no evidence that media reports influenced the interviewees in their decision-making. The principal benefits of the media identified in the interviews were the exposure of the issue of sexual violence and the encouragement of victims to come forward (107, 88), and that the media can sometimes be used to attain justice (39, 1). The main complaints made by the interviewees were that the media trivialised the issue (50), stereotyped the victims and tended to blame them (50, 3, 28), invaded the privacy of victims (23, 4) and discouraged reporting by reporting on lenient prison sentences (1). A number of interviewees reported that they found it difficult to read media reports about rape as doing so could trigger flashbacks.

The Impact of the Decision to Report

Three of the four interviewees who did not report their rape expressed ambivalence about their decision. One victim said that she wished that she had felt safe enough to make a report so that the suspect would be punished, but was too frightened of possible repercussions. Another commented:

> *I would have loved to have gone ahead and done something...and then I see on TV about these sentences or lack of sentence that offenders get and I think 'thank God, I didn't' (88).*

This interviewee further commented that the experience of a friend, whose rape case went to court but did not result in a prison sentence for the offender, provided confirmation for her decision. Rape victims who do not report may thus rationalize their decision through reference to the rarity of justice being achieved. There are repercussions for not reporting, however. One of the interviewees expressed a sense of guilt that she had not made a report as the suspect might be 'doing it to other people' (107). She also expressed frustration that she would never get answers from him about the rape:

> *It was the whole thing of not getting answers from him. Like never seeing this guy again. Obviously never wanting to see him again. But never seeing this guy again who had done this to me. And what was he thinking. What did he think? ... Did he think that he did anything wrong? That was my main problem (107).*

The interviewees who did report the rape were also often frustrated by a lack of closure. Only one rape complainant saw her case go to trial; she described how she felt 'suffocated', 'smothered', 'afraid' and 'full of fear' in the time it took for the case to go to court. She also said that her life fell apart after the trial; she said that she had great difficulty accepting the suspect's refusal to admit his guilt and take responsibility for his actions (3). Another interviewee, whose case did not go to court said:

> *I didn't get any court case. I didn't get any justice whatsoever. I didn't get any acknowledgement of what happened to me in the justice system at all, you know. It was a lot of hard work. It was a lot of unnecessary pain and disappointment and...an awful of disappointment because I really didn't think the system was so bad – such a letdown (4).*

This interviewee did not regret her decision to report the rape because she could now say that she had gone 'down every road' in addressing the issue, and she felt that making a report of the crime was necessary for her own well-being and healing (ibid.). By contrast, Interviewee 50 expressed her regret at going to the Gardaí; she said that she was humiliated by the experience of making the report and by the subsequent reaction from some of her friends and acquaintances.

Other interviewees were more positive, especially about the support they received. An interviewee whose rapist committed suicide shortly after the incident explained:

> *I can't imagine what it's like for people who don't report it. Because it must be very lonely kind of…I can't imagine if my parents didn't know about it now. It would be an awful thing really (30).*

Another interviewee was similarly grateful for the support from friends and family after they became aware of the situation through the report (48) while a third complainant argues that making the report ensured the end of her abusive marriage (23).

Dealing with the Gardaí

Several of the interviewees spoke about negative experiences in their dealings with the Gardaí. One of the principal themes concerned an apparent lack of sympathy exhibited by the interviewing Garda. One interviewee, for example, who did not make a report described how she felt like 'nobody' in the Garda Station and did not think she was being taken seriously. The Garda she spoke to:

> *… just didn't seem to have the time to listen or the time to do anything about it. She wasn't as sympathetic as I would … have expected. So I was, I was, I did feel very much alone' (28).*

Other interviewees expressed similar comments (50, 48). Temkin notes that studies have disclosed a discrepancy between victim and police needs. Police officers consider efficiency and professionalism to be of critical importance, and their focus is on getting the relevant information. Victims, by contrast, tend to look for a more supportive and personal contact and may prefer to share their story in a more holistic manner (Temkin, 2002: 270). The qualitative interviews presented here corroborate this view, suggesting that Garda compassion and support is very important to both the victims' experience and also, potentially, to the wider context of the case. For at least one victim, lack of support and empathy led to a sense of 'awkwardness' that prevented her from making a full report (50). In New York, a training programme was devised for sexual assault investigators that emphasised allowing victims to express their feelings while limiting questions to what was strictly necessary (Temkin, 2002: 273). Providing both the atmosphere and the opportunity for victims to talk about their experience, and the training for police officers to be able to glean information by listening to (as opposed to questioning) victims, may not only be supportive to the victim but may also encourage a more complete revelation of the incident.

Some of those interviewees who spoke positively about their initial experience with the Gardaí spoke of negative experiences thereafter. Interviewee 30, for example, described how she was left crying in the toilets of a local shop when she was informed on her mobile phone that the case was not proceeding because the defendant had committed suicide. Another was also given the news on her mobile phone that her case was not being prosecuted. She said that she was at her daughter's house and was emotionally unprepared for such news. She had previously been told that the news would be delivered in person and she 'would be allowed say to them – hang on one second ... I want to sit down and make myself a cup of tea or have a cigarette'. She describes being 'bluntly' told over the mobile phone that there would be no prosecution as the 'lowest point in my life' (1). These cases evidence a lack of sensitivity on the part of the Gardaí in breaking bad news. It is also of importance that the Gardaí follow through on their 'promises'; for the interviewee described above, the discord between her expectations of the manner in which she would be contacted and the reality added to her trauma and sense of injustice (1). A greater emphasis on sensitivity during Garda training and the development of a standard protocol in dealing with rape victims should be sufficient to deal with these issues.

A number of interviewees expressed dissatisfaction at the lack of communication from the Gardaí as regards the progress of the case (1, 23, 48, 50). One had no further contact with the Gardaí after making her report other than one phone call (50). Another interviewee who gave a glowing report of her experience with the Gardaí in the aftermath of the rape also spoke of the Gardaí as a negative influence, saying:

> *Well, the guards are good and the guards are bad. Ok, that was basically, I mean ... once a year we might get a phone call ... At the start I was really angry, you know, because, you know, this happened to me and I wanted it sorted and I didn't understand you know – what they were doing? Now it's like, ok, you know that there's other things, more important that the guards have to do ... I think it's the third year, yeah, and nothing. Nothing. Well, the last time they were in touch was probably a year ago, a year and a half ago, and that was about it. That was it, yeah (48).*

Poor communication between the Gardaí and victims further undermines the victim's sense of control and agency. Complaints regarding poor communication between the police and complainants are commonly reported in other studies (Temkin, 2002: 269). The absence of clear and regular information regarding their case's progress leads to a sense of being disconnected to their own experience – their rape, an ultimately personal experience, becomes public property. Compassion, sensitivity and good communication would go a long way towards providing victims with a sense of ownership over their own experience and the support and validation required to begin recovering from the ordeal of the rape.

Finally, several serious allegations were made against the Gardaí. One alleged that a number of the Gardaí were friends with the suspect and they 'lost' her complaint for months until a Superintendent ordered the complaint to be brought to him immediately (39). Another interviewee went to the Ombudsman after her complaint and forensic evidence were lost and mismanaged. She complained that the Garda in question was fined but only apologised to the Gardaí and not to her. The case never went to trial. The interviewee stated that she had received 'no satisfaction whatsoever from reporting' (1).

Experience with the Legal System

A number of the interviewees expressed reservations as to their treatment within the legal system more generally. A number of interviewees commented on their position within the system and drew bitter comparisons with the treatment given to suspects. Interviewee 39, for example, expressed frustration that she was 'only the witness in it ... as opposed to the important one' (39). Two interviewees noted that the suspect had plenty of time to get advice (39) or to think of an alibi (4). The latter interviewee was especially critical of the Garda investigation, stating that she had conducted her own investigation to discover the suspect's identity. She went on to note how little support is given to a rape victim:

> *I just found that you're extremely vulnerable and you're very broken and you're extremely sensitive ... you have to defend ... because the way the criminal justice system is ... you have to defend yourself from the minute it happens. You have to stand your ground ... you have to go through the process of ... of being examined, making statements, being questioned, being ridiculed, asking about the most private details of the assault, the rape or whatever, the attack. You get very little support ... you're in a very lonely kind of place (4).*

However, the same interviewee was allowed to give her statement some time after she gave basic information and after the medical examination, and spoke glowingly of how considerate and discreet the Gardaí were at this early stage (4). There is thus evidence that allowing victims some space to recover and gather their thoughts is beneficial to their well-being, *and* may lead to more accurate statements as they will have had time to 'make-sense' of their experience.

One interviewee that did have her case proceed to trial reported a negative experience of the trial itself. While the defendant had a 'trail of neighbours' and supporters with him, the Rape

Crisis counsellor that attended court with the victim was 'nearly thrown out' at the defence's request. The interviewee argues that the law supported the defendant (3).

> *I wasn't entitled to a solicitor as such ... I was allowed to have one just for my own ... but there's no real representation as such for victims ... I know that the accused in my case had free legal aid and had a top of the range defence team and they played a very good game.*

The interviewee further stated that she was treated poorly by the justice system, stating:

> *A victim in court is treated with very little respect and ... It was a horrible, horrific experience being up on the stand trying to defend yourself.*

This interviewee found the judge to be highly insensitive, and stated that 'the judge wished the accused a Merry Christmas and didn't even acknowledge who I was' (ibid.).

The Impact of the Rape

The impact of the rape on the mental and physical health, social activities, employment and personal relationships of the women interviewed was largely similar regardless of whether or not they had made a report. Only one interviewee had gone to trial, and her comment that her life 'came down and fell apart' after the trial suggests that the trial experience might delay the recovery of the victims (3). The trial may also exacerbate the negative impact of the rape, particularly as, in this case, the suspect was not convicted of rape. She notes that, 'the justice system and how I was treated in court is something that will always, always eat at me. It just wasn't, it wasn't right…it didn't [hold back the recovery] but it didn't help' (3). She further stated that it had taken her four years to be able to 'feel positive'. She rated herself 'around the 3 or the 4' in terms of her recovery, on a scale from 1, non-existent, to 5, complete (3). This rating was commensurate with the other interviewees' self-perceived recovery; on average they rated themselves at 3.5 and there was no evidence that making a report made any difference to this rating.

Some of the interviewees experienced a sense of isolation or disassociation from loved ones (88, 14, 50, 4, 107, 1). Four interviewees made suicide attempts or had had suicidal feelings, and one interviewee had begun to self-harm (50). Self-medicating through alcohol or prescription or illegal drugs was also common (14, 30, 3, 1). One interviewee had been admitted to the psychiatric ward of a hospital for treatment (50), while a number of the interviewees reported feeling 'numb' and 'like someone else' after the rape (4, 107, 88). The following comments are illustrative of these experiences:

Most nights, I use to buy a bottle of cider and then go up to the flat with my friends and just sit and drink it. They tried to stop me a few times and I did end up being really pathetic. Probably the lowest thing that I did was actually to take some of my mum's valiums one day ... and then ring my boyfriend to tell him 'bye'. I'm actually pretty ashamed of that (14).

I didn't feel that I was hugging my child. I had no feelings ... feelings of ... that nurturing loving mothering feeling that you have for your child ... I felt like a stranger, I felt strange because I felt numb ... I mean I looked ok but I just felt nothing, absolutely nothing ... I went through the whole process [of daughter's confirmation] and I laughed and I sat and I talked but I felt absolutely nothing. It was like I was dead inside (4).

Social interaction was affected by the rape: withdrawing from social life and being reserved when meeting new people was a common effect of the rape (50, 4, 107, 28, 1, 48).

I didn't trust myself at all. I found it very hard to trust my own judgement, you know. I found it very hard to go out in a social situation. I was doing it but it wasn't working. I would come home. I would cry my eyes out. I wanted to be on my own (107).

> *Basically some people found out like ... They said I deserved everything I got ... It was horrible. So socially, people look at me now and call me a weirdo. They look down on me. They don't know anything, they just judge you (50).*

> *I wouldn't have had a problem of being friendly before all this happened. Now, I would be wary of saying two words other than 'it's nice weather' or whatever to anyone I would meet that I didn't know (1).*

Feeling fearful and nervous in social environments was also a problem (107, 4, 1, 48, 50, 14).

> *Where I live it's in a very small rural area and I know that there would have been a lot of talk and I felt that for a long time afterwards going out and being seen and worrying about what people were saying. And, of course, I had also the fact that ... that I could bump into him anywhere in the area ... I was restricted (3).*

Two interviewees mentioned having difficulty resuming sexual relationships, while others felt distanced from people by their experience. A number of interviewees found that their friendships and other relationships were compromised by the impatience of others in relation to the time-frame of their recovery. One interviewee stated that she lost friends as they were 'fed up' with her depression, and that she 'was either getting drunk or crying all the time' (14).

Intimate relationships also ended after the rape for two interviewees (50, 88) while others felt that the rape put an ongoing strain on their intimate relationships (4, 48).

> *My boyfriend, who I really, really loved, me and him ended up breaking up because I was really insecure all the time. I thought he was going to ... I just couldn't understand why he was staying with me because I thought he could do better. You know, I think it actually affected him as well, a lot, what happened, I think that's it really (14).*

One interviewee explained that she entered into a series of 'bad relationships' after the rape (28). Another interviewee, however, listed her husband as a major support (3), and another told of how she was at the time of the interview involved in a very supportive, intimate relationship that was helping her recovery (30). Family relationships also experienced the dual aspects of increased strain and increased closeness. One interviewee described how her relationship to her mother improved, but found it difficult to relate to her father (30).

> *I'd say [my father] kind of blamed himself a little bit that he brought me back up and left me there on my own. Which wasn't his fault at all. But I've a feeling he did. I think he found that hard in his own way. But he never said it, but I know he did. Whereas my mother, she would cry or whatever. We'd talk that way. We'd have the odd crying session. But Dad wouldn't. So that way it was kind of tough for him (30).*

Yet another interviewee explained that families also need support to overcome the trauma of the rape (4), a view echoed by other participants.

> *From what I know of other people that have been through similar ... a lot of families split up and a lot of it is because there's nothing in the system to support families or let them know what to expect (4).*

Interviewees also spoke of a number of physical conditions developing as a result of the rape. These included gaining or losing weight, developing bulimia (50), insomnia, difficulty concentrating (4) and feelings of exhaustion (3). Employment was also affected as three interviewees either left or lost their job (3, 50, 39), two experienced a negative impact on their work (1, 88), and one missed a year of work (4). Two interviewees, both students, dropped out of college after the rape (30, 14) and another stated that she had lost all career motivation (48).

> *I did leave college because ... I couldn't go in because I was worried in case people started asking me questions ... I didn't want tutors asking me where I was and then start me bursting into tears and having to run away ... and it has affected me because anytime I go looking for a job – 'how come you were only in college for two years, blah, blah, blah'. And you can't say that to them (14).*

Both of the students did eventually return to college, while one of the women who lost her job, and two others whose work was negatively affected, are now in better, happier employment. Although still troubled by the negative effects of the rape, all the interviewees but one reported feeling stronger and better able to cope. Many of the interviewees noted that the relationships that survived the difficult aftermath of the rape had become closer and stronger than before; some had also made new friends through the experience (39, 88, 14, 30, 107, 28, 3). Other positive outcomes included:

- Being able to trust themselves more;
- Being more vigilant and careful;
- A rekindling of their faith;
- Being better able to cope with stress;
- Being able to disregard gossip;
- Greater recognition of the importance of family and friends;
- Improved self-esteem and the ability to say 'no';
- Being able to re-evaluate and improve their lifestyle; and
- Being able to make others more aware of potential danger (4, 107, 28, 30, 39, 23, 14).

Victim Recommendations

The interviewees were given the opportunity to express their opinion on a variety of specific issues and recommendations for the legal system, some of which have already been brought into effect. Those interviewees who expressed an opinion invariably endorsed all the options to the maximum degree possible. A number of interviewees endorsed the idea of specialist Gardaí, prosecutors and judges:

> *It's not enough to have an ordinary guard because I had a young ban Garda with me who I was feeling sorry for because she was young and embarrassed and she didn't know how to handle the situation ... she was embarrassed while I was being examined.... Yes, yes I suppose ... specialist prosecutors but then again like also ... there would need to be special settings and hearings ... [Judges] need to be kept in tune with what's going on (4).*

One interviewee was especially enthusiastic about the provision of free legal aid:

> *Now, that one I would definitely go for because if I had legal advice that could have done an awful lot to help me (39).*

The law as it stands makes provision for free legal aid to rape victims for the purpose of securing legal advice but it is unclear how often these provisions are invoked.

The complainants questioned all indicated that knowing the reasons behind the prosecutor's decision was very important, and that they should not be excluded from decisions that would have a significant impact on their life.

> *Even if he gives reasons or an explanation I think it's just the whole thing of being acknowledged again. Somebody makes a decision about the rest of you life and you're not entitled to an explanation? (4)*

The DPP is currently piloting a scheme under which reasons will be given to victims if they so choose. At present, this scheme applies only to homicide cases but if it proves successful the DPP has indicated his willingness to extend the scheme to sexual offences (Director of Public Prosecutions, 2008: 26)

Interviewees also expressed support for the provision of adequate services in court such as separation waiting facilities:

> *Separate waiting areas? Don't tell me you have to wait ... there isn't separate waiting areas is there not? ... Even with unfair dismissals they had a small room in the thing itself (39).*

> *I had to pass by the accused and his traddle of neighbours ... it was just the way the courts were set up (3).*

The new criminal courts complex in Dublin have been designed with the needs of victims in mind. In particular, provision is being made for victim support rooms and ancillary services, along with facilities for prosecution witnesses, including vulnerable witnesses in a secure area (Courts Service, 2007)

Both the interviewees that reported the rape, and those that did not, felt that current provisions for dealing with offenders were inadequate. Apart from one participant who recommended castration (4), all the women interviewed stated that offenders should be sentenced to prison, with most adding that they should be given longer sentences. Rehabilitation was mentioned by three women in conjunction with prison (4, 28, 3), while two other women argued that exposing or 'naming-and-shaming' the offender would be more effective than prison in preventing recidivism. One woman who did not report felt that 'they'll get their come-uppance in the end, whether they go to prison or not' (14). Regarding informing the victim's of the offender's release from prison, on interviewee said:

> *I know that they're supposed to have a certain amount of rights but I honestly think that there should be a system where if somebody is convicted of a sexual offence like that that there should ... there should be a probation period for when they come out of prison. That they should be monitored – tagged – and that the victims should know and that other people that they've hurt should know – people in the area. They shouldn't just be allowed back into society (4).*

Although the majority of women interviewed did not believe there was anything that could be done by the offender to help them recover, five women did say that if the offender admitted his guilt, they would feel better. One woman said, 'I imagine yes if it were to happen [offender admit guilt and explain the reason why] it would definitely have a huge ... effect' (28). Other interviewees made similar statements:

> *I just wanted him to admit what he had done and I know he never would have admitted it but I wanted to put him in the spotlight because he wasn't in the spotlight! ... I was the one in the spotlight, still was. He was never brought into the spotlight (4).*

> *Obviously I want to hear him give his reasons and tell me why but at the same time he probably doesn't even realise he did anything wrong. I suppose to make him realise he did something wrong. I'd love for him to know what he had done (107).*

Conclusion

Participants that reported the incident usually did so following immediate support and advice to that effect. This would suggest that, although victims often listed some of the reasons contained on the interviewer's card when posed directly, these motives (i.e., protecting others, wanting justice, etc.) were more likely assigned retroactively, possibly to provide the victim with a sense of agency in the decision to report. It is telling that only one interviewee cited any of the interviewer's reasons without prompt, when she claimed that she reported the rape for protection from her partner (23). Thus, although Greenberg and Ruback (1992) perceive the decision-making process as largely personal, albeit subject to social influence, the qualitative study indicates that reporting the rape initially occurs, primarily, externally to the *victim's* cognitive processes. Greenberg and Beach's more recent study (2004) similarly noted the significant rise in victim reports where victims were *advised* by others to report a crime. Nevertheless, social and contextual factors and social norms regarding the guards, rape, and reporting crimes, no doubt influence the reactions of others to the victim of rape and would thus be implicated in advice-giving. Further, in cases in which the rape was reported after a delay, it is likely that other decision-making processes do come into effect as the initial shock, and accompanying denial, begins to subside.

All the victims listed the Rape Crisis Centres as an important and positive influence in their recovery, although one victim felt that she was too tired to talk anymore and felt their help was somewhat limited (48). Another interviewee was upset at the non-directive policy of the Rape Crisis Centres under which her counsellor would not advise her as to whether she should make a report to the Gardaí (39).

There is no indication in the interviews that the experience of reporting a rape has a significantly different effect on recovery rates than the decision not to make a report. Women from both groups reported a variety of effects related to Post-Traumatic Stress Disorder. It is noteworthy that a number of rape victims expressed difficulty recalling the rape or aspects of the rape: PTSD has been shown both to damage the hippocampus causing physiological brain changes implicated in memory loss (Bremner, 2000), and cause disassociative amnesia (Biondo, 2007: 4). This is an effect that is likely to have a negative influence on the accuracy of the victim's statement (and which may also be used by defence counsel at trial to impeach the complainant's credibility). Thus, allowing a complainant some time to recuperate before taking a full statement might be in the interests of the prosecution as much as it would be in the interests of the complainant herself.

It is also worth noting the large number of women interviewed who experienced a negative impact on their employment. The economic consequences of rape may be an issue that requires further attention. Job loss, inability to work and the absenteeism associated with trauma and possible court appearances are likely to have immediate financial costs to the victim of rape and may impede their long-term career progression. Further, considering the large numbers of women who do experience rape in their adult years there may also be wider, socioeconomic consequences to rape. This again is an issue that will require further attention.

The follow-up interviews demonstrate the tremendous courage, strength and emotional dexterity possessed by these rape survivors. All of the women, both those that reported and those that did not, went through very difficult periods that impacted on their lives socially, physically, emotionally and professionally, but all perceive their recovery as progressing. There was no indication that the women who reported experienced a more difficult, or easier, recovery than those that did not. Nor was their any indication that the women who reported their rape were influenced by significantly different issues to make the report. Rather, situational circumstances appear to have a much more significant initial effect on the decision to report. The interviews indicate the importance of privacy, validation, compassion, communication, and empathy from family, friends, counsellors, guards and prosecutors to the long-term recovery from the trauma of rape. All of the victims indicate that their recovery began when they were able to start talking about what happened to them and list the Rape Crisis Centres and particularly the Rape Crisis Counsellors as the primary or secondary source of support. The remarkable resilience demonstrated by the women interviewed may be due, in part, to the fact that they all accessed help through Rape Crisis Centres. For victims of rape who have never reported, nor perhaps even disclosed the incident, it is worth considering the words of one of the interviewees:

> *I was looking for a code book, a guide book all the time for a long, long time of what to expect next so I could be prepared. And no such things exists of course, but I asked advice from the Rape Crisis Centre and I used the hotline continually which was great because you really do need people to talk to ... and as you grow, you do get stronger, you do ... you do recover ... you do ... become stronger in yourself ... you become far more appreciative of where you've been, what you've been through and who you're becoming now (4).*

Chapter 5

PROSECUTING RAPE

This chapter examines the second attrition point in the legal system – the decision by the DPP whether or not to prosecute. Finlay J., in the Supreme Court, stated:

> ... in regard to the DPP I reject also the submission that he has only got discretion as to whether to prosecute or not prosecute in any particular case related *exclusively to the probative value of the evidence* laid before him. Again, I am satisfied that there are many other factors which may be appropriate and proper for him to take into consideration (O'Higgins, 2008: 6 – emphasis added).

Due to the nature of rape cases, in which physical evidence is so often lacking, these 'other factors' may take on even greater importance. The factors that are *most* influential in the decision to prosecute a rape case, however, have remained unknown because the DPP is under no obligation to explain his prosecutorial decisions. This study was therefore designed to examine which case, complainant, and suspect characteristics were influential in the DPP's decision-making process in relation to rape complaints, using quantitative regression techniques designed to reveal significant relationships.

Describing Rape

Case Characteristics

The complainants were overwhelmingly female: 96 per cent were women, with just 4 per cent (or 22) being men. This statistic conforms to other studies that also identify adult rape as a primarily female problem (e.g., McGee et al., 2002; 65). Just over 27 per cent of complaints concerned traditional rape as defined by section 2 of the Criminal Law (Rape) Act 1981 on its own or in combination with other lesser offences, with another 52.6 per cent of offences recorded simply as 'rape'. It is likely that most of these unspecified rapes were also section two rapes. If this assumption is made, almost 80 per cent of reported rapes were classified under section two. The remainder of the cases concerned charges of rape under section four of the Criminal Law (Rape) (Amendment) Act 1990 or a combination of the two forms of rape.

Rape was most likely to occur in the complainant's own home (30.1 per cent) followed by the suspect's home (22.4 per cent) or in another private setting (16.5 per cent) such as a hotel room or the home of a friend. These figures indicate that the vast majority of rapes in Ireland (69 per cent) occur in a private setting. If the rapes that occur in private vehicles are considered also to have occurred in a private location, then 77.8 per cent of rapes occurred in a private setting. This finding is substantiated by most other studies (e.g. Myhill and Allen, 2002: 37).

Complainant/Suspect Relationship

The majority, 58.2 per cent, of rape suspects were classified as friends or acquaintances of the complainant. Further, current or past partners or spouses accounted for 12.7 per cent of suspects, and a further 3.5 per cent of suspects were involved in a dating relationship with the complainant. The figure for current spouses/ partners accused of rape is substantially lower than that found by Myhill and Allen in their survey (2002). This may indicate that domestic rape in Ireland is significantly under-reported to the Gardaí. Strangers accounted for 10.9 per cent of suspects.

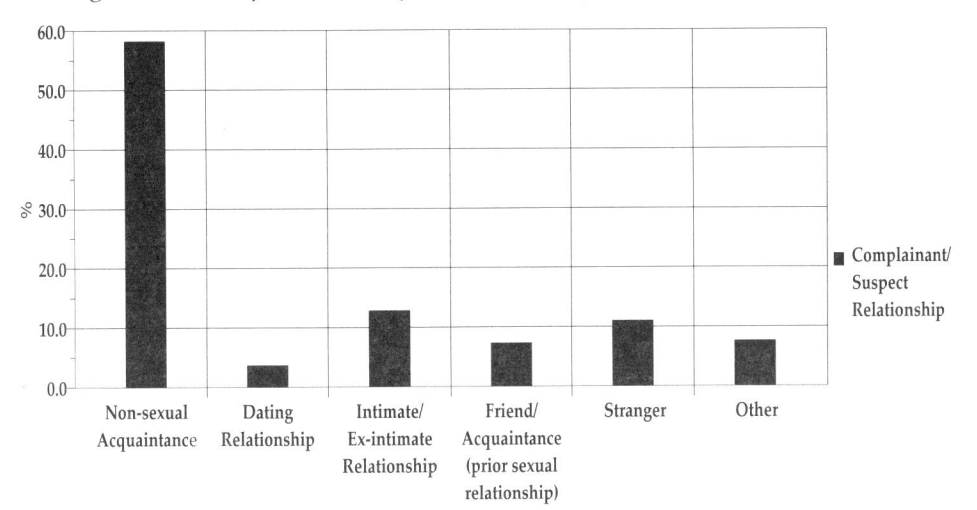

Figure 5.1: Complainant/Suspect Relationship

[Bar chart showing Complainant/Suspect Relationship percentages: Non-sexual Acquaintance ~58%, Dating Relationship ~3%, Intimate/Ex-intimate Relationship ~13%, Friend/Acquaintance (prior sexual relationship) ~8%, Stranger ~12%, Other ~8%]

In total, 45 cases involved more than one suspect or more than one victim. In five cases one complainant made complaints against more than one suspect, representing a total of ten suspects. Of these cases, five suspects were tried and convicted, another was charged, and four more were not prosecuted. County Dublin had the highest number of 'gang rapes', followed by Limerick which otherwise demonstrated a disproportionately low number of rape cases. There were also a number of cases that involved one suspect and more than one victim. Four suspects fit the description of a 'serial rapist' – committing rape against multiple victims on separate occasions. These cases were highly likely to be prosecuted and convicted: only one of the nine victims did not have her complaint prosecuted and convictions were secured in six cases, with two further cases awaiting trial.

National Distribution of Rape Cases

County Dublin had the highest rate of reported rape in Ireland at 32.3 per cent, followed by Cork with 12.3 per cent, both representing a slightly larger than expected share when compared to the population distribution (Central Statistics Office, 2002). Galway and Waterford each accounted for 4.2per cent of rapes, followed by Donegal at 4 per cent and Clare and Kildare at 3.5 per cent each. Leitrim, Offaly and Longford had the fewest reported rapes. These statistics largely echo the population distribution although some counties were over-represented. Waterford, for example, accounted for just 2.6 per cent of the Irish population but accounted for 4.2 per cent of rapes. Limerick, by contrast, accounted for 4.5 per cent of the population but accounted for just 2.9 per cent of rapes. The predominant position of Dublin and Cork accords with the finding that rape reports are made most frequently in cities (47.6 per cent), followed by towns (42.1 per cent) and then rural areas/villages which represent just 9.8 per cent of rapes in Ireland. Again, however, the low number of rapes occurring in Limerick, which has the fourth highest population density after Dublin, Louth and Kildare, stands out (ibid.). A possible explanation for this is that the presence in Dublin and Cork of Sexual Assault Treatment Units (SATU), which were not present in the west of Ireland at the time of the study, has an effect on the reporting of rapes. Indeed, it was found that in County Dublin, 17 rapes are reported per 100 000 people, as opposed to 8.5 rapes per 100,000 people in County Mayo, one of the furthest counties from a SATU.

Myhill and Allen's study in England and Wales found that women living in urban areas were fractionally more likely to report an incident of sexual victimisation than those women living in rural areas (2002: 24). However, the high disproportion between rural and urban rates of rape reporting found in this study suggests that rape is very under-reported in rural Ireland.

Figure 5.2: Frequency of Rape Offence by County

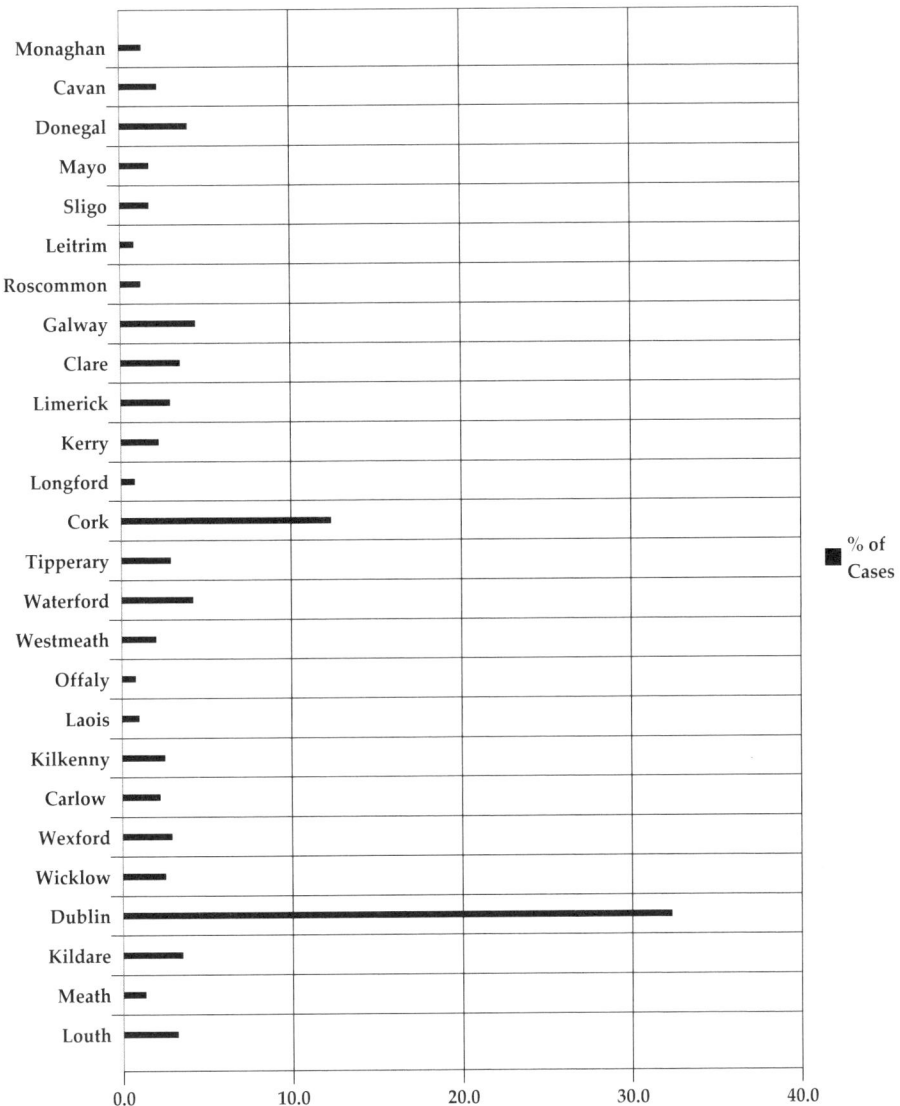

County	% of Cases
Monaghan	
Cavan	
Donegal	
Mayo	
Sligo	
Leitrim	
Roscommon	
Galway	
Clare	
Limerick	
Kerry	
Longford	
Cork	~12
Tipperary	
Waterford	
Westmeath	
Offaly	
Laois	
Kilkenny	
Carlow	
Wexford	
Wicklow	
Dublin	~32
Kildare	
Meath	
Louth	

Other Characteristics

A slight majority (38.6 per cent) of rapes were reported within an hour of the offence. A report within 24 hours was the next most common category (37.4 per cent). Complaints were withdrawn by the complainant in 27 per cent of cases, while suspected false complaints accounted for 6.1 per cent of cases. This percentage of suspected false complaints fell in the middle of the range indicated by Kelly et al. in Britain of between three and eight per cent (2005). These issues will be discussed in greater detail in the following sections. In nine cases, a review of the decision not to prosecute was requested by either the complainant or by a Garda, but the original decision not to prosecute was upheld in all nine cases.

Complainant Characteristics

Nationality

As stated, the vast majority of complainants were women. The vast majority (87.2 per cent) of complainants were of Irish nationality. Given that over 91 per cent of people in Ireland were Irish (Central Statistics Office, 2002), there is consequently a slight over-representation of non-nationals among the complainant population. The majority of non-national complainants (6.7 per cent) were from other Western European countries, 1.7 per cent were Eastern European, 0.3 per cent were from South America, and 1 per cent of complainants came from each of North America, Asia, Africa and Australia/New Zealand. Each of these categories of non-nationals were slightly over-represented compared to the population as a whole.

Age, Marital Status and Employment

Complainants were predominantly young, with almost half (49.2 per cent) under 25 and a further 28.7 per cent under 35. Thus, a full three-quarters of the complainants were under the age of 35. The majority were also single (35.3 per cent). A further 22.4 per cent were in a relationship, 15.6 per cent were married or cohabiting and 8.2 per cent were divorced or separated. It is noteworthy, however, that the marital status of 18.4 per cent of complainants was unknown, a figure that is sufficiently high that it could make a significant difference to the relationship distribution.

Complainants were also most likely to be unemployed (27.5 per cent) or in manual or unskilled employment (26.8 per cent). Just over 12 per cent of complainants were students, 11.4 per cent were employed in a professional or skilled job and 4.2 per cent of complainants were homemakers. Bailey's study similarly found that reported rapes were disproportionately high among low-income groups (1992: 335). As with marital status, a potentially significant number of complainants' employment status was unknown (17.4 per cent). These results are consistent with the age group of the majority of complainants.

These findings are consistent with those of the British Crime Survey. Myhill and Allen concluded that the typical rape victim in Britain was young, with women between 16 and 19 the most likely to be victimised and those between 20 and 24 almost equally represented among victims (2002: 21). Victims were also more likely to be from low-income households and to be single (ibid.: 23). However, Myhill and Allen also found, however, that students had the highest rate of sexual victimisation (ibid.: 24), unlike the findings in this study. It is possible that students in Ireland are less likely to report their rape to the Gardaí.

Alcohol Consumption

Alcohol consumption by complainants was demonstrably high, with over 80 per cent of complainants having consumed alcohol around the time of the commission of the offence. Further, 45.4 per cent of complainants were described as severely intoxicated at the time of the commission of the offence. Similarly, the Dublin SATU noted that in 2003, 58 per cent of its clients had consumed more than four units of alcohol (Rotunda, 2003). Approximately 20 per cent of complainants were moderately intoxicated and another 20 per cent were not intoxicated. These findings place Irish complainants at the top of the list for alcohol consumption based on previous studies carried out in the United States and in Britain (Finney, 2004: 2). Further, these finding indicate that alcohol consumption is higher than previously recorded in Irish studies of sexual violence. For instance, McGee et al. records alcohol consumption as present in approximately half of all adult sexual violence cases (2002: 100), although this figure relates to all forms of sexual violence and not just rape.

Suspect Characteristics

Nationality

Table 5.1 shows the nationality of the suspects. Although 75.1 per cent were Irish nationals, this is significantly below the 91.5 per cent expected if suspects were proportionally distributed amongst the population. With the exception of suspects from North America, whose numbers were proportionate to the population of North American nationals living in Ireland, all the other nationalities demonstrated a higher than expected frequency of being accused of rape. Particularly significant are the differences between the resident national populations of Africa and Eastern Europe and the number of individuals accused of rape from these countries. African men were approximately ten times more likely to be accused of rape than would be expected, and Eastern European suspects were over seven times more likely to be accused given the proportion of the population that comes from Eastern Europe.

Table 5.1: Nationality of Suspects

Suspect's Country of Origin	Number	%
Ireland	474	75.1
Other Western Europe	41	6.5
Eastern Europe	31	4.9
Africa	31	4.9
Asia	15	2.4
North America	4	0.6
South America	5	0.8
Australia/New Zealand	3	0.5
Unknown	27	4.3
Total	631*	100

* Due to several cases having more than one suspect, the number of suspects is higher than the number of cases.

Personal Characteristics

In 92.8 per cent of cases, the suspect was identified but a great deal of personal information was not present on the files. The relationship status, for example, of nearly one-third of suspects was unknown. If those cases were excluded, then suspects were most likely to be single, followed by married or cohabitating, and then by those in a relationship. Suspects were least likely to be divorced or separated. Of those whose employment status was known, suspects were most likely to be employed in a manual or unskilled job (35.3 per cent), with 22.3 per cent being unemployed and 12.7 per cent being employed in a professional or skilled job. Suspects tended to be somewhat older than complainants, with 36.3 per cent of defendants falling into the 25-34 year old category. A further 32.3 per cent of suspects were under 25 years old, while 22.3 per cent were between the ages of 35 and 44.

The majority of suspects have no previous convictions, although for one-fifth of suspects there was no information about prior convictions. Of those suspects who had been previously convicted, the majority had convictions for violence and/or other non-sexual offences.

Alcohol Consumption

The suspects' level of intoxication mirrors that of the complainants. The great majority of suspects were intoxicated at the time of the commission of the offence, with 40.8 per cent being severely intoxicated and a further 26.6 per cent being moderately intoxicated. About one in twelve were only mildly intoxicated and just under one-quarter (23.4 per cent) had consumed no alcohol at all. In 16 per cent of cases, the suspect's level of intoxication, if any, was unknown. These results are broadly similar to those found by studies conducted in the United States and in Britain (Finney, 2004: 2).

Defence Claims

As expected, the most popular defence offered by suspects during interrogation by the Gardaí was that the intercourse was consensual. This defence was offered by nearly half of all suspects, followed by a denial of intercourse by one-quarter of suspects. Almost one suspect in twelve made a confession during interrogation.

Table 5.2: Defences Offered by Suspects

Defence Offered by Suspect	Number	% (Rounded)
Consensual Sexual Intercourse	304	48
No Sex Occurred	151	24
Believed Consent Had Been Given	5	1
Consensual Sexual Activity Occurred but Denial of Sexual Intercourse	14	2
Confessed	42	7
Gave No Answer	32	5
Was Not Questioned	44	7
Other	39	6
Total	631	100

Aggravating and Consent Features

A number of aggravating and consent features were considered in the analysis. It was found that in just under 95 per cent per cent of cases only one suspect was involved. Weapons were used or threatened in 8.6 per cent of cases, while physical force was a common feature of rape in Ireland, present in two-thirds (66.7 per cent) of cases. In 25.8 per cent of cases the complainant incurred physical injury due to the rape or related violence. Verbal threats were alleged in 21.7 per cent of complaints, while the covert administration of alcohol or other drug (excluding the so-called date-rape drugs such as Rohypnol) was virtually non-existent with only three cases having this feature, and a further three cases in which complainants claimed to have been *forcefully* administered a drug. In 20 cases (3.4 per cent), complainants claimed that Rohypnol or other date-rape drugs were administered, although there was no corroborating medical evidence on the files.

In terms of consent features, it was found that verbal non-consent was the most common expression of refusal and was present in 68.7 per cent of cases. Physical resistance was offered in 49 per cent of cases. It should also be noted that 93 cases (15.6 per cent) had no indication of either aggravating or non-consent features. In 61 of these cases, the complainants were severely intoxicated, indicating that potentially 10 per cent of incidents involved individuals who were either unable to offer consent or express non-consent, either verbally or physically, due to incapacitation from voluntary intoxication.

Risk Factors

The term 'risk factors' denote issues identified in the literature generally as decisions by or characteristics of the complainant that facilitated the incident. It needs to be stressed that denoting certain decisions or characteristics as risk factors does not in any way indicate that the complainant was *responsible* for what happened; rather, this label is applied in a purely factual sense.

The presence of a variety of risk factors was explored:

- The complainant agreeing to accompany the suspect to his residence, car or hotel room;
- The complainant invited the suspect to her residence;
- The complainant was hitch-hiking alone;
- The complainant was walking alone at night;
- The complainant worked in the sex industry or had a history of prostitution;
- The complainant was alone in a bar;
- The complainant had a disability.

The most common such factor was the complainant agreeing to accompany the suspect to his residence (24.7 per cent of complainants). Complainants who accused a friend/acquaintance with whom they had no previous sexual relationship and those in a dating relationship were most likely to have this risk factor identified in the questionnaire supplied by the DPP. However, this may be due to Garda recording procedures – when complainants and suspects are in a current relationship it may be deemed unnecessary to record this information. Thus, while 32.6 per cent of those in a non-sexual friendship/acquaintanceship with the accused are recorded as having agreed to accompany the suspect to his residence, only 2.7 per cent of spouses had similar information recorded. A further 10.4 per cent of complainants had voluntarily invited the suspect to her place of residence. The group that most commonly demonstrated this behaviour were friends/ acquaintances with a prior sexual relationship. Over one-third of complainants had willingly gone to the private location in which the incident occurred.

Relationship	% of Complainants Who Voluntarily Accompanied Suspect to His Residence in Each Relationship Group	% of Complainants Who Invited Suspect to Her Place of Residence
Friend/Acquaintance (no prior sexual relationship)	32.6	11.8
Dating/Seeing Each Other	28.6	14.3
Current Spouse/ Partner	2.7	0
Ex-Spouse/ Partner	12.8	15.4
Friend/Acquaintance (prior sexual relationship)	20.9	20.9
Stranger	13.8	1.5

The second most common risk factor identified in this study is disability. Almost one-fifth (18.8 per cent) of complainants were recorded as having a physical or intellectual disability or a history of mental illness. Psychiatric illness was by far the most common disability, representing 13.1 per cent of the total number of cases, followed by intellectual disability at 5 per cent. Only 6 cases had evidence of physical disability.

Fewer than 10 per cent of complainants had been walking alone at night, including a small number of complainants who were working as a prostitute at the time. Nearly five per cent of complainants had been in a bar alone on the occasion of the offence, although 14.6 per cent of complainants had a history of alcohol abuse and a further 7.4 per cent had a history of drug abuse. Four per cent of cases involved complainants with a history of prostitution and a further three per cent of complainants had past criminal convictions. Only one case involved hitchhiking and a further three involved work in the sex industry (other than prostitution), making these insignificant risk factors.

Evidential Factors

Complainants made a statement to the Gardaí in 97.5 per cent of cases and 86.7 per cent of cases had evidence of notes or memos of the interview with the suspect contained in the file, making the complainant statement and the suspects interview the most common types of evidence in rape cases in Ireland. The medical examination report was contained in the file sent to the DPP in 70 per cent of cases, with forensic evidence present in the file in 49.2 per cent of complaints. Information regarding suspect identification by the complainant was contained in the file in 48.8 per cent of cases. Although DNA evidence was present in the files sent to the DPP in 14.6 per cent of cases, it was relevant in somewhat fewer, representing 12.6 per cent of rape cases. Similarly, forensic medical evidence was relevant in 44.9 per cent of rape complaints.

Prosecutions for Rape in Ireland

Figure 5.3 shows the final outcomes of all cases received by the DPP between 2000 and 2004, excluding cases in which the complainant withdrew her allegation. These cases were excluded from this aspect of the analysis because such cases are effectively unprosecutable. The DPP prosecuted 29.7 per cent of rape complaints, with 9.6 per cent resulting in a guilty plea and less than 4 per cent resulting in a conviction for rape. In total, 17.8 per cent of complaints resulted in some form of legal recognition of a crime (i.e., resulting in a conviction for some offence). A small number of cases representing 2.5 per cent of cases from this period are still awaiting trial, invariably due to an inability to locate the suspect. The results indicate that when a rape case does proceed to trial it has a nearly 60 per cent chance of resulting in a guilty plea or conviction on *some* charge, although the charge for which the offender was ultimately convicted may be significantly reduced. In two cases, the original charge of rape was down-graded to a non-sexual offence; consequently these cases could not have resulted in a rape conviction.

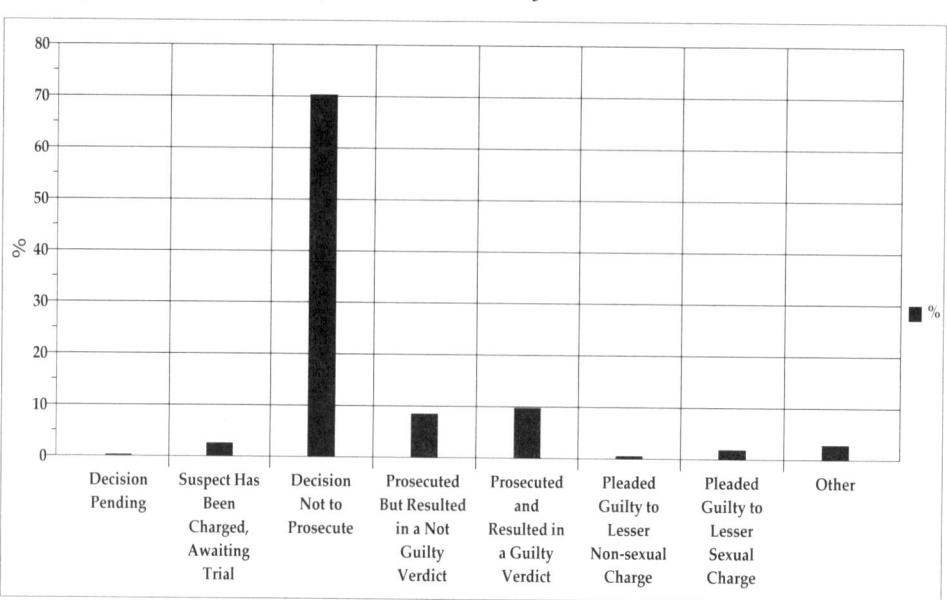

Figure 5.3: Outcomes of Cases Received by DPP, 2000-2004

N.B. Withdrawn Complaints Excluded

INFLUENTIAL FACTORS IN THE DECISION TO PROSECUTE

In order to examine the relationship between variables a number of statistical tests were used. Nonparametric correlation was utilised, with a Spearman's Rho (ϱ) correlation coefficient, to test the strength and direction of the relationship between ordinal variables and Pearson's R correlation coefficient (r) was used to test the relationship between scale variables. The Chi Square (χ^2) measure of association was used to determine the existence of a relationship between nominal variables, with Phi (Φ) used to examine the strength of the relationship in 2 x 2 tables and Cramér's V to examine the strength of the relationship in larger tables. In order to determine relationships between variables and the decision to prosecute, binary logistic regression was used. The Chi-square goodness-of-fit test was used to test the null hypothesis that the factors considered do not influence the decision to prosecute and the Hosmer and Lemeshow goodness-of-fit test was used to determine if the logistic model's estimates fit the data at an acceptable level.

Offense Location

Although the location of the offence did not demonstrate a significant relationship to the DPP's decision to prosecute a rape case, the location of the rape was significantly associated with the time lapsed between the rape and its report (χ^2 = 89.925, df 33, p<0.05, Cramér's V= 0.163, p<0.05). Although 54.7 per cent of rapes that occurred in a public place were reported within an hour of their occurrence, only 34.2 per cent of rapes that occurred in a private place were promptly reported.

Complainant Characteristics

No complainant characteristics, or combination of complainant characteristics (apart from the risk factors discussed below), had a significant influence on the decision to prosecute a rape complaint. Cases were then divided into stranger and known categories and logistic regressions were run to test whether complainant characteristics are more or less influential in each of these categories. No statistically significant relationships were found. It is also of note that no significant relationships were found when complainant characteristics were compared against discordant suspect characteristics, such as where the complainant was employed and the suspect was not.

Suspect Characteristics

Logistic regression revealed a relationship between the suspect's nationality and the likelihood of prosecution. Irish suspects were somewhat less likely to be prosecuted than non-Irish suspects (β= -0.171, S.E. 0.073, Wald 5.563, sig. 0.018, Exp(β) 0.843). The suspect's relationship status was shown to have no influence in the DPP's decision, but where the suspect was employed he was less likely to be prosecuted (professional or skilled employment: β= -0.942, S.E. 0.433, Wald 4.728, sig. 0.030, Exp(β) 0.390; manual or unskilled employment: β= -0.800, S.E. 0.363, Wald 4.852, sig. 0.028, Exp(β) 0.449). This echoes the findings of Brown et al's study (2007: 361). Where the suspect had no previous convictions, he was less likely to be prosecuted (β= -1.749, S.E. 0.260, Wald 45.072, sig. 0.000, Exp(β) 0.174), a finding similarly represented in Holmstrom and Burgess' study (1978: 43), but the type or number of previous convictions had no significant effect on the DPP's decision. The number of previous convictions was positively associated with both the number of evidentiary factors (r =0.099, n = 451, p < 0.05) and the number of aggravating factors (r = 0.152, n = 451, p<0.001). As evidentiary and aggravating factors have been shown to positively influence the decision to prosecute, there is likely to be a collinear effect between these factors.

If the suspect was known to the complainant the case was less likely to be prosecuted (β= -0.920, S.E. 372, Wald 6.111, sig. 0.013, Exp(β) 0.398). A second regression was run in which unidentified suspects were excluded to assess whether this impacted on the relationship between the suspect's relationship (known/unknown) and the decision to prosecute. It was found that the positive relationship between stranger assailants and the decision to prosecute was increased once unidentified suspect cases were excluded

(β=1.395, S.E. 0.299, Wald 21.700, sig. 0.000, Exp(β) 0.248). This result is substantiated by a number of studies conducted in other common law jurisdictions, including Adler (1987), Estrich (1987), Lievore (2005) and Klippenstine et al. (2007).

Intoxication

Logistic regression found that the suspect's level of intoxication does not significantly influence the prosecutor's decision. Similarly, the complainant's level of intoxication did not evidence an effect on the decision to prosecute; however, there was a positive relationship between the suspect's and the complainant's level of intoxication ($\rho = 0.477$, n = 486 p< 0.000) as demonstrated in Figure 5.4. Further, the younger the suspect, the more intoxicated both the complainant ($\rho = -0.94$, n = 476, p<0.05) and the suspect ($\rho = -0.124$, n = 472, p< 0.01) were, and the younger the suspect, the younger the complainant ($\rho = 0.420$, n = 472, p<0.000). There was no significant relationship found between the age of the complainant and her level of intoxication.

Figure 5.4: Comparison of Complainant's and Suspect's Levels of Intoxication

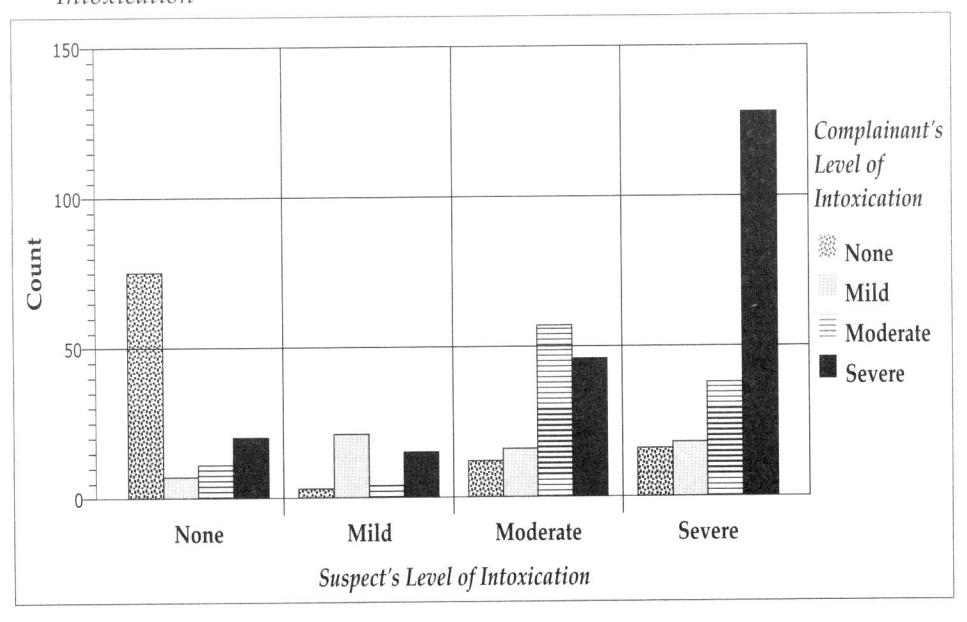

Aggravating and Consent Features

Of the aggravating and consent features considered, the use or threatened use of a weapon was the only feature that was statistically significant on its own to the decision to prosecute a rape complaint (β=1.779, S.E. 0.317, Wald 31.425, sig. 0.000, Exp(β) 5.924). Where the complainant incurred physical injury *and* was threatened with or had a weapon used against her, the DPP was also likely to prosecute the case (β=0.759, S.E. 0.093, Wald 66.359, sig. 0.000, Exp(β) 2.136). Similarly, where the complainant incurred physical injury *and* there was relevant forensic evidence, the case was more likely to be prosecuted (β=0.869, S.E. 0.110, Wald 62.370, sig. 0.000, Exp(β) 2.384). Multiple offenders, verbal non-consent, the presence of physical injury only, the use of physical force, physical resistance or the covert administration of a date-rape type drug demonstrated no relationship to the decision to prosecute. The covert or forceful administration of other drugs was excluded from the analysis due to the small number of cases expressing this feature.

Aggravating factors are significantly associated with a number of other features. The more aggravating and non-consent features that were present, the sooner the offence was likely to be reported (ϱ = -0.170, n = 564, p<0.000). The number of evidentiary features also had a positive linear relationship to the number of aggravating and consent features (ϱ = 0.313, n = 565, p<0.000). Cases that involved suspects with previous convictions were also more likely to have more aggravating features and to have offered resistance/non-consent in more ways (ϱ = 0.271, n = 449, p<0.000).

A significant association is also evident between relationship and physical injury (χ^2= 32.700, df 9, p<0.000, Cramér's *V*= 0.241, p<0.000). Although 26.8 per cent of all complainants reported physical injury, 45 per cent of complainants were injured in stranger cases, compared to 29.6 per cent of cases involving known suspects. When intimate (dating, spouse/partner, ex-spouse/partner, and sexual acquaintance) rapes were exclusively considered, the rate of injury rose to 40 per cent. There is also a significant association between verbal threats and relationship

(χ^2= 38.013, df 9, p<0.000, Cramér's V= 0.260, p<0.000). Verbal threats were most common where the complainant and suspect were dating (present in 50 per cent of these cases), followed by strangers (40 per cent), current spouses and partners (38.7 per cent) and ex-spouses and partners (27.8 per cent). Physical force was most commonly reported in rapes that involved suspects and complainants who were dating, and this relationship demonstrated a significant but weak association (χ^2=22.357, df 9, p< 0.01, Cramér's V = 0.194, p<0.01).

Figure 5.5: Complainant/Suspect Relationship and the Use of Physical Force

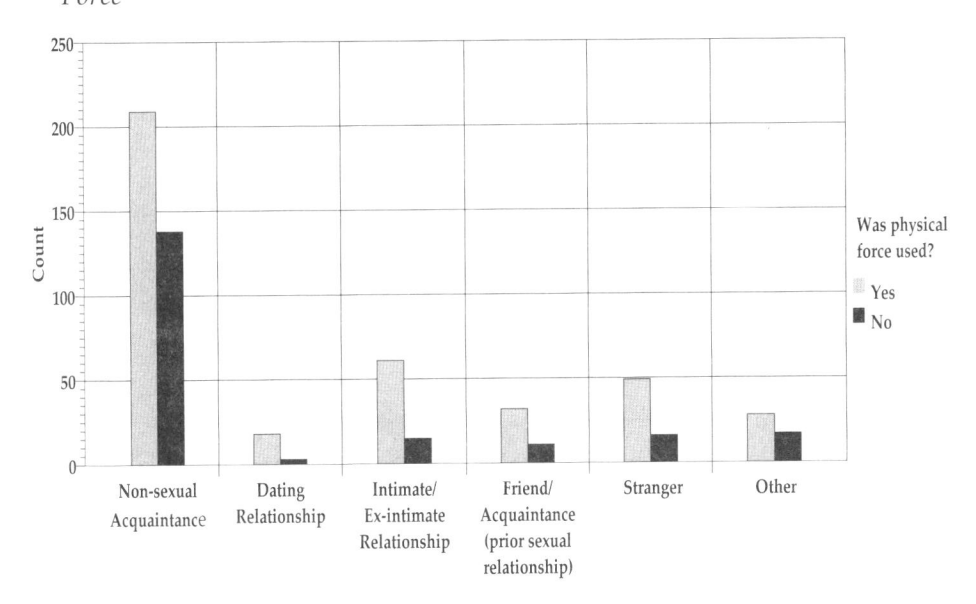

A similar situation was evident for the use of a weapon and the relationship between suspect and complainant (χ^2=20.984, df 9, p<0.05, Cramér's V= 0.188, p<0.05) with dating relationships the most likely to have the aggravating factor of a weapon present.

The presence of aggravating features had a weak but significant association with the time lapse between the rape and its report. The use of physical force (Cramér's V=0.150, p<0.01), and verbal non-consent (Cramér's V=0.144, p<0.01) had the strongest (although still weak) association with the time-lapsed before reporting.

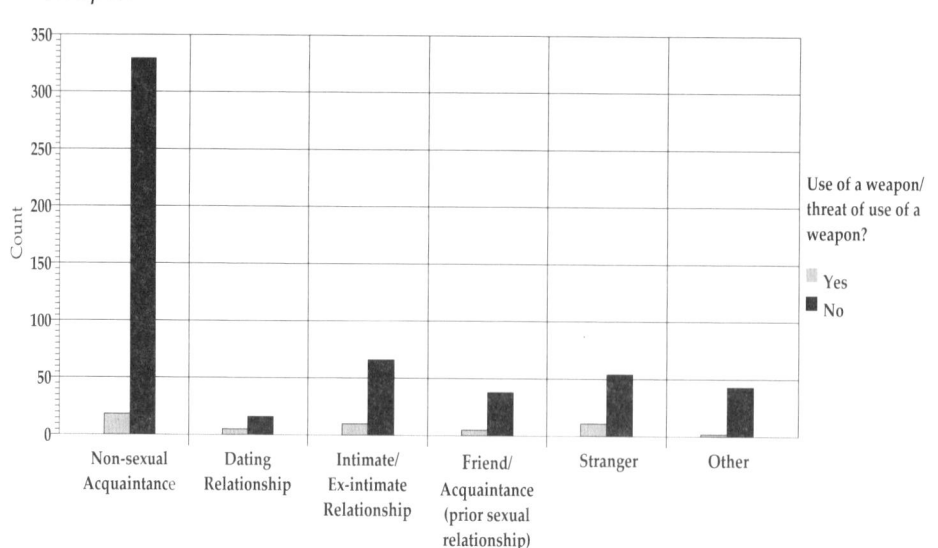

Figure 5.6: Complainant/Suspect Relationship and the Use/Threat of a Weapon

[Bar chart showing counts by relationship category (Non-sexual Acquaintance, Dating Relationship, Intimate/Ex-intimate Relationship, Friend/Acquaintance (prior sexual relationship), Stranger, Other) with Yes/No bars for use of a weapon/threat of use of a weapon.]

'Gang rapes' and multiple rapes had sample sizes too small to conduct a logistic regression. Amalgamating the files to represent a binary division between one and more than one suspect did not result in a significant association with the decision to prosecute. However, examining the files related to prosecutions does reveal a high number of successfully prosecuted cases, as discussed earlier, that involved multiple victims raped by a single suspect, indicating that both prosecutors and juries are influenced by the ratio of perpetrators to victims. Thirty-two cases involved more than one suspect, and seven of these cases (22 per cent) went to trial. Cases involving gang rapes were no more likely to involve the use of weapons or the infliction of physical injury than cases involving single perpetrators. It should be noted however that where a single perpetrator assaulted multiple women on different dates, these were most likely to be stranger rapes that fit the 'real rape' scenario, and where a single perpetrator raped multiple people on a single date they were more likely to use weapons and inflict physical injury. Half of the 26 cases that were linked to other cases, due to a single perpetrator committing multiple assaults on different victims, resulted in a conviction and another three were awaiting trial. Only five of the 26 cases of this type were not prosecuted, and a further four resulted in a not guilty verdict. A significant association was found between cases that were linked to other cases and the decision to prosecute (χ^2=76.615, df 8, p<0.000, Cramér's V= 0.357, p<0.000). Also, rapes that involved multiple victims in a single incident or multiple incidents were more likely to have evidence of the use or threatened use of a weapon. Twenty-three per cent of cases linked to other rape cases had this aggravating factor, compared to eight per cent of stand-alone cases, indicating a significant association (χ^2=7.325, df 1, p<0.01, Cramér's V= 0.111, p<0.01).

Risk Factors

The regression analysis demonstrates that of the risk factors considered, walking alone late at night, a history of alcohol abuse and the presence of a psychiatric illness affected the decision to prosecute. Voluntarily accompanying the suspect to his place of residence or car, or inviting the suspect to the complainant's own residence had no influence on the decision to prosecute. Similarly, the fact that the complainant was alone in a bar, had a history of drug abuse or past criminal convictions are not significantly associated with the decision to prosecute. The risk factors for hitchhiking and a history of work in the sex industry (other than prostitution) were excluded from the regression analysis due to their low frequency. Information regarding a past history of prostitution was found to be insignificant to the decision to prosecute, as was intellectual disability. Prosecutors were less likely to prosecute where the complainant had a history of alcohol abuse (β= -1.093, S.E. 0.446, Wald 6.013, sig. 0.014, Exp(β) .335) and more significantly where there was the presence of mental illness (β= -2.605, S.E. 0.723, Wald 12.970, sig. 0.000, Exp(β) 0.074). Where the complainant was walking alone late at night prosecutors were *more* likely to prosecute (β=.831, S.E. 0.392, Wald 4.5, sig. 0.034, Exp(β) 2.296). However, this is likely related to the strong association between walking alone and stranger rapes (χ^2=89.212, n = 592, p<0.000, Cramer's V= 0.388, p<0.000), and walking alone and rapes that occur in a public place (χ^2=62.416, n= 589, p<0.000, Cramer's V=0.326, p<0.000), both of which have evidenced a positive relationship with the decision to prosecute.

Logistic regression was also used to combine risk factors to determine if multiple factors increased the likelihood that prosecutors would or would not prosecute the case. If the risk factor walking alone late at night was combined with a history of prostitution, the strength of the positive relationship diminished (β=0.557, S.E. 120, Wald 21.572, sig .000, Exp(β) 1.746). Other combinations considered were:

- A history of alcohol abuse x walking alone;
- A history of drug abuse x prostitution x walking alone late at night;
- A history of alcohol abuse x drug abuse x prostitution;
- A history of alcohol abuse x accompanying suspect to his residence;
- Psychological disability x accompanying the suspect to his residence;
- A history of alcohol abuse x inviting the suspect to her (the complainant's) home;
- A history of alcohol abuse x psychological disability; and
- Psychological disability x inviting the suspect to her home.

None of these combinations were relevant to the decision to prosecute.

Although 78 cases involved complainants with a history of mental illness, only two cases were prosecuted. Both of these cases had a preponderance of evidence to support the allegation, including forensic evidence, and both victims suffered injuries in the assault and reported the rape within one hour. Furthermore, the DPP indicated that the suspects' accounts of the events were less credible than the victims. Both cases, however, resulted in a 'not guilty' verdict at trial. It is of note that individuals with a history of mental illness were also more likely to withdraw their case. Of the 76 complaints made by individuals with mental illness that were not prosecuted, 29 were withdrawn by the complainant, representing approximately 16 per cent of total withdrawals – a disproportionately high rate of withdrawal. A second analysis was conducted in which those complainants with mental illness who had withdrawn their complaint were excluded. This analysis marginally increased the strength of the association between prosecutions and mental illness from Cramér's $V= 0.190$, $p<0.00$ to Cramér's $V=0.200$, $p<0.00$. It was also found that the rate of prosecution in cases involving complainants with mental illness rose to 4.7 per cent from 2.5 per cent. Excluding the cases that were withdrawn, however, did not change the fact that those with mental illness were significantly less likely to have their cases prosecuted than complainants with no indication of mental illness. This result was also found by Lievore in her Australian study (2004: 41).

Those with mental illness were more likely to have their cases dropped due to insufficient evidence (45 per cent of mental illness cases as against 39.6 per cent of cases with no mental illness indications) or because it was 'unsafe' to prosecute (30.4 per cent as against 28 per cent). Those with mental illness were no more likely to have their case dropped due to unreliability. When the DPP was asked what *factors* influenced the decision, however, complainant unreliability or lack of witness credibility was the second most commonly cited factor, relevant in 25 out of 78 cases (32 per cent), after lack of evidence. This was also true for those with a history of alcohol abuse where a lack of evidence was a factor in dropping 49 per cent of these rape cases, complainant unreliability or lack of credibility in 36 per cent of cases, and inconsistencies in the statement in 32 per cent of dropped cases.[*] Complainants with a history of alcohol abuse also withdrew in 29.9 per

---

[*] As more than one reason may be given by the DPP, responses add to more than 100 per cent.

cent of cases, accounting for 16 per cent of withdrawals, making this the third most common group to withdraw.

Evidentiary Factors

Nonparametric correlation found that the older the complainant, the less evidentiary factors were present ($\varrho = -0.098$, sig. 0.020, N=560), but that the sooner the offence was reported the more evidentiary factors were identified ($\varrho = -0.263$, sig. 0.000, N=565). A relationship was also found between the time lapse between offence and report and the presence of both DNA ($\chi^2=16.580$, df 4, sig. 0.002, Cramer's V= 0.168) and, more strongly, forensic medical evidence ($\chi^2=63.035$, df 4, sig. 000, Cramer's V= 0.327, sig. 000).

Of the evidence types, a medical examination report, suspect identification and forensic evidence were all positively associated with the decision to prosecute, as demonstrated in Table 5.3. Neither the presence of DNA evidence on the file, nor the relevance of forensic evidence and DNA evidence, were predictors of the DPP's decision to prosecute.

Table 5.3: *Evidence and the Decision to Prosecute – Variables in the Equation*

		B	S.E.	Wald	df	Sig.	Exp(B)
Step 1 (a)	Idvic*	1.296	.227	32.578	1	.000	3.655
	medex**	1.078	.306	12.380	1	.000	2.939
	evidfor***	1.479	.239	38.259	1	.000	4.386

a Variable(s) entered on step 1: idvic, medex, evidfor.

There is a stranger/known suspect divide manifest in the results for evidential factors. Cases that involved strangers expressed a statistically significant likelihood of reporting the rape at an ear-

---

* Victim identified the suspect.

** The medical examination report was contained in the file.

*** Forensic evidence was contained in the file.

lier stage ($\chi^2 = 17.422$, df 4, p<0.01, V=0.172, p<0.01). Furthermore, and related to the time of reporting, stranger cases are also more likely to have DNA (χ^2=51.257, df 1, p<0.000, Φ = – 0.293, p<0.000) and forensic evidence (χ^2=14.886, df 1, p<0.000, Φ =-0.158, p<0.000) in the case file.

Reason not to Prosecute

The most common explanation given by the DPP for the decision not to prosecute a rape case was 'lack of evidence'. This explanation was relevant on its own or in combination with other factors in 42.6 per cent of all cases. In 37 per cent of cases, the complainant was deemed 'not credible' or unreliable, and in 27.8 per cent of cases not pursued, there were inconsistencies in the complainant's statement. However, in 72.2 per cent of these cases that were dropped for inconsistencies, the DPP did not return the file to Garda for clarification, suggesting that the 'inconsistencies' noted were not purely documentary and thus resolvable. This may indicate a method through which complainants who are deemed to be poor witnesses are excluded from the system. Other relevant factors included the withdrawal of the complaint, listed in 17.5 per cent of cases as the primary reason for dropping the case, an inability to establish absence of consent beyond a reasonable doubt (11 per cent), a delay in reporting (5 per cent), and previous consensual sexual activity between the complainant and the suspect (4.7 per cent). This final factor usually involved consensual kissing, petting and other activities up to and including full sex, on the occasion of the rape.

WITHDRAWING THE COMPLAINT

Who Withdraws?

A total of 27 per cent of rape complainants withdrew their complaint. Proportionally, the group most likely to withdraw were complainants who accused spouses/partners or ex-spouses/partners. Lea et al. (2003), Brown et al. (2007) and Lievore (2005) all found similar results in their studies. In fact, these groups were more likely to withdraw than not. This was significantly represented in the follow-up questionnaire submitted to the Office of the DPP to examine the reasons for withdrawals. Approximately 30 per cent of complainants who withdrew their complaint were or had been married or were cohabitating with the accused. Almost 12 per cent were or had been in a relationship with the accused at the time of the offence or prior to the offence. Thus, over 40 per cent of withdrawals involved individuals who had a current or previous intimate relationship with the suspect (see Figure 5.7). A further 4 per cent of withdrawals involved rapes allegedly committed by family members. Logistic regression revealed relationships between the decision to withdraw and the relationships of current partners/spouses (β= -2.242, S.E. 0.819, Wald 7.487, sig. 0.006, Exp(β) 0.106), ex-partners/spouses (β= -2.337, S.E. 0.817, Wald 8.193, sig. 0.004, Exp(β) 0.097), and cohabitating couples (β= -2.079, S.E. 0.981, Wald 4.495, sig. 0.034, Exp(β) 0.125).

Approximately 21 per cent of complainants who withdrew their complaints suffered from substance abuse or dependency, with alcohol being the primary substance in over 80 per cent of these cases. The relationship between mental illness and withdrawing the complaint because 'the rape did not happen' was statistically significant (χ^2=38.735, df 20, $p<0.05$, Cramér's V= 0.495, $p<0.05$). Furthermore, 21 per cent of complainants had other indications of a troubled history, including evidence of a violent or turbulent relationship, traumatic incidences in the past such as the death of a loved one or a history of sexual abuse. The risk factors of homelessness and poverty were identified in only one case, while prostitution was an issue in four cases and intellectual disability in eight cases.

Only one case was tried despite the complainant's withdrawal. This case involved a suspect and complainant who were in a relationship. The suspect was accused of rape (s.4), sexual assault and making threats to kill. The suspect threatened the victim with a weapon and used physical force, and he made a threat to kill after the complainant made her complaint to the Gardaí. The complainant continued her relationship with the suspect and at the time of the withdrawal (approximately three months after the offence and its report) was engaged to him. She claimed that he 'was sorry' and promised it would not happen again. Due to the seriousness of the incident, the DPP decided to prosecute; the complainant, however, refused to give evidence at the trial and the judge directed a 'not guilty' verdict shortly after the trial began.

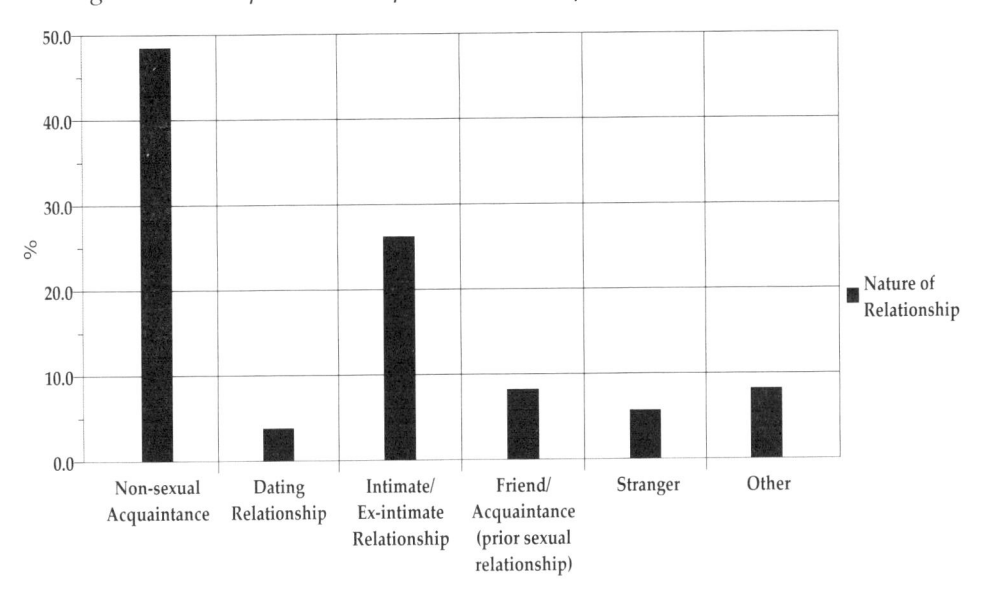

Figure 5.7: Complainant/Suspect Relationship in Withdrawn Complaints

Reasons for Withdrawal

Figure 5.8 sets out the primary reasons given for withdrawing the complaint, and Figure 5.9 sets out the stated secondary reasons. When cases in which no reason were given are excluded, the most frequent reason given for withdrawal was that the complainant wanted 'to move on' or forget about the incident (33 per cent). This result is significantly higher than that found by Holmstrom and Burgess, who reported that only nine per cent of rape complainants indicated a desire to move on with life as the reason for withdrawal (1978: 56). For 28.5 per cent of those complainants in this study who withdrew their complaint, the primary reason given concerned the court appearance and/or the trial, a figure

Figure 5.8: Primary Stated Reason for Withdrawal

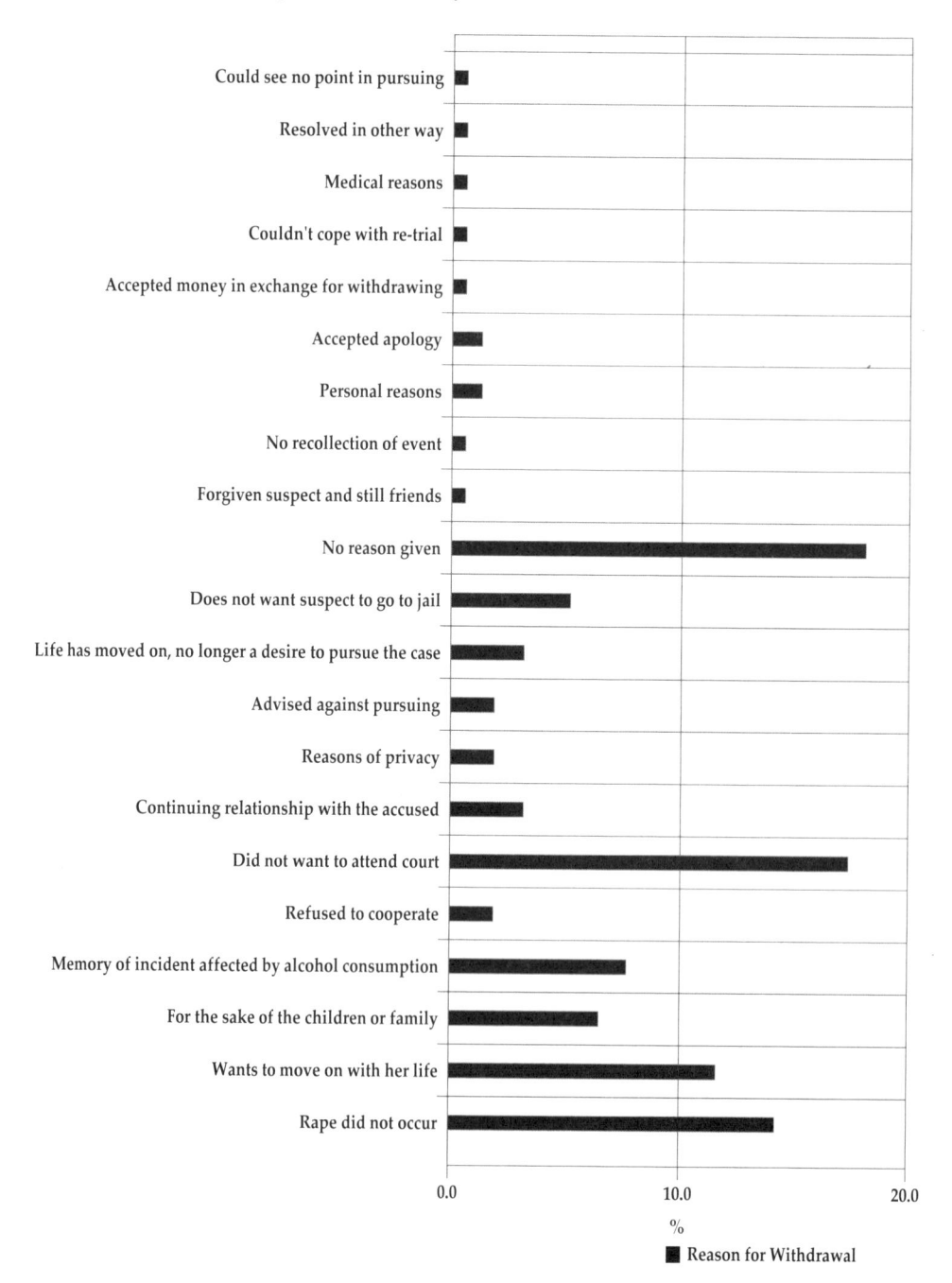

Reason	
Could see no point in pursuing	
Resolved in other way	
Medical reasons	
Couldn't cope with re-trial	
Accepted money in exchange for withdrawing	
Accepted apology	
Personal reasons	
No recollection of event	
Forgiven suspect and still friends	
No reason given	
Does not want suspect to go to jail	
Life has moved on, no longer a desire to pursue the case	
Advised against pursuing	
Reasons of privacy	
Continuing relationship with the accused	
Did not want to attend court	
Refused to cooperate	
Memory of incident affected by alcohol consumption	
For the sake of the children or family	
Wants to move on with her life	
Rape did not occur	

■ Reason for Withdrawal

Figure 5.9: Secondary Reasons for Withdrawal

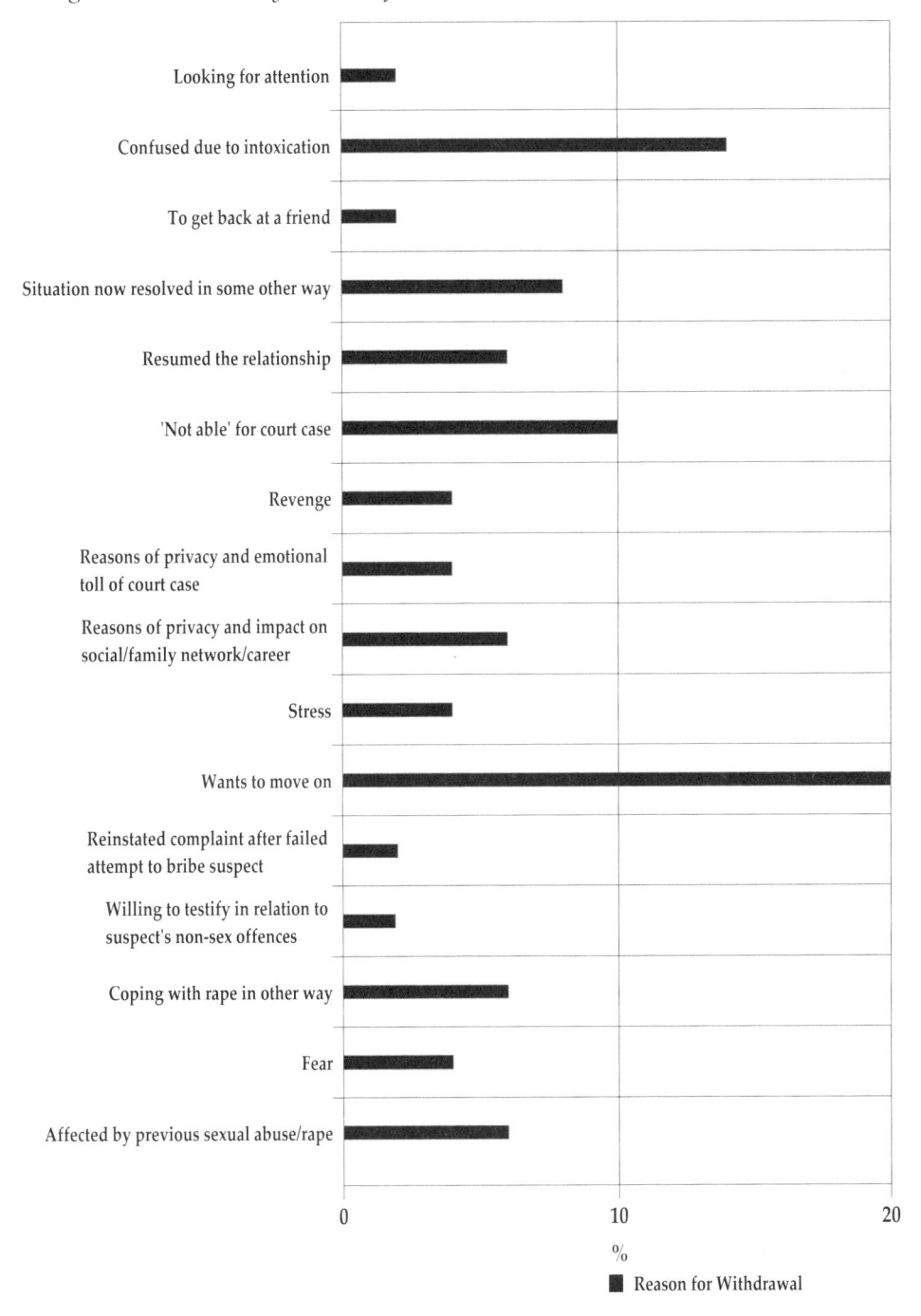

Reason	%
Looking for attention	2
Confused due to intoxication	14
To get back at a friend	2
Situation now resolved in some other way	8
Resumed the relationship	6
'Not able' for court case	10
Revenge	4
Reasons of privacy and emotional toll of court case	4
Reasons of privacy and impact on social/family network/career	6
Stress	4
Wants to move on	20
Reinstated complaint after failed attempt to bribe suspect	2
Willing to testify in relation to suspect's non-sex offences	2
Coping with rape in other way	6
Fear	4
Affected by previous sexual abuse/rape	6

■ Reason for Withdrawal

similar to that reported by Holmstrom and Burgess (ibid). Just over 12 per cent of complainants withdrew due to concerns for their children, family members or relationship. A similar percentage listed the effects of excessive alcohol consumption, giving rise to uncertainty about the event or consent, as the reason for withdrawal. Nearly 6 per cent of withdrawing complainants claimed to be dealing with the rape in some other way, such as through individual counselling, relationship counselling, or the suspect promising not to repeat the incident and to address his alcohol problems. A total of 16 per cent did not wish to proceed either because their relationship with the suspect was ongoing or had been rekindled (6 per cent), or because the complainant had feelings for the suspect or felt sorry for him.

The Effect of a Delay on Withdrawal

Of great relevance is the effect of a delay in the case coming to trial on the decision to withdraw. Out of a total of 161 rape complaints that were withdrawn, 142 cases were withdrawn within a year. Thirteen cases that were later withdrawn were initially directed 'prosecute on indictment', including three cases that were withdrawn in the first year and one case (discussed above) that was prosecuted despite the withdrawal of the complaint shortly after it was made. Of the remaining nine cases, however, that were deemed prosecutable originally, all of them were withdrawn after delays spanning one to seven years. Indeed, three-quarters of withdrawn cases, originally directed 'prosecute on indictment', were withdrawn after two years or longer. Potentially, 10 cases may have proceeded to trial had the delay been shorter. In most cases the complainants gave reasons for withdrawing that related to moving on with their life (four complainants, for example, had new babies or were pregnant), managing the trauma in some other way and did not want to re-live the incident, or were still in a relationship with the suspect. It is possible that had the complaints been brought before a jury earlier, the complainant would not have withdrawn and guilty pleas or verdicts may have been reached.

False Reports

Interpreting the rate of false reporting for rape cases is difficult. Rape complainants may maintain false reports or they may make genuine reports that they later claim were false in order to be certain that the case will not be prosecuted. Genuine complaints may be suspected by Gardaí although remain un-falsified, and false reports may be suspected but remain unproven. False reports may also be recanted. For a researcher, consideration must be given to the criteria by which the falsity of the complaint is judged. The results from various studies for the rate of false rape reports range from 1.5 per cent to 90 per cent (Rumney, 2006: 136-137) although a recent study suggests that research on false rape reporting tends to converge around 2–8 per cent (Lonsway et al., 2009). British studies have similarly placed the rate of false complaints between three per cent, where only cases that are designated by police as 'probable' or 'possible' false complaints are included, to eight per cent where all complaints designated 'false' were included (Kelly et al., 2005). The Federal Bureau of Investigation claims that approximately eight per cent of rape complaints in the United States are false, but this figure includes all 'unfounded' rapes, whose numbers may be inflated by incorrect police filing (Sampson, 2002). Academic convention, however, holds that false rape complaints are made no more often than false complaints of other crimes (Kelly et al., 2005).

In this study, either the Gardaí or the DPP indicated that the complaint may be false in approximately six per cent of cases, which is below the 9 per cent recorded for false complaints in the Daphne II study (Corr et al., 2009). In some cases this was only a 'hunch' and was not backed by corroborating evidence, while in other cases, more serious consideration was given to prosecuting the complainant for making a false complaint. This was most likely to be true when the complainant admitted making a false complaint. Just over 13 per cent of withdrawing complainants (3.7 per cent of total complainants) stated that the incident that they initially alleged was rape either was in fact consensual or had not occurred. Only six cases, however (3.8 per cent of withdrawals, or one per cent of the total sample), were deemed by the Gardaí or the DPP to be malicious. In the other cases, alcohol or mental illness affected the memory or perception of the incident. In one case the withdrawing complainant stated that 'she just wanted to say that it never happened'; however, the file indicated that there was no suggestion that this was a false report. There were a number of other cases, however, in which the Gardaí suggested that the complaint may not be truthful but had no evidence to back this claim. Legal action was not taken against any complainants for making false complaints. The reasons for this fell into one of three categories: it was not in the public interest to do so due to the complainant's 'fragile' nature, the complaint was not malicious (e.g., there was genuine confusion due to alcohol consumption or mental illness), or, despite Gardaí's suspicion that the complaint was false, the complainant never stated that she was not raped. It would appear that the DPP is only comfortable prosecuting those who make false complaints if the complainant admits the complaint was false and malicious, and the complainant is unaffected by a troubled history or mental illness.

Discussion

The analysis has demonstrated that the DPP's decision to prosecute is not influenced by complainant characteristics, such as socio-economic status, nationality or age. Further, 'risky' behaviour, such as accompanying the suspect home or inviting him into the complainant's home, does not appear to inhibit the decision to prosecute. Indeed, walking alone late at night was positively associated with the decision to prosecute, although this result likely reflects the fact that individuals who were walking alone at night were more likely to be raped by a stranger in a public place. There is some indication that where the complainant has a history of prostitution and was walking alone late at night (possibly *as* a prostitute) the DPP was less likely to press charges than if there was no history of prostitution, but this did not act to negate the positive effect of walking alone late at night on the decision to prosecute.

The result that complainant characteristics do not influence the prosecutor's decision in either stranger or acquaintance rape cases is contrary to the findings of a number of studies conducted in the United States and in Britain (e.g., La Free 1981; Spohn et al., 2001, Brown et al. 2007, Tellis and Spohn, 2008) although a minority of other studies did arrive at a similar result (e.g. Kingsnorth et al., 1998; Horney and Spohn, 1996). It is possible that more recent advances in public attitudes towards 'typical' rape complainants and a growing awareness that rape is not a crime restricted to certain types of victims has influenced these changes. Indeed, the SAVI study records a high rate of accurate public knowledge regarding female victims of sexual violence (McGee et al, 2002: 157).

While complainant characteristics and risky behaviour did not have a negative influence on the decision to prosecute, other risk characteristics did. Individuals with a history of alcoholism and/or mental illness were more likely to have their cases dropped by the DPP, almost certainly as such individuals are unlikely to be impressive witnesses. Gregory and Lees found similar practices in the Crown Prosecution Service (CPS) in their study, where a Chief Superintendent commented that 'a number of victims are not regarded by the CPS as competent witnesses because of emotional or other difficulties, so these cases don't go to court' (1996: 8). The HMCPSI/HMIC report similarly noted that the conviction rate in cases in which the complainant had vulnerabilities that relate to mental health and learning difficulties were lower than the overall conviction rate for rape cases (2007). Lievore's Australian study also found that cases involving complainants with mental health issues were less likely to be prosecuted (2004: 41). This is of some concern as it has been established that both mental illness and substance abuse put the individual at greater risk of trauma, including rape (MIMH, 2002). Automatically excluding a class of people from the protection of the law is untenable. It would be prudent (and ethical) for the DPP to consider pursuing more cases involving individuals with mental illness or alcoholism, despite a potential low probability of conviction, to test juries and expose possible prejudices against these groups. This is especially so as there is no apparent distinction made for different degrees of mental illness. Certainly, low levels of mental illness, such as a past bout of depression, should not automatically affect her credibility. It is also worth considering specialist training for Gardaí who take statements from those with mental illness, as this group may need to be treated with extra sensitivity in order to discourage withdrawing of genuine complaints.

Some suspect characteristics did have an influence on the decision to prosecute. Non-Irish individuals were more likely to be prosecuted, as were the unemployed and those with convictions. The HMCPSI/HMIC study similarly noted the greater likelihood of prosecutions being brought when the defendant had prior convictions (2007: 116). It is possible that these results are indicative of the DPP seeking for bad-character evidence and being willing to exploit jury prejudices towards non-Irish individuals although there is no evidence to confirm this. It is interesting that the number of convictions and the type of convictions did not have a significant influence. The presence of one conviction may establish the bad character that prosecutors are looking for, and thus there may be no need to take the number of convictions into account when deciding whether to pursue or drop the case.

There is strong evidence that cases are more likely to be prosecuted when the suspect is a stranger rather than known. Similar findings have been noted in the literature (e.g., Harris and Grace, 1999; Kingsnorth et al., 1999; Tellis and Spohn, 2008). This finding is, however, complicated by other factors, including the fact that cases involving strangers were more likely to be reported within one hour and to have the presence of forensic and DNA evidence. 'Simple' rapes, as discussed in the literature, are particularly complicated to prosecute as they rarely involve corroborating evidence and usually revolve around the question of consent. It is also relevant that complainants who know their attacker are more likely to withdraw their complaint; excluding withdrawals, however, from the analysis did not substantially affect the results for a positive association between prosecutions and strangers.

Prosecutors in Ireland are more likely to prosecute when the rape occurred in a public area, a factor that has also proven relevant in other jurisdictions (e.g., Brown et al., 2007: 359; Spohn et al., 2001: 226). Such rapes, however, are more likely to be committed by a stranger and are more likely to have been reported within an hour of the attack. A delay in reporting is associated with a decline in the amount of evidence, particularly forensic and DNA evidence, and this, in turn, has been associated with a decreased likelihood of prosecution (Kingsnorth et al., 2000: 287; Lievore, 2005: 41). It would seem, therefore, that the location of the rape has a secondary, rather than a primary, effect on the decision to prosecute.

The disproportionately low report of rape in rural areas of Ireland may reflect more than just a lower likelihood of being raped outside of towns and cities. Considering that approximately 41 per cent of the total Irish population in 2000 lived in rural areas (Earthtrends, 2003: 1), it would be expected that the rate of rape would be similarly distributed. It is possible that in rural areas people are more likely to know one another, and acquaintance rapes are thought to be reported less frequently than stranger rapes. In the withdrawal questionnaire, three complainants mentioned being from a small town or rural area and explained that they did not want people to know about the rape. It is also of note that in these cases, the accused was an ex-boyfriend in one case, a neighbour in the other and an acquaintance in the third. Further, sexual assault treatment centres are located in urban areas and may play a significant role in encouraging reporting. The Rotunda SATU reported in 2006 that almost all of its users were referred by the Gardaí, and furthermore, those who did not come to the SATU from the Gardaí had to make an appointment (*Irish Examiner*, 02/09/2006). There is thus a strong incentive to report a rape in areas serviced by a sexual assault treatment unit. Women living far from these services may be missing a valuable incentive to report – to receive treatment from a specialised unit. The high rates of reported rape in Waterford found in this study, where one of the few SATU centres in Ireland is located, and the very low rate of rape reporting in Limerick, where rape victims were forced to travel to Cork for treatment, provides further confirmation of the importance of accessible treatment units for the detection and prosecution of sexual crime. It is quite possible that the nearly negligent rate of rape reports in the far west of Ireland may be due, in part, to a complete lack of services in this area at the time of the study. The recent addition of a SATU in Galway may improve this situation.

Of all the aggravating factors considered, only the use or threatened use of a weapon had a significant positive effect on the decision to prosecute. When physical injury was incurred and a weapon was used, prosecutors were also more likely to prosecute, but this was not a more significant result than when only a weapon was without causing injury. It is likely, therefore, that it is the presence of a weapon rather than its use that influences the decision to prosecute. However, where a physical injury was incurred and there is relevant forensic evidence, prosecutors are more likely to prosecute indicating that injury may add credibility to a claim, but injury is not enough on its own to assure prosecution. Although other studies have also identified the importance of the use and/or presence of a weapon in the decision to prosecute a rape case, it is unusual that complainant injury is not more significant in this study, and this remains to be adequately explained. Because our data did not distinguish the degree of physical injury, it cannot be assessed whether those rape cases that demonstrate moderate or severe injuries are more likely to be prosecuted than those with minor injuries, although the literature would suggest this to be true (e.g., Frazier and Haney, 1996; Brown et al., 2007). This may explain, to some extent, the finding in this study that physical injury alone does not affect the decision to prosecute.

Evidential factors appear as highly relevant to the decision to prosecute a rape case in Ireland and studies from other states would indicate this to be true throughout the common law world (e.g., MacGregor et al., 2002; Brown et al., 2007; Spohn et al., 2001; Horney and Spohn, 1996). As one would expect, the ability to identify the suspect was very important, as was the existence of forensic medical evidence and the existence of a medical report. DNA evidence is not significantly associated with the decision to prosecute; however, this is likely explained by the fact that the primary defence offered in rape cases is that the intercourse was consensual thereby negating the evidential relevance of DNA. In general, it is only identity cases and cases in which the suspect denies any sexual contact (a much smaller percentage of cases) in which DNA evidence would be relevant.

It is significant that alcohol was present in so many rape cases. More than 45 per cent of complainants and 40 per cent of suspects were severely intoxicated on the occasion of the rape. 79 per cent of complainants and 76 per cent of suspects had consumed alcohol on the date of the offence. There is a very strong indication that alcohol consumption is implicated in rape, although some caution must be exercised in concluding that alcohol is a causal factor in the commission of rape. Those who drink heavily may be in situations that are more likely to lead to an assault, such as socialising in a pub, club or at a party. It is possible, therefore, that alcohol consumption has only a tangential effect on the commission of rape. Nevertheless, alcohol has a number of effects, including disinhibiting behaviour and increasing aggression (Abbey et al., 2001), which may increase the likelihood of an individual committing a rape. There is thus a strong incentive to tackle excessive drinking, particularly among young men.

Twenty-seven per cent of cases were withdrawn, making this a very significant factor affecting the rate of attrition of rape cases in Ireland, a result that is echoed in other states according to the literature (Bryden and Lengnick, 1997: 1377; Brown et al., 2007: 357; Temkin, 2002: 21). The relationship between the suspect and the complainant was highly relevant here, with complainants making accusations against intimate partners far more likely to withdraw the complaint – often in order to protect children, or to resume the relationship. This result is also replicated in the literature (Gregory and Lees, 1996; Lea et al., 2003; Lievore, 2005). Those suffering from mental illness and alcoholism were also more likely to withdraw than other groups. The directed acquittal of the only rape case brought to trial despite the complainant's withdrawal indicates the difficulty, if not the impossibility, of prosecuting rape cases without the support of the victim. The study identifies the importance of short delays between report and trial, as a total of 10 prosecutable cases were withdrawn after considerable delays. Overcoming a rape requires tremendous psychological strength, while the legal process in itself is stressful, time-consuming and emotionally, physically and financially costly. Expecting complainants to wait more than two years for their case to come to trial is expecting more stamina than most victims can muster. Withdrawing the complaint may be a reasonable strategic choice for women attempting to recover psychologically and put their lives back together.

CONCLUSION AND RECOMMENDATIONS

The Director of Public Prosecutions is required by statute to assess both sufficiency of evidence and the public interest in deciding whether or not to prosecute a case. The overriding conclusion in this analysis is that the DPP makes his decisions on the basis of evidential and witness and credibility issues. This is primarily as it should be. Nevertheless, there are some serious issues that require careful attention and internal investigation by the DPP, especially concerning the over-representation of non-nationals among defendants and the greater likelihood of not prosecuting allegations brought by complainants with a history of mental illness. Such results may well be evidentially justified, but care must be taken to ensure that decisions are not made about individuals on the basis of their membership of a particular class. Furthermore, where some groups, in particular those with mental illness, are seen to be excluded from the justice system due to personal attributes or disabilities a violation of human rights may have occurred (see, for instance, *X & Y v. The Netherlands*). The DPP should therefore examine procedures to ensure that all groups have access to justice.

There is evidence that the 'real rape' scenario remains a relevant motivation in the decision to prosecute, and this is of some concern. This study has found that where a complainant is attacked by a stranger in a public place and reports her rape immediately she is more likely to have her case prosecuted. An increasingly negative result was demonstrated in cases in which the rape was committed in a private place by an individual known to the complainant and the time lapse between offence and report was greater than an hour. Delays in reporting are associated with evidential difficulties, but it was also shown that this negative effect persists even when the rape was reported immediately. This result indicates that evidentiary issues may not be as relevant to the decision to prosecute as the stranger/acquaintance, public/private issues. Precisely how relevant these issues are will require further investigation.

This study has demonstrated the importance of forensic evidence to the prosecution of rape cases. Considering how quickly such evidence can degrade, and the difficult circumstances of collecting the evidence, particularly for the victim of rape, it is strongly recommended that Sexual Assault Treatment Units be established at significant locations throughout the State. At the time of the study, it could take up to 12 hours for a round-trip journey to a SATU (O'Shea, 2006: 15). Access to such units may also increase the rate of rape reporting (ibid.). Fortunately, new SATU's have since opened in Galway and Mullingar and in Limerick some forensic examination facilities are available, thus greatly reducing the distance that victims of rape must travel to access such essential services. It is highly welcome that a new SATU is to be opened in Letterkenny. Continuing to provide funding and development of these services is indispensable in helping victims and likely to minimise the rate of attrition.

Withdrawal of complaint accounts for a huge part of the rate of attrition. The rate of prosecution in Ireland was approximately 23 per cent. However, withdrawals accounted for 27 per cent of all cases not prosecuted; when withdrawals were eliminated from the analysis the rate of prosecution increased to almost 30 per cent. This is a comparatively high rate of prosecution in common law jurisdictions. Although many of the cases that were withdrawn would not have proceeded even with the victim's support, there were 10 cases that were marked for prosecution that were later withdrawn. These cases would have increased the rate of prosecution to nearly 25 per cent of all reported rape cases or almost 32 per cent of cases excluding withdrawn complaints. Particular attention must be given to the very high rate of withdrawal associated with rapes that occur in domestic situations.

Tackling the issue of complaint withdrawal is complicated. Rape victims often withdraw due to fears surrounding a court appearance. The provision of adequate victim support during the entire legal process is essential. Actively seeking the victim's wishes in decision-making, and especially maintaining communication with the victim throughout the process, may reduce the incidence of withdrawal. Victim advocates with legal experience who can liaise between Gardaí, the DPP, and the complainant may provide the complainants with a sense of security and support.

Chapter 6

THE TRIAL PROCESS

THE TRIAL COURT RECORDS

A total of 173 files out of 661 received by the Central Criminal Court between 2000 and 2005 fit the eligibility criteria established for the project (see Chapter 3). Virtually all of the other 243 sexual cases (excluding the sixteen that we were unable to locate) concerned child rape. Thus, for the first half of the first decade of the twenty-first century nearly 60 per cent of all rape cases sent to the Central Criminal Court for trial involved allegations of sexual abuse against children, with just over 40 per cent involving adult victims. The total number of complainants involved in these 173 cases was 182, with seven files having more than one complainant and one file having three complainants. The total number of defendants was 188, with eight files having more than one defendant and one file having five defendants. Thus, about 95 per cent of the eligible files contained only one complainant or one defendant.

The Parties

The records disclosed a considerable amount of information about both the complainants and the defendants.

The Complainants

Information about the complainants primarily came from their statements and, where relevant, their medical reports, both of which were contained in the Books of Evidence.

Gender. Rape is usually considered a crime that affects women, but a man can be involved in rape not only as a perpetrator but also as a victim. Table 6.1 sets out the gender breakdown of the complainants.

Table 6.1: Gender of the Complainants

	Number	%
Female	176	96.7
Male	6	3.3
Total	**182**	**100**

Until 1990, the very concept of a male rape complainant was a legal impossibility. Since the enactment of section 4 of the Criminal Law (Rape) (Amendment) Act 1990, the law now recognizes that men can suffer rape and that such rapes should be treated as seriously as female rape. As expected, however, the vast majority of rape complainants in the sample were female.

Age. The terms of reference for this study were limited to rape cases involving adult victims, so all the complainants in the sample were aged at least 18. Of the 182 complainants, data on age was collected in respect of 165 of them, or just under 91 per cent. Table 6.2 sets out the range of ages.

Table 6.2: Complainants' Age

Minimum	18
Maximum	89
Median	23
Mean	26.62

Again as expected, the mean and median ages were low, facts confirmed by the following frequency table.

Table 6.3: Age Bands of Complainants

Ages	Number	% (of those known)
18-20	56	33.94
21-30	73	44.24
31-40	17	10.30
41-50	11	6.67
51-60	5	3.03
61-70	2	1.21
≥71	1	0.61
	165	100

The age group most likely to suffer rape is that between 18 and 30, accounting for more than three-quarters of all complainants in our sample. From the age of 31 onwards, there is a substantial fall-off in the likelihood of being raped.

Occupation. Occupational information was available in respect of 119 complainants, or 65 per cent. Table 6.4 sets out the employment status of the complainants.

Table 6.4: Complainants' Employment Status

	2000	2001	2002	2003	2004	2005	Total
Employed (Professional/Skilled)	6	2	3	3	2	1	17
Employed (Manual/Unskilled)	6	9	9	8	7	1	40
Not in Paid Employment	8	6	5	5	0	2	26
Unemployed	6	10	4	1	2	3	26
Unclear/Insufficient Info.	2	2	2	2	1	1	10
Total	28	29	23	19	12	8	119

Complainants who were employed were divided into two categories: those employed in a professional or skilled capacity for which some kind of externally accredited training course or qualification was required, and those employed in a manual or unskilled capacity. The category of not in paid employment includes housewives, students and retirees. The category of unemployed includes nine complainants who were working as prostitutes when the incident occurred. In the case of ten complainants, there was insufficient information on file to categorise their employment status. About half of the complainants for whom occupational information was available were in official employment at the time of the alleged rape, two-thirds of whom had jobs of a manual or unskilled nature.

Information about the industry in which these 119 complainants were working at the time of the incident was also available and is set out in Table 6.5. The categories were borrowed from the adaptation of the NACE Rev.1 system (Eurostat, 1996) used by the Central Statistics Office in the presentation of its Quarterly National Household Survey.

Table 6.5: Complainants' Employment, by Industry

	2000	2001	2002	2003	2004	2005	Total
Agriculture, Forestry & Fishing	0	2	0	0	0	0	2
Other Production Industries	1	1	1	1	1	0	5
Construction	0	0	0	0	0	0	0
Wholesale & Retail Trade	1	2	2	4	2	0	11
Hotels & Restaurants	5	2	4	1	2	1	15
Transport, Storage & Communication	0	2	2	0	0	0	4
Financial & Other Business Services	0	1	0	3	0	0	4

The Trial Process 263

Public Administration & Defence	0	0	0	1	0	0	1
Education	0	0	0	0	0	1	1
Health	3	1	1	1	1	0	7
Other Services	2	1	2	0	3	0	8
Unemployed	5	4	3	1	2	1	26
Not in Paid Employment	9	12	6	5	0	4	26
Unclear/Insufficient Info.	2	1	2	2	1	1	9
Total	28	29	23	19	12	8	119

Again, those who were not in paid employment included housewives, students and retirees, while the unemployed category includes the nine complainants who were working as prostitutes at the time of the incident. There was insufficient information on file to categorise nine complainants. The unemployed and those who were not in receipt of remuneration account for nearly half the complainants. Those employed as waitresses, barmaids and shop assistants made up the biggest group among the complainants who were in paid employment.

The Defendants

Information about the defendants came primarily from statements given to the Garda Síochána and were included in the Books of Evidence and, for those who were convicted or who pleaded guilty, from pre-sentence reports prepared by the Probation Service.

Gender. It is theoretically possible for a woman to be charged with the commission of rape in two ways. First, a woman can be charged as a principal offender with committing rape under section 4, or second, as a secondary offender who aided, abetted, counselled or procured the commission of a rape offence. In the latter case, the Criminal Law Act 1997 provides that the woman would be liable to be indicted, tried and punished as a principal offender. In practice, however, rape remains an offence that is committed almost entirely by men, and in this sample all defendants were male.

Age. The terms of reference for this project were not limited to cases in which defendants had reached their majority, so cases in which the defendant was still legally a child were included. Of the 188 defendants in the sample, information was available on the ages of 181 of them, or just over 96 per cent. Table 6.6 sets out the defendants' age-range.

Table 6.6: Defendants' Ages

Minimum	15
Maximum	63
Median	27
Mean	28.06

The age-spread among defendants was somewhat wider than among the complainants, as Table 6.7 shows.

Table 6.7: Age Bands of the Defendants

Ages	Number	% (of those known)
<18	11	6.08
18-20	25	13.81
21-30	82	45.31
31-40	48	26.52
41-50	12	6.63
51-60	2	1.10
61-70	1	0.55
	181	100

Some 85 per cent of the defendants were aged between 18 and 40 when the alleged offence occurred, with those aged 21 to 30 making up the largest single group.

Occupation. Occupational information was available in respect of 117 of the 188 defendants in the sample, or just over 62 per cent. Table 6.8 sets out the employment status of those 117 defendants.

Table 6.8: Defendants' Employment Status

	2000	2001	2002	2003	2004	2005	Total
Employed (Professional/Skilled)	2	7	10	2	2	2	25
Employed (Manual/Unskilled)	21	14	5	7	3	3	53
Not in Paid Employment	0	0	1	0	6	1	8
Unemployed	1	3	1	5	1	3	14
Unclear/Insufficient Info.	5	5	4	1	2	0	17
Total	29	29	21	15	14	9	117

Two-thirds of the people in the sample charged with rape were employed, with the great majority of them being employed in a manual capacity. Only one in every five had a job that requires an externally validated training programme or qualification, as needed to fit the professional or skilled category.

Table 6.9 shows the breakdown of defendants by occupation, which is again based on the NACE Rev.1 system used by the Central Statistics Office.

Most of the defendants in the sample about whom occupational information was available were employed. Many were employed on a fairly casual basis in the construction industry, with others being employed as waiters, barmen and warehouse operatives.

Table 6.9: Defendants' Employment, by Industry

	2000	2001	2002	2003	2004	2005	Total
Agriculture, Forestry & Fishing	2	1	0	0	0	0	3
Other Production Industries	3	3	0	2	0	0	8
Construction	3	5	8	2	2	4	24
Wholesale & Retail Trade	1	3	2	0	1	0	7
Hotels & Restaurants	1	3	2	2	2	0	10
Transport, Storage & Communication	4	3	1	2	0	0	10
Financial & Other Business Services	0	0	0	0	0	0	0
Public Administration & Defence	1	1	2	0	0	0	4
Education	0	0	0	0	0	0	0
Health	1	1	0	0	0	1	3
Other Services	6	2	0	1	0	0	9
Unemployed	1	3	1	5	1	3	14
Not in Paid Employment	0	0	1	0	6	1	8
Unclear/ Insufficient Info.	6	4	4	1	2	0	17
Total	29	29	21	15	14	9	117

Background. Pre-sentence reports prepared for the courts by the Probation Service contained background information on 70 defendants. It needs to be stressed that these reports were prepared only in respect of defendants who had either pleaded guilty or had been convicted by a jury. Accordingly, these profiles are not necessarily representative of those defendants who were acquitted or whose trials did not proceed.

Figure 6.1 shows the principal factors identified by the Probation Service in the backgrounds of the 70 defendants (note that the numbers exceed 70 in that many defendants reported multiple factors).

Figure 6.1: Defendants' Background Factors

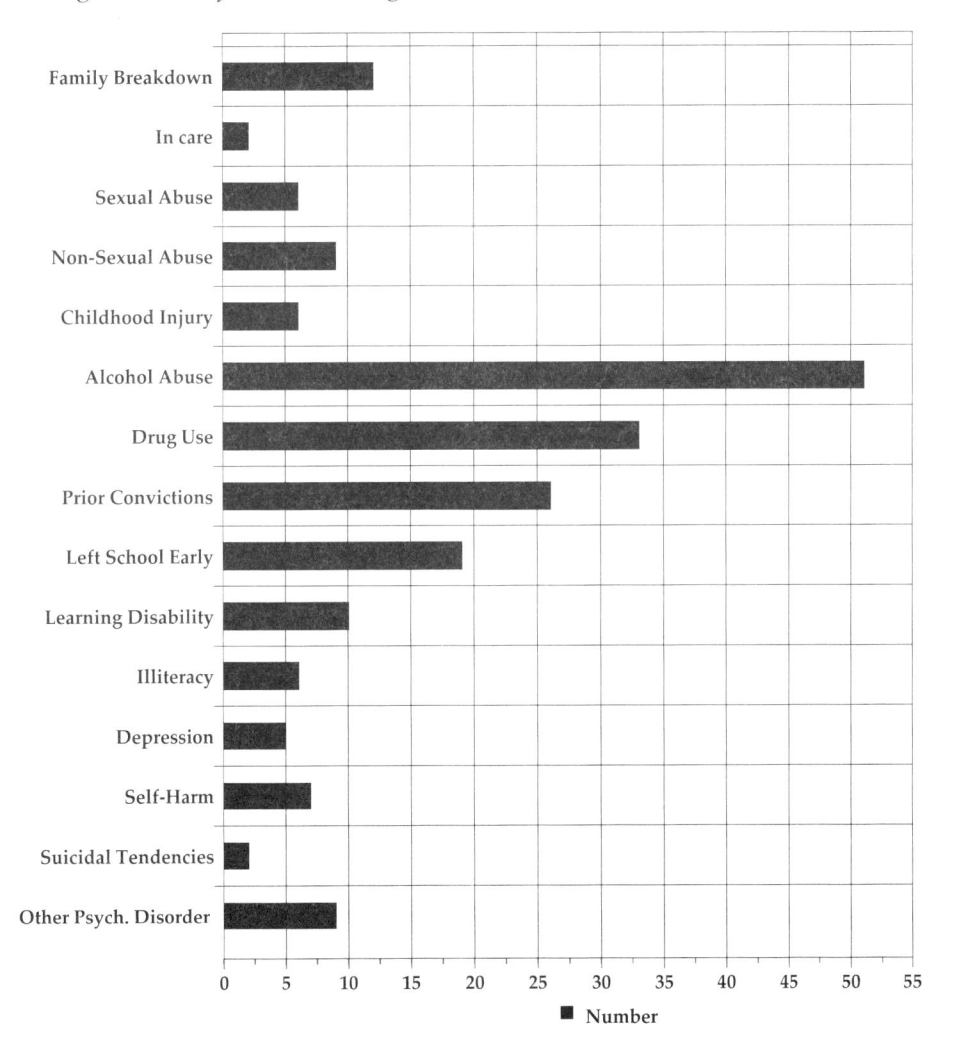

Nearly three-quarters of these defendants reported problems with alcohol, and nearly half had a history of drug abuse. Over a quarter had left school early and more than one in eight had a learning difficulty. One-third had prior convictions, with some having multiple prior convictions. The offences for which these men had been convicted ranged from road traffic offences, drugs offences and larceny to violent assaults, sexual assault and rape.

The Allegations of Rape

The Book of Evidence forms the basis of the prosecution's case against a person charged with the commission of a criminal offence. It consists of the all the witness statements, medical and forensic reports, notes from the interview with the defendant, etc. In this sample, there was a Book of Evidence on 172 of the 173 relevant files. The material contained in these Books provided a great deal of information about the circumstances of the incidents complained of.

Relationship between the Complainant and the Defendant

Broadly, there were three categories: family relationship, non-family relationship and no prior relationship. Each of these categories was then broken down as shown in Table 6.10.

These categories are based upon the complainant's description of the relationship set out in her statement to the Gardaí. The category of 'other' is used to cover situations in which the complainant did not appear to have any prior relationship with the defendant but we could not be certain. Thus, in one case, the defendant and the complainant both worked for the same company; it was unclear from the materials to hand whether there they had ever actually met prior to the incident. Further, the category of 'other' includes two cases in which the defendant was the complainant's pimp.

Nearly three-quarters of complainants reported being raped by someone with whom they had a prior relationship of some description. The largest single category is that of 'acquaintance' (i.e., persons the complainant had known prior to the incident) followed by 'just met' (i.e., met within the 24 hour period prior to the incident). In terms of family relationships, more than one in eight complainants alleged being raped by a husband, partner or ex-partner.

Table 6.10: Relationship between Defendants and Complainants

	Number	%
Family Relationship		
Husband	3	1.65
Partner	13	7.14
Ex-Partner	9	4.95
Family – Other	5	2.75
Total	30	16.49
Non-Family Relationship		
Friend	9	4.95
Family Friend	2	1.10
Neighbour	7	3.85
Acquaintance	47	25.82
Just Met	39	21.43
Total	104	57.15
No Personal Relationship		
Stranger	32	17.58
Other	16	8.79
Total	48	26.37

Location of the Incident

Information on the location of 181 of the incidents complained of was collected (where a complainant alleged more than one incident and the location for each incident was specified, each incident was counted separately).

Nearly three-quarters of incidents in which the location was specified occurred in a private place or vehicle. Over one-third of these incidents occurred in a residence occupied by the complainant, the defendant or both. Only just over one quarter took place outdoors.

Table 6.11: Locations of the Rapes

	Number	%
In a Building		
Defendant's Residence	36	19.89
Complainant's Residence	36	19.89
Mutual Residence	10	5.52
Family Residence	1	0.55
Partner's Residence	1	0.55
Residence – Other	8	4.42
Rental Accommodation	12	6.63
Building/Structure	6	3.31
Total	110	60.76
In a Vehicle		
Defendant's Vehicle	15	8.29
Complainant's Vehicle	2	1.10
Taxi	3	1.66
Other Vehicle	2	1.10
Total	22	12.15
Outdoors		
Carpark	5	2.76
Garden	3	1.66
Public Place	41	22.65
Total	49	27.07

Time of the Incident

Information was available in respect of 155 incidents. As with location, if the complainant alleged more than one incident and indicated the time at which each of the incidents occurred, each incident was counted separately.

Overwhelmingly, rape is a crime committed at night: only 27 out of these 155 incidents occurred during what would commonly be described as daylight hours; three-quarters of the incidents, by contrast, occurred between midnight and 6.00 am.

Table 6.12: Timings of the Incidents

	Number	%
Midnight – 3.00 am	50	30.26
3.00 am – 6.00 am	67	43.23
6.00 am – 9.00 am	12	7.74
9.00 am – Noon	3	1.94
Noon – 3.00 pm	4	2.58
3.00 pm – 6.00 pm	4	2.58
6.00 pm – 9.00 pm	4	2.58
9.00 pm – Midnight	11	7.10

Consumption of Alcohol and Drugs

A total of 133 complainants admitted to consuming alcohol immediately prior to the incident. Of these, 100 female complainants (75 per cent) and 4 male complainants indicated the quantity of alcohol they had consumed with sufficient specificity to allow a calculation of their standard drinks total using the matrix provided by www.drinkaware.ie. A 'standard drink' is a standardized unit that equates to 10 grams of pure alcohol and allows for equations to be made between very different kinds of drinks (HSE, 2008). In making these calculations, the complainant was given the benefit of the doubt:

- If the complainant indicated that he or she had consumed five or six drinks, the lower amount was counted;
- If the complainant gave a total in bottles and it was unclear whether they were standard or large bottles, the smaller size was counted; and

- If the complainant consumed spirits at home, each drink was equated with a pub-measure of spirits although it would almost certainly have been more.

Almost certainly, therefore, the figures presented below are under-estimates of the real totals.

Table 6.13 shows the consumption of alcohol in standard drinks of the 100 female complainants.

Table 6.13: Complainants' Consumption of Alcohol, in Standard Drinks

Standard Drinks	%
0-1	6
2-6	31
7-10	41
11-20	19
21-30	1
31-40	2

Current medical advice is for women to limit their intake of alcohol to 14 standard drinks per week, and for men to limit their consumption to 21 standard drinks per week, and for both to spread their consumption out rather than engage in binge drinking (Health Service Executive, 2008: 3). The consumption of seven units or more on a single occasion constitutes a binge. On that basis, nearly two-thirds of complainants had engaged in what is officially classified as binge-drinking prior to the incident in question. Virtually all had consumed more alcohol in a single sitting than would be advisable medically. As for the four male complainants, three had consumed between seven and ten standard drinks and the fourth had consumed in excess of 30 standard drinks. Thus most complainants were inebriated when the incident occurred.

Among the defendants, 142 admitted to consuming alcohol prior to the incident. Of these, 65 (46 per cent) indicated the quantity of alcohol they had consumed with sufficient specificity to allow for a calculation similar to that made with the complainants.

Thus, almost 88 per cent of those defendants whose alcohol consumption could be calculated had engaged in binge-drinking. Further, 17 defendants whose consumption could not be calculated admitted to being drunk at the time the incident occurred.

Table 6.14: Defendants' Consumption of Alcohol, in Standard Drinks

Standard Drinks	Number	%
<3	0	0.00
3-6	8	12.31
7-10	13	20.00
11-20	33	50.77
21-30	8	12.31
31-40	3	4.62

In terms of drug use, some 15 per cent of complainants and 12 per cent of defendants admitted to consuming illegal drugs prior to the incident in question, and in both cases, the overwhelming drug of choice (excluding alcohol) was cannabis or marijuana.

Impact of the Rape

A large amount of information was available in respect of the impact of the rape on the complainant both from the medical reports prepared for the prosecution, and also from the Victim Impact Reports prepared in connection with the sentencing process. The medical reports were generally included as part of the Book of Evidence, although occasionally they were submitted under a Notice of Additional Evidence. There were medical reports in respect of 155 complainants. Of the remainder, it is likely that no medical report was obtained due to delays in making a report to the Gardaí – six had made a complaint only after two days had elapsed and a further nine had taken even longer. This is not intended as a criticism of the complainants but simply a statement of fact. The longer the delay in making a complaint the more likely it is that any injuries occurring would have healed; a medical report in such circumstances would have been superfluous.

A total of 108 complainants reported sustaining physical injuries, or some 70 per cent of complainants about whom medical reports were prepared. The following table sets out the most common injuries (note that the totals exceed 100 per cent as complainants often reported more than one injury).

Table 6.15: Physical Injuries Reported by Complainants

Injury	No.	% of 108
General Bruising	80	74.07
Facial Bruising/Swelling/Cuts	41	37.96
Scratching	35	32.41
Vaginal Injury, Including Lacerations and Bleeding	35	32.41
Tenderness	12	11.11
Anal Injury, Including Lacerations and Bleeding	10	9.26
Pressure Marks	10	9.26
Bite Marks	7	6.48
Broken Bones	4	3.70
Knife/Stab Wounds	3	2.78
Strangulation Marks	3	2.78
Tooth Injuries	3	2.78
Other	10	9.26

Typically, where physical injuries are reported, they tend to be relatively minor in nature, although some (such as vaginal or anal bleeding) would no doubt be highly distressing. Only a small minority of complainants reported serious injuries such as broken bones, strangulation marks and knife wounds.

A further source of information concerning the impact of the rape is the Victim Impact Reports prepared for the court in connection with sentencing. In two respects, these reports are a better source of information than the medical reports. First, medical reports tend to focus on physical injuries with little mention being made of psychological issues, and therefore tend to give only a limited view of the impact that rape has on the victim. Second, as the Victim Impact Report is prepared in connection with sentencing for sexual or violent crimes, the jury must have been satisfied that such a crime occurred. There were 107 Victim Impact Reports in the sample, made in respect of 92 complainants. Typically, these reports were made by a psychologist, the Garda Síochána, Rape Crisis Centre Counsellors or by the complainant themselves.

Table 6.16: Authorship of Victim Impact Statements

Prepared By	Number	%
Psychologist	47	43.93
An Garda Síochána	19	17.76
Complainant	15	14.02
Rape Crisis Centre	12	11.21
Other	14	13.08

Table 6.17 sets out the frequency with which each of a specified kind of issue was mentioned by each of the groups of authors of Victim Impact Reports.

While physical injuries were the focus of the medical reports, such injuries are mentioned in only 34 of the Victim Impact Reports, or less than one third. Psychologists mention physical injuries only 13 per cent of the time, but it may be that they concentrate deliberately on psychological issues. Significantly, only six of the 15 Reports prepared by the complainant mentioned physical injuries, indicating that such injuries are not the complainant's primary concern. By contrast, psychological concerns are mentioned in all but two of the Victim Impact Reports. Further, issues of trust arose in 13 out of the 15 Reports prepared by the complainant, 14 out of the 19 prepared by the Gardaí and 10 out of the 12 prepared by the Rape Crisis Centres. Problems at work also arise in a significant number of Victim Impact Reports.

Table 6.17: Issues Mentioned in Victim Impact Statements

	Physical Injuries	Psychological Problems	Economic Loss	Relation-ships	Trust Issues	Family Issues	Time Off Work	Lost Job	Changed Job	Work Problems	Moved Away
Garda	10	19	7	5	14	3	6	3	2	7	9
RCC	5	12	1	3	10	1	4	2	1	5	1
Psychologist	6	47	5	3	13	2	7	2	3	8	4
Complainant	6	14	5	3	13	2	7	2	3	8	4
Other	7	13	0	3	9	1	3	1	1	5	5
Total	34	105	18	17	59	9	27	10	10	33	23

It might also be noted, finally, that a handful of complainants reported in the Victim Impact Reports that some positive changes came out of their experiences. At first sight, it seems odd that anyone would associate something positive with a rape, but such a traumatic event can be a catalyst for positive changes being made in a person's life. In some cases, the changes were positive by any standard: a couple of drug-addicted complainants who engaged in prostitution to help pay for their addiction, for example, reported that they had sought help for their addiction and no longer engaged in prostitution. It is less clear whether some other changes, such as finding religion and engaging in missionary work or learning marital arts for self-defence are entirely positive, but we have included them as positive changes in that they involve a degree of self-empowerment.

The Legal Process

An examination of the trial court records provided an opportunity to review the operation of aspects of the legal process as it applies to rape.

Investigation

The Garda Síochána is responsible for the investigation of all allegations of rape. They will take a detailed statement from the complainant and will usually arrange for her to be medically and forensically examined. They will also interview any potential witnesses and visit the scene of the alleged rape. They will search for the person either named or described by the complainant as the person responsible. Once they have located this person, they will usually exercise their powers of arrest and bring him to the Garda Station where he will be detained for questioning. Copies of all statements will be made available by the Gardaí to members of the Directing Division of the Office of the Director of Public Prosecutions, who will decide whether or not to prosecute the defendant. The Gardaí will also be responsible for conducting any follow-up enquiries needed by the DPP. If a prosecution is directed, a Book of Evidence will be produced containing all the witness statements, the medical and forensic reports, details of the

Garda interview with the defendant, and any other piece of evidence upon which the prosecution might rely. Very often, the Book of Evidence will be supplemented by further evidence disclosed by a Notice of Additional Evidence.

Of the 173 files in the sample, 172 contained a Book of Evidence. The number of statements on these Books of Evidence varied between 6 and 91, with a median number of 23 and an average number of 24.24. Each Book of Evidence contained a number of statements from members of the Garda Síochána, ranging from two to 55, with a median number of 12.5 and an average number of 13.71. This might sound like a lot of Garda statements, but it is important to remember that statements will be taken not only from the investigating Gardaí but also from any member who has any contact with the defendant. This is important in order to document arrest and detention periods and the conditions in which the defendant was detained, all of which are subject to statutory rules, a breach of which might render evidence and statements inadmissible.

All but one of the Books of Evidence contained a copy of the complainant's statements – in 27 files, the complainant made at least one supplemental statement. These statements in total varied in length from one page to 31.5 pages, with a median number of 5.5 pages and an average number of 13.71 pages. A statement from the defendant was included in 96 Books of Evidence, and in 9 of them the file contained a supplemental statement. In 81 of these 96 statements the defendant admitted to engaging in sexual activity but admitted to rape in only 34.

There was evidence that DNA tests were sought in 145 cases, or 83.82 per cent of the total number of cases. By coincidence, there was evidence of a Sex Offences Kit being used in 145 cases as well. A Sex Offences Kit is a standardised set of materials that can be used to collect samples for forensic examination tests from a person who makes an allegation of a sexual offence. Which particular elements of the kit will be used in a particular case will obviously depend upon the precise allegations being made. Figure 6.2 sets out the forensic tests done in the cases in this sample.

Swabs of some description (i.e., oral, cervical, rectal, etc.) are the most common forensic test conducted, appearing in more than 80 per cent of the cases. Tests on blood and hair are also common, as are tests on articles of clothing taken from the complainant, the defendant or the scene.

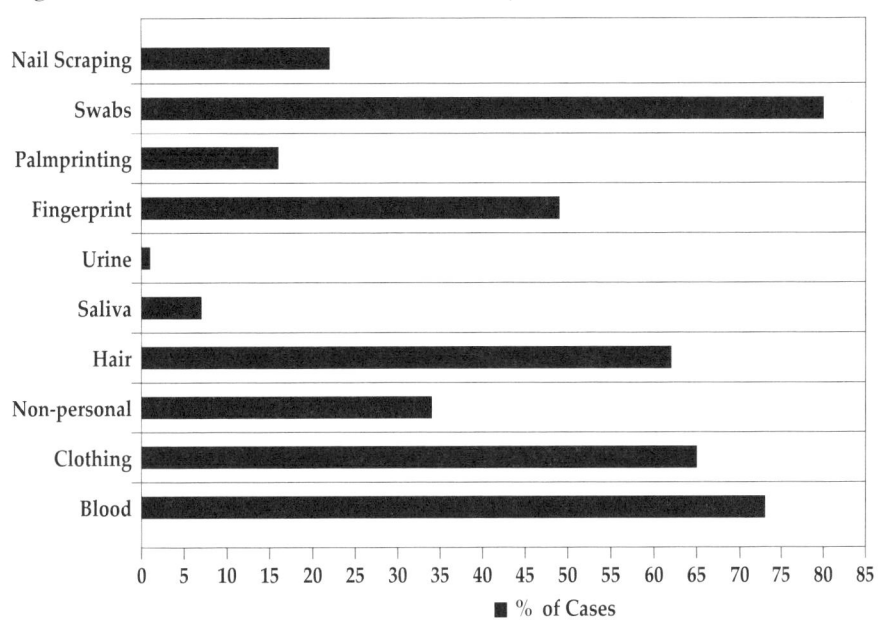

Figure 6.2: Forensic Tests Conducted in Rape Cases

[Bar chart showing % of Cases for forensic tests:
- Nail Scraping: ~22%
- Swabs: ~80%
- Palmprinting: ~15%
- Fingerprint: ~48%
- Urine: ~1%
- Saliva: ~6%
- Hair: ~62%
- Non-personal: ~33%
- Clothing: ~65%
- Blood: ~73%]

In 90 files, the Book of Evidence was supplemented by at least one Notice of Additional Evidence, although the maximum number of such Notices was eight and the median number was two. This suggests that the prosecutorial authorities do not necessarily wait until *all* the evidence has been collected before initiating a prosecution; instead, a prosecution will be initiated once *sufficient* evidence has been collected and the remainder of the evidence can be collected in the run up to trial.

Bail

Bail 'can be defined as the release of a person from custody subject to an undertaking to surrender to custody at a court or Garda station at an appointed time in the future' (Walsh, 2002: 491). In essence, bail is a mechanism that allows for two competing interests to be balanced. On the one hand, the person charged with the commission of an offence is presumptively innocent and has a legitimate interest in his own liberty. On the other hand, the State has a legitimate interest in ensuring that those charged with the commission of offences face trial on those charges. The provision of bail allows a person charged with an offence to be released from custody subject to certain conditions. Anyone charged with rape may seek bail from the District Court, whose decision can be appealed to the High Court. There is a presumption in favour of granting bail that flows from the presumption of innocence; consequently, there needs to be a good reason *not* to grant bail. A refusal of bail can only be justified on one of three grounds: that the defendant will not turn up for trial, that he will try to interfere with witnesses, evidence or jurors (*People (Attorney General) v. O'Callaghan* (1966)), or that the defendant has been charged with a serious offence and refusal of bail is reasonably considered necessary to prevent the commission of another serious offence (section 2(1), Bail Act 1997).

The primary condition imposed on a defendant seeking bail is that a sum of money will be forfeit if he absconds. Usually, the defendant will be liable for this money through entering a recognizance, but sometimes a defendant will have to find an independent surety, either instead of or in addition to a recognizance, to accept a similar liability. The law does not specify the amount of bail, but the amount required must not be set so high as to constitute an effective denial of bail (*People (Attorney General) v. O'Callaghan*, 1966). The court may also impose any further conditions it deems reasonable in the circumstances of the case. Section 6 of the Bail Act 1997, as amended by section 9 of the Criminal Justice Act 2007, imposes the conditions that those admitted to bail agree to turn up at the end of the remand period and that they commit no further offences while on bail. Additionally, section 1A of the 1997 Act, inserted by section 6 of the 2007 Act now requires all applicants for bail to provide to the court a detailed statement setting out any previous convictions, whether any prior applications for bail have been refused and whether any of the defendant's prior offences were committed while on bail. Other conditions, such as signing on at a specified Garda Station or avoiding certain specified places, may be added if the court thinks they are required. An arrest warrant can be issued on the application of a member of the Gardaí for a breach of any conditions imposed: Bail Act, 1997, section 9. Provision has also been made in the Criminal Justice Act 2007 (section 11) for the electronic tagging of certain defendants admitted to bail, although this provision has not yet been brought into force.

Of the 188 defendants in the sample, 144 (76.6 per cent) were admitted to bail at some point during the process. The overwhelming majority of these defendants (137) were admitted to bail by the District Court. Details were available on the conditions attached to the grants of bail in respect of 142 of the defendants admitted to bail.

Recognisances and Sureties. All defendants admitted to bail had to enter into a recognizance. The amounts ranged between €4 and €76,184.28, with the median being €500 and the mean €1,486.28. Note that all bail recognisances entered into prior to 2002 were converted into Euros using the standard exchange rate of IR£1 = €1.27. The following table sets out the distribution of the bail amounts.

Table 6.18: Levels of Bail

Amounts	Number	%
<€10	3	2
<€100	16	11
<€1,000	69	49
<€10,000	52	37
>€10,000	2	1
Total	142	100

It has already been noted that the majority of those charged with rape were from lower socio-economic backgrounds, and this finding is reinforced by the amounts of money set for bail. The Central Statistics Office reports that in 2006 the average industrial earnings were €575.21 per week or €2,300.84 per month.* In this sample of defendants, 130 out of 142, or 91 per cent, entered into recognisances for less than the monthly average industrial wage.

A total of 77 defendants were required to find independent sureties, and 7 defendants had to find two sureties. The amounts required from the sureties ranged between €200 and €30,000, with a median of €3,000 and a mean of €4,370.23. As with recognisances, surety values offered prior to 2002 were converted to Euros using the standard exchange rate. The following table shows the distribution of surety amounts.

Table 6.19: Levels of Sureties

Amounts	Numbers	%
<€1,000	13	17
<€10,000	59	77
>€10,000	5	6
Total	77	100

Further Conditions. A total of 112 defendants (78 per cent) were made subject to conditions other than posting a recognisance or finding a surety. Figure 6.3 shows the frequency of the different kinds of conditions imposed.

The condition to be of good behaviour was the most common condition, and it along with the condition to commit no further offences were statutory conditions imposed by the Bail Act 1997 as originally enacted and should therefore have applied in all cases. It may be that the District Courts did not specifically note these conditions on the documentation seeing as they applied anyway by operation of law. Alternatively, it may be that there was other documentation that was not included in the trial court records.

---

* The figure for the average industrial weekly wage is set out on the Central Statistics Office's website at www.cso.ie, and was last accessed on 5 August 2009.

The second most common condition was to require the defendant to sign on at a specified Garda Station. The frequency with which the defendant had to sign on varied according to the case: 10 defendants had only to sign on once per week, 29 had to sign on once every day and 14 had to sign on twice per day. Other specific conditions imposed included being barred from all licensed premises in the State, abstaining from all alcoholic drink, and keeping the Gardaí informed of changes of address.

Figure 6.3: Bail Conditions

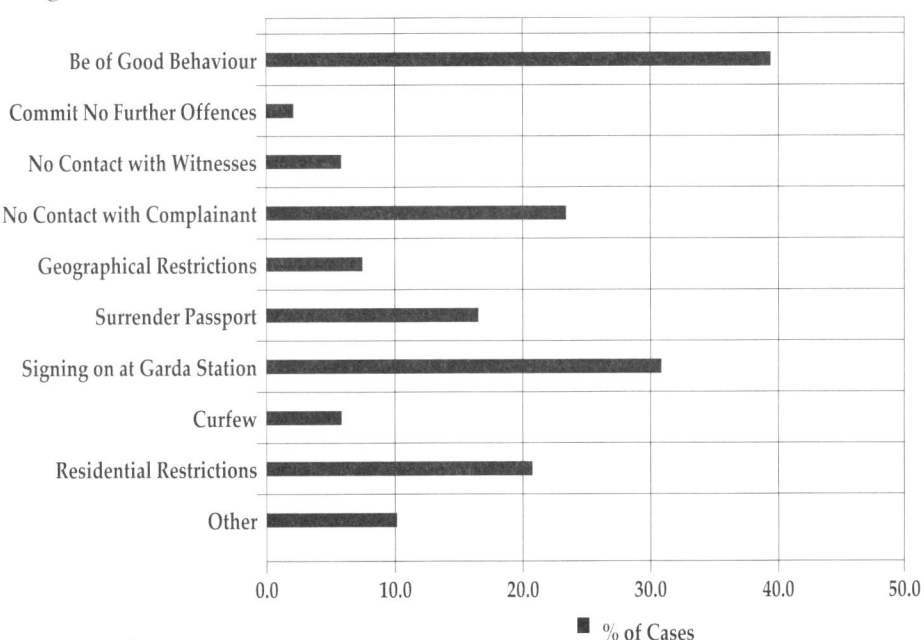

[Bar chart showing % of Cases for bail conditions:
- Be of Good Behaviour: ~40%
- Commit No Further Offences: ~2%
- No Contact with Witnesses: ~5%
- No Contact with Complainant: ~23%
- Geographical Restrictions: ~7%
- Surrender Passport: ~16%
- Signing on at Garda Station: ~31%
- Curfew: ~5%
- Residential Restrictions: ~20%
- Other: ~10%]

It is possible for these conditions to be varied at the request of the defendant. Thus, in one case, the defendant had been ordered to surrender his passport and to refrain from seeking a new one. The court ordered, however, that his passport be returned to the defendant specifically so that he could join his family on a two-week foreign holiday. The defendant subsequently returned to Ireland, stood trial and was convicted.

Absconding. Eight of the defendants admitted to bail absconded at some point during the process. This figure represents 4.26 per cent of all defendants in our sample and 5.63 per cent of all defendants admitted to bail. To put it another way, almost 95 per cent of those admitted to bail eventually stood trial. Five of the eight absconded before their trial* and the remaining three absconded after they had been convicted but before sentence had been imposed. These eight absconders were made the subjects of bench warrants for their arrest and, under the terms of the Criminal Justice Act 1984 (section 13), they may be prosecuted summarily for the offence of failing to surrender to bail.

Legal Aid

In *State (Healy) v. Donoghue* (1976), the Supreme Court accepted that a person charged with an offence had a right to be legally represented, and that such a person should receive financial assistance from the State where necessary to ensure that he is so represented. A free legal aid scheme was introduced in Ireland by the Criminal Justice (Legal Aid) Act 1962 and implemented by the Criminal Justice (Legal Aid) Regulations, 1965. This scheme 'is based on the principle of enabling the defendant to use public funds to engage the services of a professional lawyer to conduct his defence and represent his interest in the criminal proceedings against him' (Walsh, 2002: para.11-07). To qualify for legal aid at a rape trial the defendant must make an application that satisfies three criteria:

1. He has been sent forward for trial on indictment;

2. His means are insufficient to enable him to retain legal representation; and

3. It is in the interests of justice that the defendant have legal aid in the preparation and conduct of his defence, given the seriousness of the charge.

Documentation available on the trial court records shows that legal aid was granted by the District Courts to 178 defendants out of

---

* One of these five defendants was subsequently caught and brought to trial, where he was acquitted on a charge of rape and another charge of rape under section 4.

188, or some 95 per cent. This is not surprising given the seriousness of a rape charge and the fact that the majority of rape defendants are from a lower socioeconomic background. We were unable to determine the cost to the State of this level of free legal aid, although it is worth noting that the Criminal Legal Aid Review Committee (1999:32) found that the cost of the Irish legal aid scheme in 1998 was considerably less than comparable schemes in other common law jurisdictions and allowed for a greater degree of representation and choice.

Two other legal aid schemes operated by the Legal Aid Board might also be mentioned here for the sake of completeness. Complainants in rape cases are entitled to seek legal aid in order to obtain legal advice in connection with the prosecution of their complaints. This scheme, introduced by section 26 of the Civil Legal Aid Act 1995, was subject to financial eligibility criteria until the enactment of the Civil Law (Miscellaneous Provisions) Act, 2008, section 78 of which effectively removed those criteria. The Legal Aid Board was unable to inform us of the number of applications made under this provision.[*] Second, the Legal Aid Board is responsible for the administration of the separate representation scheme introduced by section 4A of the Criminal Law (Rape) Act 1981, as inserted by section 34 of the Sex Offenders Act, 2001. This scheme will be discussed more fully later on.

Juries

Rape is one of the few offences reserved for trial before the Central Criminal Court. As a result, all rape cases will be heard before, and the decision on the defendant's innocence or guilt will be made by, a jury. The jury is a group of citizens, usually twelve, drawn randomly from the community. Since the Supreme Court decision in *Attorney General v. de Burca* (1976) and the subsequent enactment of the Juries Act 1976, male and female citizens have an equal right to serve as jurors once they reach the age of 18. There is no longer any upper age beyond which a citizen cannot serve

---

[*] In correspondence with the lead author dated 6 July 2009, a copy of which has been retained on file.

(section 6 of the Juries Act 1976, as amended by section 54 of the Civil Law (Miscellaneous Provisions) Act 2008). The principle of random selection of jurors is subject to two qualifications. First, the 1976 Act contains an extensive list of persons who are disqualified, ineligible or exempt from service. So, a person who has been convicted of the commission of a serious offence is disqualified; the President, all those involved in the judicial system, the defence forces and illiterates and those with an enduring impairment that makes jury service impractical are ineligible; while politicians, local government officials, priests and those in Holy orders and most professionals are exempted from service as of right. Additionally, anyone else who is summoned may seek an exemption on the grounds of hardship. As a result, it has been suggested by the Director of Public Prosecutions that juries as empanelled are likely to contain fewer middle class and employed persons than the population as a whole (Hamilton, 2003: para.35).

Second, both the prosecution and the defence have extensive rights of challenge against potential jurors. Both sides may challenge any number of potential jurors if they can show good cause, and both sides also have up to seven peremptory challenges (i.e., challenges exercisable without any cause) that can be used at their own discretion. In the United Kingdom, the right of peremptory challenge has been abolished altogether. In the United States, several restrictions have been placed upon the use of these peremptory challenges; in particular, they cannot be used on the grounds of gender (*J.E.B. v. Alabama* (1994)) or race (*Batson v. Kentucky* (1976)). No such restrictions have as yet been imported into Irish law.

At the end of the trial, the judge will charge the jury by explaining to them the issues in the case and the relevant law, and by reviewing the evidence. The jury will then retire to consider its verdict. Jury deliberations are entirely secret, and jurors may not be questioned as to the content of their deliberations (Walsh, 2002: para.19.52). By long tradition, the jury is in the first instance required to come to a unanimous verdict, but section 25 of the Criminal Justice Act 1984 allows a trial judge to accept a majority verdict from at least ten jurors providing they have been deliberating for at least two hours. The jury may decide to acquit or to

The Trial Process

convict, or they may acquit on some charges and convict on others, or they may be unable to come to a decision on any or all charges. In the event of an acquittal, the decision is final. If the jury decides to convict the defendant on at least some charges, the defendant may seek leave to appeal the decision to the Court of Criminal Appeal. In the event of the jury being unable to agree on any or all charges, those charges may be re-tried at the discretion of the Director of Public Prosecutions.

In the sample of files in this study, 108 juries were empanelled in 92 files. There were no details of three of those juries, so the analysis below is based upon 105 juries. The total number of jurors involved was 1,256: in four juries, one juror was discharged for reasons that were unclear from the files.

Gender Composition. In total, there were 741 male jurors and 515 female jurors, or 59 per cent and 41 per cent, respectively. This split did not occur evenly through the juries, in that a male-dominated jury was by far the most likely composition.

Table 6.20: Dominance of Juries, by Gender

	Number	%
Male-dominated Juries	67	63.81
Female-dominated Juries	18	17.14
Evenly-split Juries	20	19.04

Nevertheless, male dominance of the juries was usually not overwhelming in that there were at least three members of both sexes on most juries.

In 94 juries out of 101 (93 per cent), each gender was represented by at least three members. Interestingly, women never achieved more than a two-thirds majority, whereas men achieved a higher majority in 16 juries (16 per cent). In the remaining four juries for which we collected details but which contained 11 members, two contained nine men and two women, one contained seven men and four women and one contained five men and six women.

Table 6.21: Frequency of Male/Female Breakdown of Juries

Male-Female	Frequency	%
12-0	0	0.00
11-1	2	1.98
10-2	5	4.95
9-3	11	10.89
8-4	20	19.80
7-5	26	25.74
6-6	21	20.79
5-7	8	7.92
4-8	8	7.92
3-9	0	0.00
2-10	0	0.00
1-11	0	0.00
0-12	0	0.00

Occupational Composition. Given the categories of persons excluded or exempted from jury service by the Juries Act 1976, it seemed reasonable to suppose that those with a skilled or professional occupation would be under-represented on rape juries. The actual jury cards with the jurors' names and occupations were included on the files in respect of 43 juries involving a total of 441 jurors. Table 6.22 shows the employment levels for those jurors.

Table 6.22: Employment Levels of Jurors

	Number	%
Employed (Professional/Skilled)	104	23.58
Employed (Manual/Unskilled)	233	52.83
Not in Paid Employment	34	7.71
Unemployed	13	2.95
Unclear	57	12.93
Total	441	100

As expected, those with a skilled or professional occupation, defined as one that requires an externally validated/accredited course of study or training, made up less than one-quarter of all jurors. Those whose occupations were unskilled or manual constituted the majority of jurors (over one-half). Those who were not in paid employment included housewives, students and retirees, and they and the unemployed made up just over 10 per cent of all jurors.

Table 6.23 shows the occupations of jurors according to the NACE Rev.1 system of occupational classification used by the Central Statistics Office in its Quarterly Household Surveys.

Table 6.23: Employment of Jurors, by Industry

	Number	%
Agriculture, Forestry & Fishing	1	0.23
Other Production Industries	31	7.03
Construction	43	9.75
Wholesale & Retail Trade	46	10.43
Hotels & Restaurants	16	3.63
Transport, Storage & Communications	28	6.35
Financial & Other Business Services	90	20.41
Public Administration & Defence	23	5.22
Education	10	2.27
Health	8	1.81
Other Services	41	9.30
Unemployed	13	2.95
Not in Paid Employment	34	7.71
Unclear	57	12.93
Total	441	100

The largest industry represented on the juries was financial and other business services, almost all of whose representatives were employed in clerical roles. A similarly unskilled role was had by most of those employed in the wholesale and retail trades which made up the next most represented industry. Indeed, these two industries accounted for nearly one-third of all jurors.

Jury Foremen. One of the first tasks a newly empanelled jury must perform is to select one of their number to act as foreman. Despite the gendered nature of the title, the position is open equally to male and to female jurors. Formally, the foreman speaks for the jury when giving verdict and is the conduit between the jury and the judge. The foreman, like all jurors, has only one vote and is therefore no more powerful than any other juror. In practice, however, as the foreman chairs the deliberations and decides when to hold votes, he or she is in a position to influence the deliberative process.

Gender details were available in respect of 96 jury foremen. Seventy-one (73.96 per cent) were male and twenty-five (26.04 per cent) were female. Thus male jurors were disproportionately overrepresented as foremen, accounting for less than two-thirds of jurors generally but making up almost three-quarters of all foremen. In terms of occupation, details were available on 39 foremen.

Table 6.24: Employment Status of Jury Foremen

	Number
Employed (Professional/Skilled)	14
Employed (Manual/Unskilled)	15
Not in Paid Employment	1
Unemployed	0
Unclear	9
Total	39

Those with a professional or skilled occupation were thus disproportionately likely to be chosen as foreman: professional and skilled jurors made up less than one-quarter of jurors but accounted for nearly half of all foremen. Table 6.25 shows the industrial classification of the foremen.

Table 6.25: Employment of Jury Foremen, by Industry

	Number
Agriculture, Forestry & Fishing	0
Other Production Industries	0
Construction	6
Wholesale & Retail Trade	4
Hotels & Restaurants	0
Transport, Storage & Communications	1
Financial & Other Business Services	6
Public Administration & Defence	4
Education	1
Health	3
Other Services	1
Unemployed	0
Not in Paid Employment	1
Unclear	12
Total	39

Deliberation Periods. There are no minimum or maximum deliberation periods set by the law. The jury is free to deliberate for as long as they wish, although in practical terms, the trial judge will have to call a halt once it becomes clear to him or her that the jury is unable to reach a verdict. Information on the deliberation periods was available in respect of 79 juries, and those deliberations varied between 34 minutes and 1,345 minutes (22 hours and 25 minutes) in length. The median deliberation lasted for 196.5 minutes (3 hours and 16.5 minutes), while the average lasted for 233.91 minutes (3 hours and 51.91 minutes). The standard deviation was 180.10. Table 6.26 sets out the cumulative frequency of deliberation times.

Table 6.26: Frequency of Deliberation Times

Deliberation Times (in Minutes)	Number of Cases	% of Cases
<30	0	0.00
<60	6	7.59
<90	12	15.19
<120	19	24.05
<150	26	32.91
<180	34	43.04
<210	43	54.43
<240	50	63.29
<270	55	69.62
<300	59	74.68
<330	63	79.75
<360	67	84.81
<390	70	88.61
<420	71	89.87
<450	73	92.41
<480	74	93.67
>480	79	100.00

Over half of the deliberations were completed within three and a half hours and almost three-quarters of deliberations were completed within five hours.

Verdicts. By tradition, juries are instructed to deliberate until they reach a unanimous decision. Unanimity has been a requirement since the mid-fourteenth century (Thayer, 1898 (1999): 86) but during the twentieth century, the unanimity principle came under increasing assault and many jurisdictions enacted provisions allowing for majority verdicts. In Ireland, section 25 of the Criminal Justice Act 1984 permits a trial judge to accept a majority verdict of at least 10 jurors providing the jury has been deliberating for at least two hours. This measure was controversial (Casey, 1996), but in *O'Callaghan v. Attorney General* (1993: 25), the Supreme Court accepted the constitutionality of the provision, noting that a number of advantages accrued:

> Majority verdicts such as are permitted in the impugned legislation may rebound to the advantage of the accused as well as to the prosecution on occasion; the chances of a disagreement are reduced and the aim of the zealot who glories in dissent and who may make his or her way onto a jury from time to time is defeated. Sufficient protection is provided in the legislation to give enough time to a minority to win others over to their point of view.

In the sample in this study, there were 101 verdicts given by juries on rape charges (i.e., innocence or guilt was decided by the jury on its own initiative on those charges). There were 78 other dispositions on rape charges that did not involve a voluntary jury verdict, including 53 directed acquittals, 16 hung juries and 6 instances in which rape charges were withdrawn. Of the 101 verdicts, only 13 were recorded as being majority verdicts. Six of these verdicts were at 11–1, five were at 10-2, and in two others we were unable to ascertain from the files the precise breakdown. Five of the 13 majority verdicts were for conviction and eight were for acquittal. This finding seems to vindicate the Supreme Court's assertion that majority verdicts work equally to the advantage of the defendant as to the prosecution.

Details were collected concerning the verdict patterns of 108 juries, of which all but two involved the prosecution of rape charges (the other two involved the prosecution of charges of aggravated sexual assault despite the complainant making allegations of non-consensual penetration). A total of 77 juries considered charges of rape under section 2 of the 1981 Act, 11 considered charges of rape under section 4 of the 1990 Act, and 18 juries considered charges of rape under both sections. In tabulating the decisions of the juries, the following counting rules were used:

1. If more than one jury was empanelled in a case, the verdicts of each jury were counted separately;

2. If more than one defendant was being tried by a single jury, the jury's verdicts against each defendant were recorded separately as if they were different juries;

3. In cases involving multiple charges against the same defendant, the following protocols were followed:

    a) a conviction was recorded if the defendant was convicted of at least one count of rape of either variety;

    b) if different verdicts were given in respect of different charges, we recorded the most definitive decision by the jury (i.e., if the jury was hung on one charge of rape and acquitted on another, we recorded the acquittal).

Table 6.27 sets out the results of their deliberations on the rape charges.

Table 6.27: Results of Jury Deliberations on Rape Charges

	Guilty	Not Guilty	Not Guilty by Direction	Hung	No Verdict Given	Result Unknown	Total
Rape, s.2	14	40	6	6	8	2	77
Rape, s.4	2	6	2	2	0	0	11
Both	4	10	1	0	2	1	18
Total	20	56	9	8	10	3	106

These figures demonstrate a striking reluctance on the part of juries to convict on rape charges: combining not guilty verdicts and directed not guilty verdicts, almost two-thirds of juries acquitted the defendant. Less than one in five juries convicted the defendant of at least one rape charge. Compare these figures with the verdicts presented on lesser sexual charges or non-sexual charges*

---

* Given the focus of this study, we treated the rape charges as being the most significant charges faced by the defendant. In some cases, the defendant faced

(tabulated using the same counting rules as above) as shown in Table 6.28.

Table 6.28: Results of Jury Deliberations on Lesser Sexual and Non-Sexual Charges

	Guilty	Not Guilty	Not Guilty by Direction	Hung	No Verdict Given	Result Unknown	Total
Lesser Sexual Offences	13	16	2	2	8	2	43
Non-Sexual Offences	16	10	6	0	8	2	42
Total	29	26	8	2	16	4	85

Juries that considered lesser and non-sexual offences were far more willing to convict; excluding cases in which verdicts were either not given or were unrecorded on the files, the conviction rate was some 46 per cent (29 out of 63). Further, 11 juries *convicted* the defendant of a lesser or non-sexual offence having also *acquitted* the defendant on rape charges. By contrast, where a defendant was charged with rape and other lesser or non-sexual charges, a conviction on the rape charge was invariably accompanied by a conviction on the other charges. This result did not occur on only three occasions: in one case the verdict was not recorded on the file; in the second case, the acquittal on the non-sexual charge had been directed by the trial judge; and in the third case, the acquittal on the lesser sexual charge was in respect of an attempted rape under section 4. This is significant because there is ample evidence of the reluctance of Irish juries to convict a person on a charge of rape under section 4. In this sample, 29 juries considered charges of rape under section 4. Their verdicts are set out in Table 6.29.

---

extremely serious non-sexual charges such as homicide; in any other context, charges of this nature would be considered more serious than rape.

Table 6.29: Results of Jury Deliberations on Charges of Rape under Section 4

	Guilty	Not Guilty	Not Guilty by Direction	Hung	No Verdict Recorded	Result Unknown	Total
Juries Considering s.4 Charges	4	18	3	1	2	1	29

As if to underline their reluctance to convict for rape under section 4, in one of the cases in which the jury recorded a conviction of rape under section 4, the jury also acquitted the defendant on two other similar counts.

Gender Composition and Verdict. Table 6.30, derived using the same counting rules set out above, sets out the results of the juries' deliberations on rape charges against individual defendants according to gender composition. What is being presented here are the results of the juries' deliberations on *rape* charges alone; two male-dominated juries were not required to consider rape charges and so are excluded from these figures.

The poor conviction rate on rape charges in contested cases has already been noted. What is of interest here is the conviction rate among female-dominated juries. The majority of the experimental studies reviewed in Chapter 2 suggested that female jurors are more sympathetic to complainants and are more likely than male jurors to convict a defendant. From these studies, one would expect that a female-dominated jury would be more likely to convict than a male-dominated jury. The figures presented here show no evidence to support such a contention. To the contrary, no female-dominated jury convicted a defendant of rape in our sample, which covered a six-year period. Contrary to expectations, male-dominated juries were the most likely to convict.

Table 6.30: Results of Jury Deliberations on Rape Charges, by Gender Dominance

	Guilty	Not Guilty	Not Guilty by Direction	Hung	No Verdict Given	Result Unknown	Total
Male-Dominated Juries	17	31	6	2	7	2	65
Female-Dominated Juries	0	13	0	5	0	0	18
Evenly Composed Juries	3	12	2	1	1	1	20
Unknown Composition	0	0	1	0	2	0	3
Total	20	56	9	8	10	3	106

Results

Charges were brought against 188 defendants but in the case of seven defendants all Central Criminal Court records were missing from the files. Of the remaining 181 defendants, all but four faced charges of rape whether under section 2 of the 1981 Act or section 4 of the 1990 Act. The other four defendants had originally faced charges of rape under section 4 but these charges were subsequently reduced to charges of aggravated sexual assault. A total of eleven defendants were aged under 18 at the time of the incident.

Table 6.31 sets out the results of the cases against the 188 defendants in our sample. For the purposes of this table, the following counting rules were observed:

- A defendant was deemed to have been convicted of rape if he was convicted of, or pleaded guilty to, at least one count of rape of either variety;
- If the jury returned different verdicts on different charges, we recorded the most definitive jury decision (i.e., if a jury was

hung on one count and acquitted on another count, the acquittal was recorded);

- If the jury was directed to acquit on one count and made its own decision on another count, we recorded the jury's own decision;

- In all cases, we recorded the result of the most serious charge faced by the defendant;

- The categories presented are mutually exclusive.

Ninety-nine defendants were convicted of a sexual offence, or over half of all defendants in our sample. A total of 108 defendants, or 57 per cent, were convicted of at least one charge. By contrast, over one-quarter of defendants were acquitted entirely of all charges. Of these defendants, one-sixth (eight) were fully acquitted on the direction of the trial judge. Such directions are given when the trial judge determines that the prosecution's case, viewed in the most positive light, either discloses no offence known to the law or that charged in the indictment, or that no reasonable jury could convict if properly charged (Walsh, 2002: para. 19-22). Further, the DPP decided not to proceed against nearly one in twelve of all defendants. The reasons for these withdrawals were not apparent from the files. Nevertheless, it must be a source of some concern that 20 defendants had their cases dropped by the prosecutor or removed from the jury by the trial judge. This figure represents almost 11 per cent of all the defendants in the sample, or one in nine.

Of the 70 defendants convicted of rape, 51 (73 per cent) pleaded guilty and only 19 were convicted at trial. Further, 21 defendants pleaded guilty to a lesser sexual offence and four defendants pleaded guilty to a non-sexual offence. In most cases, the guilty plea was sufficient to end proceedings entirely, which has the appearance of plea-bargaining. Plea-bargains typically involve the defendant agreeing to plead guilty either to a lesser charge (charge-bargaining) or in return for an agreed reduced sentence (sentence-bargaining). In eight cases, however, the DPP continued to press rape charges notwithstanding the defendant's plea to a lesser or non-sexual charge, which lends credence to his oft-stated claim that his office does not engage in plea-bargaining. In one case, multiple charges were brought against the defendant in respect of offences against an adult woman and her daughter. The charges in respect of the woman were dropped when the defendant agreed to plead guilty to the charges in respect of the daughter. While this appears to be a classic example of charge-bargaining, the file makes it clear that this agreement came about very much at the instigation of the adult woman.

Table 6.31: Results of Charges, by Defendant

Result	Totals	% of all Defendants
Conviction of Rape	70	37
Conviction of a Lesser Sexual Offence	29	15
Conviction of a Non-Sexual Offence	9	5
Acquittal	52	28
Defendant Absconded	4*	2
Prosecutor did not Proceed	12	6
No Trial for Technical Reasons	5	3
Documents Missing	7	4
Total	188	100

Attrition. Attrition is usually defined as the process by which cases fall out of the criminal justice system (Gregory and Lees, 1996; Lea et al., 2003). Cases can involve multiple defendants and/or multiple charges, so it makes more sense to refer to attrition by reference either to cases against individual defendants or to charges rather than to cases. Referring to cases against individual defendants, attrition occurs any time a defendant avoids a conviction for rape. Referring to charges, attrition occurs any time

---

* A fifth defendant absconded before his trial but was subsequently caught, stood trial and was acquitted on charges of rape and rape under section 4.

charges of rape are dropped, downgraded or rejected at any stage during the criminal process. On either formulation, it is apparent that attrition is not a zero-sum proposition; rather, attrition should be viewed as a continuum in which there are varying degrees. If a defendant is convicted of sexual assault instead of rape, or if a charge of aggravated sexual assault is substituted for a charge of rape, attrition has occurred but not to the same degree as if the defendant was fully acquitted or all charges were dropped. In other words, there is complete attrition and partial attrition.

Table 6.32 sets out the degrees of attrition experienced by the defendants in our sample, and is based on the results set out in the earlier table.

Table 6.32: Attrition, by Defendant

	Point of Attrition	**Numbers**
No Attrition		70
Partial Attrition		38
	Trial – Lesser Sexual Offence Conviction	29
	Trial – Non-Sexual Offence Conviction	9
Complete Attrition		73
	Trial Acquittal	52
	Trial Did Not Proceed	9
	Pre-Trial	12
Unknown		7
Total		188

The same continuum can be expressed in the form of a chart, as shown if Figure 6.4.

Figure 6.4: Attrition, by Defendant

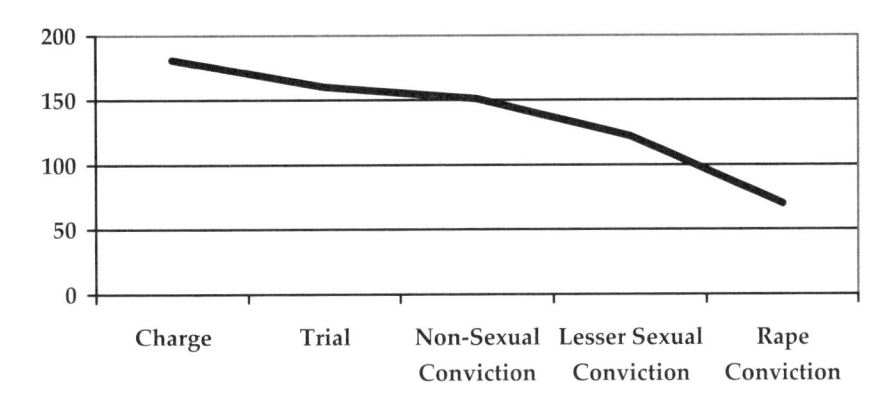

[Line chart showing values declining from ~180 at "Charge" to ~150 at "Trial" to ~150 at "Non-Sexual Conviction" to ~120 at "Lesser Sexual Conviction" to ~70 at "Rape Conviction"]

In our sample, charges were laid against 188 defendants, but documentation was missing in respect of seven of them. Of the 181 defendants for whom information as to outcome was available, 21 defendants did not go to trial and a further 52 defendants were acquitted at trial, giving a complete attrition rate of 73 defendants out of 181, or 40 per cent. Nine defendants were convicted of a non-sexual offence and a further 29 defendants were convicted of a lesser sexual offence, giving a partial attrition rate of 38 out of 181 defendants, or 21 per cent. Thus, some degree of attrition occurred in respect of 111 defendants, or 61 per cent. In respect of only 70 defendants, or 39 per cent, was there no attrition at all.

The preceding discussion considers attrition in the context of defendants. As noted above, attrition can also be considered in the context of charges. Table 6.33 sets out the degree of attrition by category of charges.

Overall, the charges actually prosecuted largely reflect the charges laid against the defendants in the initial Statements of Charges. The DPP appears reluctant to drop rape charges once they have been laid, but he is apparently willing to add extra lesser sexual offences to an indictment. Dropping non-sexual charges in rape cases appears to be quite common, but in the context of a rape case, these non-sexual offences are usually relatively minor in nature.* In terms of outcome, there is a high degree of uniformity in the attrition rate among the different categories of charges laid against defendants in our sample of rape cases: a little over one-third of each category of charges resulted in a conviction.

Table 6.33: Attrition, by Charge

	Statement of Charges	Charges Prosecuted	Charges Resulting in Conviction
No. of Rape Charges	325	319	114
No. of Lesser Sexual Offences	141	161	47
No. of Non-Sexual Offences	202	116	74
Total No. of Charges	668	596	235

Sentencing

A total of 111 sentences were imposed for rape, including sentences imposed upon five defendants aged under 18 at the time of sentencing. Excluding these juvenile offenders and their sentences, Table 6.34 sets out the range of sentences imposed for rape (there were no life sentences imposed).

These figures give a basic indication of the sentences imposed for rape, and they show that the sentences ranged between two years and 21 years. The median sentence is nine years while the average sentence is a little over nine years and three months. These figures are misleading, however, in that they do not take account of differences between the two forms of rape nor between sentences imposed on foot of a conviction and those imposed on

---

* This is not always the case: in two of the cases in this sample, the non-sexual offences included charges of homicide.

foot of a guilty plea. Table 6.35 breaks down the figures to show these distinctions.

Table 6.34: Range of Sentences Imposed for Rape

	Sentences Imposed (in months)
Minimum Sentence	24
Maximum Sentence	252
Median Sentence	108
Mean Sentence	112.37
Standard Deviation	48.38

Table 6.35: Range of Sentences, by Charge, Trial and Guilty Plea (in months)

	Rape (section 2)		Rape (section 4)	
	Trial	*Guilty Plea*	*Trial*	*Guilty Plea*
Minimum	24	36	72	36
Maximum	216	252	120	204
Median	96	102	84	114
Mean	109.04	111.55	90	118
Standard Deviation	47.99	50.69	22.98	48.38

This table throws up two issues of immediate interest. First, actions that come within the definition of rape under section 4 are relatively new additions to the broader modern definition of rape. As such, it might have been expected that rape under section 4 was not taken as seriously as the traditional formulation of rape. Using sentence as a proxy for the relative seriousness with which the two forms of rape are viewed by the courts, it is apparent that this is not the case. While the median and mean trial sentences for traditional rape are higher than those for rape under section 4, the median and mean sentences following a guilty plea are higher for rape under section 4 than for traditional rape. The starting point for rape under section 4 at trial is also three times higher than that for rape, although we had information on only two such sentences. It is possible, however, that these aggregated figures hide variations in sentences for the two forms of rape. Seventeen defendants, however, received sentences during the same trial for both rape and rape under section 4. In these cases, the circumstances of the offence and those of the offender would obviously be the same for both forms of rape, and it is noteworthy that all seventeen defendants received exactly the same sentence for rape under section 4 as for rape. The evidence suggests, therefore, that the Irish judiciary make no distinction between the two forms of rape when imposing sentence.

Second, the table shows that a guilty plea to a charge of either variety of rape will not necessarily result in an individual offender receiving a light sentence. For both forms of rape in our sample, the maximum sentence imposed after a guilty plea was substantially higher than that imposed after a trial. Further, the median and mean sentences imposed for both forms of rape are higher after a guilty plea than after a trial. At first glance this seems odd given that a guilty plea is the principal mitigating factor, and one that will usually attract a substantial discount in recognition of the fact that a guilty plea saves the complainant from having to give evidence and face cross-examination (O'Malley, 2006: para. 6-21). The English courts have indicated that an early guilty plea will typically attract a discount of one-third, and O'Malley cites evidence that the Irish courts take a similar view (2006: para. 6-32). The discount, however, is measured against the sentence that the individual defendant would otherwise have received; the discount is not measured against the median or mean sentences imposed for a particular category of offence.

Frequency of Sentences. Table 6.36 sets out the frequency with which sentences arose in different bands in our sample (excluding the sentences imposed upon five juvenile offenders)*.

Table 6.36: Frequency of Sentences

	Rape		Rape Under Section 4	
	Trial	*Guilty Plea*	*Trial*	*Guilty Plea*
≤ 24 months	0	0	0	0
≤ 60 months	4	7	0	5
≤ 120 months	14	36	2	25
≤ 180 months	2	2	0	0
≤ 192 months	1	0	0	0
> 192 months	0	5	0	3
Total	21	50	2	33

Out of 106 sentences imposed for rape and rape under section 4, only 16 (15 per cent) were for imprisonment for periods of five years or less. The very considerable majority of sentences (77 or 73 per cent) were for periods between five and ten years imprisonment. The remaining 13 sentences (12 per cent) were for periods of imprisonment of 15 years or more.

Concurrent and Consecutive Sentencing. In general, the courts have discretion to impose either concurrent or consecutive sentences, aside from certain instances where consecutive sentences

---

* The sentences imposed upon these five offenders were as follows: 120 months in St. Patrick's Institution, 108 months in St. Patrick's Institution, 96 months in St. Patrick's Institution, 48 months in Trinity House in Lusk, and 36 months in St. Patrick's Institution. The first four juvenile offenders were all sentenced for a rape they committed together with another adult offender. All five juvenile offenders pleaded guilty. Three other offenders were aged under 18 at the time of the commission of the offence but had reached majority by the time of sentencing and received prison sentences. These sentences are included in the table.

are required by statute (O'Malley, 2006: para. 7-02).* Sentencing theory holds that sentences for offences committed as part of a single transaction should run concurrently, while sentences for offences that do not form part of a single transaction should run consecutively (O'Malley, 2006: para.7-01, citing Thomas, 1979: 53). Consecutive sentences are subject to the totality principle, under which the total aggregate period to which the defendant has been sentenced should be assessed in terms of proportionality (*People (DPP) v. TB*, 1996: 298). The Irish courts, however, have displayed a marked lack of enthusiasm for consecutive sentences; in *People (DPP) v. GMcC* (1997), the Court of Criminal Appeal commented that it has 'long been the sentencing practice in this jurisdiction that a discretion in favour of consecutive sentences is exercised sparingly'. The court was especially wary of imposing consecutive sentences that 'would lead to American-type sentences of hundreds of years, which do not form part of our jurisprudence' (1997, citing with approval the comments of the trial judge). The hostility shown by the Irish judiciary towards consecutive sentences is well illustrated by *DPP v. Byrne* (1995). There, the defendant committed acts of rape against two different women in two different locations and on two different dates. He was sentenced to two terms of imprisonment of 10 years each, to run concurrently. The Court of Criminal Appeal rejected the DPP's contention that this arrangement was unduly lenient to the defendant. In *People (DPP) v. McKenna (No.2)* (2002), the Court of Criminal Appeal described as useful a submission from counsel from an earlier case that a consecutive sentence might be appropriate in cases where the defendant had engaged in 'sexual misconduct with different persons or over a much longer period of time than is the case here and that, perhaps too, the misconduct would have been attended with circumstances of depravity beyond the actual act of intercourse' (2002: 349). This comment illustrates the kind of cir-

---

* For example, section 11(1) of the Criminal Justice Act 1984 provides that if a person commits an offence while on bail, the sentence for that offence must run consecutively to any sentence imposed for the original offence.

cumstances that need to exist before an Irish court will consider imposing consecutive sentences.

In this sample, 51 defendants had multiple sentences imposed upon them, and in all cases, the sentences were to run concurrently. Only one defendant was subjected to consecutive sentences. This defendant had been convicted of raping three different women on three different occasions and in three different locations. Unusually, he was tried separately in respect of each complainant and pleaded guilty in each trial. He was sentenced to seven years imprisonment in each trial, with the final two years of each suspended, and the sentences were to run consecutively. The Court of Criminal Appeal increased each sentence to 10 years, 12 years and 15 years, respectively, but ordered that they should all run concurrently. Thus, the defendant gained nothing in practical terms as the total period of imprisonment remained at 15 years, but this case illustrates the hostility of the Irish courts to consecutive sentencing.

Suspension Periods. The judiciary has a power, developed initially at common law but now subject to statutory control (section 99 of the Criminal Justice Act 2006), to suspend any portion of a sentence of imprisonment usually in return for the offender agreeing to certain conditions (O'Malley, 2006: para. 22-01). O'Malley sets out three fundamental conditions to be complied with by a court in imposing a suspended sentence: that imprisonment is merited in the first place, that the sentence is not inflated because a portion of it is to be suspended and any conditions to be attached to the suspension must be capable of fulfilment by the offender (O'Malley, 2006: paras. 22-03-22-05). Once the sentence is suspended, it can be reactivated if the offender breaches the conditions attached to the suspension. For that reason, the power of suspension is often justified on the basis that it encourages the rehabilitation of the offender (O'Malley, 2006: para.22-09).

In our sample, 111 sentences were imposed for rape, all involving periods of imprisonment. Of these sentences, 82 (74 per cent) were made subject to a period of suspension. In terms of defendants, 44 defendants out of 70 (63 per cent) who were convicted of rape or rape under section 4 received a sentence that was at least partially suspended. Thus, a period of suspension is very much the norm in sentencing for rape. Table 6.37 sets out the range of suspension periods imposed on the sentences in our sample.

Table 6.37: Range of Suspension Periods

	Suspension Periods (in months)
Minimum Period	9
Maximum Period	72
Median Period	18
Mean Period	23.33
Standard Deviation	11.72

Table 6.38 sets out the frequency by which suspension periods were imposed.

Table 6.38: Frequency of Suspension Periods

	Suspension Period
≤ 6 Months	0
≤ 12 Months	15
≤ 18 Months	31
≤ 24 Months	17
≤ 36 Months	14
≤ 48 Months	4
≤ 72 Months	1
Total	82

The considerable majority of suspensions were for periods of between 12 and 36 months – a total of 62 suspensions, or 76 per cent. All but five of these defendants had pleaded guilty to the rape charges, and two of these five defendants were aged under 18 at the time of the commission of the offences. The vast majority of defendants sentenced for rape will serve some period in prison. Only four defendants had their sentences for rape suspended entirely, while two others had four out of five years and four out of six years suspended.

The courts have the power to attach any condition they deem fit to the suspension. At a minimum, the defendant usually has to enter a bond to be of good behaviour for the term of the suspension. In other cases, however, the court might try to tailor the conditions specifically to the defendant's circumstances. Examples of these conditions in our sample include the following requirements, imposed on different defendants:

- The defendant must abstain from the consumption of alcohol;
- The defendant must pass the European Computer Driving Licence examinations and undergo tuition in the English language; and
- The defendant must regularly attend meetings of Alcoholics Anonymous and attend a psychotherapist.

The effect that these suspension periods have upon the sentences to be served by those convicted of rape can be dramatic. Table 6.39 sets out the range of theoretical and actual sentences imposed upon defendants convicted of rape in our sample. The term 'theoretical sentence' is used to denote the maximum sentence that the defendant could serve as a result of the court's sentence. The term 'actual sentence' is used to denote the maximum sentence that the defendant will actually serve taking into account any suspension periods imposed by the court. In other words, the actual sentence is the theoretical sentence minus the suspension period.

There were only two sentences imposed for rape under section 4 following a trial and neither was subject to a suspension period. In all other categories, however, the use of suspension periods had a significant effect on the amount of time offenders would actually serve on prison – between 12 per cent and 18 per cent. The biggest impact was felt in respect of sentences imposed following a guilty plea. Consequently, offenders who plead guilty receive a double benefit: they receive a discount on the sentence they would otherwise have received, and that discount is accentuated through the use of suspension periods.

Table 6.39: Effect of Suspension Periods

	Rape (section 2)				Rape (section 4)			
	Trial		Guilty Plea		Trial		Guilty Plea	
	Th.	Ac.	Th.	Ac	Th.	Ac.	Th.	Ac.
Minimum	24	12	36	0	72	72	36	0
Maximum	216	202	252	240	120	120	204	180
Median	96	84	102	83	84	84	114	93
Mean	109.04	94.96	111.55	96.57	90	90	118	101.75
St. Dev.	47.99	50.25	50.69	55.61	22.98	22.98	48.38	50.42

Ancillary Penalties. Irish law makes provision for a number of ancillary penalties to be imposed upon those convicted of rape, all introduced by the Sex Offenders Act 2001. Part 2 of this Act imposes upon an offender convicted of any of the main sex offences under Irish law an obligation to notify the Gardaí within seven days of his name, his address and his date of birth. Section 14 of the Act requires the trial judge to certify as a sex offender any offender who is subject to the notification requirements in the 2001 Act. These requirements will remain in place indefinitely for any eligible sex offender sentenced to a term of imprisonment of two years or more, although there is provision for the offender to apply to the Circuit Court after 10 years for discharge from this obligation. Part 5 of the Sex Offenders Act 2001 made provision for the introduction of post-release supervision of sex offenders by the Probation Service. Unlike the notification requirements, post-release supervision is not mandatory but a court can impose a period of supervision if it believes that doing so is in the interests of the offender's rehabilitation and the need of the community to be protected from the offender. The court is empowered to attach any conditions it deems necessary to be observed during the period of supervision.

In this study, 98 defendants were convicted of rape or a lesser sexual offence. Evidence of certification as a sex offender was present on the files in respect of 74 defendants (75.5 per cent), which demonstrates broad compliance with the terms of the 2001 Act. Sixty of these defendants had been convicted of rape offences, 11 had been convicted of indecent or sexual assault and the other three had been convicted of aggravated sexual assault or an attempted sexual offence. It is not clear why there was no evidence of certification in respect of the other defendants, given that certification is supposed to follow automatically from a conviction for a relevant offence. Some can be explained by the fact that they were sentenced prior to the commencement of the 2001 Act, while others were convicted of indecent assault which is not eligible if the victim was an adult and the defendant is not sentenced to a penalty involving deprivation of liberty. Five defendants, however, were convicted of rape or aggravated sexual assault and were sentenced after the commencement of the Act, but there was no evidence of certification on the files. It may simply be that these defendants were in fact certified but the relevant documentation was not attached to the files.

Table 6.40: Periods of Post-Release Supervision

	Supervision Periods (in years)
Minimum Period	1
Maximum Period	10
Median Period	5
Mean Period	4.65
Standard Deviation	2.25

Thirty-four defendants were ordered to undergo a period of post-release supervision. Twenty-two of these defendants had been convicted of rape, four had been convicted of aggravated sexual assault and the remainder had been convicted of indecent or sexual assault or sexual offences against the mentally ill. Table 6.41

sets out the frequency with which various supervision periods were imposed.

Table 6.41: Frequency of Supervision Periods

Supervision Periods (in Years)	Number
1	2
2	2
3	8
4	3
5	11
6	2
7	2
8	0
9	0
10	3
Unclear	1*
Total	34

Two-thirds of supervision orders (22) were for periods of between three and five years. An offender should count himself unfortunate to receive a supervision period of more than seven years.

Finally, section 6 of the Criminal Justice Act 1993 provides that a court may impose upon a defendant a compensation order either in addition to or instead of any other penalty, unless it sees reason not to do so. The amount of compensation should not exceed the amount that might be ordered in a civil action, and the court must have regard to the defendant's means in assessing the amount of compensation payable. The trial court records con-

---

* One order was unclear due to a discrepancy in official documents – two documents set the period at four years while two other documents set the period at five years.

tained only two compensation orders, one for €6,363 and the other for €1,270. Anecdotally, however, we understand that it is not unusual for those convicted of rape to make private arrangements for the payment of compensation. There were references to such arrangements in two files; in one case, the defendant paid a sum of €10,000 to the complainant, while in the other, the defendant made a donation of furniture, electrical and household goods to the charity ALONE and a cash donation to the Dublin Rape Crisis Centre of €2,000. Information on any other private compensation arrangements that might have been made in other cases was unavailable.

Victim Impact Statements. Section 5 of the Criminal Justice Act 1993 obliges a court to take into account the impact of the crime on the victim when sentencing a person for a sexual or violent crime. To that end, the court is empowered to receive evidence as to that impact, although the Act does not specify from whom that evidence should come or who is responsible for putting that evidence before the court. In practice, the DPP has this responsibility (Director of Public Prosecutions, 2007: para. 8.14). The Act also gives to the complainant a statutory right, upon application, to address the court as to the impact of the crime. Many Irish commentators (Coffey, 2006: 16; Coen, 2006; O'Malley, 2006: 228) have expressed reservations about the effect that victim impact statements might have upon the sentencing process. In particular, it has been suggested that complainants might take the opportunity to exercise vengeance against the defendant, thereby making the criminal process harsher. The absence of sentencing figures from before 1993 makes it difficult to substantiate empirically the second part of this claim. The first part, however, can be tested.

In our sample of cases, victim impact statements were present in 85 files. Many files had more than one statement, giving a total of 107 statements. It was noted earlier that these statements were written by a variety of authors, and that they refer in the main to a variety of issues such as psychological problems, family problems and job problems. The following table sets out the number of statements, by author, in which either the defendant or some sentencing issue was mentioned.

Table 6.42: Mention of Defendant or Sentencing in Victim Impact Statements

	Defendant Mentioned	Sentencing Issues Mentioned	Total No. of Statements
Psychologist	6	6	47
Garda Síochána	2	6	19
Complainant	6	6	15
Rape Crisis Centre	1	1	12
Other	2	0	14
Total	17	19	107

The most obvious conclusion is how rare it is for complainants to even mention the defendant or his punishment. The defendant was mentioned in only 16 per cent of statements, and the complainant made reference to an appropriate punishment in only 18 per cent of statements. Such comments are most likely to occur in statements authored by the complainant herself. They are least likely to occur in statements authored by Rape Crisis Centre personnel.

Delay

In any rape case, certain key stages can be identified as the case progresses through the criminal justice system.

1. **The Report Stage**: this stage runs from the incident to the complainant's decision to make a formal complaint to the Gardaí – delays here can result in essential forensic evidence being lost or difficulties being encountered in locating the alleged perpetrator. This first stage is under the control of the complainant.

2. **The Investigative Stage**: this stage runs from the date of report to the date on which the defendant is charged. This stage is largely under the control of the Gardaí and represents the time required to interview witnesses, collect forensic evidence, etc.

3. **The Prosecution Stage**: this stage runs from the date of charge to the date on which the defendant is returned by the District Court for trial before the Central Criminal Court. This stage is run by the Director of Public Prosecutions and represents the DPP's commitment to prosecute the case – the DPP can withdraw the prosecution after the defendant has been returned for trial, but this is somewhat rare: in our sample, this happened with respect to only 12 defendants out of 188.

4. **The Court Stage**: this stage runs from the date of return for trial to the date on which the trial starts. While both sides will use this time to develop and prepare their own cases, the length of this stage is determined largely by logistical pressures within the Courts Service.

5. **The Trial Stage**: this stage arises in cases in which the defendant contests the charges against him, and represents the length of the trial. This stage is under the control of the trial judge.

6. **The Sentencing Stage**: the final stage arises where the defendant has either been convicted of, or has pleaded guilty to, at least one of the charges brought against him. This stage is nominally under the control of the trial judge, although its length will be determined by the time it takes to produce Probation Reports on the defendant and victim impact statements.

Most cases will be completed after the sentencing stage, but in a minority of cases, there will a further stage – the appellate stage. This stage is under the control of the Court of Criminal Appeal and, if the original result is quashed, may lead to the trial and sentencing stages being replayed.

From our sample of cases, information was collected on each of the preceding stages, and this information is presented below.* Table 6.43 presents the median length of each stage in months unless the length of time was so short as to make months an inappropriate measure. For the purposes of these results, a month is calculated as a period of 28 days. The National Crime Council, in presenting its own report on delays in rape and homicide cases (2006), also used the median for convincing reasons. The length of time cases take can vary widely for a variety of reasons which can lead to average figures being highly misleading. The median, however, is less susceptible to these variations, and therefore gives a more accurate picture of the amount of time each stage takes. Where relevant, if a case concerned multiple defendants or complainants, each defendant or each complainant was treated as a separate case. For that reason, totals will sometimes exceed the number of included cases in the sample. The key dates were not available in every case, and the number of cases on which our figures are based have been indicated.

The median length of time required to dispose of a rape case is almost 33 months, or two years and nine months. Cases disposed of through guilty plea typically required nine months less to reach disposition than those disposed of through a trial.

The vast majority of cases were reported to the Gardaí within 24 hours, which no doubt assisted the DPP in reaching the decision to prosecute as the immediate report would allow for the most complete collection of evidence. It typically takes almost a year to bring the case from initial report to the return of the defendant for trial. We are unable to say whether there is a possibility that this period could be reduced, perhaps through the formation of specialist investigative units around the country. The primary locus for delay is in bringing cases to trial – typically, it takes a year and a third for a case to proceed from return for trial to the start of trial. For this period, the case is under the control of

---

* The terms of reference for this project did not include the appellate courts so no information is presented about the Appellate Stage.

the Central Criminal Court, and backlogs there have ramifications for the disposition of cases.

Table 6.43: Median Time Periods, by Stage

Stage	Median Lengths	No. of Cases for which Dates were Available
The Report Stage (Incident to Report)	<1 day	180
The Investigative Stage (Report to Charge)	7.54 months	141
The Prosecution Stage (Charge to Return)	5.82 months	175
The Courts Stage (Return to Trial)	16.12 months	79
The Trial Stage (Start of Trial to Verdict)	5 days	91
The Sentencing Stage (Verdict to Sentence)	2.57 months	108

DISCUSSION AND RECOMMENDATIONS

The Parties

All the evidence collected from the trial court records indicates that rape is overwhelmingly a crime perpetrated by men against women. This is not to suggest that men do not suffer rape or to denigrate the suffering that male victims of rape go through. It is important, however, that one fundamental reality of the crime of rape is recognised: men simply do not face the same threat of sexual violence as do women. This fact suggests that the Irish legislature was correct not to follow the trend apparent in many jurisdictions by enacting a gender-neutral definition of the offence. Instead, by maintaining the traditional, gendered definition of rape while enacting a parallel form of the offence to recognise the reality of male rape, the Oireachtas has recognised the fundamental reality of the crime of rape: it is overwhelmingly (though not exclusively) a gender-based offence.

In line with the literature, Irish rape complainants tend to be young and from a lower socioeconomic background: nearly two-thirds are either unemployed or employed in unskilled positions. Similarly, and again in line with the literature, Irish rape defendants are predominantly young and also from a lower socioeconomic background. Whether this lower socioeconomic background among rape complainants and defendants is true of rape victims and perpetrators more generally (i.e., those whose cases are not reported or prosecuted) is difficult to determine. The British Crime Survey (BCS) has disclosed a victim profile that is remarkably similar to the profile disclosed by the Irish trial court records (Myhil and Allen, 2002; Walby and Allen, 2004). Unlike the trial court records, the BCS is not limited to complainants whose cases are prosecuted, but is drawn instead from the general British population. If the Irish experience of rape is similar to that in Great Britain, then the similarity in profile may be evidence that rape is a crime with a lower-socio-economic tinge. On the other hand, it may be that there are people from a higher socioeconomic background who suffer rape who have sufficient resources to access private forms of assistance, and who therefore eschew the public criminal justice system. Similarly, it may be that there are perpetrators of rape from a higher socioeconomic background who have the resources and wherewithal to more easily escape detection. The evidence at our disposal makes it impossible to draw any firm conclusions on this point.

The Case Characteristics

The characteristics of the rapes prosecuted in Ireland are also broadly in line with the international literature. Three-quarters of these rapes were committed by someone who was known by the complainant to some degree, while strangers made up less than one-third of perpetrators. The majority of rapes occurred inside a building; only one-quarter occurred outdoors. The vast majority of rapes occurred at night. The majority of complainants reported suffering physical injuries, but in most cases those injuries were of a fairly minor nature.

The major characteristic disclosed by the trial court records is the presence of alcohol. As with the international experience, there was little evidence of so-called date-rape drugs such as Rohypnol and GHB playing a major role in the incidence of rape in Ireland. This is not to suggest that vigilance against these substances should be relaxed; rather, greater vigilance needs to be accorded to the impact of the consumption of alcohol. A total of 133 complainants out of 182, and 144 defendants out of 188, reported having consumed alcohol in the period prior to the incident. It is also worthy of note that of the 70 convicted defendants in respect of whom a Probation Report was prepared, three-quarters indicated that they had a history of alcohol abuse. The sheer quantity of alcohol consumed is alarming: 75 per cent of complainants and 46 per cent of defendants stated how much they had drunk with enough specificity for us to make some broad estimates in terms of standard drinks. Virtually all had exceeded the recommended maximum daily intake of alcohol, while for two-thirds of these complainants and 90 per cent of these defendants the quantity of alcohol they had consumed reached or exceeded the level of binge-drinking (seven standard drinks). Indeed, half of the defendants for whom alcohol consumption estimates could be made had consumed between 11 and 20 standard drinks. These findings are in line with other research into Irish drinking patterns (Ramstedt and Hope, 2003; Strategic Task Force on Alcohol, 2004; Hope, 2007). Hope (2007) demonstrated that the average level of consumption of alcohol in Ireland is among the highest in the European Union. Ramstedt and Hope (2003) found that binge-drinking is the norm among Irish men and occurs in one-third of drinking sessions engaged in by Irish women. This is especially the case among young men and women – precisely the groups most at risk of suffering and committing rape. Further, twice as many Irishmen as men in any other European country studied had suffered at least one of eight listed adverse consequences due to their drinking. In particular, one in eight Irishmen reported having been involved in a violent episode due to their drinking (Ramstedt and Hope, 2003: 7)

The consumption of alcohol is linked to lowered inhibitions, loss of self-control and, at higher volumes, extreme behaviour and a much reduced ability to evaluate the consequences of one's actions (Grattan and Vogel-Sprott, 2001: 192). These effects have direct implications for society's attempt to deal with sexual violence. Intoxication increases a person's vulnerability to sexual attacks by making them less likely to appreciate dangers in a particular situation that would have been apparent to a sober person. This is especially true of cases in which the complainant had met the defendant only a short time before the rape occurred, and went with him to a lonely area where the assault occurred – such cases made up a large proportion of the cases in the trial court records.

An intoxicated person is also less able to resist the assault. There is also evidence that intoxicated people are sometimes targeted by those who wish to engage in sexual behaviour precisely because they are intoxicated (Kelly and Regan, 2001). At the same time, intoxication impacts a person's memory even at lower levels of consumption (Ling et al., 2003). An intoxicated person is consequently less likely to be able to remember the precise details of the incident, and is therefore less likely to be an effective witness. As a result, an intoxicated person is not only more vulnerable to attack but is also less likely to obtain redress through the legal system. Further, experimental studies have shown that mock jurors tend to attach more blame to complainants who were drinking at the time of the incident, making effective redress even less likely. For defendants, intoxication makes engaging in extreme and outrageous behaviour more likely. They are more likely also to misread another person's intentions. Thus, the consumption decisions made by both and women can have the effect of facilitating the incidence of rape and make its detection and prosecution more difficult. Further, the consumption of alcohol makes a successful prevention campaign more difficult to design and to achieve. Accordingly, it is strongly recommended that dealing with Ireland's drinking culture be seen both as a part of any anti-rape campaign and a pre-requisite for the success of any such campaign.

Bail

The trial court records show that three-quarters of rape defendants are admitted to bail, usually by the District Court. This is not surprising given that Irish law treats bail as an entitlement: the State bears the burden of showing why bail should *not* be granted rather than the reverse. Being arrested and charged does not alter the defendant's presumptive innocence, and admission to bail is a practical manifestation of that presumption. There is no realistic prospect of this changing, and doing so would require a constitutional amendment. The documentation on the trial court records provides evidence as to bail decisions rather than the factors that lead to those decisions. Bail was granted to the majority of defendants, and nearly 95 per cent of those defendants stood trial. These figures indicate that absconding while on bail contributes directly to the attrition rate in rape cases in only a minor way. It may be that the prospect of a defendant receiving bail might contribute to victims either not making or not maintaining a complaint; indeed, some evidence of this was provided by participants in an earlier part of this study. While not of itself grounds for the denial of bail in any particular case, the impact that bail decisions can have on the wider operation of the criminal justice system is a legitimate matter of concern for policymakers. Accordingly, it is recommended that pre-trial bail is never granted unconditionally, and that all bail conditions are rigorously enforced. Doing so should reduce the possibility of absconding as far as possible while simultaneously giving complainants (and potential complainants) confidence in this aspect of the criminal justice system. It is also recommended that the following conditions should be attached, explicitly and in writing, to all grants of bail in rape cases:

- The defendant will be of good behaviour and will not commit any offences while on bail. These conditions are already required by law but they did not always appear on the documentation in the trial court records.

- The defendant will not approach or communicate in any way with the complainant, either directly or through a third party, unless with court sanction. It is not sufficient to prohibit the defendant from approaching or communicating with *witnesses* in the case; such a prohibition does cover the complainant as she has the status of a witness but this might not be clear to the defendant. A clear and direct prohibition concerning the complainant will remove any such doubts. It might be necessary to vary this prohibition in some circumstances – where the defendant and the complainant have children together, for example, some communication will probably be essential – but in general this condition should be absolute. A number of complainants mentioned in their victim impact statements that they were upset when they saw the defendant who had been released on bail. There is no way to prevent such upset, especially when both the complainant and the defendant live in the same area, but the imposition and enforcement of this condition should reduce the level of upset that is caused without unduly interfering with the defendant's freedom of movement.

- The defendant must remain within the jurisdiction of the Irish courts at all times and must therefore surrender his passport and give an undertaking not to seek a replacement. The courts must retain the power to deal with exceptional issues that might occasionally arise – a defendant might have to travel abroad for medical treatment, for example. This power should be used only exceptionally, however; returning a passport to allow the defendant to accompany his family on a foreign holiday (as happened in one case in the trial court records) should not be permitted. This particular defendant did return to Ireland, but it is not difficult to anticipate other defendants being less conscientious. A defendant, as a presumptively innocent person, is entitled to take a holiday but that entitlement must be balanced with society's right to ensure that he stands trial. No such assurance is possible if the defendant is permitted to leave the jurisdiction of the Irish courts, and there are plenty of opportunities to take holidays within that jurisdiction.

- The defendant must be required to sign on at a Garda Station as often as is required to restrict his ability to abscond. It needs to be borne in mind that with modern communications a person could be anywhere in the world within twenty-four hours. How often a defendant should be required to sign on should depend upon his resources: the greater his resources the easier it will be for him to abscond, and therefore the more frequently he should be required to sign on.

These conditions should be the minimum conditions required of all defendants admitted to bail. They do not unduly restrict the defendant's liberty but they should make absconding more difficult while also protecting the interests of the complainant. The courts should, of course, retain the power to attach any other conditions required by the circumstances of the case.

Trial judges in the Central Criminal Court have the power to admit a defendant to bail at any point in the trial process, and this power seems to continue until sentence has commenced (Walsh, 2002: para. 10-14). As a result, a defendant who has been convicted of rape can be admitted to bail while awaiting sentence. The trial court records show that the period between verdict and sentence is about two and a half months, and that three defendants absconded at this point in the process. While this is a very small number – two per cent of those admitted to bail – each time a convicted defendant escapes punishment by absconding there is a failure to fully vindicate the rights of the complainant and those of society more generally. It is recommended, therefore, that bail should not be granted to any defendant who has been convicted of a rape offence. Such defendants should be held on remand. Defendants who are awaiting trial are presumptively innocent and are deserving of their liberty, but no such presumption attaches to a defendant who is awaiting sentencing. The only conceivable justification for granting bail after conviction is the possibility, left open by the Supreme Court in *People (DPP) v. Tiernan* (1988), of a non-custodial sentence being the most appropriate sentence in the circumstances of the case. In such a case, the argument can be made that holding the defendant on remand for any period, even for only a couple of months, is inappropriate. On the other hand, it is very much an exceptional case in which a non-custodial sentence would be warranted, as the Supreme Court pointed out in

Tiernan. Indeed, the trial court records show that only four defendants had their custodial sentences suspended in their entirety. O'Malley comments that:

> ... a combination of strong mitigating factors may justify a non-custodial sentence [such as] the general character of the accused, his youth or immaturity at the time of the offence, an immediate acceptance of responsibility, genuine remorse, the exceptional hardship which imprisonment would cause (because, for example, of a disability on the part of the accused).... Seldom will any one of those factors be sufficient in itself but a co-existence of several of them may tip the balance in favour of a non-custodial sentence (2006: para. 11-06).

Even where such a combination exists, however, it is difficult to see how remanding an offender convicted of rape for less than three months could be considered disproportionate or incorrect in principle, and it is only when one or both of these conditions exist that the sentence must be overturned.

Finally, the Victims' Charter published by the Department of Justice, Equality and Law Reform asserts that complainants will be told by the Gardaí whether a defendant is being remanded in custody or has been admitted to bail. In the latter case, the complainant will also be informed of any conditions attached to the admission to bail. The Charter has no legal basis (which is a point for discussion later) and the Charter makes no mention of any obligation on the criminal justice agencies to implement a quality control procedure to ensure that the standards in the Charter are met. The only way to enforce these standards, therefore, is the complaints procedure under which the complainant may write either to the local Superintendent or to the Garda Victim Liaison Officer at Garda Headquarters (Department of Justice, Equality and Law Reform, 1999: 9). Thus, the complainant effectively bears responsibility for ensuring that the Charter is adhered to. Not only does this place the enforcement obligation upon the service-*user* rather than the service-*provider*, but it also expects a great deal from a person who the evidence shows is likely to be in a poor psychological condition. It is recommended, therefore, that the Charter be amended to include, in addition to the complaints' procedure, an explicit commitment by all criminal justice agencies to take active measures to ensure that their responsibilities under the Charter will be properly discharged.

Juries

The trial court records demonstrated continuing male dominance of the trial juries in rape cases. Fifty-nine per cent of jurors were male, two-thirds of all juries had a majority of men, and three-quarters of all jury foremen were male. Nevertheless, the records also show that the male dominance of juries has declined since the 1980s, and this dominance is far from overwhelming. In particular, over 90 per cent of juries had at least three of each gender thereby allowing the members of the minority gender to force a hung jury if they so chose. Given the findings of the majority of the experimental studies that female jurors are more sympathetic to complainants while male jurors are more likely to excuse defendants, it was surprising that male-dominated juries were found to be the most likely to convict a defendant of rape while female-dominated juries failed to convict a defendant even once. This finding corroborates the anecdotal evidence offered by judges and barristers in several studies that in their experience female jurors were more harsh to complainants than male jurors (e.g., Harris and Grace, 1999: 37; Temkin and Krahe, 2008: 136-7). The finding also corroborates Simon's view (1968: 118) that no single characteristic such as gender can predict how a person will vote on a jury. Consequently, simply increasing the number of female jurors, as has been suggested by some law reform bodies and commentators, is unlikely to increase the conviction rate in rape cases. It is recommended that juries in rape cases continue to be chosen on the basis of random selection.

Figures from the Courts Service indicate that 235 people were convicted of rape or rape and other offences, and a further 98 were convicted of lesser sexual offences. These figures do not differentiate between adult and child cases, nor do they distinguish between convictions and guilty pleas. When these distinctions were made, it became apparent that there has been a stunning reluctance among Irish juries to convict defendants of rape, and an almost total aversion to convicting for rape under section 4. Less than 20 per cent of juries considering rape charges of either variety, and only four our of 29 juries considering charges of rape under section 4, rendered a verdict of conviction. No doubt some of these defendants in these cases deserved to be acquitted – the fact that nine juries were directed to acquit indicates that the Director of Public Prosecutions sometimes takes cases that turn out to be quite weak evidentially. Indeed, in one of these cases, the prosecution case was so weak that the Central Criminal Court awarded costs against the State, a move that rarely occurs in a criminal case. Even allowing for just acquittals, however, 84 juries were given the opportunity to convict the defendant of rape and only 20 did so. This is an exceptionally poor return.

Further, seven juries convicted the defendant of a lesser sexual offence, and four juries convicted the defendant of a non-sexual offence, having acquitted the defendant of rape charges. These appear to be highly inconsistent results: clearly, the juries in these cases accepted that there was at least some merit in the complainant's allegations but they were unwilling to convict the defendant of rape. The literature suggests that juries routinely base their decisions in rape cases on extra-legal factors such as rape myths, and these results are consistent with this suggestion. These results do not, however, *prove* that this is the case and the official policy of surrounding the jury's deliberations in secrecy makes a deeper investigation more difficult.

Difficult, but not impossible. In Great Britain, section 8 of the Contempt of Court Act 1981 makes it an offence for anyone to question jurors about the content of their deliberations. No such statutory provision exists in this jurisdiction. Irish law appears to be that as explained by the Court of Appeal in *Attorney General for England and Wales v. New Statesman* (1981), a case involving the prosecution of the defendant magazine for the publication of a series of interviews with the jurors in a high profile case against a prominent politician. The Court of Appeal ruled that the defendant company's actions did not constitute a contempt as there was no possibility of any interference with the course of justice because the interviews were conducted, in good faith, only after the trial had been concluded. This judgment clearly leaves open the possibility of conducting post-verdict interviews with jurors. Further, the New Zealand Law Commission, operating under a legal regime that is almost identical to that which exists in this jurisdiction, recently conducted and published an in-depth study of the criminal jury that featured a quantitative examination of deliberations with jurors in real cases (1999 and 2001). The publication of this study is proof that jury deliberations can be the subject of empirical study without undermining the secrecy that is required for jurors to deliberate freely and openly with each other. Our findings from the trial court records suggest that the effect of many of the legal reforms enacted over the last 25 years may have been reduced in contested rape cases by the conclusions of rape juries. Our ability to counter what appears to be the pervasive influence of rape myths is severely hampered by our ignorance of the jury's deliberative processes in rape cases. Accordingly, it is strongly recommended that an empirical study be commissioned, as a matter of urgency, into the deliberations of rape juries to determine the factors that lead these juries to their verdicts.

Such a study will take time, and rape prosecutions cannot be suspended until it is completed. Nor is it acceptable to allow the possibility that extra-legal factors continue to exert an influence on the outcome of rape trials. In the meantime, therefore, it is recommended that legislative steps be taken immediately to counter the apparent influence of rape myths in trials. In particular, trial judges should be required to instruct juries that there is a distinction between concluding that a complainant has acted foolishly and a conclusion that the complainant is therefore fully or partially responsible for the rape. A parallel could be drawn here with a person who leaves the doors and windows in his unoccupied home wide open. If he returned home to find that he has suffered a burglary, no doubt many would conclude that he had acted foolishly; they might even conclude that he was, in some sense, 'asking for it'. None would dispute, however, that he has suffered a burglary, and none would argue that a) the homeowner should share responsibility for the burglary with the burglar, or b) that the burglar's responsibility for the burglary was somehow reduced by the homeowner's actions. In other words, the homeowner's actions and those of the burglar are not connected. The evidence from the literature indicates, however, that for a large proportion of the population, no such disconnect occurs in a rape case. Jurors appear to be willing to attach at least some degree of blame to the complainant on the basis that she (or he) has acted foolishly or put herself in harm's way. A strongly worded judicial instruction to the following effect might help to counter these beliefs:

> ... if the jury is satisfied that the prosecution has proven all the elements of the crime of rape, and the jury is satisfied that the complainant's actions and decisions prior to the rape were foolish, this foolishness does not of itself make the complainant in any way responsible for the rape inflicted upon her by the defendant.

It might be objected that a legislative change has been recommended in an area of the law that is in urgent need of further research prior to the completion, or even the commissioning, of that research. There is not even any direct proof that juries are making decisions on the basis of extra-legal factors. On the other hand, even if it is subsequently shown that juries are not basing their decisions on rape myths or other extra-legal factors, the proposed judicial instruction does no more than to re-state the law as it stands. In essence, it reminds the jury that the complainant's foolishness is not legally to be regarded as a full or partial defence for the defendant's actions. More fundamentally, the possibility that jury decisions in rape cases might be based upon prejudice is so antithetical to any sense of justice that waiting for this research to be completed is not a viable option.

Attrition

The trial court records indicate that the attrition figures provided by the Department of Justice, Equality and Law Reform for Regan and Kelly's (2003) study that lead directly to this study being commissioned were unduly pessimistic. In terms of defendants,

70 out of 181 for whom the outcome of their cases was known, or 39 per cent, were convicted of rape. Assuming that the attrition rate is defined as cases that fail to result in a conviction for rape, this finding would give an attrition rate of 61 per cent. This rate is very high, certainly, but is a far cry from the figure of 99 per cent given to Regan and Kelly by the Department of Justice, Equality and Law Reform. If the attrition rate is defined in terms of cases that fail to result in any kind of conviction, the findings of this study become even more favourable to Ireland. Seventy defendants were convicted of rape and a further 38 were convicted of a lesser sexual offence or a non-sexual offence. On these figures, the attrition rate would be a little over 40 per cent.

If attrition is defined in terms of rape charges rather than defendants, the trial court records show that 114 rape charges resulted in conviction out of 325 charges originally laid. The attrition rate on these figures would be 65 per cent. If convictions on lesser and non-sexual charges are included, the records show that 235 out of 668 original charges resulted in a conviction, giving an attrition rate also of 65 per cent. Again, this rate is very high but it is still substantially better than the rate ascribed to Ireland by Regan and Kelly. Admittedly, their figures began with the number of cases reported to the Gardaí while the figures in the trial court records begin with the cases that are prosecuted. Regrettably, while Garda statistics show that nearly 2,500 cases of rape and rape under section 4 were reported to the Gardaí between 2000 and 2005 (Commissioner of An Garda Síochána, 2001-2006), these figures do not distinguish between adult and child cases. As a result, it is not possible to make a direct comparison with the figures presented by Regan and Kelly. Nevertheless, we are confident that the attrition rate in adult rape cases in Ireland is substantially lower than that suggested in the earlier report.

Sentencing

The mean sentence for rape was 105.71 months and the median sentence was 96 months. It is impossible to categorically state whether or not these figures adequately reflect the seriousness of the offence of rape. It is clear, however, that the mean sentence for rape in Ireland compares quite favourably (in terms of severity) to the mean sentences imposed in other jurisdictions. Table 6.44 sets out the average sentences imposed for rape in Ireland, England and Wales, Victoria (Australia) and New Zealand over recent timeframes.

The average sentence for rape imposed in Ireland is the most severe among these four jurisdictions. Only the United States has an average sentence for rape that is longer than that in Ireland (164 months, according to Greenfeld, 1997: 14). The evidence suggests that, at least from a comparative perspective, rape sentences in Ireland are not generally unduly lenient.

Table 6.44: Average Sentences for Rape, by Jurisdiction

Jurisdiction	Average Sentence (in months)	Time Frames
Ireland	105.71	2000-2005
England and Wales	87.22	2000-2004
Victoria, Australia	63.80	2003-2008
New Zealand	99.73	2000-2006

O'Malley notes that there have been consistent calls for the introduction of sentencing guidelines to deal with perceptions of disparities in sentencing (2006: Chapter 3). The fact that the English courts operate under a guidelines regime, and the fact that the average Irish sentence for rape is considerably higher than that in England, demonstrates that the introduction of a guidelines regime does not necessarily lead to an increase in the severity of sentences. Whether the introduction of such a regime would lead to greater consistency in Irish sentences is difficult to gauge (O'Malley, 2006: para. 3-17). The Irish courts have consistently stated that sentences should be proportionate to both the severity of the crime and the personal circumstances of the offender. Given the variety of factors that the court must consider it is unlikely that such an approach to sentencing will ever give rise to consistency in terms of outcome. The trial court records show that three-quarters of Irish sentences for rape are for imprisonment for between five and ten years with a median sentence of eight years imprisonment. These figures suggest that the majority of sentences imposed are not wildly inconsistent. Structurally, it is perhaps fortunate that only a small number of Irish judges are involved in the sentencing of rape offenders; such a small number increases the likelihood of consistency and therefore serves to limit the excesses of the individualised approach to sentencing required of Irish criminal courts.

Whether the introduction of a guidelines regime would increase the consistency of sentences imposed for rape beyond that which already exists is unclear. Much would depend on the nature of the regime imposed. To achieve complete consistency of outcome would require a regime that effectively required mandatory sentences, but it is difficult to see how such a regime would survive constitutional challenge (*People (DPP) v. Tiernan*, 1988). A regime that permits trial judges to depart from the guideline sentences would have a better chance of survival, but the existence of such discretion tends to undermine the effort to achieve consistency of outcome. This kind of regime might improve consistency of outcome to some degree, but given the relatively high degree of consistency that the Irish courts have already achieved, it is submitted that the consistency benefits of the introduction of such a regime would likely be quite minimal. Accordingly, any case for the introduction of sentencing guidelines based upon consistency is quite weak and serves to distract attention from other, more pressing sentencing issues: the use of concurrent sentences and the use of suspension periods and their interaction with post-release supervision orders.

Concurrent Sentencing

The Irish courts have regularly stated that their discretion to impose consecutive sentences should be used sparingly, and this approach was reflected in the trial court records. In every case in which more than one sentence was imposed upon a defendant they were ordered to run concurrently. The only time consecutive sentences were imposed – on a defendant who pleaded guilty in three different trials to raping three different women on three different occasions – the Court of Criminal Appeal ordered that the sentences were to run concurrently, but increased them such that the defendant would be subject to the same maximum period in prison as under the original trial court formulation. In other words, the Court of Criminal Appeal was concerned solely to remove the consecutive sentences rather than to reduce the defendant's sentence.

The courts have not explained their hostility to consecutive sentences other than to note that 'American-style' sentences of hundreds of years do not form part of Irish jurisprudence. Yet the use of consecutive sentences is fully in line with first principles when the offences in respect of which the sentences are imposed do not form part of the same incident. Take the facts of *DPP v. Byrne* (1995): the defendant was convicted of raping two unrelated women in their own homes on two different occasions. The trial court imposed a 10 year sentence in respect of each rape but ordered that the sentences should run concurrently. In these circumstances, consecutive sentences would more accurately have reflected the reality of what the defendant actually did and would more realistically have vindicated the rights of both of the victims. Further, it can be argued that the use of concurrent sentences creates an incentive to commit more rapes in that the defendant will serve only one effective sentence no matter how many rapes he commits. Given these disadvantages, it is incumbent upon the courts to explain why a person who commits offences against different people at different times and in different locations should serve only one effective sentence. A similar explanation is required when the defendant commits multiple offences against the same complainant, especially when the offences are committed on different occasions and/or in different locations.

Use of Suspension Periods

The great majority of rape sentences are subject to a suspension period, although it is rare for a defendant to have his sentence suspended entirely. The median suspension period is 18 months. These suspension periods had a dramatic effect on the actual maximum periods that the defendant could serve, especially in cases in which the defendant pleaded guilty. Nevertheless, suspension periods are justified on the basis that most people who go into prison will at some point come out again, and by suspending the final portion of their sentence these offenders will make the transition back to independent life knowing that if they commit any offence the remainder of the original sentence can be reactivated. The suspension period thus acts as an incentive to avoid further criminal activity. During the period of this study there was no statutory authority to impose a suspended sentence, but this lacuna has since been filled by section 99 of the Criminal Justice Act 2006.

The principal issue that arises in connection with suspension periods is how they interact with post-release supervision. Post-release supervision was introduced into Irish law by the Sex Offenders Act 2001 expressly to ensure that offenders who are made subject to a Post-Release Supervision Order will re-enter society under the supervision of the Probation Service. The Minister for Justice, Equality and Law Reform told the Dáil that the primary purpose of such an Order was to 'help the offender maintain self-control over his offending behaviour'.* The purpose of the suspended sentence is to induce an offender who is released from prison early to improve his behaviour through the threat of resurrecting the balance of his prison sentence should he commit further offences during the currency of the suspension period (Osborough, 1982). It is apparent that the purpose of the suspended sentence and that of the Post-Release Supervision Order are similar. To be sure, they are not the same – as its name suggests, the Supervision Order requires that the offender be closely supervised whereas an offender who is released on a suspended sentence merely enters into a bond to be of good behaviour. Similarly, the penalties for breach are different: the suspended sentence can be reactivated upon presentation to the court of credible evidence of the breach (O'Malley, 2006: para. 22-13) whereas a breach of a Supervision Order is an offence in its own right sub-

---

* Statement by the Minister for Justice, Equality and Law Reform, John O'Donoghue, TD opening the second stage of the Sex Offenders' Bill 2000 on 6 April 2000, 517 Dáil Debates 1085.

ject to a maximum sentence of 12 months imprisonment. Nevertheless, the two dispositions overlap to a great degree, and it would be worth considering whether the introduction of Supervision Orders has now effectively superseded the suspended sentence, especially when both are applied to the same offender. Suppose a rape offender is sentenced to eight years' imprisonment with the final two years suspended, and to a period of five years post-release supervision. Such a formulation is far from unusual. The offender will serve a maximum of six years in prison, although he will almost certainly serve less because of the statutory remission of 25 per cent for good behaviour. Once he is released from prison, the offender will for two years be subject to both the Damocletian sword of the suspended sentence and the close supervision of the Probation Service, which supervision will continue beyond the currency of the suspended sentence for another three years. Both dispositions are aimed at encouraging the offender to rehabilitate himself. Is it necessary to use both dispositions simultaneously? If the offender is subject to close supervision what effective role does his suspended sentence play? Further, the supervision order is only to be issued if the trial judge is satisfied that close supervision is required. But if such supervision is necessary, is this not tantamount to an admission that the offender's bond to be of good behaviour is insufficient? If so, it is surely arguable that this particular offender was an unsuitable candidate for a suspended sentence in the first place. It is not recommended that either disposition be abandoned; rather, it is recommended only that the use of these dispositions be rationalized more clearly, especially if it is proposed to use them together.

Delay

The typical adult rape case takes 33 months (two years and nine months) to complete. It took just over 13 months from the date of the incident for the defendant to be returned for trial, and another 16 months for the defendant's trial to be reached. These figures tally almost exactly with the figures published by the National Crime Council in 2006, as Table 6.45 shows (all figures rounded).

Table 6.45: Delays, by Study

Period	National Crime Council (2006)	Present Study (2009)
Arrest → Return*	11 months	13 months
Return → Trial	16 months	16 months
Trial → Sentence	3 months	3 months

The timescales in the two studies are virtually identical, but the earlier study did not distinguish between adult and child rape cases. The Council recommended that rape cases should not ordinarily take more than 54 weeks to proceed from initial arrest to the start of trial. The Council recommended that the Garda investigation should be completed within six and a half months. To that end, the Council recommended the opening of new specialist sexual assault units in major hospitals around the country, to ensure minimal delays in the processing of forensic examinations in rape cases (a similar recommendation was made earlier in this study, although for different reasons). The Council further recommended that the senior investigating Garda and a member of the Office of the DPP be made responsible for ensuring that this timeline be adhered to. Finally, the Council recommended that the defendant's trial should start within six months from the date of his return for trial. The Council noted that since their research, waiting periods in the Central Criminal Court had been reduced, and recommended the use of pre-trial hearings and that there be sufficient judges and support personnel to ensure that cases listed for trial actually go to trial. The Council also recommended the use of a common numbering system for prosecutions among all criminal justice agencies to aid communications. We endorse all the Council's recommendations and have nothing to add.

---

* The Council used the date of the defendant's first arrest as their staring point, while we used the date of incident. We found, however, that in typical cases the defendant was first arrested within 24 hours of the complainant's report who in turn typically made her report within 24 hours of the incident occurring. Consequently, there is little practical difference between the two starting points.

Victims' Rights

The Oireachtas has taken a series of steps designed to improve the lot of the complainant. One of those measures was the publication in 1999 of a Victims' Charter which sets out the standards that complainants can expect from the various agencies involved in the criminal justice system. Ireland has used this Charter to argue that it has lived up to its obligations under the EC Council Framework Decision on the Standing of Victims in Criminal Proceedings (2001). The European Commission was tasked with determining the extent of compliance among Member States, and concluded that the Victims' Charter did not discharge Ireland's obligations. In coming to this conclusion, the Commission pointed on several occasions to the fact that the Charter expressly does not create legal rights (European Commission, 2004: 6, 9, 10). Irish commentators have similarly pointed to the lack of a legal basis as a major deficiency in the Charter (Rape Crisis Network Ireland, 2005: 5; Irish Council on Civil Liberties, 2008: 19-20). It is recommended that this deficiency be corrected and that the Victims' Charter be placed upon a statutory footing. As already noted, it is also strongly recommend that in addition to the complaints procedure already in the Charter, each criminal justice agency be required to put in place a quality control procedure that will ensure that the standards set out in the Charter are delivered.

Section 5 of the Criminal Justice Act 1993 requires trial judges to take into account the impact of a sexual or violent crime upon the complainant. The trial transcripts (see below) indicate that the level of trauma suffered by the complainant is the single most common aggravating factor mentioned by the trial judges, which in turn indicates a high level of compliance with the primary requirement of section 5. This provision also gives the complainant a statutory right to address the court as to the impact of the offence. The use of victim impact statements has been controversial, with most commentators expressing the fear that the complainants would take the opportunity offered by the statement to engage in retribution. No empirical evidence has ever been offered in support of these claims, however, and the victim impact statements contained in the trial court records offer no support for them either. The offender and sentencing issues were mentioned in less than one fifth of all victim impact statements. These issues were most likely to occur in statements prepared by the complainants themselves, and the offender was usually described in uncomplimentary terms. It is hardly surprising that a complainant would have a low opinion of the man just convicted of raping her, and it seems unlikely that the judiciary would pay much attention to such descriptions. There is no doubt that these issues should not be mentioned in the victim impact statements, however, but there is no evidence that it was done maliciously. Further, this is a problem that can be fixed quite easily. The Scottish Government introduced a victim impact scheme in April 2009, and Information Packs have been produced to be sent to all victims as needed. These packs include a standardised statement form and explanatory material including a pamphlet entitled, *Making a Victim Statement*. This pamphlet includes the following section:

What Sort of Information Should Not Be Included?

Although you can refer to the crime, you should not describe what happened as the court will hear about this during the trial. Don't refer to any previous incidents. Only describe how the crime has affected you and don't include any information about how the crime may have affected other people, such as your children. Don't include any views on the accused or what sentence you think he or she should receive. The Judge or Sheriff decides the sentence after taking all of the facts into account (Scottish Executive, 2009: 4).

It is recommended that a similar publication be drafted for this jurisdiction, thereby giving complainants clear guidance on the limits of victim impact statements.

Section 6 of the Criminal Justice Act 1993 made provision for Compensation Orders to be made against defendants following conviction. The Act does not specify who is responsible for seeking compensation for the complainant or whether trial judges are supposed to exercise this power of their own volition. Among the trial court records there were only two instances of Compensation Orders being awarded. There is anecdotal evidence that private compensation is often paid but details on these arrangements are not generally available, and therein lies the problem. In enacting section 6, the Oireachtas has taken the view that compensation should be presumptively payable by offenders to their victims, with the compensation amount to be determined openly by an independent judge. Relying upon private arrangements subverts the clear intention of the Oireachtas, so it is recommended that section 6 be amended to clarify and strengthen the compensation procedures. Compensation should be considered in every case in which a rape has been shown to have been committed. To ensure that this is done, it is recommended that a specific responsibility to seek compensation be imposed upon the most relevant body. The complainant has no right of audience other than in relation to the impact of the crime, and the defendant cannot be expected to remind the court of the compensation issue. The only other party is the DPP, and accordingly it is recommended that a statutory obligation be placed upon the DPP to seek compensation on behalf of the complainant. The DPP is supposed to act independently of the complainant and this recommendation could be seen as being incompatible with that independence. Imposing this obligation, however, does not contradict the DPP's independence. Further, the DPP has already accepted responsibility for placing before the court victim impact statements, and as a matter of practicality, there is no reason why a compensation request cannot be made at the same time. It might also be useful to require the Probation Service, when ordered to complete a report on the offender, to consider his financial means. Thus, when the victim impact and Probation reports are submitted, the court will also be in a position to consider the issue of compensation without incurring extra delays.

THE TRIAL TRANSCRIPTS

A total of 75 cases were identified that appeared to fit the eligibility criteria of the project and transcripts of those cases were sought to examine the nature of the complainants' evidence, the nature of the defence evidence, the judge's charge and any comments on sentencing made by the judge. Only 38 transcripts could be produced, three of which were found not to fit the eligibility criteria and so were excluded. Of the 35 valid transcripts only nine were complete. The following table shows which elements of the transcripts were available to us.

Table 6.46: Elements of Transcripts Available

	Complete	Partial
Complainant's Evidence	31	4
Defence Evidence	24	4
Judge's Charge	13	2
Sentencing Comments	12	0

The following analysis of this material clearly cannot be considered definitive given the small numbers involved and should be taken as indicative only.

Order and Nature of the Evidence

The transcripts gave details of the type and number of witnesses called in rape cases. Due to their incomplete nature, it was not possible to ascertain the number of witnesses called in nine cases. In the remaining 26 cases, a total of 461 witnesses were called to give evidence, ranging from 1[*] to 37 in individual cases. The mean number of witnesses in each case was 17.7 while the median was 16.5. Not surprisingly, the complainant gave evidence in every case; indeed, it would have been amazing to find a case in which the complainant did not give evidence. In respect of both the mean and median, the complainant was the third witness called, although she was called first in 11 cases and fifth in two cases. The prosecution case was bolstered by Garda witnesses and medical experts in 34 cases, and by forensic experts in 18 cases. Aside from these groups of witnesses, the prosecution called other witnesses

---

[*] The only case in which a single witness was called collapsed after the complainant was called to the stand. The next lowest number of witnesses was six.

in 26 cases, the largest group of which were independent witnesses who were called to give evidence in 11 cases.

On the defence side, the defendant chose to give evidence in 23 cases, and did not do so in six cases. In the remaining cases, it was not possible to ascertain whether the defendant gave evidence due to the incomplete transcripts. The defence called no further witnesses in 12 cases. In 16 cases, other defence witnesses were called, usually comprising members of the defendant's family and his friends, although in two cases, members of the Gardaí were called to give evidence for the defence.

Finally, statements were presented to the court in 18 cases, ranging in number from 1 to 11. The mean number of statements presented in each of the 18 cases was 2.5, while the median number of statements in these cases was 1.5. Given the common law's traditional preference for oral testimony, the comparative rarity of written statements compared to the number of witnesses is scarcely surprising.

The Complainant's Evidence

As noted earlier, the complainant was called to give evidence in every case and typically was the third witness called. The complainant's evidence is central to the prosecution's case so her presence in every case is unsurprising. The transcripts were not time-coded so we were unable to calculate the exact amount of time that complainants spent in the stand giving their evidence. The transcripts did, however, indicate when the breaks in the hearings occurred. Typically, there are two evidence sessions in each trial day, the first running from 11.00 a.m. until 1.00 p.m., and the second running from 2.00 p.m. until 4.00 p.m. With this in mind, it was possible to calculate in 29 cases across how many sessions the complainant was in the stand. The shortest period was one session, while the longest period was 15 sessions. In the mean case, the complainant was in the stand for 2.86 sessions, while in the median case, she was in the stand for two sessions.

The transcripts showed that in all but one case the complainant was cross-examined by a professional barrister. The one exception was a case in which the two defendants decided to conduct their cross-examination of the complainant personally. This case was complicated by the fact that both defendants and the complainant were foreign nationals (all from the same country), and the cross-examination was conducted in their own language which was then translated for the court.

Sexual History Evidence

The literature on rape trials is almost uniform in its criticism of the introduction into evidence of the complainant's prior sexual history. Most common law jurisdictions have enacted legislative restrictions on the introduction of such evidence, and Ireland is no different. In essence, the Criminal Law (Rape) Act 1981, as amended by the Criminal Law (Rape) (Amendment) Act 1990 and the Sex Offenders Act 2001, requires the defence to apply to the court for permission of the court to introduce such evidence. Ideally, this should be done in advance of the trial, although the law does permit the defence to make an application during the trial itself. When such applications are made, the complainant is entitled to be legally represented in her own right. It seems that the DPP or his representatives arrange for this separate representation.* The following table shows the number of cases in which separate representation for the complainant was provided.

Table 6.47: Separate Representation Sought, 2002-2005

Year	Number of Cases
2002	16
2003	8
2004	10
2005	5

Source: Legal Aid Board.

---

* Correspondence from the Chief Executive of the Legal Aid Board with the lead author; copy on file with the lead author.

Thus, separate representation was provided in 39 cases between 2002 (the relevant legislation only came into effect the end of 2001) and 2005. When applications for separate representation are made in a rape case, the complainant is entitled to representation without restriction. Consequently, the number of applications for separate representation also indicates the number of times that defendants in rape cases seek permission to introduce evidence of the complainant's sexual history. It was not possible to ascertain how successful these applications were as this information is not recorded by the Legal Aid Board. The sample of transcripts in this study showed that seven applications were made to introduce this evidence during the trials. In three cases the application was made on the first day of trial, three were made on the second day of trial and the last application was made on the seventh day of trial. The primary reason advanced by defence counsel for making the application was to question the complainant about prior consensual sexual activity, and in three cases, the application was made with the consent of the prosecution (in one case, the prosecution agreed only if the questioning was strictly limited). In only one case did the defence explain why the application had not been made in advance of trial: the requirements of the 2001 Act had been overlooked inadvertently. One application was denied and the other six were granted. In granting these applications, three judges limited their permission to specific questions. Three judges noted that the prosecution had agreed to the application, while the following reasons were noted by one judge each:

- The application was relevant to the defendant's defence;

- The interests of fairness required admission and the judge did not want to preclude the defendant from offering a defence;

- The judge could see no reason not to grant the application.

Even though applications were made to the trial judge in seven cases, it was found that the complainant was asked about her sexual history in 13 cases; no such evidence was introduced in 19 cases, and in two cases it was not possible to ascertain whether such evidence was introduced. In 10 cases, the complainant was asked about her sexual history by the prosecution. Whether from the prosecution or from the defence, the number of sexual history questions ranged between 1 and 76; the mean number of such questions was 19.5, while the median number was 9.

Appearance

The complainant was asked about her appearance in 13 cases, and no such questions were asked in 17 cases. In the remainder of cases it was not possible to ascertain whether such questions were asked. The number of questions asked about the complainant's appearance ranged between 1 and 21, with a mean number of 7.38 and a median number of seven.

Behaviour

The complainant was asked about her behaviour in 24 cases, and no such questions were asked in seven cases. In the remainder of the cases it was not possible to ascertain whether such questions were asked. The precise number of behaviour questions asked was unclear in two cases (they were over 70 and 100, respectively). Aside from those cases, the number of questions ranged between 3 and 117. The average number of questions was 44.4, while the median number was 43.

The literature on rape trials suggests that complainants are asked about her behaviour in one of four contexts: her behaviour with the defendant at the time of the alleged rape, her behaviour with the defendant prior to the alleged rape, her behaviour generally at the time of the alleged rape, and her behaviour generally prior to the alleged rape. Table 6.48 shows that this categorisation is true in Ireland.

It is apparent from this table that the complainant's behaviour with the defendant at the time of the alleged incident is of greatest interest to the defence: this issue arises more frequently than any other form of issue concerning the complainant's behaviour. Indeed, this issue arises in more cases than does the complainant's prior sexual history.

Table 6.48: Questions on Behaviour

Type of Question	Number of Cases	Range	Number
Behaviour with Defendant at Time of the Incident	23		
		Minimum	5
		Maximum	98
		Median	20.5
		Mean	27.65
Behaviour with Defendant Prior to the Incident	11		
		Minimum	2
		Maximum	42
		Median	8
		Mean	13.67
Behaviour Generally at the Time of the Incident	14		
		Minimum	2
		Maximum	45
		Median	14
		Mean	14.64
Behaviour Generally Prior to the Incident	9		
		Minimum	2
		Maximum	30
		Median	15
		Mean	12.67

Objections

Both prosecution and defence counsel are entitled to raise objections to the questions asked or issues raised, or indeed about the general tactics utilised, by the other side. In the sample of transcripts in this study, the defence raised objections to the complainant's evidence in 14 cases. Usually no more than one or two objections were raised in any one case, although in two cases the defence raised six objections. Objections were raised in two cases to the allegedly excessively emotional manner in which the complainant gave her evidence. Objections were also raised in individual cases to leading questions from the prosecution, to the complainant taking a break in giving her testimony, and to an expert's opinion. A specific objection was raised in one case to the complainant having a friend in court, despite this being the complainant's statutory entitlement. The defence counsel alleged that the complainant's friend, a counsellor from a Rape Crisis Centre, was coaching the complainant in her evidence, having been seen speaking to the complainant during a break in the proceedings. Given that complainants are entitled to a have a friend in court and that it is not uncommon for friends to speak with one another, it is not surprising that the objection was overruled by the trial judge.

The prosecution raised objections to the cross-examination conducted by the defence in nine cases. The mean number of prosecution objections in any one case was four, while the median number was three. In one case, the prosecution objected 12 times to the defence asking the complainant unfair questions. In another case, the prosecution objected twice to the defence asking the complainant confusing questions, while in yet another case the trial judge acceded to a prosecution demand that the defence counsel stop shouting at the complainant.

The Defendant's Case

It has already been noted that the defendant gave evidence in 23 cases, and that in 16 cases the defence case was bolstered by the testimony of other witnesses who were usually either members of the defendant's family or his friends. It was possible to ascertain the primary defence strategy in 28 cases, as set out in Table 6.49.

By far the most common defence strategy was to argue that the complainant had consented to sexual intercourse. An honest belief defence was apparent as a secondary strategy in only one case.* In some cases, the basis of the consent defence was patently offensive. In two unrelated cases involving a defendant and a complainant with considerably disparate ages, the defendant argued, via his counsel, that the fact that the complainant was overweight and physically unattractive corroborated his contention that the sexual intercourse was consensual. In essence, the argument was that these complainants must have consented to sexual intercourse because their physical unattractiveness made them desperate for sexual relations. Significantly, both defendants were acquitted, although it is not possible to be sure of the basis of the acquittals.

Table 6.49: The Primary Defence Strategy

Nature of Defence	Number of Cases
Consent to Sex	18
Denial of Sex	2
Consent on Some Charges; Denial on other Charges	7
Consent to Sexual Activity but Denial of Sex	1

The law generally prohibits the introduction of evidence concerning the defendant's character on the grounds that such evidence is unduly prejudicial (McGrath, 2006: para. 9-12). Nevertheless, there are occasions when the law will permit this kind of evidence, especially in cases in which the defendant has attacked the character of the complainant or that of a prosecution witness. Evidence as to aspects of the defendant's character was evident in five cases, including questions about the defendant's prior use of

---

* The honest belief defence originated with the decision of the House of Lords in *DPP v. Morgan* (1976). There, the Lords ruled that the defendant must be acquitted if the jury accepts that the defendant honestly believed that the complainant was consenting to sexual intercourse, even though in fact she was not consenting and the defendant's belief was unreasonable. This defence is still possible under Irish law, but is no longer possible under English law by virtue of the Sex Offences Act 2003, which requires that a belief in consent be reasonable.

prostitutes, questions about a previous encounter between the defendant and the Gardaí, and a note that the defendant's girlfriend was three month's pregnant at the time of the alleged rape. There were also references to the defendants' prior convictions in three cases, two of which related to non-sexual offences only. Indeed, in one of these cases, it was the defence that raised the prior convictions in order to show that they were not sexual in nature.

The Judge's Charge

Once all the evidence has been presented and counsel on both sides have given their closing arguments, the judge must instruct the jury as to their duties. These instructions, known as the 'charge', will usually consist of a review of the evidence and an explanation of the applicable law (Walsh, 2002: para. 19-43). Trial judges are entitled to comment upon the evidence but they must make it clear to the jury that they are free to draw their own conclusions and can reject the judge's comments. A major issue about the charge to the jury in rape cases concerns corroboration. Until 1990, a common law rule existed that required a trial judge to warn the jury of the danger of convicting a person charged with a sexual offence on uncorroborated evidence (Hanly, 2001). Commentators were especially critical of this rule on the grounds that it suggested that complainants in sexual cases were peculiarly untrustworthy. The Criminal Law (Rape) (Amendment) Act 1990 made this rule discretionary rather than mandatory. In the transcripts, a corroboration warning was given in only three cases. In two of these cases, the trial judge gave a warning because he was concerned that the evidence did not entirely corroborate the complainant's allegations. In two other cases, the trial judge made mention of corroboration in discussion with counsel. In one, the trial judge stated that he did not generally give corroboration warnings but that he would point out to the jury that the evidence did not provide corroboration of the complainant's allegation. In the other, the trial judge refused to give a warning as such but agreed to point out to the jury that the prosecution's case came down to the complainant's evidence and that the State bears the burden of proof. No corroboration warning was given in nine cases and in three other cases the position was unclear.

Sentencing Factors

Counsel for both sides have an obligation to assist the court in determining the appropriate sentence in every rape case. Defence counsel generally has some latitude in making submissions concerning mitigation of punishment (O'Malley, 2006: para. 31-30), although prosecuting counsel is under an obligation to challenge the defence if a mitigation argument can be proven to be incorrect (Director of Public Prosecutions, 2007: para.8.16). The prosecutor must ensure that the court is aware of all relevant legislation and precedents and to assist the court in avoiding any appealable errors in the determination of sentence (Director of Public Prosecutions, 2007: para. 8.14). The prosecutor should also ensure that:

> ... the court has before it all the relevant evidence available to the prosecution concerning the accused's circumstances, background, history, and previous convictions, if any, as well as any available evidence relevant to the circumstances in which the offence was committed which is likely to assist the court in determining the appropriate sentence (Office of the Director of Public Prosecutions, 2007: para. 8.14).

As the defence generally can be relied on to introduce evidence in mitigation, in practice the prosecution must ensure that the court is aware of all relevant evidence relating to aggravating factors. The prosecutor's traditional role was not, however, to argue for a particular sentence. The DPP himself has suggested that this appears to be changing, and the practice of trial courts today is to request an opinion on the appropriate sentence from the prosecuting counsel (Hamilton, 2008: 16).

The transcripts give a good indication of the kind of factors highlighted by defence counsel in arguing for mitigation of sentence as set out in Table 6.50.

Table 6.50: Mitigating Factors Highlighted by Defence Counsel

Grouping	Particulars	Times Raised
Responsibilities		
	Supporting a Child	1
	Supporting a Wife	2
	Employed	1
	Good Work Record	1
Good Background		
	Not a Drug Addict	1
	Created No Further Trouble Since	1
	Prior Good Character	1
	Good Family	1
Co-operation		
	Willing to Undergo Treatment	1
	Voluntary Attendance with Gardaí	1
	Kept Bail	1
	Acknowledged His Presence at Scene	1
Poor Background		
	Psychiatric Troubles	1
	Alcohol	4
	Difficult Upbringing	1
	Involved in Drugs/Crime at Early Age	1
	Traveller Family	3
Foreign National		
	Refugee from a War-torn Country	1
	May Have Asylum Status Revoked	1
	Language Problems Would Make Prison More Difficult	1
Other		
	Recent Family Tragedy	1
	Time Already Served	2
	Prior Consensual Activity Prior to Rape	1

On foot of factors such as these, defence counsel made arguments for lenient sentences such as the avoidance of a custodial sentence, concurrent rather than consecutive sentences, and that the trial judge should consider the principal of rehabilitation in arriving at the appropriate sentence.

The transcripts were rather lighter in contributions from prosecuting counsel. The contributions that they made tended to emphasise the defendants' prior convictions and to remind the trial judge of the possibility of post-release supervision. There was no evidence in the transcripts of a prosecutor ever seeking compensation, although in one case the trial judge insisted, over the objections of the complainant, that the defendant pay compensation of €5,000 in weekly payments of €50. In another, the defendant offered to pay the complainant €10,000 in compensation in two instalments but this was a spontaneous offer from the defendant and the trial judge refused to take the offer into account in determining the appropriate custodial sentence.

The trial judge occasionally explained his choice of mode of punishment. In two cases, the trial judge insisted that a custodial sentence was warranted due to the offence being very serious. In another case, by contrast, the trial judge justified suspending the defendant's sentence in its entirety on the grounds that a suspended sentence was still a real sentence but was one that allowed the defendant to get on with his life.

The trial judges also identified a variety of mitigating factors, as set out in Table 6.51.

Two other cases in which mitigating factors were identified deserve mention. In one case the trial judge described the rape as opportunistic and a once-off and appeared to treat that description as a form of mitigation. In a second case, the trial judge noted that the defendant pleaded guilty and concluded that there was no evidence that the defendant was a threat to women. He further indicated that the rape was not very serious in that it caused no injury to the woman beyond the rape itself.

Table 6.51: Mitigating Factors Identified by Judiciary

Groupings	Particulars	Times Raised
Responsibilities		
	Defendant's Work Record	1
	Defendant's Financial Support for His Family	1
	Financially Dependant Mother	1
Good Background		
	Defendant's Good Character	1
	No Prior Sexual Convictions	1
Poor Background		
	Defendant's Mental Impairment	1
	Defendant's Difficult Home Life	1
	Defendant's Vulnerability and Poor Coping Skills	1
Foreign National		
	Political Persecution in Home Country	1
	Defendant Risked Losing Asylum Status	1
	Defendant's Language Difficulties	1
Co-operation		
	Defendant Kept Bail Even Though Living in UK	1
	Defendant Voluntarily Returned to Ireland	1
	Defendant Kept Bail	2
Other		
	Prison is More Harsh for a Traveller	1
	No Aggravating Factors Present	1

The trial judges also identified a variety of aggravating factors, as set out in Table 6.52.

Table 6.52 Aggravating Factors Identified by Judiciary

Groupings	Particulars	Times Raised
Nature of the Rape		
	Level of Violence Used	4
	Rape Was Premeditated	3
	Defendant made Threats to Complainant	2
	Violated Complainant's Home	1
	Took Advantage of a Single Mother	1
Complainant		
	Level of Trauma Suffered by Complainant	5
Defendant		
	Previous Convictions	3
	Contested the Case	2
	Claim that the Complainant Set Him Up	1
	No Discount for a Guilty Plea	1
	Patronising Attitude to Wife and to his Entitlements as a Husband	1
	Good Family – Should have Known Better	1

The precise effect that any of these factors had on the judges' sentencing decisions is difficult to ascertain. It seems certain that some of these factors would not have any impact, especially the comments about the defendant choosing to contest the charges laid against him. These comments could not justify an increased sentence: doing so would effectively punish the defendant for exercising his right to a jury trial (O'Malley, 2006: para. 6-25). Likewise, factors such as the defendant knowing better or the defendant's bad attitude to his wife seem more descriptive than punitive and are unlikely to have had any real aggravating effect on the sentences imposed.

Discussion and Recommendations

The trial court records threw light on the operation of different aspects of the criminal justice system, but it was the trial transcripts that allowed an analysis of rape trials. There were two primary goals in conducting this analysis:

1. To determine objectively the nature and severity of the ordeal that rape complainants go through at trial; and,

2. To determine the effect of the legislative changes made since 1981 to improve the position of the rape complainant.

The small number of transcripts available, and the fact that many of them were incomplete, means that this analysis cannot be considered authoritative. Rather, the analysis should be viewed as indicative.

The Nature and Severity of the Complainant's Ordeal

The complainant will typically be in the stand for two sessions, which corresponds to one full trial day. In that time she will give her evidence and be cross-examined. It is rare for a defendant to conduct the cross-examination personally, but it does happen occasionally as it did in one of the cases in the sample in this study. To face cross-examination by the person accused by the complainant of raping her (or him) must be a terrible experience. In *R v. Edwards* (1996), the defendant conducted a cross-examination of his victim, Julia Mason, that stretched over six days (see Rock, 2004: 346-52). Following the trial, Ms. Mason said:

> At least when a barrister is asking questions he is doing it to get to the truth. When a rapist is asking the questions he knows what he's done and he's furthering the act. From the moment he opened his mouth the filth and degradation of my ordeal was replayed in violent and vivid detail (Rock, 2004: 348-9).

This case attracted a great deal of publicity and ultimately helped to usher in a change in the law in Britain. This publicity, which no doubt created the impression that personal cross-examinations happen more frequently than they do, in turn must have an effect upon the willingness of a person to engage with the criminal justice system. At the very least, such cases can hardly inspire confidence in potential complainants. It is strongly recommended, therefore, that such personal cross-examinations be abolished immediately as has been done in a number of common law jurisdictions, most recently in England and Wales (section 34 of the Youth Justice and Criminal Evidence Act 1999).

Protecting the Complainant

The Oireachtas, as with legislatures throughout the common law world, has attempted to restrict the introduction of evidence of the complainant's prior sexual history. The trial transcripts indicate that this effort has met with only limited success. The legislation indicates that applications to permit the introduction of such evidence should be made prior to the trial, but the transcripts show that applications were made during seven trials, usually on the first or second day. The intention behind the legislation is to ensure that sexual history evidence will not be used to ambush the complainant, and its introduction will have been signalled well in advance. For the most part, it seems that this intention is being largely met, and there is no way that late applications can be prohibited altogether. Further, the introduction of prior sexual history evidence is not automatic: one application was refused and three others were strictly limited. This suggests that, as the law demands, the judiciary is considering the purpose behind the application and the effects of granting the application. Comments from some trial judges provide cause for concern, however, especially the decision by one judge to grant an application to admit prior sexual history evidence because he could see no reason not to do so. This decision is of concern because it suggests that this judge has a low threshold of admission. The law is quite clear, however, that permission should be granted only if refusing permission might result in a conviction while granting permission might result in an acquittal. In other words, permission should be granted only if the introduction of the evidence is of critical importance to the defendant's case.

In total, sexual history evidence was admitted in 13 cases even though applications were evident in the transcripts in only seven cases. It is possible that pre-trial applications were made and granted, or it might be that this evidence is being admitted despite the restrictions in the law. One important deficiency in the law is that the restrictions on the admission of this evidence apply only to the defence; there is no restriction at all on the prosecution asking the complainant about her sexual history. It might seem odd that the prosecution would make use of evidence that has been shown to be so prejudicial to its own efforts, but they did so in ten of the transcripts in this study. Indeed, in one case, the prosecution raised the complainant's sexual history after the trial judge had refused permission for the defence to do so. Given the impact of this evidence, both upon the complainant and upon jurors, it is recommended that the existing restrictions be extended to the prosecution. Alternatively, if this recommendation is rejected and the prosecution is to be permitted to continue to introduce this evidence, protocols should be developed to ensure that whenever the prosecution intends to do so the complainant will be made aware of this well in advance.

Nevertheless, it must be noted that sexual history evidence was not present in 19 cases. This suggests that a complainant has roughly a 60 per cent chance of not being subjected to questioning of this nature. There is no research showing how common the introduction of this evidence was prior to the restrictions enacted in 1981, making a comparison impossible. The trial transcripts indicate, however, that the approach of the modern Irish courts is to prohibit or to restrict the admission of this kind of evidence, thereby following the intention of the Oireachtas. While prior sexual history evidence has garnered the most attention, however, the transcripts indicate that the focus of the defence is more likely to be on the complainant's behaviour (questions asked in 24 cases). Further, when asked about her behaviour, the complainant is likely to be asked many more questions (median of 20.5 questions) than when she is asked about her sexual history (median of nine questions).

Finally, the transcripts contain some evidence that the prosecution barristers make some attempt to protect the complainant at least from the worst excesses of the adversarial process. In nine cases, the prosecution lawyer intervened during the cross-examination, in one case both forcefully and frequently to protest about unfair questions being asked of the complainant. There is also evidence that the trial judges, while clearly giving some latitude to defendants to present a robust defence, will intervene if the defence goes too far. In one case, for example, the trial judge instructed the defence lawyer to stop shouting at the complainant. These examples indicate that while the Irish trial system is adversarial in nature, and the complainant is not formally represented as a party, there are limits to the ordeal to which she will be subjected. Nevertheless, the complainant will not be molly-cuddled, and the trial transcripts indicate that the defence has ample opportunity to engage in highly offensive and distressing strategies. In two cases, for example, the defence pursued a similar line of argument that made explicit reference to the complainant's weight and appearance. The suggestion was made that the complainants' appearance made them more likely to have consented to sexual intercourse. It is noteworthy that in both cases the defendants were acquitted although the basis for these acquittals is unknown. No factual basis was shown for the contention that a lack of physical attractiveness makes it more likely that, on the facts of one of these cases, a 20-year-old woman will agree to have sexual intercourse with a 63-year-old man. Plainly, the defendant in this and the other case were addressing their arguments to social prejudice, and it appears that they read their respective juries correctly. The essence of the common law system is that those charged with criminal offences must be permitted to test the evidence against them and to present their defence. It is essential that they be permitted to do this and to present to the jury a robust defence. It is equally essential that the law does not restrict the defendant's strategic options on the basis of ideology and political correctness. This does not mean, however, that defendants should be permitted to utilise *any* strategy to avoid a conviction. In particular, strategies that are based upon unsubstantiated assumptions derived from the complainant's membership of a particular group meet the very definition of prejudice. Prejudice represents the antithesis of any understanding of the concept of justice, and accordingly has no place in a judicial system. It is recommended, therefore, that an expert group be convened to consider the acceptable limits of cross-examination and defence strategy in criminal cases generally, and rape cases in particular. This expert group should also consider the introduction of specialist training for barristers and, indeed, for judges as is now the norm in England and Wales (Temkin and Krahe, 2008: 191-194). Such education, especially if it involves a consideration of broader contextual issues, would help to alert members of the judiciary and the Bar to the effect that unsubstantiated and offensive defence strategies can have upon complainants and potential complainants.

Chapter 7

CONCLUSION

SUMMARY OF THE STUDY

Purpose

This study was conceived in the light of a comparative European report that concluded that Ireland has the highest rate of attrition in rape cases (Regan and Kelly, 2003). With the cooperation of the Rape Crisis Centres, over one hundred Irish rape victims, the Office of the Director of Public Prosecutions and the Courts Service, the researchers have had an unrivalled overview of the manner in which the Irish criminal justice system responds to the crime of rape. This in turn gave us the opportunity to develop a more accurate profile of rape incidents in this country, along with the characteristics of the individuals involved in those incidents, and to examine the operation of key aspects of the Irish criminal justice system. This information is essential if the effectiveness of Ireland's response to the problem of rape is to be assessed, and it is this assessment that is the ultimate purpose of this study: an investigation into the cause of attrition in rape cases in Ireland.

Profile of Rape in Ireland

Information about the characteristics of rape, rape victims and perpetrators was gleaned from three distinct sources: rape victims themselves, prosecution files held by the DPP and the trial court records. These sources provide a mutually-reinforcing profile of the typical incident of rape in Ireland:

The complainant is a young Irish woman, most likely under the age of 25, but almost certainly under the age of 35. She is unemployed or in a low-skilled job. The defendant is male and somewhat older, usually between 25 and 35 years old, and has somewhat better socio-economic circumstances but is also employed in a low-skilled job. He is Irish, has no previous convictions but possibly has a troubled background. The complainant and suspect know each other in some way: they may have been friends, acquaintances, or they may have met in a pub or at a party on the night of the incident. They may have engaged in some level of sexual interaction such as kissing. For whatever reason, they went away together, on their own or with other friends, to either his or her home. They were both severely intoxicated through the consumption of alcohol. When the incident occurred, the complainant asked the defendant to stop. The defendant ignored her and probably used a low level of force; he did not threaten her, injure her, drug her or use a weapon against her. He simply disregarded her will. Afterwards, the complainant did not report the rape to Gardaí immediately, but did make a report within 24 hours. When questioned, the defendant tells the Gardaí that the sex was consensual. The chances are good that this rape will not be prosecuted.

This is rape in Ireland. It is worth considering how this profile stacks up against the real rape stereotype. The stereotype holds that rapes are committed outdoors by strangers, with high levels of force or weapons being used, and physical resistance being offered by the victim resulting in serious physical injury. If drugs were used, the victim would have consumed Rohypnol or GHB, probably surreptitiously. In every respect this stereotype is contradicted by the reality of rape in Ireland. This reality is similar to the profile that emerges from the international literature (e.g. Estrich, 1987; Harris and Grace, 1999; Myhill and Allen, 2002; Walby and Allen, 2004; Feist et al., 2007).

Operation of the Criminal Justice System

If the typical rape incident just described does result in a prosecution, the defendant has a 75 per cent chance of being admitted to bail. He will probably be required to be of good behaviour and to sign on at a Garda Station at least once per week. It will take about a year from the date of the complainant making a report for the defendant to be returned for trial. There is a greater than 40 per cent chance that the defendant will plead guilty to at least some of the charges. There is also a one in four chance that the complainant will withdraw her complaint. If this happens, the DPP will be left with no real option but to drop the charges against the defendant. If the complainant maintains her complaint and the defendant continues to deny the charges, the trial will start over a year after the defendant was returned for trial by the District Court. The defendant will continue to argue that the sexual intercourse was consensual. The complainant will be required to give evidence and she will be in the stand for two trial sessions (i.e., one day). She will be cross-examined by defence counsel during which she will likely be questioned about her behaviour and her prior sexual history. The chances are good that the male-dominated jury will acquit the defendant on the charges of rape but might convict him of a lesser sexual offence or a non-sexual offence if that option exists. If the defendant is convicted of rape, he will likely receive a sentence of seven or eight years imprisonment with the final 18 months suspended unconditionally, followed by five years post-release supervision.

This profile represents a typical rape case as it progresses through the various stages of the criminal justice system. That progress is slow and depends to a large degree on the complainant being willing to see it through. If she does, there is a good chance that the case will be disposed of through a guilty plea, but if a trial does happen the odds are very much on the defendant's side. Much of the reason for this is the reluctance of Irish juries to convict for rape or, even more so, rape under section four. Opinion polls suggest that there is a high degree of rape myth acceptance in Irish society (McGee at al., 2002: 158; Ryan, 2008; Amnesty International, 2008), and almost certainly these attitudes will be represented on the jury. The extent to which these attitudes influence the jury's verdict needs to be researched further as a matter of urgency.

Causes of Attrition in Ireland

Attrition is defined as the process by which cases fall out of the criminal justice system as they progress through that system (Gregory and Lees, 1996; Lea et al., 2003). In Ireland, the three major points of attrition are the decision to report, the decision to prosecute and the trial process.

The Decision to Report

All the evidence suggests that the considerable majority of rape victims choose not to make a report (e.g., McGee et al., 2002). The most common reasons given by participants in this study for not making a report included:

- Psychological factors, such as not feeling strong enough to retell their experiences;

- Social considerations, including concern at how making a report might affect their families; and

- Concerns about the criminal justice system, especially the fear of not being believed.

Clearly, some complainants made a personal choice that pursuing a prosecution would cost more than would be gained. Others, however, appear to have made their decision out of fear of the criminal justice system. There is also evidence that some might have been deliberately encouraged by the Gardaí not to make or maintain a formal complaint. Those who made a report to the Gardaí did so with the support of family or friends primarily out of a desire that justice should be done. For the most part, these complainants were satisfied with the Gardaí at least at the initial stage of the investigation; these levels of satisfaction tended to drop off dramatically as the investigation progressed usually due to a lack of ongoing contact. This increasing level of dissatisfaction may have contributed to the withdrawal of some complaints.

The Decision to Prosecute

The DPP decides whether charges should be laid against the suspect, but the complainant has a role to play in this decision. In this study, one-quarter of complainants withdrew their complaints, thereby rendering their cases effectively unprosecutable. The DPP prosecuted one of these cases despite the complainant's withdrawal, and it is telling that the case ended with a directed acquittal. The principal reasons for withdrawal were:

- A desire to get on with life;
- Fear of the upcoming court appearance; or
- Concerns about the impact of the case on the complainant's children, family members or upon a relationship.

The last two reasons give cause for concern. That the criminal justice system has assumed such terrible proportions in the minds of some rape victims that they would prefer to forego any prospect of justice rather than engage with it is quite an indictment of the level of support provided to victims. The provision of proper support systems might have encouraged some of these complainants to stay the course.

In the case of complaints that were not withdrawn, evidential factors weighed heavily in the making of the prosecutorial decision. There is a correlation between the real rape stereotype and the decision to prosecute, but cases that resemble the stereotype tend to be stronger in evidential terms and are therefore more likely to be prosecuted anyway regardless of stereotypical views. Intoxication does not appear to affect the DPP's decision but it is of concern that there is such a correlation between the incidence of rape and the consumption of alcohol. Over three-quarters of complainants and defendants had consumed alcohol on the occasion of the rape, and nearly half of both groups were severely intoxicated at the time.

Some findings give rise for concern, especially the fact that non-nationals are disproportionately likely to be prosecuted.

Whether this is *because* they are non-nationals is unclear and requires further investigation. Another troubling finding is that complainants with a history of mental illness are almost certain to have their cases dropped. There are going to be obvious evidential problems with such people, but care must be taken to ensure that cases are dropped only because of an evidential assessment of that particular complainant and not simply because she has mental illness issues.

The Trial Process

It was found that three-quarters of defendants were admitted to bail. There was no evidence that this contributed directly in any significant way to the attrition rate as less than five per cent of defendants absconded. Bail can also be granted to defendants who have been convicted and are awaiting trial; it is recommended on principle that this practice be ended.

Trials typically involved the complainant being in the stand for two trial sessions during which she was cross-examined by a defence barrister. The primary line of defence offered by defendants was that the sexual intercourse was consensual which led to a focus on the complainant's behaviour. There was evidence that the judiciary are largely applying the restrictions on the introduction of prior sexual history evidence as the Oireachtas intended, but the evidence also showed that these restrictions are insufficient especially as they do not apply to the prosecution. The transcripts also indicate that corroboration warnings are given only in a minority of cases but the number of relevant transcripts was very small so no definitive conclusions can be drawn.

All rape trials are determined by juries, giving them what is arguably the most important role in the trial process. The juries were typically dominated by males in numerical terms but that dominance was rarely overwhelming. There was no evidence that this male dominance had any impact on the juries' verdicts: female-dominated juries did not convict any defendant of rape. Indeed, male-dominated juries were the most likely to register a conviction on rape charges. Accordingly, there is no evidence that the gender composition of juries contributed to the attrition rate, and thus there is no reason to impose jury gender quotas

Drawing from both the trial court records and the prosecutorial files, about 60 per cent of cases that were prosecuted resulted in a conviction for something. On this basis, the attrition rate was 40 per cent. If confined to convictions for rape only, the trial court records disclose an attrition rate of 61 per cent. The majority of these convictions, however, occur through guilty pleas rather than jury verdicts. The trial court records show that only 19 defendants out of 70 were convicted at trial, while 52 defendants were acquitted. Out of all jury verdicts less than 20 per cent were for convictions for rape. There was also a marked reluctance among jurors to convict for rape under section 4 – only four defendants out of 29 so charged were convicted.

The use of victim impact statements is common, although most of them are prepared by professionals rather than by the complainants themselves. The statements show that complainants rarely mention the defendant or sentencing; accordingly there is little evidence to substantiate the fears expressed by commentators that complainants would use their statements in a retaliatory fashion. The trial transcripts show evidence that the judiciary regularly take the impact of the rape into account in determining sentences as required by the Criminal Justice Act 1993. The median sentence in a contested rape case is 8 years imprisonment and 8.5 years imprisonment after a guilty plea. In respect of rape under section 4, the median sentences are 7 years imprisonment and 9.5 years, respectively.

DEALING WITH ATTRITION

The common law trial system has certain fundamental requirements that must be met before it will allow a conviction to be imposed: the defendant's guilt must be established by evidence beyond a reasonable doubt, with the prosecution bearing the burden of proof. The defendant must be given the opportunity to test the evidence against him, and the decision on his guilt should be made by a jury that represents the judgment of the community. These requirements exist to reduce the possibility of a mistaken conviction, but also to encourage confidence in any convictions that are imposed. It follows, therefore, that cases that cannot meet these requirements will not be permitted to proceed to conviction. As Bryden and Lengnick point out (1997: 1208), the criminal justice system operates a filtering system that identifies cases that do not meet its standards for progression and removes them. Such cases will form part of the attrition rate, but it is difficult to characterise as flawed a process designed to protect against unjust conviction. Thus, not all attrition can be considered an evil: some attrition is proper and some is improper.

Improper attrition is attrition that arises from non-evidential, illegitimate grounds. This category includes all cases that are pushed out of the criminal justice system for any of the following reasons: fear, prejudice, poor investigation or procedures, weariness/frustration or unjustifiable legal rules. Thus, incidents of rape that are not reported because the complainant is scared of the legal process or of what people might think should be considered examples of improper attrition. Similarly, cases that are withdrawn because the complainant has been alienated from the legal system by delays, poor investigative practices, pressure or lack of ongoing contact have been lost to improper attrition. Cases in which reporting or withdrawal decisions are made on the basis of rape myths, even if they are made in good faith, have also been lost to improper attrition, for the basis of the decision is untenable.

Proper attrition, by contrast, is attrition that reflects the evidential requirements of the criminal justice system. Cases that are not prosecuted because the complainant cannot remember what happened on account, perhaps, of the fact that she was intoxicated and where there is no other forms of reliable evidence, have been lost to proper attrition. It is difficult to argue that the defendant in such a case should be put at risk of a conviction. To so argue would be to dispense with the need for reliable evidence, which in turn would constitute a rejection of the very foundation of the criminal justice system. Further, a case in which the victim decides that making or maintaining a complaint is not in her best interests is also an example of proper attrition. In such a case the complainant's decision should be respected notwithstanding the inevitable consequence that society will be unable to bring a rapist to justice. The complainant's decision should take precedence over society's need to prosecute because it is the complainant who is the one who will have to pay the price demanded by the criminal justice system. Under no circumstances should the complainant be compelled to make a complaint

None of this is to suggest that proper attrition is desirable in a broader social sense. An allegation that lacks an evidential foundation may well be entirely genuine and a rapist may be able to avoid responsibility for what he has done. This is an injustice; in an ideal world, it would be possible always to distinguish between the innocent and the guilty. But this world is far from ideal. We have chosen to insist upon credible and reliable evidence as a foundation for conviction, and the existence of proper attrition is a necessary consequence of that choice.

The analysis in this study, summarised above, suggests that both forms of attrition are present in Ireland's criminal justice system. There is evidence that rape complainants choose not to go to the Gardaí out of fear, that the Gardaí and others will sometimes put pressure on complainants in more problematic cases to withdraw their complaints, and that complainants sometimes withdraw their complaints out of a sense of frustration, isolation or outright alienation. There are also indications that jury decisions may be derived from untenable rape myths. These are all examples of improper attrition, and we have made a series of recommendations aimed at them. There is also evidence, however, that the Directing Officers in the Office of the DPP make their prosecutorial decisions largely on the basis of the evidence in the case, and that the risk factors identified in the literature as supposedly leading prosecutors to make prejudiced decisions have limited impact in this jurisdiction. We suggest that cases that do not progress due to weak evidence have been properly filtered out of the system. Further, it can be argued that not filtering these cases out of the system could be unfair to *complainants*. The court experience has been shown to cause severe anxiety to those who go through it: in some cases, the mere prospect of having to go to court has resulted in complainants withdrawing their complaints. To bring a prosecution, in a case whose evidential base is so weak that there is no prospect of a conviction, thereby requiring the complainant to undergo the rigours of the trial process with no prospect of the compensation of seeing the defendant convicted, surely would be a poor use of prosecutorial discretion.

THE WAY FORWARD

There are many improvements that can be made to the operation of the criminal justice system and we have made a series of recommendations in this regard throughout this study. Improving post-report communications between the Gardaí and the complainant may help to reduce the rate of complaint withdrawal. The Charter requires the Gardaí only to inform the complainant of all relevant information such as decisions on bail, the charges being brought, trial dates, etc. In other words, the Charter effectively creates a right to *information*. No doubt passing on this information is important, but it is insufficient because the Charter fails to recognise the true sense of isolation that is so apparent in the comments given to us by the participants in Strand I. For the bulk of the trial process (possibly lasting as much as two years) no new information will arise and the Gardaí therefore have no obligation to keep in touch with the complainant during this period. Thus, by framing the obligation in terms of *information*, the Charter actually reinforces the very problem it was designed to solve. The Charter should be re-drafted in terms of a right to *ongoing contact*, of which a right to information is merely a part. Contacting the complainant at regular intervals, regardless of whether there is any new information, should help to dispel any sense of isolation felt by the complainant. Further, as the absence of such contact is the primary reason given by participants in Strand I for dissatisfaction with the Gardaí, taking this small step should also result in an improvement in their satisfaction ratings.

The rigours of the trial process have been alluded to on several occasions, and to help complainants deal with those rigours a comprehensive system of victim support services is required. At present, those services are offered by a variety of non-governmental organisations on a somewhat ad-hoc basis (Amnesty International, 2004: 7). These services need to be available to complainants throughout the process and throughout the country. Further, as forensic evidence has been shown to be of such importance, specialist treatment units should be established at locations through the country. Ideally, a Sexual Assault Treatment Unit should be easily accessible from anywhere in the country.

There is room for improvement also at the prosecutorial stage. It is essential that Directing Officers should maintain an awareness that 'real rape' scenarios continue to dominate the prosecution record, even though they make up a minority of rape incidents. Efforts should be made to eliminate any inherent bias towards the prosecution of any kind of rape incident. In particular, this study has revealed a small number of issues that need to be addressed by the Office of the DPP and doing so may help to reduce the attrition rate. Although good witnesses are an obvious necessity, too many cases are being dropped due to complainant 'unreliability' based on mental illness. It is essential that every individual in the state have equal access to the protection of the law. Not only are the mentally ill especially vulnerable, but this study demonstrates they are also most unlikely to receive justice if they are raped. Of the 78 cases involving a complainant with a history of mental illness, only two cases were prosecuted and both of these had overwhelming physical and forensic evidence. The DPP should investigate mental illness cases to determine whether new protocols could be developed to increase the number of cases being prosecuted.

Various other recommendations were made to improve different aspects of the trial process: improvements to the bail laws, for example, or changes to some aspects of sentencing practice. While these changes will have little direct affect on the attrition rate, they may help to improve confidence in the criminal justice system among victims without which the system cannot survive (Royal Commission on Criminal Justice, 1993: para. 5.44).

The role of the jury has also been considered, and it is recommended that further research be conducted without delay into the issues that influence jury deliberations. The analysis of the trial court records shows results that are consistent with the view that juries are unduly influenced by complainant behaviour, particularly behaviour that is deemed foolish or inappropriate. It is suspected that juries assign contributory fault to complainants whose behaviour does not conform to the 'real rape' scenario. To counter this possibility, pending the results of the jury research just mentioned, it is recommended that legislation be enacted requiring judges to 'remind' the jury that foolish behaviour on the part of the complainant does not imply responsibility for the subsequent rape.

Even if all these measures are introduced, however, the nature of the crime of rape suggests that absence of evidence is a regrettable reality and will likely continue to negatively influence the prosecutorial decision. This leads to an unpalatable truth: some – perhaps many – instances of rape will never proceed through the criminal justice system. Sometimes this will be at the choice of the complainant, and sometimes it will arise by operation of the system itself. As a result, it is not tenable to continue to rely *exclusively* upon the criminal justice system as a means of dealing with rape, as Irish society has hitherto been doing. What is needed is a broader approach in which the criminal justice system is but one prong of a three-pronged initiative.

The second prong concerns the range of support systems available to those who have been raped, regardless of whether or not they have made a formal complaint. These services, especially the SATU units, need to be made available to anyone who needs them. Currently, immediate access to most SATU units may still require Garda accompaniment, although there is increasing recognition of the need for general access to these services and to the expertise that they provide. Open access should be the best practice goal of SATUs. Further, developing these support systems would represent a visible commitment to the welfare and recovery of *victims of rape*, something that often gets overshadowed by the desire to find and punish the *perpetrators of rape*.

The third prong of the initiative is a multi-faceted media campaign. The media is a powerful tool; while it has often been associated with perpetuating false impressions about relationships, sex, violence and rape, the media can also be used to counteract those impressions. This project recommends a public campaign of a magnitude and time-frame similar to that initiated against the problem of drink-driving. Considering the extensive negative social and economic effects of rape, including family breakdown, job loss, psychiatric disturbance, hospitalisation, drug and alcohol abuse and more, the potential benefits of reducing the rate of rape would more than justify the cost of the campaign.

The campaign should contain three primary elements. First, steps need to be taken to address the continuing vitality of rape myths. Although these myths have been demonstrated to have some influence on prosecutors they are most prevalent among the general public, including rape victims and most likely jurors in rape trials. There is a wealth of information regarding the realities of rape as opposed to 'real rape', and this information should be made part of the public campaign. It needs to be stressed, however, that this aspect of the campaign is factual rather than ideological. It is not proposed that any particular ideology be adopted or endorsed. Rather, we suggest that the studies and information that already exists should form the basis of an education campaign to counteract perceptions of 'real rape'.

The second element of the campaign should be directed to encouraging victims to come forward. Early reporting increases the chances of recovering medical and forensic evidence, which in turn increases the chances that a prosecution and a conviction will follow. Further, participants in Strand I reported the importance to their recovery of close friends and family knowing about the rape. An experienced third-party can mediate between the traumatised victim and her family in the immediate aftermath of the rape. Emphasis should also be laid on the high levels of satisfaction that complainants reported to us in making their statements to the Gardaí. This should help to moderate the fear that is common among victims that they might be mistreated by the Gardaí. Putting the (re-drafted) Victims' Charter on a statutory footing, and requiring each criminal justice agency to establish quality control procedures, would assist in this effort as a visible commitment to dealing fairly with victims. Establishing, and then rigorously adhering to, a high standard that victims can expect should diminish fears surrounding the legal process.

Finally, the campaign must address behaviour. This study has shown that alcohol is an extremely common factor in rapes. The effects of alcohol, and the manner in which the consumption of alcohol can facilitate the commission of rape, were noted earlier: lowering inhibitions, encouraging risky behaviour, increasing aggression and confusing social signals. Men, and particularly young men, must be made aware that rape is a possible consequence of binge-drinking. They need to be reminded that they are responsible for their own actions, and that voluntary intoxication does not relieve them of that responsibility, morally or legally. Addressing the drink culture that exists in this country is an important step in preventing sexual violence. It is possible to diminish (although not altogether eliminate) some of the risk factors for perpetration and victimisation: intoxication makes it less likely that danger signals will be noted or acted upon quickly. Further, members of society should be encouraged to be proactive in increasing their safety, by challenging inappropriate behaviour (if it is safe to do so) and by engaging in prudent risk management. No one should have to sacrifice their freedom or happiness out of fear of crime.

Appendix I

Ethical Guidelines

The research operated in accordance with the Code of Ethics published by the British Psychological Society (BPS). The information was read to telephone participants and detailed in the instructions for the postal and on-line surveys. Participants were not asked to sign consent forms, as these are not normally used with postal or telephone surveys. This approach also allowed respondents to remain anonymous if they wished.

The guidelines are:

Confidentiality: The information provided by participants will be kept strictly confidential and will only be seen by the researchers. After the questionnaires are analysed, they will be locked away until the research report is published. The questionnaires will then be destroyed.

Anonymity: Participants will not be named or identified in the final report.

Participation is voluntary: Participants are free to withdraw from the research at any time and do not have to answer any question that they do not feel comfortable answering.

Participant Distress
Studies have shown that participation in research on sexual violence does not impact negatively on respondents in the long-term. In *SAVI Revisited* (McGee et al., 2005) an overwhelming majority

of those interviewed said that they benefited from talking about their abuse, did not regret taking part in the research, felt their contribution would benefit others and would recommend participation to others.

In order to minimise participant distress, the following steps were taken:

- A protocol, based on the work of McGee et al. (2002), was drawn up to deal with any participant distress that arose. The procedure in such situations was to listen, stabilise the person and locate a source of assistance, if necessary.

- Additionally, a research helpline was set up for participants, which they could contact if they had any questions about the research.

- A phone list of agencies was drawn up and offered to participants where appropriate.

- Participants were informed that counselling was available through local Rape Crisis Centres.

- Follow-up 'care' calls: A week after participation in the survey, respondents were re-contacted to check that they were not negatively affected by participation.

Appendix 2

SURVEY QUESTIONNAIRE

Thank you for participating in this survey, which is being undertaken by the National University of Ireland, Galway. The study aims to find out what people consider when deciding whether to report a sexual offence to the Gardaí and, for those who do report, the problems they may experience with the criminal justice process.

Your contribution is important – the more people who complete the survey, the more we will be able to say about how our society responds to sexual violence and how to improve that response.

The Questionnaire

This questionnaire should take about 20 minutes to complete. It is possible that some parts of the questionnaire will not apply to your experiences. In this case, there may be some questions you do not need to answer. Throughout the questionnaire, there are instructions to guide you about which questions to answer.

You may find some of the questions intrusive but it is important we ask them this way so as to be clear about what we mean. It is alright to opt out of answering any question that you do not feel comfortable answering.

Confidentiality

All the information you provide will be kept strictly confidential. After the questionnaires are analysed, they will be locked away until the research report is published. The questionnaires will then be destroyed. A reference code will be assigned to you so that your name will not be recorded on the questionnaire.

Normally we would ask people to sign a consent form but we understand that some people may wish to remain anonymous. By filling in the survey and returning it to us, you are indicating your willingness to participate.

Assistance

If you have any questions or would like to discuss the questionnaire in more detail, please phone Deirdre Healy on (091) 495374 (Tues to Thurs: 10.00 am – 12.00 noon). Outside these hours, please leave a message and I will return your call. I will also be happy to accept reverse charge telephone calls.

I understand that talking about your experience may be distressing. If you need support, please note that your nearest Rape Crisis Centre can provide free and confidential counselling (a list of centres is provided on our website).

Returning the Questionnaire

You can either:

- Email your completed questionnaire to Deirdre.Healy@ nuigalway.ie as an attachment

- Print the survey and post it to: Deirdre Healy, Faculty of Law, NUI Galway, Co. Galway.

Survey Questionnaire

SECTION 1: VIEWS ON CRIME

We would like to know your views on crime and punishment in Ireland. Please consider the following statements and circle the number that most closely represents your view.

Question 1					
	Strongly Agree		Neither Agree Nor Disagree	Strongly Disagree	
Crime has increased in the past 12 months.	1	2	3	4	5
The Gardaí are doing a good job at controlling crime.	1	2	3	4	5
The government is too soft on crime.	1	2	3	4	5
Incidents of sexual violence have increased in the past 12 months.	1	2	3	4	5
There is enough support available for victims of crime.	1	2	3	4	5
Rehabilitation programmes for sex offenders will stop them re-offending.	1	2	3	4	5
The government is paying enough attention to the problem of sexual violence.	1	2	3	4	5
Media coverage of sexual violence is damaging to victims.	1	2	3	4	5
Sentences imposed on sex offenders are too lenient.	1	2	3	4	5

The following sections deal with your personal experience. If you have experienced more than one incident, please refer to the most recent incident when answering these questions.

Remember all your answers are totally confidential and will not be seen by anyone other than the researchers

Survey Questionnaire

SECTION 2: TELLING SOMEONE

Question 2.1		
Were the Gardaí informed about the incident?	☐	Yes, I reported it
	☐	Yes, someone else reported it
	☐	Yes, the Gardaí found out some other way
	☐	No, the incident was not reported by anyone

Question 2.2
Why did you report/not report the incident to the Gardaí?

Question 2.3		
Have you ever told anyone else about the incident?	☐	Yes
	☐	No

Question 2.4		
If you have told someone about the incident, who was the *first* person you told?	☐	Have never told anyone
	☐	Friend
	☐	Partner
	☐	Family member
	☐	Gardaí
	☐	Support agency
	☐	Other, please specify _____

Question 2.5						
We would like to know how this person responded when you told them. Were they:						
Unsupportive	1	2	3	4	5	Supportive

If the incident *WAS* reported to the gardaí, please proceed to Section 3 of the questionnaire. If the incident *WAS NOT* reported, please skip to Section 7.

Section 3: Reporting the Offence

Question 3.1		
How long after the incident were the Gardaí informed?	☐	Within one hour
	☐	Within 24 hours
	☐	Within one week
	☐	Within one month
	☐	Other, please specify _____

Question 3.2		
If you delayed reporting the incident, what was the reason for your hesitation?	☐	No delay
	☐	Unsure whether to report until someone else suggested it
	☐	Scared of Gardaí's response
	☐	In shock/numb
	☐	Thought I could handle it myself
	☐	Scared of offender
	☐	Scared about other people's reactions
	☐	Was not sure if it was a crime at first

Question 3.3		
Did you make a statement to the Gardaí?	☐	Yes
	☐	No

If 'No', why did you not give a statement to the Gardaí?
(Go to Q3.11)

Question 3.4		
When did you make your statement?	Month	Year

Question 3.5		
Where did you make your statement?	☐	In Garda station
	☐	At my home
	☐	Other, specify _____

Question 3.6		
When making your statement, were you interviewed by:	☐	A male Garda only
	☐	A female Garda only
	☐	Both

Question 3.7		
Were you given the option of being interviewed by someone of the same gender as you?	☐	Yes
	☐	No

Question 3.8						
Please rate the Garda who took your statement on the following scales:						
Hostile	1	2	3	4	5	Warm
Unsympathetic	1	2	3	4	5	Sympathetic

Question 3.9						
Could you describe the atmosphere during the interview?						
Cold/ clinical	1	2	3	4	5	Warm/ supportive

Question 3.10							
Please rate your overall satisfaction with the Garda who took your statement.							
Dissatisfied	1	2	3	4	5	Satisfied

Please give reasons for your answer.

Question 3.11		
Was an internal medical examination performed?	☐	Yes
	☐	No

If not, why not?

If a medical examination *WAS* performed, please proceed to Section 4. If a medical examination *WAS NOT* performed, please skip to Section 5.

SECTION 4: MEDICAL EXAMINATION

Question 4.1		
Were you examined in:	❏	A specialist rape trauma unit
	❏	Hospital casualty department
	❏	GP's office
	❏	Other, specify _____

Question 4.2		
Was the medical examination was carried out by:	❏	A female doctor
	❏	A male doctor

Question 4.3		
Were you given the option of being examined by someone of the same gender as you?	❏	Yes
	❏	No

Question 4.4
Please rate the doctor who examined you on the following scales:

Hostile	1	2	3	4	5	Warm
Unsympathetic	1	2	3	4	5	Sympathetic

Question 4.5
Could you describe the atmosphere during the examination?

Cold/clinical	1	2	3	4	5	Warm/supportive

Question 4.6
Please rate your overall satisfaction with the medical examination.

Dissatisfied	1	2	3	4	5	Satisfied

Please give reasons for your answer.

Please proceed to Section 5.

SECTION 5: FOLLOW-UP CONTACT WITH THE GARDAÍ

Question 5.1		
Did the Gardaí provide you with information about support services available to you?	☐ ☐	Yes No

Question 5.2		
Did the Gardaí explain to you what would be involved in an investigation of your complaint?	☐ ☐	Yes No

Question 5.3		
Did the Gardaí explain to you what would be involved in proceeding with your complaint to court?	☐ ☐	Yes No

Question 5.4		
Have you at any stage seriously considered withdrawing the complaint?	☐ ☐	Yes No

If 'Yes', why did you consider withdrawing the complaint?

Question 5.5		
Have you at any stage been encouraged to withdraw the complaint?	☐	Yes
	☐	No

If yes, who encouraged you to withdraw?	☐	Gardaí
	☐	State prosecutor
	☐	Family/friends
	☐	Suspect/accused
	☐	Other, specify _____

Question 5.6		
Did you withdraw your complaint?	☐	Yes
	☐	No

Question 5.7		
Was there an investigation of your complaint (e.g. Gardaí took witness statements, visited crime scene, etc.)?	☐	Yes
	☐	No
	☐	Don't know

Question 5.8		
Was anyone taken in for questioning over this offence?	☐	Yes
	☐	No
	☐	Don't know

Question 5.9		
Did you experience any difficulty in obtaining information from the Gardaí about the progress of your case?	☐	Yes
	☐	No

Question 5.10						
Please rate the degree of difficulty you experienced.						
Easy to obtain	1	2	3	4	5	Difficult to obtain

Question 5.11						
Please rate your overall satisfaction with the investigation of your case by the Gardaí.						
Dissatisfied	1	2	3	4	5	Satisfied

Please give reasons for your answer

Question 5.12		
Has anyone been charged with the offence?	❑	Yes
	❑	No
	❑	Don't know

If 'No', what do you think was the main reason?	❑	Offender was not identified
	❑	I withdrew my statement
	❑	Insufficient evidence to proceed
	❑	Gardaí did not believe me
	❑	Other, specify _____

If someone *HAS BEEN* charged, please proceed to Section 6. Otherwise, please skip to Section 7.

SECTION 6: BEFORE THE TRIAL

Question 6.1		
What was the most serious offence with which the offender was charged?	❒	Rape
	❒	Sexual assault
	❒	Aggravated sexual assault
	❒	Gross indecency
	❒	Rape Section 4
	❒	Incest
	❒	Assault
	❒	Other, specify _____
	❒	Don't know

Question 6.2		
Were the charges downgraded?	❒	Yes, specify to what _____
	❒	No
	❒	Don't know

Question 6.3		
Has the accused been granted bail?	❒	Yes
	❒	No
	❒	Don't know

Question 6.4		
Is your case going to trial?	❒	Yes
	❒	No, case has been dropped
	❒	No, offender pleaded guilty
	❒	Don't know

Question 6.5		
If known, what is your trial date?	_____ Month	_____ Year

Please proceed to Section 7.

Section 7: About the Assault

Question 7.1	
What age were you at the time of the incident?	

Question 7.2		
When did the incident occur?	Month	Year

Question 7.3		
Where did the incident happen?	❏	In your own home
	❏	At the offender's home
	❏	At work
	❏	At school/ university
	❏	In a pub/ nightclub
	❏	On the street
	❏	In a park/ other open public space
	❏	Other, specify _____

The next question asks about the type of assault you experienced. We would like to apologise for the graphic nature of the language but this is the only way we can accurately categorise your experience.

Question 7.4	
Which of the following best describes what happened to you? (please tick all that apply)	
Someone made you have sex without your consent. *(By sex, we mean penetration of your vagina by a man's penis)*	❏
Someone made you have oral sex without your consent. *(By oral sex, we mean a man putting his penis in your mouth)*	❏

Someone made you have anal sex without your consent. *(By anal sex, we mean a man putting his penis in your anus)*	❏
Someone put fingers in your vagina without your consent	❏
Someone put another object in your vagina without your consent	❏

Question 7.5		
How many people did this to you?	❏	One
	❏	Two
	❏	Three or more

Question 7.6		
What was your relationship to the offender? *(If there was more than one, please tick the box that refers to the offender you knew best)*	❏	Stranger
	❏	Acquaintance
	❏	Friend
	❏	Workmate/ colleague
	❏	Someone you were on a date with
	❏	Boyfriend/ girlfriend
	❏	Spouse/ partner
	❏	Ex-spouse/ ex-partner
	❏	Ex-boyfriend/ ex-girlfriend
	❏	Other, specify _____

Sexual assaults don't always involve any or all of the possibilities listed next. Please tell us which of the following, if any, you experienced.

Question 7.7		
At the time of the incident, were you verbally threatened or intimidated (e.g. offender threatened you with physical harm if you did not comply)?	☐ ☐	Yes No

Question 7.8		
Was physical force used against you (e.g. were you hit, punched or held down)?	☐ ☐	Yes No

Question 7.9		
Did the offender have a weapon?	☐ ☐	Yes No

If 'Yes', what kind of weapon?	☐	Gun
	☐	Knife or other stabbing weapon
	☐	Stick or other hitting weapon
	☐	Other, specify _____

Question 7.10		
It is often not possible to resist unwanted sex, but we would like to know if you were able to do any of the following?	☐	Use physical force toward attacker
	☐	Attempt to persuade attacker
	☐	Try to escape/ run away
	☐	Scream
	☐	Other, please specify _____

Question 7.11		
Sexual assaults do not always result in additional physical injury. Did you suffer any further physical injuries?	☐	None (go to Q7.13)
	☐	Minor (e.g. bruises, cuts, scratches)
	☐	Severe (e.g. knocked unconscious, broken bones, internal injuries)
	☐	Other, please specify _____

Survey Questionnaire

Question 7.12		
Were you injured to the extent that you required medical care?	☐	Yes
	☐	No

If 'Yes', did you stay overnight in hospital?	☐	Yes
	☐	No

Question 7.13		
Had you been drinking at the time of the incident?	☐	No
	☐	Yes, 2 drinks or less
	☐	Yes, 3-5 drinks
	☐	Yes, 6 drinks or more

Question 7.14		
Had the offender been drinking at the time of the incident?	☐	No
	☐	Yes, a little
	☐	Yes, moderately
	☐	Yes, a lot
	☐	Don't know

Question 7.15		
Altogether, how many times has this type of incident happened to you in the past 12 months?	☐	Once
	☐	Twice
	☐	Three or more

Question 7.16					
Looking back, how did this assault affect your:	Little impact				Severe impact
Relationships with family and friends	1	2	3	4	5
Romantic relationships	1	2	3	4	5
Employment	1	2	3	4	5
Emotional state	1	2	3	4	5
Physical health	1	2	3	4	5

Question 7.17		
What stage is your case at now?	❒	Never reported offence to gardaí
	❒	Statement made to gardaí
	❒	Offender charged, waiting for trial
	❒	Trial completed

Question 7.18					
Please indicate whether you agree or disagree with each of the following statements.	Strongly disagree				Strongly agree
The criminal justice system treats rape victims fairly.	1	2	3	4	5
If a friend told me they had been raped, I would advise them to report it to the Gardaí.	1	2	3	4	5
Rapists are rarely convicted by the courts.	1	2	3	4	5

Question 7.19	
What percentage of convicted rapists do you think are sent to prison?	_____%

Question 7.20					
What do you think is the usual prison sentence length received by a convicted rapist?					
2 yrs or less	3-5 yrs	6-10yrs	11-20 yrs	20 yrs and over	Life

Please proceed to Section 8.

Section 8: Details

Question 8.1				
Please indicate your gender.	Male	❏	Female	❏

Question 8.2	
Please indicate your age.	

Question 8.3	
Please indicate your country of origin (e.g. Ireland).	

Question 8.4

Which of the following best describes your domestic arrangements?

❏	Single	❏	Separated/Divorced
❏	Living with a partner	❏	Widowed
❏	Married	❏	Living with parents

Question 8.5

Which of the following best describes the place in which you live?

❏	Rural/Village	
❏	Town	
❏	City	

Question 8.6	
What county are you from?	

Question 8.7	
What is your current occupation?	

Survey Questionnaire

Question 8.8
What is the highest level of education that you have successfully completed (e.g. Junior Certificate, Leaving Certificate, Bachelor's Degree, etc.)?

Thank you for participating in this survey. Your response will provide valuable information on sexual violence in Ireland and how the criminal justice system responds to it. We are very grateful for the time and effort you have given to complete this questionnaire.

SURVEY EVALUATION

We are interested in hearing your views about this survey. I would be grateful if you would take a few extra moments to comment on your experience of completing the survey.

1. How long did it take you to complete the questionnaire?	_____minutes

2. Did you find the questions:

Easy to understand		Neither easy nor difficult		Difficult to understand
1	2	3	4	5

3. Did completing this survey make you feel upset?

Not upset		No difference		Very upset
1	2	3	4	5

4. Did the questionnaire give you a chance to say everything you wanted to say?

Not at all				Very much
1	2	3	4	5

5. Are there any other topics you think should have been included?
_____
_____
_____

6. How did you hear about this study?
_____
_____

Survey Questionnaire

FOLLOW-UP STUDY

(Please complete this form and enclose with your questionnaire)

Over the next few months, we will be conducting follow-up studies to explore some further issues relating to the problem of sexual violence. We are interested in hearing your opinions about the help and support you received (or would like to have received) in the months that followed the assault. If you have reported the crime to the Gardaí, we would like to talk to you about your experiences with the criminal justice system as your case progresses.

Are you willing to be contacted again for the follow-up study?
Yes ❑   No ❑   (Tick as appropriate)

---

1. Contact Details

We understand that some people may feel uneasy about giving us their name and address. Please remember, you do not have to give your full details – just enough for us to be able to contact you (for example, your first name and phone number or email address.

Name: _____

Address: _____

_____

_____

Tel: _____

Email: _____

2. Would you prefer to be interviewed by:

A female researcher ❑   A male researcher ❑

3. Please tell us how you would like us to contact you:

Post ❑   Telephone ❑   Email ❑

Appendix 3

DPP FILE SURVEY

FILE INFORMATION

1. Offence classification: _____

2. Date offence occurred: _____

3. Date gardaí were notified: _____

4. Date file first received from gardaí: _____

5. Date DPP decision made: _____

6. Number of times file was returned to gardaí: _____

7. Dates of return(s):   8. Description of information sought:

(a) _____   _____

(b) _____   _____

(c) _____   _____

7. What evidence was contained in the file?

- ❐ Complainant statement
- ❐ Notes/memo of interview with suspect (exclude no comments)
- ❐ DNA evidence
- ❐ Suspect identification by victim/ witness
- ❐ Medical examination report
- ❐ Forensic evidence

8. Was forensic evidence relevant to this case?   ❐ Yes   ❐ No

9. Was DNA evidence relevant to this case?   ❐ Yes   ❐ No

10. What was the final outcome for this case?
- ☐ Decision pending
- ☐ Decision not to prosecute
- ☐ Suspect has been charged, awaiting trial
- ☐ Prosecuted but resulted in a not guilty verdict
- ☐ Prosecuted and resulted in a guilty plea
- ☐ Prosecuted and resulted in a guilty verdict
- ☐ Decision to prosecute but trial stayed following a judicial review
- ☐ *Result to date* _____

11. What was the trial date, if applicable? _____

COMPLAINANT CHARACTERISTICS

1. Gender ☐ Male ☐ Female
2. Age at time of offence _____
3. Country of origin: _____

4. Relationship status of injured party (time of offence):
- ☐ Single
- ☐ In relationship
- ☐ Married/cohabiting
- ☐ Divorced/separated
- ☐ Information not on file

5. Employment status (time of offence):
- ☐ Employed (professional/skilled)
- ☐ Employed (manual, unskilled)
- ☐ Student
- ☐ Unemployed
- ☐ Farmer/agricultural worker
- ☐ Retired
- ☐ Information not on file

6. Has this complainant made other complaints?
- ☐ No
- ☐ Previous complaints
- ☐ Subsequent Complaints

SUSPECT CHARACTERISTICS

1. Age at time of offence _____
2. Country of origin: _____

DPP File Survey

3. Relationship status of suspect (time of offence):
- ☐ Single
- ☐ In relationship
- ☐ Married/cohabiting
- ☐ Divorced/separated
- ☐ Information not on file

4. Employment status (time of offence):
- ☐ Employed (professional/skilled)
- ☐ Employed (manual, unskilled)
- ☐ Student
- ☐ Unemployed
- ☐ Farmer/agricultural worker
- ☐ Retired
- ☐ Information not on file

5. Previous convictions: (Tick all that apply)
- ☐ No previous convictions
- ☐ Prior sex   Number: _____
- ☐ Prior violence   Number: _____
- ☐ Prior other (e.g. theft)   Number: _____

INCIDENT AS ALLEGED

1. In what county did this offence occur: _____

2. Which of the following best describes where the offence took place?
- ☐ Rural/Village
- ☐ Town
- ☐ City

3. Complainant/suspect relationship:
- ☐ Friend/acquaintance (no prior sexual relationship)
- ☐ Friend/acquaintance (prior sexual relationship)
- ☐ Dating/seeing each other
- ☐ Cohabitee
- ☐ Current spouse
- ☐ Stranger
- ☐ Ex-spouse/partner
- ☐ Other (please specify) _____

4. Where did the offence take place?
- ☐ Complainant's home
- ☐ On the street
- ☐ Suspect's home
- ☐ Park/other open public space
- ☐ At work
- ☐ In a pub/nightclub
- ☐ At a party
- ☐ In a vehicle
- ☐ At school/college
- ☐ Other (please specify) _____

5. Were any of the following elements present in the rape? (Tick all that apply)
- ❏ Use/threat of use of a weapon
- ❏ Physical force
- ❏ Verbal threats
- ❏ Physical resistance
- ❏ Verbal non-consent
- ❏ Injury to the complainant
- ❏ Covert administration of date rape drug (e.g. Rohypnol) to the complainant
- ❏ Covert administration of other drugs/alcohol to the complainant

6. What was the complainant's level of intoxication (i.e. through alcohol/drug use)?
   ❏ None   ❏ Mild   ❏ Moderate   ❏ Severe

7. What was the suspect's level of intoxication (i.e. through alcohol/ drug use)?
   ❏ None   ❏ Mild   ❏ Moderate   ❏ Severe

8. How soon after the incident was the offence reported to the gardaí?
- ❏ Within one hour   ❏ Within one month
- ❏ Within 24 hours   ❏ Other (please specify)
- ❏ Within one week   _____

CASE CHARACTERISTICS

1. Offence classification by gardaí: _____

2. Garda recommendation: ❏ Prosecute   ❏ Do not prosecute

3. Any additional evidence to support the complainant's allegations (beyond injury, threat or force)? Please tick all that apply.
- ❏ Defendant confession
- ❏ Witness statement
- ❏ DNA evidence
- ❏ Suspect identification by victim/ witness
- ❏ Forensic medical examination
- ❏ Other forensic evidence

DPP File Survey

4. What was the nature of the suspect's defence?
- ☐ No sexual intercourse occurred
- ☐ Consensual sexual intercourse occurred
- ☐ Believed consent had been given
- ☐ Other, please specify _____

FACTORS

1.

(a) Does the file contain information about the following behaviours by the complainant *at the time of the incident*:
- ☐ Walking alone late at night
- ☐ Hitchhiking
- ☐ Agreeing to accompany the suspect to his residence
- ☐ Inviting the suspect to his/ her home
- ☐ In a bar alone

(b) Does the file contain information about the following characteristics of the complainant (please tick all that apply):
- ☐ History of alcohol abuse
- ☐ History of drug abuse
- ☐ Work history in sex industry (e.g. massage parlour)
- ☐ Prostitution
- ☐ Significant criminal convictions, specify _____
- ☐ Evidence of physical or intellectual disability, please specify _____

CASE OUTCOME

1. Prosecutor decision: ☐ Prosecute   ☐ Do not prosecute

2. Reason given for decision: _____

3. What were the main factors involved in reaching this decision?
_____
_____
_____
_____

4. (a) Did the complainant request a review of this decision? ☐ Yes ☐ No

(b) If 'yes', what was the outcome of the review?
_____

5. If not prosecuted for Rape or Rape s.4, was there prosecution for another sexual offence committed at the time of the incident? ☐ Yes ☐ No

6. If not prosecuted for a sexual offence, was there a prosecution for another non-sexual offence committed at the time of the incident? ☐ Yes ☐ No

7. If the case was prosecuted for any offence, please list all of the offences charged _____
_____

8. IF COMPLAINT WAS WITHDRAWN:

(a) When was the complaint withdrawn? _____ (DD/MM/YY)

(b) What reason did the complainant give for withdrawing?
_____

9.

(a) Were there allegations of the complainant making a false complaint?

☐ Yes ☐ No

(b) What was the outcome? _____

Appendix 4

WITHDRAWAL OF COMPLAINT SUPPLEMENTARY QUESTIONNAIRE

1. Case Number _____

Withdrawal

1. Stated reason for withdrawal:

_____
_____
_____
_____
_____
_____

Dates

1. Date of Alleged Offence: _____
2. Date of File Receipt _____
3. Date of Direction (on rape): _____
4. Date of Communication of Direction to Gardaí: _____
5. Date of Communication of Direction to Complainant: _____ or unknown ❐
6. Date of Withdrawal: _____

False Reporting

1. Did the complainant subsequently admit that the sex was consensual?
❐ Yes ❐ No ❐ Unknown

2. Was legal action taken against the complainant?
❏ Yes   ❏ No   ❏ Unknown

Vulnerability

Was the complainant vulnerable due to:
- ❏ Poverty
- ❏ Homelessness
- ❏ Substance abuse/dependency
- ❏ Drugs ❏ Alcohol
- ❏ Relationship with Accused: Family member/Spouse/Other
  _____
- ❏ Prostitution
- ❏ Mental Illness

Appendix 5

RAPE TRIAL RECORDS QUESTIONNAIRE

Identification

1. Case Code _____

Initiation of Action

1. Date of Report to Gardai _____   2. Date of Defendant's Arrest _____
3. Date of Defendant's Charge _____
4. Bail
   o Was bail granted to the defendant at any time? Y ☐   N ☐
   o Gardai ☐   Court ☐   Specify Court _____
   o Date of Bail _____
   o Conditions _____
   _____
   _____
   _____

   o If bail denied, date of defendant's remand in custody _____

District Court Hearing

1. Date of Return for Trial _____
2. Statement of Charges
      a) Charges   b) Counts

   _____   _____
   _____   _____

_____   _____

_____   _____

_____   _____

3. Legal Aid Granted Y ☐ N ☐   4. Date Cert Granted: _____

Book of Evidence

1. Date Served on Defendant _____ 2. Total Number of Statements _____
3. Victim statement   Y ☐ N ☐   Date made _____
   - Length of Statement _____
   - Date(s) of Incident _____
   - Location(s) of incident _____
   - Age of Victim at Incident _____
   - Victim Occupation _____
   - Relationship to Defendant _____
   - If unrelated, how they met _____
   - Allegation:

     Offence   Number   Date

     s.2 ☐   _____   _____

     s.4 ☐   _____   _____

     Other:

     _____ _____ _____

     _____ _____ _____

4. Garda statements   Y ☐ N ☐   Number of Statements _____
5. Defendant Details:
   - Date of Birth _____
   - Age _____
   - Occupation _____
   - Consumption of Alcohol Y ☐ N ☐ 7. Quantity _____
6. Defendant's History
   a) Poor Family Background Y ☐   N ☐

      Nature _____

   b) Substance Abuse   Y ☐   N ☐

Substance _____
Duration _____
Treatment _____
   c) Psychiatric History   Y ☐   N ☐
      Problem _____
      Duration _____
      Treatment _____
   d) Other _____
       _____
       _____
       _____

7. Defendant statement   Y ☐   N ☐   Date made _____
   - If yes, did defendant admit the allegation(s) of rape?   Y ☐   N ☐
   - If not, did defendant admit that sex occurred with victim?   Y ☐   N ☐
   - Notice of Alibi Evidence   Y ☐   N ☐
8. Exhibits   Y ☐   N ☐
   - Nature _____
9. Forensic Evidence
   - DNA evidence   Y ☐   N ☐
     Details: _____
     _____
     _____
   - Sex Offences Kit   Y ☐   N ☐
     Details: _____
     _____
     _____
   - Other forensic tests (e.g., clothing tests)
     Details: _____
     _____
     _____

10. Medical Report   Y ☐   N ☐   Date made _____
    - Physical Injuries   Y ☐   N ☐
      - If yes, specify _____
    - Alcohol use noted   Y ☐   N ☐
      - Alcohol Level _____

- Drug use noted Y ☐ N ☐
  - Which drug(s) _____
  - Quantity _____
11. Witness Summonses
  - From the Court Y ☐ N ☐ Number _____
  - From the Prosecution Y ☐ N ☐ Number _____
  - From the Defence Y ☐ N ☐ Number _____

Trial Court

1. Date of Arraignment _____
2. Guilty Plea Y ☐ N ☐   3. If yes, date entered _____
4. Before which Court _____ 5. Location of Court _____
6. Date(s) of Trial Hearing _____
   _____
   _____
   _____

7. Charge(s) actually Prosecuted   Number of Counts
   _____   _____
   _____   _____
   _____   _____
   _____   _____

8. Adjournment(s)
   Date   Sought by Whom   Reason
   _____   _____   _____
   _____   _____   _____
   _____   _____   _____
   _____   _____   _____

9. Motions
  - Application for Dismissal Y ☐ N ☐ Date_____
    - Result _____
  - Introduction of Prior Sexual History Y ☐ N ☐ Date_____
    - Result _____
  - Notice of Additional Evidence Y ☐ N ☐ Date_____
  - Other Motions

• Specify	Date	Sought By	Result
_____	_____	_____	_____
_____	_____	_____	_____
_____	_____	_____	_____
_____	_____	_____	_____

10. Date Case went to Jury _____ 11. Length of Deliberations _____

12. Composition of Jury:

       1. Gender _____ Occupation _____
       2. Gender _____ Occupation _____
       3. Gender _____ Occupation _____
       4. Gender _____ Occupation _____
       5. Gender _____ Occupation _____
       6. Gender _____ Occupation _____
       7. Gender _____ Occupation _____
       8. Gender _____ Occupation _____
       9. Gender _____ Occupation _____
       10. Gender ____ Occupation _____
       11. Gender ____ Occupation _____
       12. Gender ____ Occupation _____

  Foreman: Gender ____Occupation _____

13. Verdict

Charge	Verdict	Unan./Maj./Hung
_____	_____	_____
_____	_____	_____
_____	_____	_____
_____	_____	_____

14. Victim Impact Statement   Y ☐   N ☐
    - Made by Whom: _____
    - Read in Court: Y ☐   N ☐ Unspecified ☐

15. Date of Sentencing _____

16. Sentence(s) Imposed

    - Count   Sentence

_____	_____
_____	_____
_____	_____
_____	_____

- Sentences to run concurrently   Y ☐   N ☐
- Ancillary sentences
  - Specify _____
  _____
  _____
  _____
- Date from which sentence is to begin: _____
- Compensation Order: Y ☐   N ☐   Amount:_____

Appeal

1. Date of Notice of Appeal _____   2. Date of Appeal Hearing(s) _____
   _____

3. Appeal by Defendant   Y ☐   N ☐
   - Appeal against sentence only   Y ☐   N ☐
   - Appeal against conviction only   Y ☐   N ☐
   - Appeal against conviction and sentence   Y ☐   N ☐
4. Appeal by Prosecution   Y ☐   N ☐
   - Without Prejudice Appeal   Y ☐   N ☐
   - Appeal against Undue Leniency   Y ☐   N ☐
5. Date of Appeal Decision _____
6. Appeal Upheld   Y ☐   N ☐   Retrial Y ☐   N ☐
7. New Sentence(s) Imposed   Y ☐   N ☐
8. New Sentences
   - Count   New sentence
     _____   _____
     _____   _____
     _____   _____
     _____   _____
   - Ancillary Sentence   Variation
     _____   _____

9. Further Appeal   Y ☐   N ☐   10. Permitted by Whom _____

11. Result

_____
_____
_____
_____
_____
_____

VICTIM IMPACT STATEMENTS

Case Information

1. Case Code _____   2. Date of Statement _____
3. Statement prepared by: Complainant ☐
                             Doctor   ☐
                             Psychologist ☐
                             Other   ☐   Specify _____
4. Length of Statement (in lines) _____   5. Typed? Y ☐   N ☐
6. Read out in court? Y ☐   N ☐   U ☐   7. Date read in Court _____

Impact of the Rape

1. Was physical impact of the rape mentioned? Y ☐   N ☐
   - Hospitalization for physical injuries?   Y ☐   N ☐   Unspecified ☐
     - If yes, how many times? _____
     - For how long on each occasion
       _____
     - Nature of injuries treated?
       _____
       _____
     - How long did the recovery take? _____
2. Was psychological impact of the rape mentioned?   Y ☐   N ☐
   - Psychological problems mentioned:
     _____
     _____
     _____
     _____
   - How long did these problems last? _____
   - Hospitalization for psychological injury? Y ☐   N ☐   Unspecified ☐
     - If yes, how many times? _____
     - For how long on each occasion? _____
     - Symptoms requiring hospitalization? _____

Rape Trial Records Questionnaire

_____
_____
_____

- o Psychiatric out-patient treatment?   Y ☐   N ☐   Unspecified ☐
  - How long did treatment last? _____
- o Psychiatric medication prescribed?   Y ☐   N ☐   Unspecified ☐
  - How long did treatment last? _____
- o Self-harm inflicted?   Y ☐   N ☐
  - Injuries inflicted: _____

_____
_____
_____

3. Were relationship problems mentioned?   Y ☐   N ☐
   - o Separated from husband/wife?   Y ☐   N ☐
     - If so, how long after the rape? _____ Unspecified ☐
   - o Broke up with boyfriend/girlfriend?   Y ☐   N ☐
     - If so, how long after the rape? _____ Unspecified ☐
4. Were trust problems mentioned?   Y ☐   N ☐
   - o Difficulties trusting people generally? Y ☐   N ☐   Unspecified ☐
   - o Difficulties trusting men?   Y ☐   N ☐   Unspecified ☐
   - o Difficulties trusting women?   Y ☐   N ☐   Unspecified ☐
5. Were any problems mentioned other than those already covered?
   Y ☐   N ☐
   - o Family problems?   Y ☐   N ☐
     - Specify: _____

_____
_____
_____

- o Work problems?   Y ☐   N ☐
  - Took time off work?   Y ☐   N ☐
    - If yes, how much time? _____
  - Did complainant lose job?   Y ☐   N ☐
    - If yes, was a reason specified?   Y ☐   N ☐
    - Specify: _____

_____
_____

- Voluntarily changed job because of the rape?　　Y ☐　　N ☐
  - If yes, how many times? _____
  - If yes, what was complainant's original job? _____
  - What is her/his current job? _____
  o Location changes (i.e., moved home)?　　　Y ☐　　N ☐
    - If yes, why? _____
    _____
    _____
    _____

6. Were any consequences described as positive for the complainant?

　　　　　　　　　　　　　　　　　　　　　　Y ☐　　N ☐

  o If so, what were they? _____
  _____
  _____
  _____
  _____

Support Services Accessed

1. Which of the following support options were accessed by the complainant (tick any that apply):

o Husband/wife	☐	Helpful?	Y ☐	N ☐
o Boyfriend/ girlfriend	☐	Helpful?	Y ☐	N ☐
o Parents	☐	Helpful?	Y ☐	N ☐
o Friends	☐	Helpful?	Y ☐	N ☐
o Employer	☐	Helpful?	Y ☐	N ☐
o Rape Crisis Centre	☐	Helpful?	Y ☐	N ☐
o Doctor	☐	Helpful?	Y ☐	N ☐
o Other	☐	Helpful?	Y ☐	N ☐

  - Specify: _____

2. Were any of these support services singled out as especially helpful?
_____
_____
_____

Invalid Evidence

1. Any attempt made to introduce further factual evidence not related to the impact of the rape?   Y ☐   N ☐
   Specify: _____
   _____
   _____
   _____
   _____
   _____

Criminal Justice System

1. Complaints about the criminal justice system?
   - Treatment by members of the Gardai   Y ☐   N ☐
     - Specify: _____
       _____
       _____

   - Treatment at trial by defence lawyers   Y ☐   N ☐
     - Specify: _____
       _____
       _____

   - Treatment at trial by prosecution lawyers   Y ☐   N ☐
     - Specify: _____
       _____
       _____

   - The trial generally   Y ☐   N ☐
     - Specify: _____
       _____
       _____

   - Delays   Y ☐   N ☐
     - Specify: _____
       _____
       _____

2. Compliments for the criminal justice system?
   - Treatment by members of the Gardai   Y ☐   N ☐
     - Specify: _____
       _____
       _____

   - Treatment at trial by defence lawyers   Y ☐   N ☐
     - Specify: _____
       _____
       _____

   - Treatment at trial by prosecution lawyers Y ☐   N ☐
     - Specify: _____
       _____
       _____

   - The trial generally   Y ☐   N ☐
     - Specify: _____
       _____
       _____

3. Sentencing
   - General demand for vindication or validation by the criminal justice system?
                                                Y ☐   N ☐
   - Specific demands
     - Specific sentence demanded? _____
     - Minimum sentence demanded? _____
     - Specific form of penalty demanded? _____
   - Request for leniency?   Y ☐   N ☐
     - Reason given:
       _____
       _____
       _____
       _____

4. Overall
   - Any description of the criminal justice system?
     _____
     _____

Rape Trial Records Questionnaire 421

_____
_____

- o Regrets expressed about bringing matters to official attention? Y ☐ N ☐
- o Recommend others go through the criminal justice system?   Y ☐ N ☐
- o Expectations of the criminal justice system mentioned?

_____
_____

5. Defendant
   - o Any description of the defendant?

_____
_____
_____
_____

   - o Acknowledgement of defendant's guilty plea?   Y ☐ N ☐
     - ▪ Impact of the guilty plea: _____

_____
_____
_____

Appendix 6

TRIAL TRANSCRIPTS

Identification

1. Case Code: _____

Introductory Material

1. Charges being tried:

   Count No. *Charge* *Legislation* *Verdict* *Unanimous?*
   _____
   _____
   _____
   _____

2. Total number of witnesses giving evidence: _____
   (Only include those witnesses called to give oral testimony at trial)

3. Witnesses giving evidence:

   Prosecution
   - ☐ Complainant
   - ☐ Gardai
   - ☐ Doctor
   - ☐ Forensic specialist
   - ☐ Others; please specify:
     _____
     _____

   Defence
   - ☐ Defendant
   - ☐ Others; please specify:
     _____
     _____
     _____

4. Was complainant the first witness to give evidence? Y ☐   N ☐
   o If not, indicate number of complainant among witnesses _____

5. Were statements read into evidence? Y ☐   N ☐
   o If so, indicate number of such statements _____

Complainant's Evidence

1. Across how many sessions was complainant giving evidence, including examination, cross-examination and re-examination: _____
(Trials normally have two sessions per day, one in the morning from 11-1, and one in the afternoon from 2-4; include in the count here all sessions in which complainant is in the stand even if for only a very short period)

2. Location of incident _____ 3. Age at incident _____

4. Relationship to defendant _____

5. Consumption of chemical substances:
    - Alcohol Y ☐   N ☐   Quantity _____
    - Drugs   Y ☐   N ☐   Quantity _____

6. Was cross-examination conducted by a barrister?   Y ☐   N ☐

7. Was Complainant questioned about her prior sexual history evidence?
    Y ☐   N ☐
    - Total number of questions asked _____
      (Include all valid queries to which counsel expected an answer; exclude any questions that the trial judge prohibits)
    - If there was an application to admit prior sexual history evidence, date of application _____
    - Reasons for application   _____
                                         _____
    - Reasons why application is late _____
                                         _____
    - Reasons for granting permission   _____
                                         _____
                                         _____
                                         _____

    - Did prosecution ask complainant about her prior sexual history?
      Y ☐   N ☐

8. Was Complainant questioned about her appearance?   Y ☐   N ☐
    - Total number of questions asked _____

9. Was Complainant questioned about her behaviour?   Y ☐   N ☐
    - Total number of questions asked _____
    - Was complainant asked about:

Her behaviour with defendant?
- ○ At the time in question   Y ☐   N ☐
  Total number of questions asked _____
- ○ Prior to the time in question   Y ☐   N ☐
  Total number of questions asked _____

Her behaviour generally?
- ○ At the time in question   Y ☐   N ☐
  Total number of questions asked _____
- ○ Prior to the time in question   Y ☐   N ☐
  Total number of questions asked _____

10. Objections to presence in court of Complainant's friend   Y ☐   N ☐
    - ○ At what point in the trial? _____
    - ○ Reasons for objection _____
      _____
      _____
    - ○ Result of objection: Upheld ☐   Overruled ☐
    - ○ Judge's reasoning _____

11. Total number of objections raised by defence (excl. 9) _____
    - ○ Note anything unusual:
      _____
      _____
      _____

12. Total number of objections to cross-examination raised by prosecution _____
    - ○ Note anything unusual:
      _____
      _____
      _____

Defendant's Evidence

1. Did defendant give evidence?   Y ☐   N ☐   _____

2. Age at incident _____   3. Relationship to complainant _____

4. Consumption of chemical substances:
   - Alcohol Y ☐   N ☐   Quantity _____
   - Drugs   Y ☐   N ☐   Quantity _____

5. Defence strategy   Primary   Secondary
   - Denial of sexual intercourse   ☐   ☐
   - Consensual sexual intercourse   ☐   ☐
   - Honest Belief in consensual sexual intercourse ☐   ☐
   - Other; please specify   ☐   ☐
   - _____
   _____
   _____

6. Was defendant questioned as to his character?   Y ☐   N ☐

7. Was Defendant questioned as to previous convictions?   Y ☐   N ☐
   - State the prior convictions _____
   _____
   _____
   _____

Trial Transcripts 427

Judge's Charge

1. Corroboration warning given?   Y ☐   N ☐
   o Reasons for the warning _____
      _____
      _____

   o Definition of corroboration _____
      _____
      _____
      _____

   o Potentially corroborative evidence identified   Y ☐   N ☐
      Specify _____
      _____
      _____
      _____

2. Requisitions made on Corroboration:
   o By Whom   Prosecution ☐   Defence ☐
   o Were the Requisitions accepted   Y ☐   N ☐
   o If Yes, what effect did the Requisition have? _____
      _____
      _____
      _____

Sentencing

1. Defence Counsel's Arguments
    - Mitigating Factors _____
      _____
      _____
    - Sentencing Suggestions _____

2. Prosecution Counsel's Arguments
    - Aggravating Factors _____
      _____
      _____
    - Sentencing Suggestions _____
    - Demand for Compensation Y ☐   N ☐   Amount _____

3. Primary sentences imposed
        Count No.   *Charge*   *Sentence*
    _____
    _____
    _____
    _____

4. Sentences to run concurrently   Y ☐   N ☐   N/A ☐

5. Ancillary sentences imposed
    _____
    _____
    _____
    _____
    _____

6. Compensation for Complainant   Y ☐   N ☐   Amount _____

7. Reasons for Sentence
    - Mode of Punishment explained by judge   Y ☐   N ☐
        Specify _____
        _____
        _____
        _____
    - Mitigating Factors identified by judge   Y ☐   N ☐
        Specify _____
        _____
        _____
        _____

- Aggravating Factors identified by judge   Y ☐   N ☐
    Specify _____
    _____
    _____
    _____

BIBLIOGRAPHY

Abbey, A., Clinton, A.M., McAuslan, P., Zawacki, T., and Buck, P.O. 2002. Alcohol-Involved Rapes: Are They More Violent? in *Psychology of Women Quarterly*, Vol. 26(2), pp. 99-109.

Abbey, A. and Harnish, R. 1995. Perceptions of Sexual Intent: The Role of Gender, Alcohol Consumption and Rape Supportive Attitudes in *Sex Roles*, Vol. 32, pp. 297-313.

Abbey, A. Zawacki, T., Buck, P.O., Clinton, A.M., McAuslan, P. 2001. Alcohol and Sexual Assault in National Institute on Alcohol Abuse and Alcoholism (NIAAA), *Alcohol Health and Research World*, Vol. 25(1) [www.document] at http://www.athealth.com/Practitioner/ceduc/alc_assault.html (accessed 19/05/09).

Abracen et al., 2000. Alcohol and Drug Abuse in Sexual and Nonsexual Violent Offenders, in *Sexual Abuse: A Journal of Research and Treatment*, Vol. 12(4), pp. 263-274.

Abrahamson, M. 2004. Alcohol in Courtship Contexts: Focus Group Interviews with Young Swedish Women and Men in *Contemporary Drug Problems*, Vol. 31, pp. 3-29.

Abramson, J.B. 2000. *We, the Jury: The Jury System and the Ideal of Democracy*, Harvard University Press, Cambridge, MA.

Acock, A. and Ireland, N. 1983. Attribution of Blame in Rape Cases: The Impact of Norm Violation, Gender and Sex-Role Attitude in *Sex Roles*, Vol. 9, pp. 179-193.

Adler, F. 1973. Socioeconomic Factors Influencing Jury Verdicts in *New York University Review of Law and Social Change*, Vol. 3(1), pp.1-10.

Adler, Z. 1982. Rape – The Intention of Parliament and the Practice of the Courts in *Modern Law Review*, Vol. 45, pp. 664-675.

Adler, Z. 1985. The Relevance of Sexual History Evidence in Rape: Problems of Subjective Interpretation in *Criminal Law Review*, Vol. 769, pp. 769-780.

Adler, Z. 1987. *Rape on Trial*, Routledge and Kegan Paul, London and New York.

Adler, Z. 1991. Picking up the Pieces in *Police Review*, Vol. 99, pp. 1114-1115.

Advisory Group on the Law of Rape. 1975. *Report*, HMSO, London (The Heilbron Committee).

Albonetti, C.E. 1987. Prosecutorial Discretion: The Effects of Uncertainty in *Law and Society Review*, Vol. 21(2) pp. 291-313.

Alicke, M.D. 2000. Culpable Control and the Psychology of Blame in *Psychological Bulletin*, Vol. 126, pp. 556-574.

Amir, M. 1971. *Patterns in Forcible Rape*, University of Chicago Press, Chicago.

Amnesty International UK. 2008. Violence Against Women: The Perspective of Students in Northern Ireland, London.

Amnesty International, Irish Section. 2004. Summary Report – Justice and Accountability: Stop Violence Against Women, Dublin.

Anderson, K.B., Cooper, H. and Okamura, L. 1997. Individual Differences and Attitudes toward Rape: A Meta-Analytic Review in *Personality and Social Psychology Bulletin*, Vol. 23, pp. 295-315.

Anderson, L.A. and Whiston, S.C. 2005. Sexual Assault Education Programs: A Meta-Analytic Examination of their Effectiveness in *Psychology of Women Quarterly*, Vol. 29, pp. 374-388.

Anon. 1968. Police Discretion and the Judgment that a Crime has been Committed – Rape in Philadelphia in *University of Pennsylvania Law Review*, Vol. 117, pp. 277-322.

Anon. 1970. Note: The Corroboration Rule and Crimes Accompanying a Rape in *University of Pennsylvania Law Review*, Vol. 118, pp. 458-472.

Ashworth, A. 1993. Victim Impact Statements and Sentencing in *Criminal Law Review*, pp.498-509.

Ashworth, A. 2000. Victims' Rights, Defendants' Rights and Criminal Procedure in Crawford, A. and Goodey, J., eds., *Integrating Victim perspectives in Criminal Justice*, Ashgate, London.

Auld, Lord Justice. 2001. *A Review of the Criminal Courts of England and Wales*, Home Office, London.

Australian Bureau of Statistics. 1999. *Crime and Safety*, Canberra.

Bachman, R. and Paternoster, R. 1993-1994. A Contemporary Look at the Effects of Rape Law Reform: How Far have we Really Come? in *Journal of Criminal Law and Criminology*, Vol. 84, pp. 554-574.

Bachman, R. 1993. Predicting the reporting of rape victimisations: Have reforms made a difference? in *Criminal Justice and Behavior*, Vol. 20(3), pp. 254-270.

Bachman, R. 1998. The Factors Related to Rape Reporting Behavior and Arrest: New Evidence from the National Crime Victimization Survey in *Criminal Justice and Behavior*, Vol. 25(1), pp. 8-29

Bacik, I., Maunsell, C. and Gogan, S. 1998. *The Legal Process and the Victims of Rape*, Dublin Rape Crisis Centre, Dublin.

Bailey, W.C. 1999. The Socioeconomic Status of Women and Patterns of Forcible Rape for Major U.S. Cities in *Sociological Focus*, Vol. 32(1), pp. 43-63.

Balance in the Criminal Law Review Group. 2007. *Final Report*, Department of Justice, Equality and Law Reform, Dublin.

Baldwin, J. and McConville, M. 1980. Juries, Foremen and Verdicts in *British Journal of Criminology*, Vol. 20(1), pp.35-44

Batchelder, J.S., Koski, D.D. and Byxbe, F.R. 2004. Women's Hostility toward Women in Rape Trials: Testing the Intra-Female Gender Hostility Thesis in *American Journal of Criminal Justice*, Vol. 28(2), pp. 181-200.

Beckham, B and Aronson, H. 1978. Selection of Jury Foremen as a Measure of the Social Status of Women in *Psychological Reports*, Vol. 43, pp. 475-478.

Beichner, D. and Spohn, C. 2005. Prosecutorial Charging Decisions in Sexual Assault Cases: Examining the Impact of a Specialized Prosecution Unit in *Criminal Justice Policy Review*, Vol. 16, pp. 461-498.

Bellis, M.A., Hughes, K., Calafat, A., Juan, M., Ramon, A., Rodriguez, J.A., Mendes, F., Schnitzer, S., Phillips-Howard, P. 2008. Sexual Uses of Alcohol and Drugs and the Associated Health Risks: A Cross-Sectional Study of Young People in Nine European Cities in *BMC Public Health*, Vol. 8, p. 155.

Benedict, J. and Klein, A. 1997. Arrest and Conviction Rates for Athletes Accused of Sexual Assault in *Sociology of Sport Journal*, Vol. 14, pp. 86-94.

Benight, C. and Bandura, A. 2004. Social Cognitive Theory of Post-Traumatic Recovery: The Role of Perceived Self-Efficacy in *Behaviour Research and Therapy*, Vol. 42(10), pp. 1129-1148.

Benlevy, S. 2000. Venus and Mars in the Jury Deliberation Room: Exploring the Differences that Exist among Male and Female Jurors during the Deliberation Process in *Southern California Law and Womens' Studies*, Vol. 9, pp. 445-447.

Berger, R., Searles, P. and Neuman, W.L. 1988. The Dimensions of Rape Reform Legislation in *Law and Society Review*, Vol. 22, pp. 329-357.

Biondo, A. 2007. Memory Loss at *Your Total Health*. [www.document] http://yourtotalhealth.ivillage.com/memory-loss.html 04/30/07, pp. 1-8 (accessed 08/06/09).

Blackstone, W. 1765 (1979). *Commentaries on the Laws of England*, Vol. 1, University of Chicago Press, Chicago, Il.

Blair, Ian. 1985. *Investigating Rape – A New Approach*, Croom Helm, London.

Blumenthal, J.A. 1998. The Reasonable Woman Standard: A Meta-Analytic Review of Gender Differences in Perceptions of Sexual Harassment in *Law and Human Behavior*, Vol. 22, pp. 33-57.

Bohmer, C. and Blumberg, A. 1975. Twice Traumatized: The Rape Victim and the Court in *Judicature*, Vol. 58, pp. 390-399.

Borgida, E. and White, P. 1978. Social Perceptions of Rape Victims – the Impact of Legal Reform in *Law and Human Behaviour*, Vol. 2, pp. 339-351.

Bornstein, B.H. 1999. The Ecological Validity of Jury Simulation: Is the Jury Still Out? in *Law and Human Behavior*, Vol. 23, pp. 75-91.

Branscombe, N.R. and Weir, J.A. 1992. Resistance as Stereotype Inconsistency: Consequences for Judgments of Rape Victims in *Journal of Social and Clinical Psychology*, Vol. 11, pp. 80-102.

Brecklin, L.R. and Ullman, S.E. 2001. The Role of the Offender's Alcohol Use in Rape Attacks: An Analysis of National Crime Victimisation Survey Data in *Journal of Interpersonal Violence*, Vol. 16(1), pp. 3-21.

Bremner, J. D. 2000. The Invisible Epidemic: Post-Traumatic Stress Disorder, Memory and the Brain in *The Doctor Will See You Now*. [www.document] http://www.thedoctorwillseeyounow.com/articles/behavior/ptsd_4/ (accessed 08/06/09).

Brems, C. and Wagner, P. 1994. Blame of Victim and Perpetrator in Rape versus Theft in *Journal of Social Psychology*, Vol. 13, pp. 363-374.

Brereton, D. 1993. Rape Prosecutions in Victoria in Esteal, P., ed., *Without Consent: Confronting Adult Sexual Violence*, Canberra.

Bright, D.A. and Goodman-Delahunty, J. 2006. Gruesome Evidence and Emotion: Anger, Blame and Jury Decision-Making in *Law and Human Behavior,* Vol. 30, pp. 273-286.

Broeder, D.W. 1965. Occupational Expertise and Bias as Affecting Juror Behavior: A Preliminary Look in *New York University Law Review,* Vol. 40, pp. 1079-1100.

Brown, B., Burman, M. and Jamieson, L. 1993. *Sex Crimes on Trial: The Use of Sexual History Evidence in Scottish Courts,* Edinburgh University Press, Edinburgh.

Brown, J.M., Hamilton, C. and O'Neill, D. 2007. Characteristics associated with rape attrition and the role played by scepticism or legal rationality by investigators and prosecutors in *Psychology, Crime and Law,* Vol. 13(4), pp. 355-370.

Brownmiller, S. 1976. *Against Our Will: Men Women and Rape,* Penguin Books, Harmondsworth.

Bryden, D.P. and Lengnick, S. 1997. Rape in the Criminal Justice System in *The Journal of Criminal Law and Criminology,* Vol. 87(4), pp. 1194-1384.

Bufkin, J. and Eschholz, S. 2000. Images of Sex and Rape: A Content Analysis of Popular Film in *Violence against Women,* Vol. 6, pp. 1317-1344.

Burgess, A.W. and Holmstrom, L.L. 1984. Rape Trauma Syndrome and Post Traumatic Stress Response in Burgess, A.W., (ed.), *Rape and Sexual Assault: A Research Handbook, Volume I,* Garland, New York, NY, pp. 46-60.

Burgess, A.W. and Holmstrom, L.L. 1979. *Rape Crisis and Recovery,* Robert J. Brady and Co., Bowie, MD.

Burgess, A.W. and Holmstrom, L.L. 1974. Rape Trauma Syndrome in *American Journal of Psychiatry,* Vol. 131, pp. 981-986.

Burt, M. and Albin, R.S. 1981. Rape Myths, Rape Definitions and Probability of Conviction in *Journal of Applied Social Psychology,* Vol. 11(3), pp. 212-230.

Burt, M. R. 1980. Cultural Myths and Supports for Rape in *Journal of Personality and Social Psychology,* Vol. 38, pp. 217-230.

Burton, S., Kitzinger, J., Kelly, L. and Regan, L. 1998. Young People's Attitudes towards Violence, Sex and Relationships: A Survey and Focus Group Study, Edinburgh.

Calhoun, L.G., Selby, J.W. and Warring, L.J. 1976. Social Perception of the Victim's Causal Role in Rape: An Exploratory Examination of Four Factors in *Human Relations,* Vol. 29(6), pp. 517-526.

Cameron, C.A. and Stritzke, W.G.K. 2003. Alcohol and Acquaintance Rape in Australia: Testing the Presupposition Model of Attributions About Responsibility and Blame in *Journal of Applied Social Psychology*, Vol. 33(5), pp 983-1008.

Campbell, J., Rose, L., Kub, J. and Nedd, D. 1998. Voices of Strength and Resistance: A Contextual and Longitudinal Analysis of Women's Responses to Battering in *Journal of Interpersonal Violence*, Vol. 13, pp. 743-763.

Campbell, R., Wasco, S. M., Ahrens, C.E., Sefl, T., and Barnes, H.E. 2001. Preventing the 'Second Rape': Rape Survivors' Experiences with Community Service Providers in *Journal of Interpersonal Violence*, Vol. 6(12), pp. 1239-1259.

Caringella-MacDonald, S. 1985. The Comparability in Sexual and Nonsexual Assault Case Treatment in *Crime and Delinquency*, Vol. 31, pp. 206-222.

Carney, P. 2007. The Role of the Victim in the Irish Criminal Process, speech delivered to UCC Law Society, Cork on 10th Oct. 2007 the text of which was reported in full in the *Irish Times*, 11th Oct. 2007, p. 16.

Casey, J. 1996. Interpretation of Constitutional Guarantees: An Antipodean History Lesson? in *Irish Jurist (n.s.)*, Vol. 31, pp. 102-109.

Casey, R. 2000. The Good, the Bad, and the Ugly: The Effect of Composition of Juries on Verdict in *Trinity College Law Review*, Vol. 3, pp. 3-31.

Central Statistics Office. 2002. *Census 2002*, The Stationery Office, Dublin.

Central Statistics Office. 2004. Quarterly National Household Survey: Crime and Victimisation 1998 and 2003, The Stationery Office, Dublin.

Chalmers, J., Duff, P. and Leverick, F. 2007. Victim Impact Statements: Can Work, Do Work (For Those Who Bother to Make Them) in *Criminal Law Review*, pp.360-379

Chambers, G. and Millar, A. 1983. *Investigating Sexual Assault*, HMSO, Edinburgh.

Christie, N. 1977. Conflicts as Property in *British Journal of Criminology*, Vol. 17(1), pp. 1-15.

Clay-Warner and Harbin-Burt. 2005. Reporting Rape after Reforms in *Violence against Women*, Vol. 11(2), pp. 150-176.

Coaker, V. 2006. Written Answer to a Parliamentary Question on Rape Sentencing, House of Commons, 12 July 2006.

Coen, R. 2006. The Rise of the Victim – A Path to Punitiveness in *Irish Criminal Law Journal*, Vol. 16, pp. 10-14.

Coffey, G. 2006. The Victim of Crime and the Criminal Justice Process in *Irish Criminal Law Review*, Vol. 16, pp. 15-20.

Cohen, J. 1988. Statistical Power Analysis for the Behavioral Sciences, 2nd ed., Erlbaum, Hillsdale, NJ.

Coid, J., Petruckevitch, A., Feder, G., Chung, W., Richardson, J., Moorey, S. 2001. Relation between Childhood Sexual and Physical Abuse and Risk of Re-victimisation in Women: A Cross-Sectional Survey in *The Lancet*, Vol. 358(9280), pp. 450-454.

Commissioner of An Garda Síochána. 2001-2006. *Annual Reports*, Dublin.

Commonwealth Secretariat. 2001. Report of the Expert Working Group on Evidence, London.

Commonwealth Secretariat. 2002. Commonwealth Best Practice Guidelines for the Treatment of Victims of Crime, London.

Connor, K., Davidson, J. and Lee, L. 2003. Spirituality, Resilience and Anger in Survivors of Violent Trauma: A Community Survey in *Journal of Traumatic Stress*, Vol. 16(5), pp. 487-494.

Constantini, E., Mallery, M. and Yapundich, D.M. 1983-1984. Gender and Juror Partiality: Are Women More Likely to Prejudge Guilt? in *Judicature*, Vol. 67, pp. 121-133.

Corr, M., O'Mahony, P., Lovett, J. and Kelly, L. 2009. Different Systems, Similar Outcomes? Tracking Attrition in Reported Rape Cases in Eleven Countries, Country Briefing: Ireland, April, 2009.

Courts Service. 2000-2008. *Annual Reports*, Dublin.

Courts Service. 2007. Press Release: €120 Million Dublin Criminal Courts Complex Revealed, 4 May 2007.

Cowan, S. 2008. The Trouble with Drink: Intoxication, (In)capacity, and the Evaporation of Consent to Sex in *Akron Law Review*, Vol. 41(4), pp. 899-922.

Criminal Law and Penal Methods Reform Committee of South Australia. 1976. *Special Report: Rape and Other Sexual Offences*, Adelaide (Mitchell Committee).

Criminal Law Revision Committee. 1984. *Fifteenth Report: Sexual Offences* (Cmnd.9213), HMSO, London.

Criminal Legal Aid Review Committee. 1999. *First Report: An Examination of the Feasibility of Introducing a Public Defender System for Ireland*, Department of Justice, Dublin.

Criminal Legal Aid Review Committee. 2002. *Final Report*, Department of Justice, Equality and Law Reform, Dublin.

Crisis Pregnancy Agency. 2006. *The Irish Study of Sexual Health and Relationships*, Department of Health and Children, Dublin.

Crowe, L.C. and George, W.H. 1989. Alcohol and Human Sexuality: Review and Integration in *Psychological Bulletin*, Vol. 105, pp. 374-86.

Crown Prosecution Service: Rape Policy Document. Consultation on the Handling of Rape Cases. [www.document] at http://www.cps.gov.uk/publications/prosecution/rapepolicy.html (accessed 27/02/09).

Crown Prosecution Service. 2005. *Charging Standards*, Oxford University Press, Oxford.

D'Alessio, S. J. and Stolzenberg, L. 2003. Race and the Probability of Arrest in *Social Forces*, Vol. 81(4) (June), pp. 1381-1397.

Davis, R.C. and Smith, B.E. 1994. The Effects of Victim Impact Statements: A Test in an Urban Setting in *Justice Quarterly*, Vol. 11, pp. 453-469.

Davis, R., C., Smith, B.C., and Nickles, L. 1997. *Prosecuting Domestic Violence Cases With Reluctant Victims: Assessing Two Novel Approaches in Milwaukee*, Final Report, Grant Nos. NIJ 94–IJ–CX–0052 and NIJ 95–IJ–CX–0105, submitted to the U.S. Department of Justice, National Institute of Justice. NCJ 169111.

Deitz, S.R., Littman, M. and Bentley, B.J. 1984. Attribution of Responsibility for Rape: The Influence of Observer Empathy, Victim Resistance and Victim Attractiveness in *Sex Roles*, Vol. 10, pp. 261-280.

Denkers, A. and Winkel, F. 1998. Crime Victims' Well Being and Fear in a Prospective and Longitudinal Study in *International Review of Victimology*, Vol. 5, pp. 93-140.

Deosaran, R. 1984. Toward a Social Psychology of Trial by Jury in *British Journal of Criminology*, Vol. 24, pp. 343-360.

Department of Justice, Canada. 1990. *Sexual Assault Legislation in Canada: An Evaluation: Overview*, Department of Justice, Canada, Ottawa.

Department of Justice, Equality and Law Reform. 1999. *Victims Charter and Guide to the Criminal Justice System*, The Stationery Office, Dublin.

Department of Justice, Victoria. 1997. *The Crimes (Rape) Act 1991: An Evaluation Report*. Rape Law Reform Evaluation Project No. 2, Melbourne.

Devine, D.J., Clayton, L.D., Dunford, B.B., Seying, R. and Pryce, J. 2001. Jury Decision-Making: 45 Years of Empirical Research on Deliberating Groups in *Psychology, Public Policy and Law*, Vol. 7, pp. 622-727.

Devlin, P. 1956. *Trial by Jury*, Stevens and Co., London.

Diamond, S. and Casper, J.D. 1992. Blindfolding the Jury to Verdict Consequences in *Law and Society Review*, Vol. 26(3), pp. 513-563.

Diamond, S.S. 1997. Illuminations and Shadows from Jury Simulations *Law and Human Behavior*, Vol. 21, pp. 561-571.

Director of Public Prosecutions. 1999. *Annual Report of the Office of the Director of Public Prosecutions, 1999*, Office of the DPP, Dublin.

Director of Public Prosecutions. 2001. *Statement of General Guidelines for Prosecutors*, Office of the DPP, Dublin.

Director of Public Prosecutions. 2008. *Report on Prosecution Policy on the Giving of Reasons for Decisions*, Office of the DPP, Dublin

Dripps, D. 2008. After Rape Law: Will the Turn to Consent Normalize the Prosecution of Sexual Assault? in *Akron Law Review*, Vol. 41(4), pp. 957-980.

Duborg, R., Hamed, J. and Thorns, J. 2005. *The Economic and Social Costs of Crime against Individuals and Households 2003/04*, Home Office Online Report 30/05.

Dukes, R.L., and Mattley, C.L. 1978. Predicting Rape Victim Reportage in *Sociology and Social Research*, Vol. 62, pp. 63-84.

Du Mont, J., Miller, K., and Myhr, T. 2003. The Role of 'Real Rape' and 'Real Victim' Stereotypes in the Police Reporting Practices of Sexually Assaulted Women in *Violence against Women*, Vol. 9(4), pp. 466-486.

EarthTrends. 2003. Population, Health and Human Well-Being, Ireland in *Earth Trends: Country Profiles*. [www.document] at http://earthtrends.wri.org/country_profiles/fetch_profile.php?theme=4andfilename=pop_cou_372.PDF (accessed 27/04/2009).

Easteal, P. 1994. *Voices of the Survivors*. Spinifex, Melbourne.

Edwards, A. 1996. *The Criminal Justice Response to Sexual Assault Victims*, New South Wales Bureau of Crime Statistics and Research, Sydney.

Elias, R. 2003. *Victims Still: The Political Manipulation of Crime Victims*, Sage, London.

Ellison, L. and Munro, V.E. 2009b. Reacting to Rape: Exploring Mock Jurors' Assessment of Complaint Credibility in *British Journal of Criminology*, Vol. 49, pp. 202-219.

Ellison, L. and Munro, V.E. 2009. Turning Mirrors into Windows? Assessing the Impact of (Mock) Juror Education in Rape Trials in *British Journal of Criminology*, Vol. 49, pp. 363-383.

Ellison, L. 2002. Rape and the Adversarial Culture of the Courtroom in Childs, M. and Ellison, L. (eds.), *Feminist Perspectives on Evidence*, Routledge Cavendish, London, p. 39.

El Sohly, M.A. and Salamone, S.J. 1999. Prevalence of Drugs Used in Cases of Alleged Sexual Assault in *Journal of Analytical Toxicology*, Vol. 23, pp. 141-146.

Erez, E. and Rogers, L.1999. Victim Impact Statements and Sentencing Outcomes and Processes in *British Journal of Criminology*, Vol. 39 (2), pp. 216-239.

Erez, E., Roeger, L. and Morgan, R. 1997. Victim Harm, Impact Statements and Victim Satisfaction with Justice: An Australian Experience in *International Review of Victimology*, Vol. 5, pp. 37-60.

Esteal, P., (ed.) 1998. *Balancing the Scales: Rape, Law Reform and Australian Culture*, Federation Press, Sydney.

Estrich, S. 1987. *Real Rape*, Harvard University Press, Cambridge, MA.

European Commission. 2004. *Report from the Commission on the Basis of Article 18 of the Council Framework Decision of 15th March 2001 on the Standing of Victims in Criminal Proceedings* {SEC(2004)102}.

European Council. 2001. *Framework Decision on the Standing of Victims in Criminal Proceedings*, Brussels.

Eurostat. 1996. *N.A.C.E. Rev. 1: Statistical Classification of Economic Activities in the EC*, Office for Official Publications of the European Communities, Luxembourg.

Expert Group on Crime Statistics. 2004. *Report*, Dublin.

Falshaw, L., Bastes, A., Patel, V., Corbett, C., and Friendship, C. 2003. Assessing Reconviction, Re-Offending and Recidivism in a Sample of UK Sex Offenders in *Legal and Criminological Psychology*, Vol. 8, pp. 207-215.

Feild, H.S. and Barnett, 1978. Simulated Jury Trials: Students Versus 'Real' People as Jurors in *Journal of Social Psychology*, Vol. 104, pp. 287-293.

Feild, H.S. and Bienen, L.R. 1980. *Jurors and Rape: A Study in Psychology and Law*, Lexington Books, New York, NY.

Feild, H.S. 1978. Attitudes towards Rape: A Comparative Analysis of Police, Rapists, Crisis Counselors, and Citizens in *Journal of Personality and Social Psychology*, Vol. 36, pp. 156-179.

Feild, H.S. 1978. Juror Background Characteristics and Attitudes toward Rape: Correlates of Jurors' Decisions in Rape Trials in *Law and Human Behavior*, Vol. 2, pp. 73-93.

Feild, H.S. 1979. Rape Trials and Jurors' Decisions: A Psycho-Legal Analysis of the Effects of Victim, Defendant and Case Characteristics in *Law and Human Behavior*, Vol. 3(4), pp. 261-284.

Feist, A., Ashe, J., Lawrence, J., McPhee, D. and Wilson, R. 2007. *Investigating and Detecting Recorded Offences of Rape*, Home Office Online Report 18/07.

Feldman-Summers, S. and Linder, K. 1976. Perceptions of Victims and Defendants in Criminal Assault Cases in *Criminal Justice and Behavior*, Vol. 3, pp. 135-149.

Feldman-Summers, S. and Norris, J. 1984. Differences Between Rape Victims Who Report and Those Who Do Not Report to a Public Agency in *Journal of Applied Social Psychology*, Vol. 14(6), pp. 562-573.

Felson, R., Messner, S., Hoskin, A., and Deane, G. 2002. Reasons for Reporting and Not Reporting Domestic Violence to the Police in *Criminology*, Vol. 40(3), pp. 617-647.

Finch, E. and Munro, V.E. 2005. Juror Stereotypes and Blame Attribution in Rape Cases involving Intoxicants in *British Journal of Criminology*, Vol. 45, pp. 25-38.

Finch, E. and Munro, V.E. 2006. Breaking Boundaries? Sexual Consent in the Jury Room in *Legal Studies*, Vol. 26(3), pp. 303-320.

Finney, A. 2004. *Alcohol and Sexual Violence: Key Findings from the Research*. Home Office, London.

Finney, A. 2006. *Domestic Violence, Sexual Assault and Stalking: Findings from the 2004/05 British Crime Survey*, Home Office Online Report 12/06.

Firth. 1975. Interrogation in *Police Review*, 28 Nov. 1975.

Fitzgerald, J. 2006. The Attrition of Sexual Offences from the New South Wales Criminal Justice System. *Crime and Justice Bulletin* No. 92, BOSCAR, Sydney.

Fischer, G.J. 1997. Gender Effects on Individual Verdicts and on Mock Jury Verdicts in a Simulated Acquaintance Rape Trial in *Sex Roles*, Vol. 39, pp. 491-501.

Fisher, B.S., Cullen, F.T. and Turner, M.G. 2000. *The Sexual Victimization of College Women*. Research Report NJL 182369, United States Department of Justice, Washington, DC.

Foa, E. and Riggs, D. 1995. Post-Traumatic Stress Disorder Following Assault: Theoretical Considerations in Current Directions in *Psychological Science*, Vol. 4(2), pp. 61-65.

Foa, E. B., Riggs, D. S., Dancu, C. V. and Rothbaum, B. O. 1993. Reliability and Validity of a Brief Instrument for Assessing Post-Traumatic Stress Disorder in *Journal of Traumatic Stress*, Vol. 6(4), pp. 459-473.

Frazier, P. and Borgida, E. 1988. Juror Common Understanding and the Admissibility of Rape Trauma Syndrome Evidence in Court in *Law and Human Behaviour*, Vol. 12(2), pp. 101-122.

Frazier, P.A., Conlon, A. and Glaser, T. 2001. Positive and Negative Life Changes Following Sexual Assault in *Journal of Consulting and Clinical Psychology*, Vol. 69(6), pp. 1048-1055.

Frazier, P.A. and Haney, B. 1996. Sexual Assault Cases in the Legal System: Police, Prosecutor, and Victim Perspectives in *Law and Human Behaviour*, Vol. 20(6), pp. 607-628.

Frazier, P.A., Candell, S., Arikian, N and Tofteland, A. 1994. Rape Survivors and the Legal System in Costanzo, M. and Oskamp, (eds.), *Violence and the Law*, Sage, Thousand Oaks, CA, pp. 135-158.

Frohmann, L. 1991. Discrediting Victims' Allegations of Sexual Assault: Prosecutorial Accounts of Case Rejections in *Social Problems*, Vol. 38(2), (May), pp. 213-226.

Frohmann, L. 1997. Convictability and Discordant Locales: Reproducing Race, Class, and Gender Ideologies in Prosecutorial Decisionmaking in *Law and Society*, Vol. 31(3), pp. 531-555.

Frohmann, L. 1998. Power in Sexual Assault Cases: Prosecutorial Strategies for Victim Management in *Social Problems*, Vol. 45(3) (August), pp. 393-407.

Gabora, N.J., Spanos, N.P. and Joab, A. 1993. The Effects of Complainant Age and Expert Psychological Testimony in a Simulated Sexual Abuse Trial in *Law and Human Behavior*, Vol. 18, pp. 103-119.

Galvin, J. and Polk, K. 1983. Attrition in Rape Case Processing in *Journal of Research in Crime and Delinquency*, Vol. 20, pp. 126-156.

Gardner, J. 1990. *Victims and Criminal Justice*, South Australian Office of Crime Statistics, Attorney-General's Department, Adelaide.

Garrison, A.H. 2000. Rape Trauma Syndrome: A Review of Behavioral Science Theory and its Admissibility in Criminal Trials in *American Journal of Trial Advocacy*, Vol. 23, pp. 591-657.

Garson, G. D. 2009. Mutliple Regression. [www.document] at http://faculty.class.ncsu.edu/garson/PA765/regress.htm (accessed 02/06/09).

Gartner, R. and Macmillan, R. 1995. The effect of victim-offender relationship on reporting crimes of violence against women in *Canadian Journal of Criminology*, Vol. 37(3), pp. 393-429.

George, W.H., Gourmic, S.J. and McAfee, M.P. 1988. Perceptions of Post-Drinking Female Sexuality: Effects if Gender, Beverage Choice and Drink Payment in *Journal of Applied Social Psychology*, Vol. 18, pp. 1295-1317.

Gerber, G.L., Cronin, J.A. and Steigman, H. 2004. Attributions of Blame in Sexual Assault to Perpetrators and Victims of Both Genders in *Journal of Applied Social Psychology*, Vol. 34, pp. 2149-2165.

Giacopassi, D. and Dull, R.T. 1986. Gender and Racial Differences in the Acceptance of Rape Myths within a College Population in *Sex Roles*, Vol. 15, pp. 63-75.

Gobert, J.J. 1997. *Justice, Democracy and the Jury*, Ashgate, Surrey.

Goldberg, D.P. 1978. *The Manual of the General Health Questionnaire*, Nfer, Windsor.

Goldberg, D. 1978. *The 12-Item General Health Questionnaire*, NFer-Nelson, Windsor.

Goldberg, D. and Williams, P. 2004. *A User's Guide to the General Health Questionnaire*, NFer-Nelson, London.

Golding, J., Siegel, J., Sorenson, S., Burnam, M. A., and Stein, J. A. 1989. Social Support Sources Following Sexual Assault in *Journal of Community Psychology*, Vol. 17, pp. 92-107.

Gottfredson, M. and Gottfredson, D. 1988. *Decision-Making in Criminal Justice: Toward the Rational Exercise of Discretion*, Plenum Press, New York, NY.

Goudriaan, E., Lynch, J. and Nieuwbeerta, P. 2004. Reporting to the Police in Western Nations: A Theoretical Analysis of the Effects of Social Context in *Justice Quarterly*, Vol. 21(4), pp. 933-969.

Grace, S., Lloyd, C. and Smith, L. 1992. *Rape: From Recording to Conviction*. Research and Planning Unit Paper, No. 71. HMSO, London.

Grattan, K.E., and Vogel-Sprott, M. 2001. Maintaining Intentional Control of Behaviour under Alcohol in *Alcoholism: Clinical and Experimental Research*, Vol. 25(2), pp. 192-7.

Greenberg, M. and Beach, S. 2004. Property Crime Victims' Decision to Notify the Police: Social, Cognitive and Affective Determinants in *Law and Human Behaviour*, Vol. 28(2), pp. 177-186.

Greenberg, M. and Ruback, R. 1992. *After the Crime: Victim Decision-Making*. Plenum Press, New York, NY.

Greenfeld, L.A. 1997. *Sex Offenses and Offenders*, Bureau of Justice Statistics, U.S. Department of Justice, Washington DC.

Greer, E. 2000. The Truth Behind Legal Dominance Feminism's 'Two Percent False Rape Claim' Figure in *Loyola of Los Angeles Law Review*, Vol. 33, pp. 947-972.

Gregory J. and Lees, S. 1994. In Search of Gender Justice: Sexual Assault and the Criminal Justice System in *Feminist Review*, No. 48, The New Politics of Sex and the State (Autumn), pp. 80-93.

Gregory J. and Lees, S. 1996. Attrition in Rape and Sexual Assault Cases in *The British Journal of Criminology*, Vol. 36, pp. 1- 17.

Grublin, D. and Gunn, J. 1990. *The Imprisoned Rapist and Rape*, Department of Forensic Psychiatry, Institute of Psychiatry, London.

Guiry, R. 2006. Who is the Victim? – The Use of Victim Impact Statements in Murder and Manslaughter Cases in *Irish Criminal Law Journal*, Vol. 16(2), pp. 2-9.

Hale, M. 1736 (2003). *History of the Pleas of the Crown, Volume I*, Lawbook Exchange Ltd., Clark, NJ.

Hall, C. 1988. Rape: The Politics of Definition in *South African Law Journal*, Vol. 105, pp. 67-82.

Hamilton, J. 2008. The Prosecutor's Role at Sentencing Hearings, unpublished paper presented at the 3rd Annual Thomson Round Hall Criminal Law Conference, 12 April 2008.

Hamilton, J. 2003. Review of the Criminal Justice System Arising from Public Concern at Recent Developments: Submission by the Director of Public Prosecutions, Oireachtas Joint Committee on Justice, Equality, Defence and Women's Rights, Dublin.

Hammock, G.S. and Richardson, D. 1997. Perceptions of Rape: The Influence of Closeness of Relationship, Intoxication, and Sex of Participant in *Violence and Victims*, Vol. 12, pp. 237-246.

Hanley, K. 2006. Law of Rape: Lack of Conviction in *Law Society Gazette*, Vol. 20, 20 July, 2006.

Hanly, C. 2001. Corroborating Rape Charges in *Irish Criminal Law Journal*, Vol. 11(2), pp. 2-11.

Hans, V.P. and Brooks, N. 1977. Effects of Corroboration Instructions in a Rape Case on Experimental Juries in *Osgoode Hall Law Journal*, Vol. 15, pp. 701-716.

Hans, V.P. and Vidmar, N. 2001. *Judging the Jury*, Perseus, New York, NY.

Harris and Grace. 1999. *A Question of Evidence? Investigating and Prosecuting Rape in the 1990's*. Home Office Study No. 196, London.

Hastie, R, Penrod, and S. Pennington, N. 1983. *Inside the Jury*, Harvard University Press, Cambridge, MA.

Hattem, T. 2000. *Survey of Sexual Assault Survivors*. Department of Justice, Canada, Ottawa.

Health Service Executive. 2008. *Less Alcohol is More Money, Energy and Control*, Department of Health, Dublin.

Henning, T. and Bronnitt, S. 1998. Rape Victims on Trial: Regulating the Use and Abuse of Sexual History Evidence", in Easteal, P., (ed.), *Balancing the Scales, Rape Law Reform and Australian Culture*, Federation Press, Sydney.

Henning, T. 1996. *Occasional Paper 4: Sexual Reputation and Sexual Experience in Tasmanian Proceedings relating to Sexual Offences*, University of Tasmania Law Press, Hobart.

Henriques, J., Hollway, W., Urwin, C., W., Venn, C., and Walkerdine, V. 1984. *Changing the Subject: Psychology, Social Regulation and Subjectivity*, Methuen, London.

Herman, J.L. 1992. *Trauma and Recovery*, Basic Books, New York, NY.

Higgins, P.L., Heath, W.P and Granneman, B.D. 2007. How Type of Excuse Defense, Mock Juror Age, and Defendant Age Affect Mock Jurors' Decisions in *Journal of Social Psychology*, Vol. 147(4), pp. 371-392.

Hingson, R., Heeren, T., Winter, M., Wechsler, H. 2005. Magnitude of Alcohol-Related Mortality and Morbidity among U.S. College Students Aged 18-24: Changes from 1998 to 2001 in *Annual Review of Public Health*, Vol. 26, pp. 259-279.

HMCPSI and HMIC, 2002. *A Report on the Joint Inspection into the Investigation and Prosecution of Cases involving Allegations of Rape*, Her Majesty's Crown Prosecution Service Inspectorate/Her Majesty's Inspectorate of Constabulary, London.

HMCPSI and HMIC, 2007. *Without Consent: A Report on the Joint Review of the Investigation and Prosecution of Rape Offences*, Her Majesty's Crown Prosecution Service Inspectorate/Her Majesty's Inspectorate of Constabulary, London.

HMCPSI and HMIC. 2006. *Raising the Standard: Justice in Policing, Joint Thematic Report*, Her Majesty's Crown Prosecution Service Inspectorate/Her Majesty's Inspectorate of Constabulary, London.

Hodge, J.E. 1993. Alcohol and Violence in Taylor, P.J., (ed.), *Violence in Society*, Royal College of Physicians, London.

Holmstromm, L. and Burgess, A. 1978. *The Victim of Rape: Institutional Reactions*. John Wiley and Sons, Hoboken, NJ.

Home Office. 1998. *Speaking Up for Justice: Report of the Interdepartmental Working Group on the Treatment of Vulnerable and Intimidated Witnesses in the Criminal Justice System*, Home Office, London.

Home Office. 2001. *Making Punishments Work: Report of a Review of the Sentencing Framework for England and Wales*, Home Office, London (The Halliday Report).

Home Office. 2002. *Justice for All*, Home Office, London.

Hope, A. 2007. *Alcohol Consumption in Ireland, 1986-2006*, Health Service Executive – Alcohol Implementation Group, Dublin.

Horney, J. and Spohn, C. 1991. Rape Law Reform and Instrumental Change in Six Urban Jurisdictions in *Law and Society Review*, Vol. 25, pp. 117-154.

Horney, J. and Spohn, C. 1996. The Influence of Blame and Believability Factors on the Processing of Simple Versus Aggravated Rape Cases in *Criminology*, Vol. 34(2), pp. 135-162.

Horowitz, I. 1988. The Impact of Judicial Instructions, Arguments and Challenges on Jury Decision-making in *Law and Human Behavior*, Vol. 12, pp. 439-453.

Howard, D.E., Griffin, M., Boekeloo, B., Lake, K. and Bellows, D. 2007. Staying Safe While Consuming Alcohol: A Qualitative Study of the Protective Strategies and Informational Needs of College Freshmen in *Journal of American College Health*, Vol. 56, pp. 247-254.

Howard League for Penal Reform. 1985. *Unlawful Sex: Offences, Victims and Offenders in the Criminal Justice System in England and Wales*, Waterloo, London.

Howard, W.G. and Refering, D. 1983. The Dynamics of Jury Decision-Making: A Case Study in *Social Behavior and Personality*, Vol. 11, pp. 83-89.

Hoyle, C., Cape, E., Morgan, R. and Sanders, A. 1998. *Evaluation of the 'One Stop Shop' and Victim Statement Pilot Projects*, Home Office, London.

Irish Council for Civil Liberties. 2008. *A Better Deal: The Human Rights of Victims in the Criminal Justice System*, Dublin.

Irish Council for Civil Liberties. 2008b. *Taking Liberties: The Human Rights Implications of the Balance in the Criminal Law Review Group Report*, Dublin.

Irish Examiner. 09/02/2006. *Rape Services in Crisis*. [www.document] http://archives.tcm.ie/irishexaminer/2006/02/09/story282847934.asp (accessed 11/06/09).

Irving, T. 2008. Decoding Black Women: Policing Practices and Rape Prosecution on the Streets of Philadelphia in *NWSA Journal*, Vol. 20(2) (summer), pp. 100-120.

Jackson, J.D., Quinn, K. and O'Malley, T. 1999. The Jury System in Contemporary Ireland: In the Shadow of a Troubled Past in *Law and Contemporary Problems*, Vol. 62, pp. 203-232.

Jackson, R. M. 1937. The Incidence of Jury Trial during the Past Century in *Modern Law Review*, Vol. 1, pp. 132-144.

Jacobson, M.B. 1981. Effects of Victim's and Defendant's Physical Attractiveness on Subjects' Judgments in a Rape Case in *Sex Roles*, Vol. 7, pp. 247-255.

James, R.M. 1959. Status and Competence of Jurors in *American Journal of Sociology*, Vol. 64(6), pp. 563-570.

Jamieson, L., Burman, M., Grundy, S. and Dyer, F. 1998. *The 'Attrition' of Sexual Offences in the Criminal Justice System: A Report of a Pilot Study Monitor-*

ing Cases from First Report to the Police Final Outcome. Unpublished Report submitted to the Scottish Office.

Johnson, J. 1994. The Effect of Rape Type and Information Admissibility on Perceptions of Rape Victims in *Sex Roles*, Vol. 30, pp. 781-792.

Johnson, J.D., Jackson, L.A., Gatto, L., and Nowak, A. 1995. Differential Male and Female Responses to Inadmissible Sexual History Information regarding a Rape Victim in *Basic and Applied Social Psychology*, Vol. 16, pp. 503-513.

Johnsons, H. and Sacco, V. 1995. Researching Violence Against Women: Statistics Canada's National Survey in *Canadian Journal of Criminology*, Vol. 37(3), pp. 281-304.

Joint Oireachtas Committee on Women's Rights. 1987. *Fourth Report: Sexual Violence* (PL 4697), Dublin.

Jordan, J. 2001. *True 'Lies' and False 'Truths': Women, Rape and the Police*, unpublished Ph.D. dissertation, Victorian University of Wellington, New Zealand.

Jordan, J. 2004. Beyond Belief? Police, Rape and Women's Credibility in *Criminal Justice*, Vol. 4, pp. 29-59.

Kahneman, D., Slovic, P. and Tversky, A. 1982. *Judgment under Uncertainty: Heuristics and Biases*, Cambridge University Press, Cambridge.

Kalven, H. and Zeisel, H. 1966. *The American Jury*, Little, Brown and Co., Boston, MA.

Kanin, E. 1994. False Rape Allegations in *Archives of Sexual Behavior*, Vol. 23, pp. 81-92.

Katz, S. and Mazur, M.A. 1979. *Understanding the Rape Victim: Synthesis of Research Findings*, John Wiley, New York, NY.

Kaukinen, C. 2002. The Help-Seeking Decisions of Violent Crime Victims: An examination of the direct and conditional effects of gender and the victim-offender relationship in *Journal of Interpersonal Violence*, Vol. 17, No. 432, pp. 432-456.

Kelly, L. and Regan, L. 2001. *Rape: The Forgotten Issue? A European Attrition and Networking Study*, CWASU, London.

Kelly, L. 2001. *Routes to (In)justice: A Research Review on the Reporting, Investigation and Prosecution of Rape Cases*, Home Office, London.

Kelly, L., Temkin, J. and Griffith, S. 2006. *Section 41: An Evaluation of New Legislation Limiting Sexual History Evidence in Rape Trials*, Home Office Online Report 20/06.

Kelly, L., Lovett, J. and Regan, L. 2005. *A Gap or a Chasm? Attrition in Reported Rape Cases*, Home Office Research Study 293, Home Office, London.

Kennedy, H. 1992. *Eve was Framed: Women and British Justice*. Vintage, London.

Kerr, N. L., Harmon, D. L., and Graves, J. K. 1982. Independence of Multiple Verdicts by Jurors and Juries in *Journal of Applied Social Psychology*, Vol. 12, pp. 12-29.

Kerstetter, W. and van Winkle, B. 1990. Who decides? A study of the complainant's decision to prosecute in rape cases in *Criminal Justice and Behaviour*, Vol. 17(3), pp. 265-283.

Kerstetter, W.A. 1990. Gateway to Justice: Police and Prosecutorial Response to Sexual Assaults Against Women in *Journal of Criminal Law and Criminology*, Vol. 81(2), pp. 267-312.

Kibble, N. 2004. *Judicial Perspectives on Section 41 of the Youth Justice and Criminal Evidence Act 1999*, A Research Report for the Criminal Bar Association of England and Wales, London.

Kilpatrick, D.G. 2000. *Mental Health Impact of Rape* at National Violence Against Women Prevention Research Center, 2000 [www.document] at http://www.musc.edu/vawprevention/research/mentalimpact.shtml accessed 27/02/09.

Kingsnorth, R., Lopez, J., Wentworth, J., Cummins, D. 1998. Adult Sexual Assault: The Role of Racial/Ethnic Composition in Prosecution and Sentencing in *Journal of Criminal Justice*, Vol. 26(5), pp. 359-371.

Kingsnorth, R.F., MacIntosh, R.C. and Wentworth, J. 1999. Sexual Assault: The Role of Prior Relationship and Victim Characterisation in Case Processing in *Justice Quarterly*, Vol. 16(2), pp. 275-302.

Klemmack, S.H. and Klemmack, D.L. 1976. The Social Definition of Rape in Walker, M.J. and Brodsky, S.C., eds., *Sexual Assault*, D.C. Health and Co., Lexington, MA.

Klippenstine, M.A., Schuller, R.A. and Wall, A-M. 2007. Perceptions of Sexual Assault: The Expression of Gender Differences and the Impact of Target Alcohol Consumption in *Journal of Applied Social Psychology*, Vol. 37(11), pp. 2620-2641.

Koski, D.D. 2002. Jury Decision-Making in Rape Trials in *Criminal Law Bulletin*, Vol. 38, pp. 21-159.

Koss, M. and Harvey, M. 1991. *The Rape Victim: Clinical and Community Interventions*, Sage, London and Thousand Oaks, CA.

Koss, M.P., Dinero, T.E. 1988. Stranger and Acquaintance Rape: Are there Differences in the Victims' Experiences? in *Psychology of Women Quarterly*, Vol. 12, pp. 1-24.

Koss, M.P. and Oros, C. 1982. Sexual Experiences Survey: A Research Instrument Investigating Sexual Aggression and Victimisation in *Journal of Consulting and Clinical Psychology*, Vol. 50, pp. 455-457.

Krahé, B., Temkin, J., Bieneck, A. and Berger, A. 2008. Prospective Lawyers' Rape Stereotypes and Schematic Decision-Making About Rape Cases in *Psychology, Crime and Law*, Vol. 14(5) (October), pp. 461-479.

Kramer, K. 1994. Rule by Myth: The Social and Legal Dynamics Governing Alcohol Related Rape in *Stanford Law Review*, Vol. 47, pp. 115-160.

Krulewitz, J. and Nash, J. 1979. Effects of rape victim resistance, assault outcome and sex of observer on attributions about rape in *Journal of Personality*, Vol. 47(4), pp. 557-574.

Krulewitz, J.E. and Payne, E. 1978. Attributions about Rape: Effects of Rapist Force, Observer Sex and Sex Role Attitudes in *Journal of Applied Social Psychology*, Vol. 8, pp. 291-305.

L'Armand, K.L. and Pepitone, A. 1982. Judgments of Rape: A Study of Victim-Rapist Relationship and Victim Sexual History in *Personality and Social Psychology Bulletin*, Vol. 8, pp. 134-139.

La Free, G. 1981. Official Reaction to Social Problems: A Case Study of Police Decisions in Sexual Assault Cases in *Social Problems*, Vol. 28, pp. 582-594.

La Free, G. 1989. *Rape and Criminal Justice: The Social Construction of Sexual Assault*, Wadsworth, Belmont, CA.

La Free, G.D., Reskin, B.F. and Visher, C.A. 1985. Jurors' Responses to Victims' Behavior and Legal Issues in Sexual Assault Trials in *Social Problems*, Vol. 32(4), pp. 389-407.

LaFree, G.D. 1980. The Effect of Sexual Stratification by Race on Official Reactions to Rape in *American Sociological Review*, Vol. 45 (October), pp. 842-854.

Langan, P.A. and Farrington, D.P. 1998. *Crime and Justice in the United States and in England and Wales, 1981-96*, United States Department of Justice, Bureau of Justice Statistics, Washington DC.

Langbein, J. 1978. Criminal Trials Before the Lawyers in *University of Chicago Law Review* Vol. 45, pp. 263-316.

Law Reform Commission of Canada, 1978. *Report No.10: Sexual Offences*, Ottawa.

Law Reform Commission of Tasmania. 1976. *Reducing Harassment and Embarrassment of Complainants in Rape Cases*, Hobart.

Law Reform Commission of Victoria. 1976. *Report No.5: Rape Prosecutions (Court Procedures and Rules of Evidence)*, Melbourne.

Law Reform Commission of Victoria. 1986. *Discussion Paper No.2: Rape and Allied Offences – Substantive Aspects*, Melbourne.

Law Reform Commission of Victoria. 1987. *Discussion Paper No.5: Rape and Allied Offences – Procedure and Evidence*, Melbourne.

Law Reform Commission of Victoria. 1988. *Report No.13: Rape and Allied Offences – Procedure and Evidence*, Melbourne.

Law Reform Commission. 1996. *Report on Sentencing* (LRC 53-1996), Dublin.

Law Reform Commission. 1987. *Consultation Paper on Rape*, Dublin.

Law Reform Commission. 1988. *Report on Rape* (LRC 24-1988), Dublin.

Law Reform Commission. 1993. *Consultation Paper on Sentencing*, Dublin.

Law Reform Commission. 1996. *Report on Sentencing* (LRC 53-1996). Dublin.

Law Reform Commissioner of Victoria. 1976. *Rape Prosecutions: Court Procedures and Rules of Evidence*. Report No. 5, Melbourne.

Lea, S.J., Lanvers, U., and Shaw, S. 2003. Attrition in rape cases: Developing a profile and identifying relevant factors in *British Journal of Criminology*, Vol. 43, pp. 583-599.

Leanne, M., Ryan, S. Fennell, C. and Egan, E. 2001. *Attrition in Sexual Assault Offence Cases in Ireland: A Qualitative Analysis*, Department of Justice, Equality and Law Reform, Dublin.

Lees, S. and Gregory, J. 1993. *Rape and Sexual Assault: A Study of Attrition*. Islington Police and Crime Prevention Unit, Islington.

Lees, S. 1993. Judicial Rape in *Women's Studies International Forum*, Vol. 16, pp. 11-36.

Lees, S. 1996. *Carnal Knowledge: Rape on Trial*, Hamish Hamilton, London.

Lees, S. 2002. *Carnal Knowledge: Rape on Trial*, 2nd ed., Women's Press, London.

Lees, S., 1997. *Ruling Passions: Sexual Violence, Reputation and the Law*, Open University Press, Milton Keynes.

Lefcourt, H. 1991. Locus of control in Robinson, J. et al. eds. *Measures of Personality and Social Psychological Attitudes*, Academic Press, London.

Levenson, H. 1981. Differentiating among Internality, Powerful Others, and Chance in Lefcourt, H. ed., *Research with the Locus of Control*, Vol 1, Academic Press, New York, NY, pp. 15-63.

Levin, H. Y. and Emerson, J.W. 2005-2006. Is there a Bias against Education in the Jury Selection Process? in *Connecticut Law Review,* Vol. 38, pp.325-353.

Lewis-Herman, J. 2005. Justice from the Victim's Perspective in *Violence against Women*, Vol. 11(5), pp. 571-602.

Lievore, D. 2003. *Non-Reporting and Hidden Recording of Sexual Assault: An International Literature Review*, Commonwealth Office of the Status of Women, Canberra.

Lievore, D. 2005. Prosecutorial Decision in Adult Sexual Assault Cases in *Trends and Issues in Crime and Criminal Justice*. No. 291 (January), pp. 1-6.

Lievore, D. 2004. *Prosecutorial Decision in Adult Sexual Assault Cases: An Australian Study,* Australian Government Office of the Status of Women, Canberra.

Ling J, Heffernan TM, Buchanan T, Rodgers J, Scholey AB and Parrott AC. 2003. Effects of Alcohol on Subjective Ratings of Prospective and Everyday Memory Deficits in *Alcoholism: Clinical and Experimental Research* Vol. 27, pp. 970-4.

Lizotte, A. 1985. The Uniqueness of Rape: Reporting Assaultive Violence to the Police in *Crime and Delinquency*, Vol. 31(2), pp. 169-190.

Lloyd, C. and Walmsley, R. 1989. *Changes in Rape Offences and Sentencing*. Home Office Research Study No. 105. HMSO, London.

Loh, W.D. 1979-1980. The Impact of Common Law and Reform Rape Statutes on Prosecution: An Empirical Study in *Washington Law Review*, Vol. 55, pp. 591-653.

Lonsway, K.A. and Fitzgerald, L.F. 1994. Rape Myths in *Psychology of Women Quarterly,* Vol. 18, pp. 133-164.

Lonsway, K.A., Archambault, J. and Lisak, D. 2009. Moving Beyond the Issue to Successfully Investigate and Prosecute Non-Stranger Sexual Assault in *The Voice* Vol. 3(1), pp. 1-11.

LSE Jury Project. 1973. Juries and the Rules of Evidence in *Criminal Law Review*, pp. 208-223.

Luginbuhl, J. and Mullin, C. 1981. Rape and Responsibility: How and How Much is the Victim Blamed? in *Sex Roles,* Vol. 7, pp. 547-559.

MacCoun, J. 1989. Experimental Research on Jury Decision-Making in *Science,* Vol. 244, pp. 1046-50.

MacLean, N.M. 1979. Rape and False Accusations of Rape in *Police Surgeon,* pp. 29-40.

Mahony, P. 1999. High Rape Chronicity and Low Rates of Help-Seeking Among Wife Rape Survivors in a Non-Clinical Sample in *Violence against Women*, Vol. 5(9), pp. 993-1016.

Majority Staff of the United States Senate Judiciary Committee. 1993. *The Response to Rape: Detours on the Road to Equal Justice*, U.S. Senate Judiciary Committee, Washington, DC.

Malloch, M.S. 2004. 'Risky' Women, Sexual Consent and Criminal 'Justice' in Cowling, M. and Reynolds, P., eds., *Making Sense of Sexual Consent*, Ashgate Publishing Ltd., Hantshire, pp. 111-127.

March, J., Geist, A. and Caplan, N. 1982. *Rape and the Limits of Law Reform*, Auburn House, Boston, MA.

Marder, N.S. 1987. Gender Dynamics and Jury Deliberations in *Yale Law Journal*, Vol. 96(3), pp. 593-612.

Martin, D. Vieraitis, L.M. and Britto, S. 2006. Gender Equality and Women's Absolute Status: A test of the feminist models of rape in *Violence Against Women*, Vol. 12(4), (April), pp. 321-339.

Martin, S.E. 1992. The Epidemiology of Alcohol-Related Interpersonal Violence in *Alcohol, Health and Research World*, Vol. 16(3), pp. 231-237.

Masher, D.L. and Anderson, R.D. 1986. Macho Personality, Sexual Aggression and Reactions to Guided Imagery of Realistic Rape in *Journal of Research in Personality,* Vol. 20, pp. 77-88.

Maxwell, C., Robinson, A. and Post, L. 2003. The Impact of Race on the Adjudication of Sexual Assault and Other Violent Crimes in *Journal of Criminal Justice*, Vol. 31(6), pp. 523-538.

McAdams, D. 1995. The Life Story Interview. [www.document] www.letus.org/foley/instruments/interview.html (accessed 12/05/09).

McGee, H., Garavan, R. de Barra, M., Byrne, H. and Conroy, R. 2002. *The SAVI Report: Sexual Abuse and Violence in Ireland*, The Liffey Press, Dublin.

McGee, H., Garavan, R. Leigh, C., Ellis, C., and Conroy, R. 2005. *SAVI Revisited: Long-Term Effects of Disclosure of Sexual Abuse in a Confidential Research Interview*, Dublin Rape Crisis Centre, Dublin.

McGrath, D. 2006. *Evidence*, Thomson Round Hall, Dublin.

McGregor, M.J., Du Mont, J. and Myhr, T.L. 2002. Sexual Assault Forensic Medical Examination: Is Evidence Related to Successful Prosecution? in *Annals of Emergency Medicine*, Vol. 39(6) (June), pp. 639-647.

McHugh,. 1988. Juror's Deliberations, Jury Secrecy, Public Policy and the Law of Contempt in Findlay, M. and Duff. P., eds., *The Jury Under Attack*, Butterworths, London.

McLendon, K., Foley, L.A., Hall, J., Sloan, L. Wesley, A. and Perry, L. 1994. Male and Female Perceptions of Date Rape in *Journal of Social Behavior and Personality*, Vol. 9, pp. 421-428.

Menard, K. 2005. *Reporting Sexual Assault; A Social Ecology Perspective*, LFB Scholarly Publishing, New York, NY.

Mills, C.J. and Bohannon, W.E. 1980-1981. Juror Characteristics: To What Extent are they Related to Jury Verdicts? in *Judicature*, Vol. 64, pp. 23-31.

Mills, E.S. 1962. A Statistical Study of Occupations of Jurors in a United States District Court in *Maryland Law Review*, Vol. 22, pp. 205-214.

Mills, E.S. 1969. A Statistical Profile of Jurors in a United States District Court in *Law and the Social Order*, pp. 329-339.

MIMH. 2002. *Trauma Among People with Mental Illness and/or Substance Abuse Disorders*. The Missouri Institute of Mental Health: Fact Sheet. (November). [www.document] www.mimh.edu/pie (accessed 27/04/09).

Mohler-Kuo, M., Dowdall, G.W., Koss. M.P. and Wechsler, H. 2004. Correlates of Rape while Intoxicated in a National Sample of College Women in *Journal of Studies on Alcohol*, Vol. 65, pp. 37-45.

Morgan, R. and Sanders, A. 1999. *The Uses of Victim Statements*, Home Office, London.

Morrison, B., Soboleva, N. and Chong, J. 2008. *Conviction and Sentencing of Offenders in New Zealand, 1997 to 2006*, Ministry of Justice, Wellington.

Morway, R. 2006. Date Rape Stories and Media Coverage in *Associated Content*, October 6th. [www.document] at http://www.associatedcontent.com/article/66523 (accessed 20/05/09).

Mouzos, J. and Makkai, T. 2004. *Women's Experiences of male Violence: Findings from the Australian Component of the International Violence Against Women Survey*. Australian Institute of Criminology, Canberra.

Muehlenhard, C.L. 1988. 'Nice Women Don't Say Yes and 'Real' Men Don't Say No: How Miscommunication and the Double Standard Can Cause Sexual Problems in *Women and Therapy*, Vol. 7, pp. 95-108.

Muir, G. and MacLeod, M.D. 2003. The Demographic and Spatial Patterns of Recorded Rape in a Large UK Metropolitan Area in *Psychology, Crime and Law*, Vol. 9(4) (December), pp. 345-355.

Muir, J. 1990. *Victim Impact Statements in Canada: Evaluation of the Calgary Project*, Department of Justice Canada, Ottawa.

Myhill, A. and Allen, J. 2002. *Rape and sexual assault of women: The extent and nature of the problem*: Findings from the British Crime Survey, Home Office Research Study 237, Home Office, London.

National Crime Council. 2006. *An Examination of Time Intervals in the Investigation and Prosecution of Murder and Rape Cases in Ireland from 2002 to 2004*, The Stationery Office, Dublin.

National Victim Center and Crime Victims' Research and Treatment Center. 1992. *Rape in America: A Report to the Nation*, Medical University of South Carolina.

Neame, A. 2003. *Briefing Paper No.2: Beyond 'Drink Spiking' – Drug and Alcohol Facilitated Sexual Assault*, Australian Centre for the Study of Sexual Assault, Australian Institute of Family Studies.

Neddermeyer, D. 2004-2009. *Sexual Assault: Rape – Healing is Possible* at Women's Web. [www.document] http://www.womensweb.ca/violence/ rape/healing.php (accessed 27/04/09).

Negrusz, A., Adamowicz, P., Saini, B.K., Webster, D.E., Juhascik, M.P., Moore, C.M. and Schlemmer, R.F. 2005. Detection of Ketamine and Norketamine in Urine of Nonhuman Primates after a Single Dose of Ketamine using Microplate Enzyme-Linked Immunosorbent Assay (ELISA) and NC1-GC-MS in *Journal of Analytical Toxicology*, Vol. 29, pp. 163-168.

Nelligan, P.J. 1988. The Effects of Gender of Jurors on Sexual Assaults Verdicts in *Journal of Sociology and Social Research*, Vol. 72, pp. 249-251.

Nemeth, C., Endicott, J. and Wachtler, J. 1976. From the '50s to the '70s: Women in Jury Deliberations in *Sociometry*, Vol. 39(4), pp. 293-304.

New South Wales Department for Women. 1996. *Heroines of Fortitude: The Experiences of Women in Court as Victims of Sexual Assault*, Canberra.

New Zealand Law Commission. 1999. *Report 55: Evidence, Volume I – Reform of the Law*, Wellington, New Zealand.

New Zealand Law Commission. 2001. *Report 69: Juries in Criminal Cases*, Wellington, New Zealand.

Nietzel, M.T., McCarthy, D.M., and Kern, M.J. 1999. Juries: The Current State of the Empirical Literature", in Roesch, R., Hart, S.D. and Ogloff, J.R.P., eds., *Psychology and Law: The State of the Discipline*, Kluwer, New York.

Northern Ireland Office. 2004. *Victims' and Witness' Views on their Treatment in the Criminal Justice System*. NIO Research and Statistics Report, No. 10, Northern Ireland Office, Belfast.

Note. 1967. Corroborating Charges of Rape in *Columbia Law Review*, Vol. 67, pp. 1137-1148.

O'Dwyer, K., Kennedy, P. and Ryan, W. 2005. *Garda Public Attitudes Survey 2005*. Research Report No. 01/05. An Garda Síochána, Templemore.

O'Higgins, M. 2008. *Reviewing Prosecutorial Decisions*. 9th Annual National Prosecutors' Conference. 24 May 2008, Dublin Castle Conference Centre, Dublin.

O'Keefe, S. 2003. Police Decision-making in Investigations of Rape. [www.document] www.sexualviolence.ie (accessed 17/05/09).

O'Malley, T. 1993. Punishment and Moral Luck: The Role of the Victim in Sentencing Decisions in *Irish Criminal Law Review*, Vol. 3, pp. 40-60.

O'Malley, T. 2006. *Sentencing Law and Practice*, 2nd ed., Thomson Round Hall, Dublin.

O'Shea, A. 2006. *Sexual Assault Treatment Services: A Review*, National Steering Committee on Violence Against Women and The Department of Health and Children, Dublin.

Office for Criminal Justice Reform. 2006. *Convicting Rapists and Protecting Victims – Justice for Victims of Rape: A Consultation Paper*, HMSO, London.

Office of Criminal Justice Reform. 2007. *Convicting Rapists and Protecting Victims – Justice for Victims of Rape: Response to Consultation*, HMSO, London.

Olsen-Fulero, L. and Fulero, S. 1997. Commonsense Rape Judgments: An Empathy-Complexity Theory of Rape Juror Story-Making in *Psychology, Public Policy and Law*, Vol. 3, pp. 402-427.

Ong, A.S.L. and Ward, C. 2006. The Effects of Sex and Power Schemas, Attitudes to Women, and Victim Resistance on Rape Attributions in *Journal of Applied Social Psychology*, Vol. 29(2), pp. 362-376.

Orth, U. 2003. Punishment goals of crime victims in *Law and Human Behaviour*, Vol. 27(2), pp. 173-186.

Orth, U. and Maerchker, A. 2004. Do trials of perpetrators retraumatise crime victims? in *Journal of Interpersonal Violence*, Vol.19(2), pp. 212-227.

Osborough, N. 1982. A Damocles' Sword Guaranteed Irish: The Suspended Sentence in the Republic of Ireland in *Irish Jurist (n.s.)* Vol. 17, pp. 221.

Paciocco,. 1999. *Getting Away with Murder: The Canadian Criminal Justice System*. Irwin Law, Toronto.

Painter, K. 1991. *Wife Rape, Marriage and the Law – Survey Report: Key Findings and Recommendations.* Manchester: Faculty of Economic and Social Studies, University of Manchester.

Payne, D.L., Lonsway, K.A. and Fitzgerald, L.F. 1999. Rape Myth Acceptance: Exploration of its Structure and its Measurement using the Illinois Rape Myth Acceptance Scale in *Journal of Research in Personality*, Vol. 33, pp. 27-68.

Pennington, N. and Hastie, R. 1992. Explaining the Evidence: Tests of the Story Model for Juror Decision-Making in *Journal of Personality and Social Psychology*, Vol. 62, pp. 189-206.

Peretti, P. and Cozzens, N. 1983. Characteristics of Female Rapees Not Reporting and Reporting the First Incident of Rape in *Corrective and Social Psychology*, Vol. 29, pp. 82-87.

Peterson, Z. and Muehlenhard, C. 2004. Was it Rape? The Function of Women's Rape Myth Acceptance and Definitions of Sex Labelling Their Own Experiences in *Sex Roles*, Vol. 51, pp. 129-144.

Phillips, C and Brown, D. 1998. *Entry into the Criminal Justice System: A Survey of Police Arrests and their Outcome*, Home Office, London.

Pino, N. and Meier, R. 1999. Gender Differences in Rape Reporting in *Sex Roles*, Vol. 40, pp. 979-990.

Purdon, S. and Erens, B. 1995. *Chapter 12: Psychological Wellbeing in The Scottish Health Survey 1995*, Vol. 1.[www.document] at http://www.sehd.scot.nhs.uk/publications/sh5/sh512-01.htm (accessed 26/05/09).

Ramstedt, M. and Hope, A. 2003. *The Irish Drinking Culture: Drinking and Drinking-Related Harm – A European Comparison*, Dublin (available on www.meas.ie).

Rape Crisis Network Ireland. 2005. *Agenda for Justice: Towards Ending Injustice for Survivors of Sexual Violence,* Rape Crisis Network Ireland, Galway.

Rape Crisis Network Ireland. 2005. *National Rape Crisis Statistics 2004.* Rape Crisis Network Ireland, Galway

Rape Crisis Network Ireland. 2007. *Agenda for Justice III: The Investigation of Sexual Violence – Priority Recommendations*, Rape Crisis Network Ireland, Galway.

Rape Crisis Network Ireland. 2007. *RCNI National Rape Crisis Statistics 2007*, Rape Crisis Network Ireland, Galway.

Reed, J.P. 1965. Jury Deliberation, Voting and Verdict Trends in *Southwestern Social Science Quarterly*, Vol. 58, pp. 390-399.

Reed, J.P. and Reed, R.S. 1977. Liberalism-Conservatism as an Indicator of Jury Product and Process in *Law and Human Behavior*, Vol. 1, pp. 81-86.

Regan, L. and Kelly, L. 2001. *Teenage Tolerance: The Hidden Lives of Irish Young People*, Women's Aid, Dublin.

Regan, L., and Kelly, L. 2003. *Rape: Still a Forgotten Issue*, Child and Woman Abuse Studies Unit, London Metropolitan University, London.

Resick, P.A. 1987. Psychological Effects of Victimization: Implications for the Criminal Justice System in *Crime and Delinquency*, Vol. 33, pp. 468-478.

Reskin, B.F. and Visher, C.A. 1986. The Impacts of Evidence and Extra-Legal Factors in Jurors' Decisions in *Law and Society Review*, Vol. 20(3), pp. 423-438.

Roberts, J.V. and Edgar, A. 2002. Victim Impact Statements at Sentencing: Perceptions of the Judiciary in Canada in *International Journal of Victimology*, Vol. 1, *available* at www.jidv.com.

Roberts, J.V. and Edgar, A. 2006. *Victim Impact Statements at Sentencing: Judicial Experiences and Perceptions – A Survey of Three Jurisdictions*, Department of Justice Canada, Ottawa.

Roberts, J.V. 2003. Victim Impact Statements and the Sentencing Process: Recent Developments and Research Findings in *Criminal Law Quarterly* Vol. 47, pp. 365-396.

Roberts, J.V. 1996. Sexual Assaults in Canada: Recent Statistical Trends in *Queens Law Journal*, Vol. 21, pp. 395-421.

Rock, P. 1993. *The Social World of the English Crown Court*, Clarendon Press, Oxford.

Rock, P. 2004. *Constructing Victims' Rights: The Home Office, New Labour and Victims*, Clarendon Press, Oxford.

Roizen, J. 1997. Epidemiological Issues in Alcohol-Related Violence, in Galanter, M, (ed.), *Recent Developments in Alcoholism – Volume 13: Alcohol and Violence*, Vol. 13(7), pp. 7-40.

Rotunda Hospital. 2003. *Clinical Report, 2003*. Dublin: Rotunda.

Royal Commission on Criminal Justice. 1993. *Report*, Home Office, London (Runciman Commission).

Royal Commission on Human Relationships. 1977. *Report*, Canberra.

Ruch, L., Davidson-Coronado, J., Coyne, B. J., and Perrone, P. A. 2000. *Reporting Sexual Assault to Police in Hawaii*, Crime Prevention and Justice Division Hawaii.

Ruch, L.O. and Leon, J.L. 1983. Type of Sexual Assault Trauma: A Multidimensional Analysis of a Short Term Panel in *Victimology*, Vol. 8, pp. 237-250.

Rumney, P.N.S.2006. False Allegations of Rape in *Cambridge Law Journal*, Vol. 65, pp.128-158.

Rumney, P.S. 2001. The Review of Sexual Offences and Rape Law Reform: Another False Dawn? in *Modern Law Review*, Vol. 64(6), pp. 890-910.

Rumsey, M.G and Rumsey, J.M. 1977. A Case of Rape: Sentencing Judgments of Males and Females in *Psychological Reports*, Vol. 41, pp. 459-465.

Ruparel, C. 2004. *The Nature of Rape of Females in the Metropolitan Police District*, Home Office Findings 247, Home Office, London.

Russell, D.E.H. 1984. *Sexual Exploitation – Rape, Child Sexual Abuse and Workplace Harassment*, Sage, Beverly Hills, CA.

Russell, D.E.H. 1990. *Rape in Marriage*. Macmillan, New York, NY.

Ryan, C. 2008. 25% Think Judge Right to Let Rapist Walk Free in *Irish Examiner*, 27 March 2008, p. 11.

Ryan, C. 2008. Majority have Confidence in Courts in *Irish Examiner*, 26 March, 2008, p. 7.

Ryan, C. 2008. Rape: Our Blame Culture in *Irish Examiner*, 26 March 2008, p. 1.

Ryan, C. 2008. Victims' Greatest Fear – Not Being Believed in *Irish Examiner*, 26 March, 2008, pp. 6-7.

Ryan, C. At least there is a consensus on minimum sentences – six years in *Irish Examiner*, 27 March 2008, pp. 10-11.

Ryan, K.M. 1998. Rape and Seduction Scripts in *Psychology of Women Bulletin*, Vol. 12, pp. 237-245.

Sampson, R. 2002. Acquaintance Rape of College Students, *Guide No. 17*, at Centre for Problem-Oriented Policing. [www.document] at http://www.popcenter.org/problems/rape/ (accessed 05/06/09).

Sanders, W.B. 1980. *Rape and Women's Identity*, Sage, Beverly Hills, CA.

Schafer, D. and Kerwin, J. 1992. On Adhering to Judicial Instructions: Reactions of Dogmatic and Nondogmatic Juries to the Judge's Charge in an Entrapment Case in *Journal of Applied Social Psychology*, Vol. 22, pp. 1133-1147.

Schissel, B. 1996. Law Reform and Social Change: A Time Series of Sexual Assault in Canada in *Journal of Criminal Justice*, Vol. 24(2), pp. 123-138.

Schulhofer, S. 1998. *Unwanted Sex: The Culture of Intimidation and the Failure of the Law*, Harvard University Press, Cambridge, MA.

Schuller, R.A. and Hastings, P.A. 2002. Complainant Sexual History Evidence: Its Impact on Mock Jurors' Decisions in *Psychology of Women Quarterly*, Vol. 26, pp. 252-261.

Schuller, R. A. and Stewart, A. 2000. Police responses to sexual assault complaints: The role of perpetrator/complainant intoxication in *Law and Human Behaviour*, Vol. 24, pp. 535-551.

Schult, D. and Schneider, L. 1991. The Role of Sexual Provocativeness, Rape History, and Observer Gender in Perceptions of Blame in Sexual Assault in *Journal of Interpersonal Violence*, Vol. 6, pp. 94-101.

Schutte, J. W. and Hosch, H.M. 1997.Gender Differences in Sexual Assault Verdicts: A Meta-Analysis in *Journal of Social Behavior and Personality*, Vol. 12(3), pp. 759-772.

Scott-Ham, M. and Burton, F.C. 2005. Toxicological Findings in Cases of Alleged Drug-Facilitated Sexual Assault in the United Kingdom over a Three-Year Period in *Journal of Clinical Forensic Medicine*, Vol. 12, pp. 175-188.

Scottish Executive. 2000. *Redressing the Balance: Cross-Examination in Rape and Sexual Offence Trials – A Pre-Legislative Consultation Document*, Edinburgh.

Scottish Executive. 2009. *Making a Victim Statement*, Edinburgh.

Scronce, C. and Corcoran, A. 1995. The Influence of Victims' Consumption of Alcohol on Perceptions of Stranger and Acquaintance Rape in *Violence against Women*, Vol. 1(3), pp. 241-253.

Sealy, A.P. and Cornish, W.R. 1973. Jurors and their Verdicts in *Modern Law Review*, Vol. 36(5), pp. 496-508.

Sentencing Advisory Council. 2009. *Sentencing Snapshot No.26: Sentencing Trends for Rape in the Higher Courts of Victoria, 2003-04 to 2007-08*, Melbourne.

Sentencing Advisory Panel. 2002. *Rape: The Panel's Advice to the Court of Appeal*, May 2002. [www.document] www.sentencing-guidelines.gov.uk/docs/rape.pdf (accessed 25/10/2009).

Sentencing Guidelines Council, 2007. *Sexual Offences Act 2003: Definitive Guideline*, London.

Shapland, J. and Hall, M. 2007. What do we Know about the Effects of Crime on Victims? in *International Review of Victimology*, Vol. 14, No. 2, p. 175-217.

Shapland, J., Wilmore, J., and Duff, P. 1985. *Victims in the Criminal Justice System*, Gower, Aldershot.

Shields, R. 2008. Report Calls for Changes to Rape Coverage in *The Independent*, 24/03/3008. [www.document] http://www.independent.co.uk/news/media/report-calls-for-changes-to-rape-coverage-786543.html (accessed 20/05/09).

Shoham, E. 2000. The Battered Wife's Perception of the Characteristics of Her Encounter with the Police in *International Journal of Offender Therapy and Comparative Criminology*, Vol. 44(2), pp. 242-257.

Simon, R. 1967. *The Jury and the Defence of Insanity*, Little, Brown and Co., Boston, MA.

Simon, R. 1968. The Effects of Newspapers on the Verdicts of Potential Jurors in Simon, R., (ed.), *The Sociology of Law*, Chandler, San Francisco.

Sinclair, H. C. and Bourne, L. E. 1998. The Cycle of Blame or Just World: Effects of Legal Verdicts on Gender Patterns in Rape Myth Acceptance and Victim-Empathy in *Psychology of Women Quarterly*, Vol. 22(4), pp. 575-588.

Slaughter, L. 2000. Involvement of Drugs in Sexual Assault in *Journal of Reproductive Medicine*, Vol. 45, pp. 425-30.

Smart, C. and Smart, B. 1978. Accounting for Rape: Reality and Myth in Press Reporting in Smart, C. and Smart, B., eds., *Women Sexuality and Social Control*, Routledge and Kegan Paul Books, London.

Smart, C. 1976. *Women, Crime and Criminology*, Routledge, London.

Smith, S.J. 1989. *The Politics of 'Race' and Residence*. Polity Press, Cambridge, MA.

Sommers-Flanagan, R., Sommers-Flanagan, J. and Davis, B. 1993. What's Happening on Music Television? A Gender Role Content Analysis in *Sex Roles*, Vol. 28, pp. 745-753.

Soothill, K. and Jack, A. 1975. How Rape is Reported in *New Society*, 19th June.

Soothill, K., Walby, S. and Bagguley, P. 1990. Judges, The Media and Rape in *Journal of Law and Society*, Vol. 17(2), pp. 211-233.

Soothill, K., Way, C. and Gibbens, T.C.N. 1980. Rape Acquittals in *Modern Law Reform*, Vol. 43(2), pp. 159-172.

South Australian Police Department. 1986. *Rape: A Four-Year Study of Victims*, Adelaide.

Spanos, N.P., Dubreuil, S.C. and Gwynn, M.I. 2001.The Effects of Expert Testimony Concerning Rape on the Verdicts and Beliefs of Mock Jurors in *Imagination, Cognition and Personality*, Vol. 11, pp. 37-51.

Spohn, C. and Holleran, D. 2004. Prosecuting Sexual Assault: A Comparison of Charging Decisions in Sexual Assault Cases Involving Strangers, Acquaintances, and Intimate Partners available online at www.ncjrs.gov (accessed on 25/10/2009).

Spohn, C., Beichner, D. and Davis-Frenzel, E. 2001. Prosecutorial Justifications for Sexual Assault Case Rejection: Guarding the 'Gateway to Justice' in *Social Problems*, Vol. 48(2), pp. 206-235.

Spohn, C.C. and Horney, J. 1996. The Impact of Rape Law Reform on the Processing of Simple and Aggravated Rape Cases in *Journal of Criminal Law and Criminology*, Vol. 86(3), pp. 861.

Spohn, C.C. 1998-1999. The Rape Reform Movement: The Traditional Common Law and Rape Law Reforms in *Jurimetrics*, Vol. 39, pp. 119.

SPSS, 15.0.1 (22 Nov. 2006). *SPSS, 15.0 for Windows*. 1989-2006.

Stanko, E.A. 1982. Would You Believe this Woman? in Rafter, N. and Stanko, E.A., eds., *Judge, Lawyer, Victim, Thief*, Northeastern University Press, Boston.

Steblay, N.M., Hosch, H.M., Culhane, S.E. and McWethy, A. 2006. The Impact on Juror Verdicts of Judicial Instructions to Disregard Inadmissible Evidence: A Meta-Analysis in *Law and Human Behavior*, Vol. 30, pp. 469-492.

Stewart, C.H. 1981. A Retrospective Survey of Alleged Sexual Assault Cases in *Police Surgeon*, pp. 28-32.

Stith, K. and Cabranes, J. 1998. *Fear of Judging: Sentencing Guidelines in the Federal Courts*, University of Chicago Press, Chicago.

Strategic Task Force on Alcohol. 2004. *Second Report*, Department of Health and Children, Health Promotion Unit, Dublin.

Strodtbeck, F. L., Rita M. James and Charles Hawkins. 1957. Social Status and Jury Deliberations in *American Sociological Review*, Vol. 2, pp. 713-19.

Strodtbeck, F.L. and Hook, L.H. 1961.The Social Dimensions of a Twelve Man Jury Table in *Sociometry*, Vol. 24, pp. 397-415.

Strodtbeck, F.L., James, R.M. and Hawkins, C. 1957. Social Status in Jury Deliberations in *American Sociological Review*, Vol. 22, pp. 713-719.

Sturman, P. 2000. *Report on Drug Assisted Sexual Assault*, Home Office, London.

Survive.Org. 1998. Post Traumatic Stress Disorder in Rape Survivors at Survive.Org [www.document] http://survive.org.uk/PTSD.html (accessed 20/05/09).

Talja, S. 1999. Analyzing qualitative interview data: The discourse analytic method. *Library and Information Science Research*, Vol. 21(4), pp. 459-477.

Tasmanian Task Force on Sexual Assault and Rape. 1998. *Report of the Task Force on Sexual Assault and Rape in Tasmania*, Department of Justice, Hobart.

Taylor, N. and Mouzos, J. 2006. *Community Attitudes to Violence against Women Survey*, Australian Institute of Criminology, Canberra.

Taylor, N. 2007. *Trends and Issues in Crime and Criminal Justice: Juror Attitudes and Biases in Sexual Assault Cases*, Australian Institute of Criminology, Melbourne.

Tedeschi, R., Park, C. and Calhoun, L. (eds.). 1998. *Post-Traumatic Growth: Positive Changes in the Aftermath of Crisis,* Erlbaum, Mahwah, NJ.

Tellis, K.M. and Spohn, C. C. 2008. The Sexual Stratification Hypothesis Revisited: Testing Assumptions About Simple Versus Aggravated Rape in *Journal of Criminal Justice,* Vol. 36, pp. 252-261.

Temkin, J. 2000b. Rape and Criminal Justice at the Millennium in Nicolson, D. and Bibbings, L., eds., *Feminist Perspectives on Criminal Law,* Cavendish Press, London, pp.183-203.

Temkin, J. and Ashworth, A. 2004. The Sexual Offences Act 2003: Rape, Sexual Assault and the Problem of Consent in *Criminal Law Review,* pp. 328-346.

Temkin, J. 1982. Toward a Modern Law of Rape in *Modern Law Review,* Vol. 45, pp. 399-419.

Temkin, J. 1997. Plus ca change: Reporting Rape in the 1990's in *British Journal of Criminology,* Vol. 37(4), pp. 507-528.

Temkin, J. 2000. Prosecuting and Defending Rape: Perspectives from the Bar in *Journal of Law and Society,* Vol. 27(2) (June), pp. 219-248.

Temkin, J. 2002. *Rape and the Legal Process,* 2nd ed. Oxford University Press, Oxford.

Temkin, J. 1999. Reporting Rape in London: A Qualitative Study in *Howard Journal of Criminal Justice,* Vol. 38, pp. 17-41.

Temkin, Jennifer and Krahe, B. 2008. *Sexual Assault and the Justice Gap: A Question of Attitude,* Hart, Oxford.

Testa, M. and Parks, M.A. 1996. The Role of Women's Alcohol Consumption in Sexual Victimisation in *Aggression and Violent Behavior,* Vol. 1(3), pp. 217-234.

Thayer, J. B. 1898 (1999) *A Preliminary Treatise on Evidence at the Common Law,* Rothman Reprints Inc., 2nd Reprinting, South Hackensack, NJ.

Theilade, P. and Thomsen, J. 1986. False Allegations of Rape in *Police Surgeon,* Vol. 30, pp. 17-22.

Thomas, C. 2007. *Diversity and Fairness in Juries,* Ministry of Justice, London.

Thomas, D.A. 1979. *Principles of Sentencing,* 2nd ed., Heinemann, London.

Tjaden, P. and Thoennes, N. 1998. *Prevalence, Incidence and Consequences of Violence against Women: Findings from the National Violence against Women Survey,* U.S. Department of Justice, Washington, DC.

Tjaden, P. and Thoennes, N. 2006. *Extent, Nature, and Consequences of Rape Victimization: Findings form the National Violence against Women Survey*, U.S. Department of Justice, Washington DC.

Tomlinson, D. 1999. *Police-Reporting Decisions of Sexual Assault Survivors: An Exploration of Influential Factors* (available from Calgary Communities Against Sexual Abuse, Calgary, Alberta, Canada).

Truman, D.M., Tokar, D.M. and Fischer, A.R. 1996. Dimensions of Masculinity: Relations to Date Rape Supportive Attitudes and Sexual Aggression in Dating Situations in *Journal of Counseling and Development*, Vol. 74, pp. 555-62.

Tur, R.H.S. 1996. Subjectivism and Objectivism: Towards Synthesis, in Shute, S., Gardner, J. and Horder, J., *Action and Value in the Criminal Law*, Oxford University Press, Oxford.

U.S. Department of Justice. Table 42. *Personal Crimes of Violence, 1996-2005*. [www.document] at www.ojp.usdaj.gov/bjs/ (accessed 09/03/09).

Ullman, S. and Filipas, H. 2001. Correlates of Formal and Informal Support Seeking in Sexual Assault Victims in *Journal of Interpersonal Violence*, Vol.16(10), pp. 1028-1047.

Ullman, S.E., Townsend, S.M., Filipas, H.H., and Starzynski, L. L. 2007. Structural Models of the Relations of Assault Severity, Social Support, Avoidance Coping, Self-Blame, and PTSD Among Sexual Assault Survivors in *Psychology of Women Quarterly*, Vol. 31, pp. 23-37.

United Nations. 1985. *Declaration of Basic Principles of Justice for Victims of Crime and Abuse of Power* (GA Res. A/Res/40/34).

United States Department of Justice. 2005. *Criminal Victimisation in the United States in 2003*, U.S. Department of Justice, Washington DC.

Van Kesteren, J., Mayhew, P., and Nieuwbeerta, P. 2000. *Criminal Victimisation in Seventeen Industrialised Countries: Key Findings from the 2000 International Crime Victims Survey*, Ministry of Justice, The Hague.

Vasschs, A. 1994. *Sex Crimes*, Arrow Books, New York.

Vaughan, A.E. 2003. The Association Between Offender Socio-Economic Status and Victim-Offender Relationship in Rape Cases – revised in *Sexualities, Evolution and Gender*, Vol. 5(2), pp. 103-105.

Vera Institute of Justice. 1981. *Felony Arrests: Their Prosecution and Disposition in New York City's Courts*, New York.

Vidmar, N. and Hans, V.P. 2007. *American Juries: The Verdict*, Prometheus Books, New York, NY.

Villemur, N.K. and Hyde, J.S. 1983. Effects of Sex Defense Attorney, Sex of Juror, and Age and attractiveness of the Victim on Mock Juror Decision-Making in a Rape Case in *Sex Roles*, Vol. 9, pp. 879-889.

Visher, C.A. 1987. Juror Decision-Making: The Importance of Evidence in *Law and Human Behavior*, Vol. 11, pp. 1-17.

Walby, S. and Allen, J. 2004. *Domestic Violence, Sexual Assault and Stalking: Findings from the British Crime Survey*. Home Office Research Study, No. 276. HMSO, London.

Wall, A.M. and Schuller, R.A. 2000. Sexual Assault and Defendant-Victim Intoxication: Jurors' Perceptions of Guilt in *Journal of Applied Social Psychology*, Vol. 30, pp. 253-274.

Walsh, D. 2002. *Criminal Procedure*, Roundhall, Dublin.

Ward, C. 1988. The Attitudes toward Rape Victim Scale: Construction, Validation, and Cross-Cultural Applicability in *Psychology of Women Quarterly*, Vol. 12, pp. 127-146.

Ward. C. 1995. *Attitudes Toward Rape*, Sage, London.

Warner, J.C. and Burt, C.H. 2005. Rape Reporting after Reforms: Have Times Really Changed? in *Violence against Women*, Vol. 11(2), pp. 150-176

Watson, D. and Parsons, S. 2005. *Domestic Abuse of Men and Women in Ireland: Report on the National Study of Domestic Abuse*, National Crime Council, Dublin.

Weir, J.A. and Wrightsman, L.S. 1990. The Determinants of Mock Jurors' Verdicts in a Rape Case in *Journal of Applied Social Psychology*, Vol. 20, pp. 901-919.

Wenger, A.A. and Bornstein, B.H. 2006. The Effects of Victim's Substance Use and Relationship Closeness on Mock Jurors' Judgments in an Acquaintance Rape Case in *Sex Roles*, Vol. 50, pp. 547-555.

Weninger, R. 1978. Factors Affecting the Prosecution of Rape: A Case Study of Travis County, Texas in *Virginia Law Review*, Vol. 64, pp. 357-397.

Wessel, E., Drevland, G.C.B., Eilertsen, D.E. and Magnussen, S. 2006. Credibility of the Emotional Witness: A Study of Ratings by Court Judges in *Law and Human Behavior*, Vol. 30, pp. 221-230.

Whatley, M.A. 2005. The Effect of Participant Sex, Victim Dress and Traditional Attitudes on Causal Judgments for Marital Rape Victims in *Journal of Family Violence*, Vol. 20(3), pp. 191-200.

Whitehead, E. 2001. *Witness Satisfaction: Findings from the Witness Satisfaction Survey, 2000*. Home Office Research Study, No. 230. HMSO, London.

Wiehe, V. and Richards, S. 1995. *Intimate Betrayal: Understanding and Responding to the Trauma of Acquaintance Rape*, Sage, Newbury Park.

Wiener, R.L., Feldman-Wiener, A.T. and Grisso, T. 1989. Empathy and Biased Assimilation of Testimonies in Cases of Alleged Rape in *Law and Human Behavior*, Vol. 13, pp. 343-355.

Wiener, R.L., Habert, K., Shkodriani, G. and Staebler, C. 1991. The Social Psychology of Jury Nullification: Predicting when Jurors Disobey the Law in *Journal of Applied Social Psychology*, Vol. 21, pp. 1379-1401.

Wild, C.T., Graham, K. and Rehm, J. 1998. Blame and Punishment for Intoxicated Aggression: When is the Perpetrator Culpable? in *Addiction*, Vol. 93(5), pp. 677-687.

Williams, G. 1962. Corroboration — Sexual Cases in *Criminal Law Review*, p. 662.

Williams, L. 1984. The Classic Rape: When do Victims Report? in *Social Problems*, Vol. 31(4), pp. 459-467.

Willis, C.E. and Wrightsman, L.S. 1995. Effects of Victim Gaze Behavior and Prior Relationship on Rape Culpability Attributions in *Journal of Interpersonal Violence*, Vol. 10(3), pp. 367-77.

Winkel, F.W. and Koppelaar, L. 1991. Rape Victims' Style of Self-Presentation and Secondary Victimization by the Environment in *Journal of Interpersonal Violence*, Vol. 6, pp. 29-40.

Wissler, R. and Saks, M.J. 1985. On the Inefficacy of Limiting Instructions: When Jurors Use Prior Conviction Evidence to Decide on Guilt in *Law and Human Behavior*, Vol. 9(1), pp. 37-48.

Woods, G.D. 1981. *Sexual Assault Law Reforms in New South Wales*. Department of the Attorney-General and Department of Justice, Sydney.

Wright, C.A. and Graham, K.W. 1980. *Federal Practice and Procedure*, Vol. 22, Thomson West, Eagan, MN.

Wright, R. 1980. The English Rapist in *New Society*, 17 July 1980.

Wright, R. 1984. A Note on the Attrition of Rape Cases in *British Journal of Criminology*, Vol. 24, p. 399.

Yarmey, A.D. 1985. Older and Younger Adults' Attributions of Responsibility toward Rape Victims and Rapists in *Canadian Journal of Behavioral Science*, Vol. 17, pp. 327-338.

Yescavage, K. 1999. Teaching Women a Lesson: Sexually Aggressive and Nonaggressive Men's Perceptions of Acquaintance and Date Rape in *Violence against Women*, Vol. 5, pp. 796-812.

yfg.ie. 2006. Sexual Assault Treatment Unit. Young Fine Gael. 28/05/2006. [www.document] http://www.yfg.ie/print.php?sid=743 (accessed 11/06/09).

York, E. and Cornwell, B. 2006. Social Characteristics and Influence in the Jury Room in *Social Forces*, Vol. 85, 455.

Young, W. 1983. *Rape Study Vol.1: A Discussion of Law and Practice*, Department of Justice and Institute of Criminology, Wellington, New Zealand.

Young, W., Cameron, N. and Tinsley, Y. 1999. *Preliminary Paper No. 37 – Part II: Juries in Criminal Trials, Part II – A Summary of the Research Findings*, Wellington, New Zealand.

Zander, M. and Henderson, P. 1993. *Crown Court Study*. Royal Commission on Criminal Justice Research Study No.9, HMSO, London.

Table of Cases

Attorney General v. De Burca [1976] I.R. 38.

Attorney General v. New Statesman [1981] 1 Q.B. 1.

Batson v. Kentucky 476 U.S. 79 (1976).

Croissant v. Germany (1993) 16 E.H.R.R. 135.

DPP v. Haugh [2000] 1 I.R. 184

DPP v. Byrne [1995] 1 I.L.R.M. 279.

DPP v. Morgan [1976] A.C. 182.

Faretta v. United States 422 U.S. 806 (1975)

J.E.B. v. Alabama 511 U.S. 127 (1994).

Martinez v. United States 528 U.S. 152 (2000)

Mistretta v. United States. 488 U.S. 361 (1989).

O'Callaghan v. Attorney General [1993] 2 I.R. 17.

People (Attorney General) v. O'Callaghan [1966] I.R. 501.

People (DPP) v. Drought 2007 I.E.H.C. 310.

People (DPP) v. GMcC, unreported Court of Criminal Appeal, 31st October 2003.

People (DPP) v. McKenna (No.2) [2002] 2 I.R. 345.

People (DPP) v. TB [1996] 3 I.R. 294.

People (DPP) v. Tiernan [1988] I.R. 250.

R v. A [2001] 3 All E.R. 1.

R v. Baskerville [1916] 2 K.B. 658.

R v. Billam [1986] 1 W.L.R. 349.

R v. Connor: R v. Mirza [2004] 1 All E.R. 925.

R v. Graham (1910) 4 Cr. App. Rep. 218.

R v. Makanjuola; R v. Easton [1995] 2 Cr. App. Rep. 469.

R v. Millberry [2003] 2 All E.R. 939.

Re *Freedom of Information Act 1997; Minister for Justice, Equality and Law Reform v. The Information Commissioner* [2002] 2 I.L.R.M. 1.

State (Healy) v. Donoghue [1976] I.R. 325.

United States v. Booker 543 U.S. 220 (2005).

X and Y v. The Netherlands [1985] 8 E.H.R.R. 235.

INDEX

Advisory Group on the Law of Rape, 70, 77, 92, 94
ALONE, 313
Attorney General v. de Burca, 285
Attorney General for England and Wales v. New Statesman, 326
attrition, xxiii, xxx, 1, 4, 7–10, 15, 34, 35, 47, 51, 54, 108, 113, 116, 117, 121, 139, 140, 157, 182, 184–90, 192–3, 255, 257–8, 299–302, 321, 328–9, 359
  causes of, 362–5
  dealing with, 365–8

bail, xxx, xxxiii, 5, 123, 279–84, 321–5, 364, 368

Batson v. Kentucky, 286
Book of Evidence, 5, 122, 268, 273, 277–9
British Crime Survey, 318
Brownmiller, Susan, 33, 91–2

Central Criminal Court, 5, 6, 123, 124
Charleton J., 105, 106
Civil Law (Miscellaneous Provisions) Act 2008, 285, 286
Civil Legal Aid Act 1995, 285
Coaker, Vernon, 101

Commission for the Support of Victims of Crime, 86
Compensation Orders, 313, 337
Contempt of Court Act 1981, 326
corroboration, 60, 71, 73, 76, 80–2, 86, 347, 364
Cosc, xx, 87
Court of Criminal Appeal, xxxi, 6, 7, 307, 315, 326, 332
Courts Service, 103–4, 121–2, 125, 315, 325
Crime and Disorder Act 1998 (UK), 99
Criminal Justice Act 1984, 286
Criminal Justice Act 1993, xxxiv, 7, 86, 312, 313, 336, 337
Criminal Justice Act 1999, 5
Criminal Justice Act 2006, 333
Criminal Justice and Public Order Act 1994 (UK), 81
Criminal Justice (Legal Aid) Act, 1962, 284
Criminal Law Act 1997, 263
Criminal Law (Rape) Act 1981, xxiii, 1, 50, 85, 110, 123, 220, 285, 341
Criminal Law (Rape) (Amendment) Act 1990, xxiii, 2, 5, 50, 85, 110, 123, 220, 341, 347

Criminal Legal Aid Review Committee, 285
Criminal Procedure Act 1967, 5
Crisis Pregnancy Agency, 80
Crown Prosecution Service, 8, 50, 55, 59, 69, 251

Department of Justice, Equality and Law Reform, xx, 1, 86, 173, 324, 328
Director of Public Prosecutions (DPP), xxiii, xxiv, xxviii, xxxiii, 4, 5, 7, 47, 48, 52, 53, 55, 119, 177, 180, 188–9, 193, 195, 214, 219, 230–1, 233–4, 236, 240–3, 250–2, 256–8, 277, 298, 301, 313, 315–6, 326, 338, 341, 348, 361, 363, 369, *see also* Office of Director of Public Prosecutions
District Court, 5
DNA, 231, 242, 255, 278
DPP v. Byrne, 306, 332
DPP v. Morgan, 52, 73
Dublin Rape Crisis Centre, 313
Dublin Sexual Assault Treatment Unit, 138

Edwards, Ralston, 82
European Convention of Human Rights, 83

Faretta v. United States, 83
Federal Sentencing Guidelines (US), 99
Finlay J., 219
forensic evidence, 3, 4, 49, 51, 71, 72, 207, 231, 236, 240, 242, 254, 314, 369, 371

gang rapes, 57, 221, 238
Garda Victim Liaison Officer, 324

General Health Questionnaire (GHQ-12), 113, 184–5, 192, 193
GHB, 21, 26, 27, 319

Hale, Lord Matthew, 16
Heilbron Committee, *see* Advisory Group on the Law of Rape
Home Office (UK), 17, 77, 99, 101
House of Lords, 78
Human Rights Act 1998, 79

Irving, Toni, 67

J.E.B. v. Alabama, 286
juries, 52–4, 88–98, 285–302, 325–8
  attitudes to rape, 91–2
  deliberation periods of, 291–2
  foremen of, 290–1
  gender composition of, 287–8, 296–7
  increasing female presence in, 94–6
  male dominance of, 92–4, 296–7
  occupational composition of, 288–90
  verdicts of, 292–9
Juries Act 1976, 285, 286, 288

Law Reform Commissioner of Victoria, 17, 18, 77
legal aid, 284–5
Legal Aid Board, 285
Levenson's Locus of Control Test, 115–6, 184, 187–90
London Rape Crisis Centre, 25

Making a Victim Statement, 337
Mason, Julia, 82, 353
Martinez v. United States, 84
medical evidence, 56, 70–1, 75, 228, 231, 255
mens rea, 52

Mitchell Committee, 81
National Crime and Victimisation Survey, 40
National Crime Council, xxxiv, 107, 316, 334–5
National Domestic Violence and Sexual Assault Investigations Unit, 87
New Zealand Law Commission, 327
'no-criming', 17, 48
Notice of Additional Evidence, 5, 278, 279

O'Callaghan v. Attorney General, 293
Offences against the Person Act 1861, 1
Office for Criminal Justice Reform (UK), 97
Office of the Director of Public Prosecutions, xxiv, 47, 54, 109, 119–20, 243, 335, 359, 367, 369
Directing Division, 4, 277, 367
Solicitors' Division, 4

People (Attorney General) v. O'Callaghan, 280
People (DPP) v. Drought, 105
People (DPP) v. GMcC, 306
People (DPP) v. McKenna (No.2), 306
People (DPP) v. TB, 306
People (DPP) v. Tiernan, 5, 103, 323, 331
plea-bargaining, 298
Post-Traumatic Life Change Questionnaire, 114, 184–6, 192
Post-Traumatic Stress Disorder (PTSD), 25, 39, 98, 113, 115, 186, 187, 190–1, 193–4, 201, 217
and passage of time, 191
Post-Traumatic Stress Disorder Symptom Scale – Self Report (PSS–SR), 115, 184, 186–7, 198, 217
Probation Reports, 6
Probation Service, 310, 333–4
Prosecution of Offences Act 1974, 4

R v. A, 78
R v. Baskerville, 80
R v. Billiam, 99
R v. Connor, 89
R v. Easton, 81
R v. Edwards, 353
R v. Graham, 80
R v. Makanjuola, 81
R v. Millberry, 99, 100
R v. Mirza, 89
rape
  alcohol and, xxvii–xxix, 27, 30, 61–2, 66, 137–8, 146, 167, 174, 181, 225, 239–41, 244, 271–3, 319–20, 360, 363, 371, 372
  allegations of, 268–77
  and attempts at reform of criminal process, 10–12
  characteristics of, 131–7, 359–60
  complainants
    alcohol consumption and, 195, 210, 225, 241, 250, 252, 255, 271–3
    appearance, 31
    characteristics of, 63–70, 224–5, 260–3
    contact with police, 43–7
    evidence at trial, 340–5
    non-cooperation, 54–6
    protecting, 84–8, 354–7
  conviction rate for, 8–10, 294–302

rape (cont'd)
  defendants
    alcohol and drug consumption and, 271–3, 267, 309
    case at trial, 345–7
    characteristics of, 263–8
    self-representation by, 82–4
  definition of, 1–4, 49–54
  drug-assisted, 26–8, 146–7
  force and, 23–4, 135, 228, 237
  Gardaí response to, 160, 163–72, 201–2, 205–8
  impact of, 209–13, 273–7
  injury and, 24–6, 56–7, 136–7, 274
  investigation of, 172–81, 277–9
  legal system and, 10–12, 208–9, 277–317, 360–2
    delays in, 314–7
  location of, 22–3, 59, 132, 269–70
  marital, 41, 55
  media impact on, 33–4, 202–3
  mental illness and, 240–1
  multiple assailants, 57, 238
  myths, 15–34
    false accusations, 16–19
    impact of on reporting, 42
    prevalence of, 31–4
  prosecuting, 47–69, 219–58
    factors in decision to, 233–43, 363–4
      aggravating and consent features, 236–9
      complainant characteristics, 233–4
      intoxication, 235
      suspect characteristics, 234–5
    impact of jury on, 52–4
  reason not to, 243
  race and, 66–8
  relationship with offender, 133–5, 147–8, 220–1, 237–8, 268–9
  risky behaviour and, 65–6
  sexual history and, 63–5, 76–80, 341–3, 355
  'real', 3, 19–29
  repeated, 58
  resistance to, 24–6, 135
  reporting, 34–47, 127–218
    decision to, 37–43, 196–200, 362
    delay in, 59–60, 156–7, 334–5
    false, 249–50
    impact of, 203–5
    reasons for, 148–56
    reasons for not, 140–8
    withdrawal, 157–62, 243–9
      effect of delay on, 248–9
      reasons for, 245–8
  'simple', 3
  stranger, 21–2
  suicide and, 210
  supportive attitudes, 29–31
  suspects
    alcohol consumption and, 227
    characteristics of, 226–8
    defences offered by, 227–8
  time of, 22–3, 270–1
  trials, 70–108, 260–357, 364–5
    defence tactics during, 73–84
    delay in, 107–8
    evidentiary difficulties, 70–2
    judge's charge in, 347–8
    transcripts of, 338–53
  use of weapons and, 23–4, 56–7, 237–8
  victims' evidence, 26

Index

rape cases
  attrition rates, 299–302
  characteristics, 220
  evidential factors in, 231
  national distribution of, 221–4
  outcomes, 232
Rape Crisis Centres, 111–12, 163, 217, 218
Rape Crisis Network Ireland, 1, 35, 108, 132
Rape Myth Acceptance Scale, 32–3
Rape Shield Laws, 11, 77
Rape Trauma Syndrome (RTS), 25, 98
'real rape' stereotypes, 19–29, 69, 175, 257
Rohypnol, 21, 26, 27, 228, 319

sentencing, 98–108, 302–14, 329–34
  ancillary penalties and, 310–3
  concurrent and consecutive, 305–7, 331–2
  effect of Victim Impact Statements on, 313–4
  factors, 348–53
  frequency of, 305
  in Ireland, 103–7
  length of, 101–3
  suspension periods, 307–10, 332–4
Sentencing Advisory Panel (UK), 99, 100
Sentencing Guidelines Council, 99

Sexual Assault Treatment Units (SATU), xxxii, 222, 225, 253, 254, 257, 369–71
Sex Offenders Act 2001, 86, 285, 310, 333, 341
Sex Offences Kit, 278
Sexual Abuse and Violence in Ireland study (SAVI), 10, 42, 46, 127, 134, 139
Sexual Offences Index, 26
socio-demographic factors, 38–9, 67–8, 127
State (Healy) v. Donoghue, 284
Statement of Charges, 4, 5
Statements of General Guidelines for Prosecutors, 48

Timmerton, Tracy, 58

United States v. Booker, 99

Victims' Charter, xxxii, xxxiii, 86, 172–4, 182, 324, 336, 368, 372
Victim Impact Statements, xxx, xxxiv, 6, 87, 88, 122, 273, 275, 277, 313–4, 322, 336–8, 365
  authorship of, 275
victim-precipitation, 30
victim
  recommendations, 213–6
  rights, 336–8
  risk factors, 229–31, 239–41
Violence against Women Survey (Canada), 41
Women's Task Force on Rape (US), 11
Woolmington v. DPP, 72

X & Y v. The Netherlands, 256